Form Follows Feeling

The Acquisition of Design Expertise and the Function of Aesthesis in the Design Process

Terrence M. Curry
Delft University of Technology, Faculty of Architecture and the Built Environment, Department of Urbanism

Architecture
and the
Built environment

abe.tudelft.nl

Design: Sirene Ontwerpers, Rotterdam

ISBN 978-94-92516-63-3
ISSN 2212-3202

© 2017 Terrence M. Curry

Form Follows Feeling

The Acquisition of Design Expertise and the Function of Aesthesis in the Design Process

Proefschrift

ter verkrijging van de graad van doctor
aan de Technische Universiteit Delft,
op gezag van de Rector Magnificus prof. ir. K.C.A.M. Luyben,
voorzitter van het College voor Promoties,
in het openbaar te verdedigen op 3 juli 2017 om 15:00 uur

door

Terrence Michael CURRY
M. Div., Jesuit School of Theology at Berkeley, United States of America
Th. M., Xavier University of Louisiana, United States of America
geboren te Brooklyn, United States of America

This dissertation has been approved by the

promoter: Prof.ir. H. C. Bekkering

Composition of the Doctoral Committee

Rector Magnificus   chairman
Prof.ir. H. C. Bekkering   Delft University of Technology

Independent members

Prof.dr. P. G. Badke-Schaub   Deft University of Technology
Prof.dr. R. Cavallo   Deft University of Technology
Prof.dr.ir. V.J. Meyer   Deft University of Technology
Prof.dr.ir. C.H. Dorst   Eindhoven University of Technology
Prof.dr.ing. C. Gänshirt   Xi'an Jiaotong-Liverpool University

This research was supported by the UNE Province of the Society of Jesus, USA and a research grant from Tsinghua University, School of Architecture, P.R. China.

The artist must suffer sleepless nights, purify himself without ceasing,
voluntarily abandon fertile places, full of insecurity.
Maritain

Acknowledgements

First, I want to express my gratitude to the Technical University of Delft, the School of Architecture and the Built Environment, and the Department of Urbanism, for the invitation to pursue my doctorate and for the generous hospitality they extended to me over these past 6 years. None of this research would have been possible without the help and support of my friend, colleague and promoter Henco Bekkering and his partner Ria Wiegman, Ralf Weber who first introduced me to empirical aesthetics, and Roger Haight who helped me transform my first musings into a cohersive argument. I am indebted to my brother Jesuits who supported and encouraged me throughout this five year journey in the USA, the Netherlands and in China. I am grateful for my colleagues at Delft University of Technology, Tsinghua University, Budapest University of Technology and Economics, and at the University of Detroit Mercy, as well as my own design teachers at the Pratt Institute. I thank my students who have taught me and given me more than they can ever imagine. Finally I am indebted to my family, my mother, my brothers and my sisters, especially my grandfather Theodore Grupinski who taught me how and to love making stuff.

AMGD

Contents

Preface

This thesis is fundamentally about the cognitive processes involved in learning to become a designer.

To give this thesis context it is probably best to start is by explaining the title: *Form Follows Feeling*. The title did not occur to me until well after the first draft was completed. Up until then the title was: *The acquisition of design expertise and the function of aesthesis in the design process*. Admittedly, not a particularly catchy title.

The title is an obvious reference to Louis Sullivan's famous, often misquoted, out of context and sometimes misattributed quote, "Whether it be the sweeping eagle in his flight, or the open apple blossom, the toiling work-horse, the blithe swan, the branching oak, the winding stream at its base, the drifting clouds, over all the coursing sun, *form ever follows function*, and this is the law." (Sullivan, 1869, p. 408). The quote comes from an article written by Sullivan entitled "The tall building artistically considered." In this article Sullivan makes a passionate and eloquent plea for the legitimization of a new building type – the tall building – on its own terms. He argues against the use of the "classical column" as the true prototype, against "the beauty of prime numbers," against the "logical statement," against organic justification found in the "vegetable kingdom" (p. 406). Sullivan, referring to how in nature "the essence of things is taking shape in the matter of things," makes his point again:

It is the pervading law of all things organic and inorganic, of all things physical and metaphysical, of all things human and all things superhuman, of all true manifestations of the head, of the heart, of the soul, that the life is recognizable in its expression, that form ever follows function. *This is the law...* And thus the design of the tall office building takes its place with all other architectural types made when architecture, as has happened once in many years, was a living art." (p. 408)

His was not an argument against decoration, as can easily be seen by looking at any of his buildings. Nor was he arguing for a from of *technical rationalism*, though he does argue for a kind of inevitability "if we follow our natural instincts without the thought of books, rules, precedents, or any educational impedimenta..." His argument, not unlike Kahn's conversation with a brick (Kahn & Twombly, 2003), is founded on the belief that the truth of a thing is found by recognizing the essence of a thing, feeling into it, letting it be what it wants to be.

Unfortunately, Sullivan's passionate plea to embrace a new building type "for the transaction of business," and made possible by "the intervention and perfection of the high-speed elevator..., development of steel manufactures has shown the way to safe, rigid, economical constructions..., and so on, by action and reaction, interaction and inter-reaction" (p. 403), has been perverted as a justification for a kind of technical rationalism and functional determinism. Sullivan is not arguing for technical rationalism or functional determinism, but rather he is arguing for a kind of passionate essentialism.

The technical rationalism and functional determinism that the phrase *form follows function* has come to embody has been embraced by architecture design students[1] across the world as if it is a self-evident truth. This, along with the *cult of the concept* (where it is believed that all design solutions have their genesis in a concept) and the banishment of the concept of the aesthetic (dismissed due to a naive understanding of subjective relativism) has led to a kind of intellectual abstraction of the design process that no longer recognizes that the proper end of design is not a concept for or a representation of a possible building or built environment: The proper end of architecture design is a building, a built environment made of the stuff of the earth.

Somehow architecture design has become a disembodied activity, not unlike Cartesian dualism, where the mind has an existence without the body, where the concept for a building is more important than the building itself. I suppose that if one accepts that one's true existence as a person is as a disembodied mind, then it follows that the end of architecture design should be a disembodied idea/concept for a building. But if one does not accept mind/body dualism, but rather embraces an embodied view of human existence, where mind means nothing more than human cognition, and the body is understood as not only a way of interaction with the world, but as a way, perhaps the primary way of knowing the world, then architecture design is about making places for human dwelling that engages the body and takes into account fleshy, smelly, sensuous, romantic, tender, ingenious, vulnerable beings that humans are. Thus I argue, *form follows feeling*.

---

1   For the purpose of simplicity, I will refer to the "designer" as a person. This is not to suggest that I am talking about the Howard Roark (a character from [the nemesis of Peter Keating] Ayn Rand's *The Fountainhead,* 1996) like individual who alone knows what is good and what is right. Rather I recognize that the designer often includes many people who actively participate in the design process throughout its many phases: from defining the problem, through the production/implementation of the solution. The designer can be understood to be an individual, a group or a series of individuals and groups. Dong (2009) discusses this issue in terms of *agency,* who is permitted to claim the role of designer. Acknowledging the role that the user plays in defining the problem, the need for large teams of designers when working on large-scale systems, and the expectations by which we identify who a designer is as opposed to who engages in "designerly actions," he observes that the "boundary between being in/within the process of design and outside of what is considered designing is artificial" (pp. 5-7).

My motivation for writing this thesis comes from and is grounded in 25 years of professional practice and making stuff; but perhaps more so from a genuine love of teaching and of my students. For the past 15 years I have been spending most of my time helping students learn to design at architecture schools in the USA, Hungary and China. It is surprising how similar the basic structure of the programs are, and the kinds of challenges that students have to face. In architecture schools there are several models of teaching design, including critic, coach, and instructor (Adams, R., 2016). Each has its strengths and weaknesses. I prefer the instructor model, as it emphasizes "showing how." I work closely with students trying to understand what they are trying to do, showing them how to approach a design problem, suggesting multiple methodologies and strategies, and helping them to discover their own voice. Some things work, some things don't. It often depends on the student, their learning preferences, group dynamics, skill sets, etc. I often find myself trying to put myself in their place, and try to recall what it was like when I was a student. And when I need a little humility I take out a project I did when I was their age. Sometimes I forget that I had to learn to design too.

Several years ago I began to notice a pattern in the design studio. There would be 12 eager students in a second-year studio. As it was a selective school, the students tended to be of above average intelligence, highly motivated and hard working. They were enthusiastic and curious. All of the students were given exactly the same project, with clearly defined learning objectives, and plenty of personal attention. Even so, while most of the students seemed to understand the problem, actively engage in seminar-type discussions on design theory and methodology, completed all the exercises, there were always three or four students whose work would stand out. They were not always the "smartest," or the hardest working students. But their work always seemed to have "that something extra" that a design instructor is always looking for. For years I just assumed, like many of my colleagues, that these students just had "natural talent," and it was my responsibility to identify it, nurture it and to draw it out. But then I wondered, what about the other students? How does one draw out what isn't there? Would they ever be able to produce work that also possessed that something special?

Often I would encounter some of the same students a few years later in an upper level studio. By this time, they were familiar. I knew their work. But I noticed something very interesting; some of the work of students who seemed to possess natural talent in the second year no longer stood out; while some of the work of students who just didn't seem to get it in the second year now had that something special. As I reflected on this phenomenon over the years, I tried to make sense of it.

The theory that students who are able to produce design solutions that had that "something special" where just naturally talented was not satisfying. This explanation did not adequately explain those other students who seemed to develop a sense of design later on.

Was it that their talent was laying dormant waiting to be drawn out as Socrates draws out knowledge from Meno's slave boy? (Plato, *Meno, 1956*). Research on the topic of nature versus nature does not bear this theory out. I began to consider what if there is no real connection between a sense of design and talent? What if a sense of design is not a natural God-given gift that some have and some do not, but rather a learned ability, a kind of connoisseurship, that plays a critical function in the design process? What if talent had nothing to do with developing a sense of design?

As I explored this possibility, I learned that while certain psychological, physiological, and cognitive predispositions do offer an advantage, and while some students do benefit from a more privileged environment, none of these guarantee that one can or will achieve expert levels of performance. This observation resonated with my experience. Further, research in the area of the acquisition of expert performance showed that what determines if one will ever achieve a level of expert performance (in any discipline) is not natural talent, but years of deliberate practice that reshapes and reinforces cognitive and physical abilities required for that discipline (Ericcson, 2016). It is an embodied *feel for what to do* – a complex, embodied, cognitive ability to assess a situation, identify a strategy and then implement it in an apparently effortless manner – that is essential to being an expert more so than propositional knowledge, technical rationality or so-called talent.

What I have learned working with some extraordinary students over the world is that more than technical knowledge, problem-solving ability, representational skill, previous experience, hard work and motivation, what is necessary for a student to produce work that has that something special is a sense of design. And that a sense of design heavily depends on the ability to know feelingly (aesthesis) and identify the quality of a built environment (atmosphere). It is not functional analysis that determines good design or the inevitability of functional determinism. Neither is intended by Sullivan's famous quote. Functional determinism is a fiction that promises if a design solution is true to the functional requirements of the design brief, then the design solution will be inevitably good and possess desirable aesthetic qualities. But there is no inevitability in design (Rittel, 1988). While *form follows function* and Mies van der Rohe's *less is more* (another so-called self-evident truth of architecture education), taken in a historical context, provided a new way to think about design, that took into account the reality of post-war Europe, new materials and methods of construction; in contemporary design education these function as naïve slogans and empty epithets. In fact, there is no function that is necessarily associated with a particular form (Pye, 1978). Sure, one can conceive a form that is better suited to a particular task, but that relies on a very specific definition of a task and/or form. A certain kind of hammer while being well suited to driving a particular type of nail into a particular type of material, can also make a very effective weapon.

Like many designers and design instructors who have gone before me, my problem has been that while I have learned much about how students learn and what is necessary to be a good designer, what I know is mostly in the form of tacit knowledge. That is, a kind of knowledge where I know more than I can say (Polanyi, 1975). This thesis is an attempt to correct this situation. To do this I have spent a good deal of the past six years in an effort to find a way *to say what I know*.

The following is an attempt to understand what is involved in learning to design and to propose a theoretical framework that explains how design expertise is acquired and why a highly developed sense of design is necessary to acquire design expertise. It's a multi-disciplinary work that looks at the topic from theoretical, philosophical, psychological, historical, evolutionary and cognitive science points of view. There is no doubt that some will take issue with how I describe design, what I claim is the proper end to design, how I define expertise, what I identify as normative performance expectations, my argument in favor of tacit knowledge and embodied cognition over technical rationality, whether one really can experience qualia in mental representations, the developmental model of the acquisition of expertise, my use of the word aesthesis, and the importance of aesthetic resonance in the design process. Even so, there are many valuable concepts and ideas presented here that are worth considering and that offer insight into how students learn to design.

It is my hope that this work will prove to be useful to others who desire to and are committed to helping others learn to design; and for those who simply would like to read what they already know about being a designer but have yet to find the words.

Samenvatting

1   Onderzoekvraag

Terwijl het voor het oplossen van een ontwerpprobleem een basale vereiste is rekening te houden met functionele en technische criteria, zowel als met een gevoel voor samenhang, is het vermogen een bedoelde esthetische ervaring op te roepen het kenmerk van ontwerpexpertise. Dit vermogen is wat bedoeld wordt met een gevoel voor ontwerpen. Expert-ontwerpers hebben een sterk ontwikkeld gevoel voor ontwerpen, dat in dit onderzoek "aesthesis" wordt genoemd. Reflectie op 25 jaar ontwerponderwijs in de Verenigde Staten, Hongarije en China heeft tot de observatie geleid dat de meeste succesvolle ontwerpstudenten, meer dan intellectuele vaardigheid, de vaardigheid om te tekenen en maquettes te maken of een sterke motivatie, allen leken te beschikken over wat een intuïtief gevoel voor wat een goed ontwerp is genoemd kan worden. Het is niet dat zij al weten hoe te ontwerpen, of dat ze van nature ontwerpers zijn, maar zij hebben een meer ontwikkeld gevoel voor aesthesis. Dit onderzoek hanteert een multidisciplinaire benadering om een theoretisch raamwerk te ontwikkelen dat beschrijft wat het inhoudt om ontwerpexpertise te verwerven, wat de rol is van aesthesis in het ontwerpproces, en om te bepalen of wat een intuïtief gevoel voor ontwerpen lijkt te zijn een natuurlijk talent is of een verworven vaardigheid.

2   Onderzoekmethode

De methodologie van onderzoek omvat: (1.) kritische reflectie op 25 jaar ontwerponderwijs, ontwerppraktijk en bouwen; (2.) testen van de inzichten die uit deze reflectie voortkomen aan relevant onderzoek en theorie, inclusief ontwerponderzoek, psychologie, filosofie, cognitiewetenschap en evolutionaire biologie; en (3.) discussie met collega's.

3   Resultaten

Het onderzoek startte met onderwerpen uit de ontwerpmethodologie, wat vragen opriep gerelateerd aan de cognitieve psychologie, in het bijzonder probleem-oplossingstheorieën. Diepgaande studie van het onderzoek naar belichaamde cognitie resulteerde in argumenten tegen de ontkoppeling van lichaam en geest, en een herintroductie van het lichaam als een essentieel onderdeel van de menselijke cognitie.

Dit heeft geleid tot nader onderzoek naar aanverwante onderwerpen als: voor-verbale kennis, de cognitieve architectuur van het brein, de mechanismen van gevoel en waarneming, beperkingen in en typen van het vermogen tot herinnering en de verwerkingscapaciteit van het brein, en in het bijzonder de werking van emoties/gevoelens in kennisverwerving, die tezamen inzicht bieden in hoe ontwerpen werkt als cognitief proces.

4 Conclusie

Het onderzoek laat zien dat ervaren ontwerpers in plaats van te vertrouwen op technisch rationele kennis alleen, vertrouwen op een sterk ontwikkelde impliciete belichaamde kennis om tot beslissingen en oordelen te komen. Hierdoor weten ze meer dan wat ze kunnen uitdrukken. Dit is het kenmerk van experts op vele gebieden. Het komt echter niet voort uit een natuurlijk talent, maar uit een ontwikkelingsproces dat jaren van bewuste oefening vergt. Dit is noodzakelijk voor het herstructureren van het brein en het trainen van het lichaam op een manier die uitzonderlijk functioneren mogelijk maakt. Voor expert ontwerpers vormt aesthesis een soort meta-vuistregel waarmee complexe problemen schijnbaar moeiteloos opgelost kunnen worden. Aesthesis is een vermogen dat iedereen heeft, maar dat expert ontwerpers ver hebben ontwikkeld. Dit maakt het mogelijke gebouwen en de bebouwde omgeving te produceren die de beoogde kwaliteit van esthetische ervaring bij de gebruiker oproepen (een gevoel voor ontwerpen). Het is een cognitieve vaardigheid die het zowel mogelijk maakt het ontwerpprobleem te (her-)structureren en de oplossing te evalueren; en het is tevens een vaardigheid om zich met zijn gevoel in te leven in de ontwerp-wereld, op zoek naar esthetische resonantie die anticipeert op de kwaliteit van de omgeving die de gebruiker waarschijnlijk zal ervaren. Deze vaardigheid is cruciaal voor het verwerven van ontwerpexpertise.

Summary

1   Research Question

....

While the consideration of functional and technical criteria, as well as a sense of coherence are basic requirements for solving a design problem; it is the ability to induce an intended quality of aesthetic experience that is the hallmark of design expertise. Expert designers possess a highly developed sense of design, or what in this research is called aesthesis. Reflection on 25 years teaching design in the USA, Hungary, and China led to the observation that most successful design students, more than intellectual ability, drawing, model making or drive, all seemed to possess what may be called an intuitive sense of good design. It is not that they already know how to design, or that they are natural designers, it is that they have a more developed sense aesthesis. This research takes a multi-disciplinary approach to build a theory that describes what is involved in acquiring design expertise,identifies how aesthesis functions in the design process, and determines if what appears to be an intuitive sense of design is just natural talent or an acquired ability.

2   Research Methods

....

The methodology used for this research includes: (1.) Critical reflection on 25 years of teaching, design practice, and making; (2.) Testing insights gained from this reflection against related research and theoretical work, publications, including design research, psychology, philosophy, cognitive sciences and evolutionary biology; (3.) Discussion with colleagues. (4.) (4.) Externalizing results of research.

3   Results

....

The research started with topics related to design methodology, which led to questions related to cognitive psychology, especially theories of problem-solving. An in-depth review of research in embodied cognition challenged the disembodied concept of the mind and related presuppositions, and reintroduced the body as an essential aspect of human cognition. This lead to related topics including: pre-noetic (pre-verbal) knowledge, the cognitive architecture of the brain, sense mechanisms and perception, limitations and types of memory as well as the processing capacity of the brain, and especially how emotions/feelings function in human cognition, offering insight into how designing functions as a cognitive process.

4 Conclusion

The research provides evidence that more than technical rationality, expert designers rely heavily on a highly developed embodied way of knowing (tacit knowledge) througout the design process that allows them to know more than they can say. Indeed, this is the hallmark of expert performers in many fields. However, this ability is not to be understood as natural talent, but as a result of an intense developmental process that includes years of deliberate practice necessary to restructure the brain and adapt the body in a manner that facilitates exceptional performance. For expert designers it is aesthesis (a kind of body knowledge), functioning as a meta-heuristic, that allows them to solve a complex problem situation in a manner that appears effortless. Aesthesis is an ability that everyone possesses, but that expert designers have highly developed and adapted to allow them to produce buildings and built environments that induce an intended quality of aesthetic experience in the user. It is a cognitive ability that functions to both (re)structure the design problem and evaluate the solution; and allows the designer to inhabit the design world feelingly while seeking aesthetic resonance that anticipates the quality of atmosphere another is likely to experience. This ability is critical to the acquisition of design expertise.

Propositions

1   Talent is way over-rated

2   Experts normally do not make good teachers

3   Design is a kind of *making*: an action that results in an artifact" [for human use], not planning or problem-solving.

4   The primary manner in which we know the world is through our bodies, not our *minds*

5   Without a direct experience of the properties and characteristics of materials, one can never truly master architecture design.

6   While human behavior not predictable, it is however consistent.

7   The hallmark of a true craftsman is not to be found in his hands, but rather in his ability to feel the grain, density, and irregularities of a piece of wood through the edge of the blade of the plane in his hands.

8   While beauty may be in the eye of the beholder, it all depends on how one defines *the beholder*.

9   The current world-wide trend to require a PhD to teach (design) at the university level is having a deleterious effect on design education.

10 There is only so much bad design that people can handle, at some point they simply stop seeing the world they live in.

1 Introduction[2]

A critical, but rarely discussed ability necessary for design expertise, that functions within the design process as both a *means* of assessment and a *desire* to be satisfied is a kind of body knowledge called **aesthesis**. Aesthesis is used here in the Greek sense (αἴσθησις) that Perez-Gomez (2016) describes, "referring not only to visual perception but to apprehension by all the senses, enabling an understanding through non representative concepts of that which is perceived by embodied consciousness" (p. 17).

Design expertise involves more than technical rationality, problem-solving, technical competency, and the ability to produce a coherent solution often associated with the dictum– *form follows function*. While these components of design are necessary, they are not sufficient. From the theory of tacit knowledge and embodied cognition, I will argue that the desire for and the seeking of aesthetic quality (and aesthetic experience itself), rather than being simply one of many design criteria, operates as an overarching unifying function that provides focus and motivation throughout the design process. One might call this kind of knowledge a *sense of design*. As the human body is the primary means for knowing the world, the ability to determine and assess the experiential quality of the design solution (aesthesis) is essential for design expertise. More than functional efficiency, technical feasibility and a sense of coherence, the ability to induce an intended aesthetic experience (create an atmosphere) determines the quality of a design solution. Thus the title of this work: *Form Follows Feeling*. What this means and how it functions in the design process are central to this thesis.

To describe what designers do and what is involved in learning to be a designer, I have framed the problem as: **the acquisition of design expertise and the function of aesthesis in the design process**.

---

2   English language is burdened with not having an inclusive pronoun. Traditionally "he" was, for better and for worse, considered to be inclusive. Contemporary sensibilities and the desire to be inclusive in academic language has left us with the unfortunate problem of choosing a pronoun. S/he, Her/his, is awkward. They, and one, are equally awkward. Recently, the recognition of the fluidity of gender identity has made this question of the inclusive pronoun even more complicated. In light of this, I will fall back on the traditional standard of using he, though I am quite aware that soon almost half of students studying architecture design in the USA will be women (See NAAB 2016 Annual Report, sec. 03 "Overall Enrollment in accredited programs."). My apologies to anyone who may be offended by this choice.

§ 1.1 Some Clarifications

The sub-title of the thesis contains some terms that need clarification. **Acquisition of design expertise:** This research is not about how to teach design,[3] but rather how design expertise is *acquired* (learned). Menon asks Socrates (Plato, *Meno*, 1956), "Can you tell me, Socrates—can 'virtue' be 'taught'? Or if not, does it come by practice? Or does it come neither by practice nor by teaching, but do people get it by nature, or in some other way?" (p. 28). Replace the word "virtue" with "design," and "taught" with "learned," and the question posed to Socrates by Menon encapsulates the question I am asking. "Tell me, can design be learned? Or if not, does it come by practice? Or does it neither come by practice nor by learning, but do people get it by nature or in some other way?" Design (knowledge), like virtue (in the Aristotelian sense), is not acquired in the same explicit way as propositional knowledge. Its acquisition is more implicit, learned by doing, hard to define, *tacit*.

The function of aesthesis in the design process: This research is not about aesthetics *per se*, but rather about the *function* of aesthesis – hedonic body knowledge – in the design process. This research does not attempt to define what good design is, or propose a normative standard for evaluating a design in the sense of criticism. This research proposes a theoretical basis for understanding how design expertise is acquired.[4] It is founded upon extensive research literature, and critical reflection on 25 years of architecture professional practice and teaching architectural design at the university level. To adequately describe my observations and defend my thesis, the research takes a multidisciplinary approach to the problem, including: design theory and methodology; philosophy, psychology and cognitive science;[5] and the relatively new fields of expert performance theory, and neuroaesthetics.

---

[3] Though it is my intent that this research will provide new insights that will influence how design is taught.

[4] The insight that a deeper understanding how design expertise is acquired would benefit the teaching of design is not new. Cross (1990) suggests that "it is through understanding the nature of design ability that we can begin to construct an understanding of the intrinsic values of design education." This research however is not specifically intended to form the basis for a new theory or critique of design education. Rather it is asking how design expertise is acquired and what role does aesthetic judgment play in the design process.

[5] Gardner (1985) describes *cognitive science* as a (then) emerging interdisciplinary study of mind and intelligence that includes philosophy and psychology as well as neuroscience, artificial intelligence, linguistics, anthropology, and evolutionary biology.

Designing occurs in various disciplines, such as architecture, interior design, urban design, landscape design, product/industrial design, engineering and others. This research recognizes that while certain theories, principles, methodologies and methods are relevant across disciplines, design expertise, as it is practiced, tends to be domain specific (situated). The focus of this research is on the domain of architecture design, where (normally) a building/built environment is the expected outcome. The presupposition is that **the proper** (normative) **end** (purpose) **of architectural design is a buildable building/built environment that provides a coherent solution for the design problem and evokes intended aesthetic qualities**. It is understood that this is not the only end of architectural design (architects do much more than design buildings), but it is the working definition for this research.

Other terms that are central to this thesis include: **Tacit knowledge** (Ryle, 1949), knowing more than you are able to say. **Boundedness** (Simon, 1972), the acknowledgment of the limits of cognitive capacity that influence how we think and structure problems. **Extension** (Clark), the way things and external mechanisms are recruited to increase the cognitive capacity; for example sketching. **Einfühlung** and **mirror-neurons**, (Wölfflin, 1884; Rizzolatti, 2004) the cognitive mechanisms that allow us to *feel into* a thing, as well as feel the feelings someone else is likely feeling. **Inhabiting the problem space feelingly** (Polanyi, 1974), how experts are able to know how to instantaneously respond to complex situations. **Aesthesis** (Perez-Gomez), the mechanism that is critical in assessing the aesthetic experience (quality) of an *atmosphere*. **Representations** (Newell), how pre-noetic cognitive data is structured in the mind to facilitate comprehension. **Functional representation** (Habraken, 1985), the proximate end (product) of designing that results in a building/built environment. **Exaptation**(Gould, 1982), how attributes that were acquired through evolutionary processes for one purpose adapt to become useful for something else as the environment changes. **Pre-structuring** (Hillier, 1972), the presuppositions and biases one brings to the problem situation which help to both define the problem space and frame the problem. **Appreciative system** (Schön, 1985), the values, norms, beliefs and preferences that facilitate decision-making and judgments. **Deliberate practice** (Ericsson, 2008), what is necessary for a person to effectively adapt his cognitive capacity and body that allows him to perform at an exceptional level. These concepts, as well as others included in the text, led to proposing the concept of **aesthetic resonance**, an emotional state experienced by the designer where he assesses the congruence between the intended quality of aesthetic experience and the quality of aesthetic experience as he inhabits the design world feelingly.

§ 1.2   Methodology

The methodology used for this research includes: (1.) Critical reflection on 25 years of teaching, design practice, and making; (2.) Testing insights gained from this reflection against related research and theoretical work, publications, including design research, psychology, philosophy, cognitive sciences and evolutionary biology; (3.) Discussion with colleagues. (4.) Externalizing results of research

As will be discussed below, knowing how to do something (tacit knowledge) is different than knowing what (propositional knowledge). Tacit knowledge is described as *knowing more than you can say* (Polanyi, 1974). Its a kind of implicit knowing. The challenge in this research was to engage in critical reflection on my experience teaching design to try to make explicit what I have come to know without conscious deliberation (van Dooren, K. et al., 2013). While I know much about how students learn to design, and about how to design, as a result of years of deliberate practice supported by theory and research, and while I can substantiate my claim to success as a teacher of design and as a professional designer (see attached CV), I have not systematically documented the insights and knowledge I've acquired in a manner that could be considered quantitative research. Rather, the (tacit) knowledge that I have gained from teaching design functions as a way to structure and *enter into the problem space feelingly* (Polanyi, 1974), to frame the questions and how to know which paths of evidence to follow. It is a dialectical approach where I test what I know from doing against the evidence that I encountered in the research. The dialectic gave direction to the research. Sometimes the research confirmed what I suspected, sometimes the research provided new categories, vocabulary and concepts to better express what I know, and sometimes the research forced me to rethink how I thought about my experience. My research methodology follows that recommend by Schön (1991) in the tradition of Dewey (1938/2015), which proposes building theory on experience through *reflective practice*. This approach is sometimes referred to as a *designerly way of knowing* (Cross, 2001).

As the nature of the topic is inter-disciplinary, so is the research, as is the thesis. In discussion with colleagues knowledgeable in the field, and through publication (Curry, T., 2014; 2014a) I identified key issues I wanted to explore. To test my assumptions against empirical research, I started by (re-)reading Broadbent (1973), Bloomer & Moore (1977), Jones (1992), Weber (1995), Rowe (1987), Alexander (1964), Cuff (1992). Then I discovered Schön (1991), Cross (2011), Dorst and Lawson (2009), Margolin and Buchannan (1995), McCormick (2004). These led to Simon (1996), Popper (1996), Rittel (1988; Protzen & Harris, 2010), Polanyi (1974), Ryle (1949), Goldschmidt (2003), Arnheim (2009), Csikszentmihalyi (1996), Finke et al. (1992), Akin (1986) and Brawne (2003).

As I began to focus I found Lakoff & Johnson (1999), Mallgrave (2011; 2013), Thagard (2002), Ramachandran (2011), Damasio (1994), Chatterjee (2014), Ericsson (2016) and Gänshirt (2007), and others, as well as much cross-referencing, many leads and dead ends. It became clear that the only way to see the whole picture was to look at it across disciplines, including: design theory, philosophy, psychology and a good deal of cognitive science. This research uncovered a world I had suspected existed, but that I knew little of. The research confirmed some of my beliefs, forced me to rethink others, and led to still entirely new ways of thinking. After diagramming and examining the relationships between knowledge from experience, discussion with colleagues and review of relevant research, confirmed observations and new ways of thinking about the topic, the final methodology was to externalize what I knew as a linear narrative that makes sense. Externalizing mental representations is always useful, it not only exposes the holes in thinking that the mind is happy to pretend do not exist, it provides feedback, and forces one to be as clear and precise as possible, lest one's intended meaning is lost. In many ways it is not unlike designing a building.

§ 1.3 Claims

This thesis makes five claims. (1.) Designing is an acquired skill that (though tacit in nature) can be described (not defined) by well-established models of expert performance. (2.) Architecture design is fundamentally about making buildings/ built environments for human use and habitation, which are (primarily) experienced through our body's sense systems, not (only) as abstract ideas (concepts), but rather as tactile, actual, built objects. (3.) A successful design is not only a coherent solution (one that "makes sense") that solves clearly defined (functional, technical, environmental, economic) criteria and constraints (that is problem-solving), but also one that induces intended aesthetic experience (a hedonic quality/body knowledge) in the user. (4.) Along with the seeking of coherence, an evolving knowledge of (feel for) the quality of the intended aesthetic experience plays a critical, overarching, motivational role throughout the design process; a kind of seeking. (5.) The ability to assess/anticipate the quality of the intended aesthetic experience (aesthesis) of a design proposal (anticipating the experience it will induce after it is built) within the design process (aesthetic resonance), with a reasonable level of reliability (a kind of emotional intelligence), is essential for the acquisition of design expertise.

§ 1.4 Argument

In making these claims I argue for the importance of understanding the developmental process that students of architecture design typically move through from beginner to the acquisition of design expertise; the need to challenge *Cartesian dualism* that promotes abstract formalism to the exclusion (or devaluation) of body experience; the importance of *embodied cognition* (body knowing) in designing; a need to rethink how we normally think about aesthetics (as quality of experience rather than the quality of an object), based on principles of *empirical aesthetics*; and the importance of emotion (feeling) as a motivational factor in the design process. These claims and supporting concepts may be met with objections by others, such as: whether my definition of designing is accurate; whether buildings are or should be considered the proper end to architectural design; whether (gifted) students do just have what it takes to be designers (talent/innate ability) and some do not; whether the design process is definable, or observable; whether the primary standards for assessing a design solution should be rational, programmatic, functional; whether aesthetic judgment is fundamentally/ultimately little more than subjective opinion; whether it is actually possible to learn to be an expert designer.

The following provides a theoretical framework (argument) that both supports my claims and answers the objections. I have divided it into ten chapters. There is a good deal of overlap and perhaps some repetition of ideas between the chapters. This is the result of translating a way of thinking about this topic that is multidimensional, to a two-dimensional narrative. For the sake of a coherent narrative, I have made ample use of footnotes and citations. These both provide support for the argument and provide the reader with references should he want to pursue an idea in more depth.

Chapter 2 locates this research in the domain of architecture design as an occupation that possesses well-defined performance expectations. After reviewing how others have described design, I propose a description of design that will function as a basis for the following chapters. **Chapter 3** provides a brief overview of the history and objectives of design research as a discipline, especially the early attempts at scientising design. This leads to an in-depth review of some theories of problem solving, tacit knowledge and embodied cognition. A main emphasis of this chapter is to (re-) establish the importance of the body in cognition. Arguments are presented from philosophy, evolutionary biology and cognitive science. Many of the ideas contained in this overview have shaped and continue to influence how we talk about designing. It is the foundation for what follows. **Chapter 4** looks at the ways designing can be described as a process, and the influence the concepts of heuristics and systems theory have had on the development of design methodologies. This chapter identifies the three meta-components of designing: the problem, the solution and the problem-framing/solution-seeking process that is at the core of designing. An important point in this chapter is that designing is *not* a process. Process is a cognitive approximation used to describe designing. Designing is a cognitive ability.

Chapters 5, 6, 7, and 8, focus on the three meta-components of the design process. **Chapter 5** looks at the problem in terms of who defines the problem, the structure of the problem and the problematic nature of design problems. **Chapter 6** looks at the solution, who defines the solution, the function of representations, and what is meant by the four normative performance expectations related to design practice that are established by the profession. These expectations are of two types: demonstrable and experiential. The demonstrable expectations are satisfying functional criteria and constraints and technical competency. The experiential expectations induce a sense of coherence and an intended quality of aesthetic experience. The remainder of the chapter is spent on describing these with an in-depth discussion on the importance of a sense of coherence and its evolutionary roots in human cognition.

Chapter 7 explains the meaning and function of aesthesis in the design process, and the historical development of how we understand and experience the aesthetic. Aesthetic is described as a kind of hedonic (body) experience that is induced, that involves sensations, emotions and meaning. And an argument from evolutionary biology and cognitive science is given for inter-subjectivity. **Chapter 8** gets into the heart of what designers do. The chapter describes several ways of thinking about design methodology, presents some representative examples, and finally provides a synthesis that frames a way of describing design that takes into account the function of aesthetic judgment.

With the above establishing what is involved in designing, the following two chapters look at how design expertise is acquired. **Chapter 9** is about expertise. It starts with the question, who can be a designer? The question is explored in terms of personality, character traits, and aptitude. The research suggests that there are very few indicators that suggest that one person over the other is more likely to be successful at design, except for general intelligence, problem-solving ability, personal drive, and access to resources. However, one aptitude does stand out: visio-spatial thinking and problem solving ability. There is no mention of *natural* talent. The chapter ends with a theory of technical ability and a developmental model that describes the stages involved in acquiring expertise.

Chapter 10, after an overview of the argument up until now, introduces the concept of aesthetic resonance. Aesthetic resonance describes how aesthesis functions in the design process, as both a means for assessing internal/external representations, and by pre-structuring the design problem through determining a quality of atmosphere the designer wants to induce in the user. The expression used to describe how aesthesis works in the design process is *inhabiting the design world feelingly*. It is this ability that allows the designer to anticipate how the building/built environment will be experienced by the end user. It is this highly-developed ability to enter feelingly into the design world that is critical to acquiring design expertise.

Structure of the argument

The proper end of architecture is buildings or built environments for human use
 Built environments are made of materials → Humans experience the world through
their bodies → The quality of an architectural solution is determined by both
demonstrable and experiential criteria → Demonstrable criteria have to do with
functional and technical requirements → Experiential requirements have to do with
the sense of coherence and experience of aesthetic qualities of a design solution
→ These are considered to be performance expectations of (architecture) design
practice → The ability to design buildings that exceed the performance expectations
of practice requires design expertise → Design expertise is acquired over time with
years of deliberate practice → Fundamental to design expertise – in addition to being
able to design a building that solves for the demonstrable criteria – is the ability
to make buildings that induce an intended hedonic (aesthetic) experience → The
ability to assess the quality of an aesthetic experience is called aesthesis → Aesthetic
experience is dependent on having a (human) body → Humans have the psychological/
physiological ability to anticipate how another will experience a situation (empathy) →
To achieve (induce) an intended quality of aesthetic experience requires refining the
ability to (accurately) anticipate how another is likely to experience the building/built
environment → Aesthetic resonance is the ability to inhabit a design world "feelingly"
and to anticipate how another is likely to experience the design solution when it is
built → Aesthetic resonance is a fundamental ability necessary for the acquisition of
(architectural) design expertise.

2 What is designing?

A designer makes things.

(Schön, 1991, p. 78)

Like a design problem, writing about designing requires setting a problem space →
framing the problem → finding a way to communicate the ideas in an effective manner.
Like a building design this research is inter-dependent and multi-dimensional.
Conceptually, it is more multi-dimensional rather than two. But, as a means of
transferring information, language typically relies on narrative and a narrative is
basically linear, that is two-dimensional. I need to start somewhere. So, I am starting
with setting the broad boundaries of the problem space.

This chapter locates design expertise in the context of an established profession
or occupation: architectural design practice. As a presupposition it is a given that
the proper end of architectural designing is the production of buildings/built
environments. While it is true that professional architectural design practice involves
more than the designing of buildings and built spaces, including alternative forms
of practice, designing is the focus of this research. The presupposition is that the
act of designing results in objects (artifacts) and it is by the quality of these objects
that a designer's ability (expertise) is judged. There are reasons for starting with this
presupposition that will become clear below.

It will be argued that while the proximate end of architectural the design process is the
making of *representations* – drawings, physical and digital models, documents, etc.
– whose purpose is to facilitate the making of buildings, the proper end (telos) of the
architecture design process is the production of buildings.[6]

---

6   Though I feel in debt to Prof. Rittel for all I have learned about design from his writing, in these ways I hazard
to respectfully disagree with him. (1.) Rittel (1968) declares design is "an activity, aiming at the production of
a plan." As pointed out above and as will be discussed in detail later, the proper end to architectural design as
an activity is a building. It is not a plan. When the end of architectural design is thought to be a plan, it results
in several unintended consequences. These will be discussed below. (2.) He (1988) argues that "Since design
is intentional, purposeful, goal-seeking, it decisively relies on reasoning" (p. 2). I will argue below, that to the
contrary, designing – as a tacit way of knowing and as a function of embodied cognition – decisively relies on
feelings (body knowledge) or aesthesis. (3.) Rittel (1988), who was a philosopher and planner, also argues that
"Design terminates with a commitment to a plan which is meant to be carried out" (p. 1). Here again Rittel
seems to miss the point. Designers *make* things. I will explain what I mean by this below.

Designing, as an action, in this thesis is understood to be teleological. That is, designing as an action is not seen as a *good* (value) in itself. The value of designing as an action is to be found in the quality of the proper end of the action; where activities and all proximate ends contained within the action are directed toward achieving its end. As the quote from Schön above says, "a designer makes things."

With these boundaries established, I will explore what might be meant by designing as an activity[7] and the goals of design research. I will not try to define designing, rather I will offer a working description. The purpose of this first chapter is to establish the context, to define the problem space and frame the problem.

§ 2.1   The Designer's Context

This research is not about designing in its most basic sense, as in "everyone can design."[8] Or as Cross calls it "run-of-the-mill designing" (1990, p. 129), or "lower level design ability" (2007, p. 38).[9] **This research is about design expertise – designing practiced as a recognized occupation** (profession) **in a manner that** (significantly) **exceeds (normative) performance expectations established by a profession** (domain).[10]

---

[7] As this research is not about providing a prescriptive definition of or methodology for how to design, but rather to understand how design expertise is acquired, I am intentionally not going to provide a definition of design. I am however going to describe what I mean by design.

[8] "All men are designers. All that we do, almost all the time, is design, for design is basic to all human activity. The planning and patterning of any act toward a desired, foreseeable end constitutes the design process... Design is composing an epic poem, executing a mural, painting a masterpiece, writing a concerto. But design is also cleaning and reorganizing a desktop drawer, pulling an impacted tooth, baking an apple pie, choosing sides for a back-lot baseball game, and educating a child... Design is the conscious effort to impose meaningful order" (Papanek, 1984, p.3).

[9] "Although professional designers might naturally be expected to have highly developed design abilities, it is also clear that non-designers also possess at least some aspects, or lower levels of design ability. Everyone makes decisions about arrangements and combinations of clothes, furniture, et However, in other societies, especially non-industrial one's, there is often no clear distinction between professional and amateur design abilities – the role of the professional designer might not exist" (Cross, 2007 p. 38).

[10] Winch (2010) explains that expertise as it is related to practical activity "involves mastery of an occupation, profession or activity" (p. 1). Expertise is a level or quality of performance that is evaluated against an accepted norm. Performance expectations are established by and/or accepted by the occupation. It is not possible to talk about expertise without referring to a field within which it takes place. To put this important point into context Winch refers to MacIntyre's influential book, *After Virtue* (2007) where "practice" is described as a recurrent social activity characterized by four key features:

>>>

As noted above, this research is not about professional designers in general, but designing as it is practiced (situated) within the specific discipline (domain) of architecture. As such, it is the *performance expectations* as found/established within the domain of architectural design (as a recognized practice) that will define the problem space for this research.

As an occupation (or profession) architectural design serves both personal and social goods, and possesses expectations[11] that are well-established by historical tradition, professional associations and society in general.[12] It is not understood as simply a skill, ability or a "way of knowing" that is practiced in isolation. In this way, design expertise is understood to possess characteristics in common with other types of expert performance. "Architectural design," understood as an occupation or profession, does not exist in isolation. In many ways architectural design as an occupation is a *social construct*.[13]

>>>

1. It has goals or *telos* (internal/intrinsic goods), criteria for the achievements of which constitute the of excellence available in that practice. The activities involved in achieving and the fulfillment of the criteria of excellence are both seen as intrinsic goods.
2. It is historically constituted and involves taking into account of a developing tradition or activity aimed at attaining intrinsic goods.
3. A practitioner understands the significance of his life and worthiness in relation to the practices in which he is located
4. In addition to internal goods a practice also possesses external goods that have extrinsic value, i.e.: the ability to make money. (p. 11)

11   The terms *norms* and *performance expectations* as described by Winch(footnote 12) are used in this research not in the sense of rules, but rather as *reasonable expectations* or basic criteria. In this case performance expectations refer to, in general terms, the reasonable expectations has for the work a particular practice. Or the criteria one can use which describes the scope of service one might normally expect from an occupation.

12   In the report, *Building Community: A future for architecture education and practice* Boyer writes, "Membership in any profession, whether law, medicine, teaching, journalism, accounting, or architecture, entails not only the mastery of a body of knowledge and skills but at its best the honoring of a social contract to advance basic human values… In the case of architecture, the larger purposes relate not only to building competently and fulfilling the wishes of the clients, but to helping to foster, through design, more wholesome neighborhoods, safer streets, more productive work places, a cleaner environment, and more cohesive communities" (Boyer & Mitgang, 1996 p. 31).

13   "Social constructs or social constructions define meanings, notions, or connotations that are assigned to objects and events in the environment and to people's notions of their relationships to and interactions with these objects. In the domain of social constructionist thought, a social construct is an idea or notion that appears to be natural and obvious to people who accept it but may or may not represent reality, so it remains largely an invention or artifice of a given society" (Ozor, 2008).

Expertise implies above average performance as measured against an accepted norm. This means that there must be normative (implied or explicit) performance expectations against which performance is measured.[14] Like it or not, a designer's performance, insofar as he is deemed to be performing at an expert level, is so only insofar as his performance is evaluated against normative performance expectations that are established by historical tradition, professional associations and the society (culture) in general. Expertise is a relative term.

Without reference to such expectations (of practice) it is impossible to discuss levels of expertise or expert performance. The difficulty in this case is explicitly stating, establishing and/or codifying said performance expectations for architecture design. While there have been numerous attempts to do this over the centuries, through treatises, codes of professional practice promoted by professional societies, regulations and licensing by government authorities, the primary way by which a practitioner learns the professional expectations of practice is by participating in and becoming part of the professional culture.[15] These expectations are more implicit than explicit in practice, descriptive than prescriptive, acquired more by being incorporated into the culture of the practice than by imposition from outside.[16]

---

14   Csikszentmihalyi (1996, p. 27) in identifying not what creativity is, but where it is to be found identifies three criteria, "…the idea must be couched in terms that are understandable to others, it must past muster with experts in the field, and finally it must be included in the cultural domain to which it belongs." Further, he writes, "A person cannot be creative in a domain to which he or she is not exposed. No matter how enormous mathematical gifts a child may have, he or she will not be able to contribute to mathematics without learning its rules." Csikszentmihaly's point is that a truly "creative" (as opposed to "novel") act, idea or way of thinking can only legitimately be considered as such within a particular domain, recognized by its gate-keepers, and be the work of an individual or group of individuals working within the domain. This is not to say that it is not possible for an individual working outside the domain to stumble upon a genuinely creative, culture changing idea, that either is or is not accepted or rejected as such by the field (gate-keepers). It is only to say that this is not the norm and should be seen as the standard. See also Gardner (1993).

15   These are so numerous that it would be impossible to provide a comprehensive list of references here. A Google search of "architecture standards of professional practice" resulted in over 84,000,000 results in 0.37 seconds. Some examples of what I am referring to would be from Vitruvius, *On Architecture*, Books 1-10 (1998); (Vitruvius, 1998); Palladio, *Four Books of Architecture* (1997); Semper, *The Four Elements of Architecture* (1989); to UIA International Standards of Professional Practice (2014), AIA Handbook of Professional Practice (2014); the UK Architects Registration Board's *Architects Code: Standards of Professional Practice* (2009); RIBA Code of Practice for Chartered Practices (2005); Royal Institute of Dutch Architect's, *The Architecture Profession in the Netherlands* (2006).

16   In this way the profession is seen as the gate-keeper. The American Institute of Architects revised and enacted the *Standards of Professional Practice*, at the 86th Convention held in Boston. The following quote makes the point: "There is one aspect of our responsibility that no one else can discharge for us. Where we as individuals live and practice our profession. The profession and all architects are judged by us. No program of national publicity or public relations will avail if in our own community we fail to do a good job. Here is a responsibility we cannot shirk. Upon us personally and individually rests the yoke of the discipline of our profession" (Cummings, 1955).

In much of the world this involves the *rite of passage* associated with most professions: completing an accredited professional degree program, a professional internship, qualifying and passing a licensing/registration exam, and years of practice. Specifying what these expectations are and providing an in-depth description of how these expectations are assimilated is beyond the scope of this research. The point here is simply that expertise in **architecture design as a profession or occupation is defined by performance expectations** that, though not static, exist in a social/historical/cultural context. And anyone who professes to be a designer as a professional architect practices within this context.

Having located design expertise in the context of an occupation or practice, where an established occupation (legitimately) imposes performance expectations of practice, we can now get on to describing what is meant by (the practice of) designing.

Describing Designing

Describing design, as an activity, can be an elusive task. Over the years there have been numerous attempts.[17] Each description takes a particular point of view that emphasizes some aspect, function, purpose, or personal opinion about what designing might be.[18] None are completely adequate or exhaustive. This being the case, I have decided that I am not even going to attempt to "define" designing.

Rather I propose, as a working description, that architectural design is **a kind of solution-driven problem-solving process that results in the making of a functional representation for a building/built environment that solves for design criteria and constraints within an acceptable range, that is technically competent, coherent, and induces intended aesthetic qualities**. The meaning and the implications of this description will unfold in the following chapters.

Four components of designing are identified in this description that function as performance expectations.[19] These components are of two types: demonstrable and experiential. The demonstrable components describe the quantitative, measurable (perhaps objective) aspects of the design solution. The experiential components describe the qualitative (perhaps subjective) aspects of the design solution. Most design/problem-solving theories (implicitly) suggest three performance standards: (1.) A successful design solution should satisfy design criteria and constraints within an acceptable range, (2.) be technically feasible (possible to build), (3.) and possess some level of coherence (makes sense).

---

17   Buchanan writes, "No single definition of design, or branches of professional practice such as industrial or graphic design, adequately covers the diversity of ideas and methods gathered together under the label" (1995, p.3). In describing the pluralism of definitions, diverse ideas, meanings and claims about design in the design literature Buchanan and Margolin (1995, p. xiii) write: "Young designers are rightfully confused about the pluralism of competing ideas, and they struggle to form their own concepts and find a place in the design professions... At its best ... debate about the meaning and definition of design has gradually broadened the subject matter under discussion, revealing new aspects of products and suggesting alternative paths for exploration, practice and reflection."

18   Some of these will be reviewed below.

19   These will be discussed in detail below. Though I rearranged them, these four performance expectations are derived from Vitruvius (1998), Book I. c. III, 2: "Now these should be so carried out that account is taken of strength [*firmitatis*], utility [*utilitatis*], grace [*venustatis*]. Account will be taken of *strength* when the foundations are carried down to solid ground, and when from each material there is a choice of supplies without parsimony; of *utility*, when the sites are arranged without mistake and impediment to their use, and a fit and convenient disposition for the aspect of each kind; of *grace*, when the appearance of the work shall be pleasing and elegant, and the scale of the constituent parts is justly calculated for symmetry." Criteria and constraints refers to *utilitatis*; technical competency refers to *firmitatis*; and coherence and aesthetic quality refers to *venustatis*.

Most do not (even implicitly) identify inducing intended aesthetic quality as a separate component.[20] This may have to do with the desire within design research to be inclusive of those design disciplines for which a design solution is not necessarily an artifact – thus making it difficult to talk about aesthetic qualities as an independent component of designing. More likely, I will argue, is the desire, promoted by the Modernists (still prevalent within the schools and the profession) and argued for by the design methods movement, that designing can be, even ought to be, scientised.

---

20   There is a presupposition, attributed to modernism, that if a design solution optimizes functional/technical requirements, and is governed by reason and "mathematical calculation", the solution will (implicitly) possess *meaning* and/or aesthetic qualities. From this point of view there is no need to be explicitly concerned with determining intended aesthetic experience, as long as the design is rationally defensible. This concept, usually misquoted and wrongly attributed to Sullivan's (1896) famous aphorism "form ever follows function" (Leslie, 2010; Mumford, 1989), which is often mis-attributed to Le Corbusier (Rawsthorn, 2009) who promoted a kind of *machine aesthetic* (See Banham, 1980, p. 188 quoting van Doesburg, "The new possibilities of the machine have created an aesthetic expressive of our time, that I once called the 'machine aesthetic'.") famously described in by his "five points" (Corbusier, 1926/1970). In *Towards a New Architecture* Le Corbusier (1923/1986) writes "the Engineer's Aesthetic and Architecture are two things that march together and follow one from the other: the one being now at its full height, the other in an unhappy state of retrogression" (p. 17). He goes further to insist that the architect should follow the engineer who "inspired by the law of Economy and governed by mathematical calculation" achieves harmony (p. 102). And that by doing so, "The Architect, by his arrangement of forms, realizes an order which is a pure creation of his spirit; by forms and shapes he affects our senses to an acute degree and provokes plastic emotions; by relationships which he creates he wakes profound echoes in us, he gives us the measure of an order which we feel to be in accordance with that of our world, he determines the various movements of our heart and of our understanding; it is then that we experience the sense of beauty" (p. 20). Perez-Gomez (1992) writes, "Many years have passed since architects began their search for a universal theory grounded in absolute rational certainty. Gottfried Semper, for one, drawing on some of the insights first expressed by Durand, postulated functionalism as a fundamental premise of architectural intentionality. Semper clearly attempted to make the process of design analogous to the resolution of an algebraic equation. The 'variables' represented the manifold of reality that architecture had to take into account; the solution was simply a 'function' of these variables. This reductionist strategy has since become the fundamental framework of architecture theory and practice, whether one examines the forms of structural determinism or more subtle attempts to utilize psychological, sociological, or even aesthetic variables. More recently, various sophisticated methodologies and even computers have been applied to design, always failing, however, to come to terms with the essential question of meaning in architecture" (p. 469). For Perez-Gomez, meaning is analogous to what I mean by aesthetic quality, it is the ability of architecture, as to evoke a particular kind of experience that imbues architecture with meaning. Johnson, (2015) describing human beings as "complex, bodily and social animals... [whose locus of all] experience, meaning, thought, valuing, communicating, and action is a series of ongoing organism-environment interactions," argues that the "meaning" of "any object or event arises in the processes of organism-environment interaction that mutually define ourselves and our world. The meaning of any object, person or event is what it affords us or points to by way of some experience we might have – either past or present, or future possible experience" (p. 27). Meaning in this sense has to do with the significance of our (embodied) interaction with the world (simulation semantics) as opposed to abstract inference (conceptual semantics). Meaningful interaction with the world relies on the "affordances" that "arise from the ways my body-mind can engage that object or event" (p. 28). See Gibson (1986). In this way, the experience of the world has aesthetic meaning, or as Dewey writes, meaning "that presents itself directly as possessions of objects which are experienced... the meaning is as inherent in immediate experience as is that of a flower garden" (1994, p. 41). Maier & Fadel (2009) write "in the context of engineering design, we define an affordance as a relationship between two subsystems in which a potential behavior can occur that would not be possible with either subsystem in isolation" (p. 226).

I will argue, however, that for an architectural design solution to exhibit expert qualities it must satisfy four performance expectations:

1   Solve for (functional) design criteria/constraints[21]
2   Be technically competent (possible to implement with available technology and materials)
3   Appear to be coherent (make sense to the user)
4   Induce (intended) quality of aesthetic experience

Further, I will argue that, in architectural design, these four performance expectations function together in a manner that is **interdependent and incommensurable**. To do so an expert designer must possess multiple cognitive abilities, skills and competencies to produce design solutions that satisfy (all) these performance expectations. How this is achieved, how the various performance expectations function in the design process, and how the ability to satisfy them is learned/acquired is the question of this research.

§ 2.3   Designing as an Object of Study

The purpose of researching design/design behavior/design cognition is to gain a deeper understanding of what happens when designers design, to identify/codify methodologies and methods that can inform how designing is taught, with the goal of improving the effectiveness and efficiency of the design process and to increase the likelihood of producing better quality design solutions.

Cross (2007) writes that knowledge about designing comes from three sources: (1.) People, (2.) Processes, and (3.) Products.[22]

---

21   This component of design is most like problem-solving. It refers to the functionalism postulated by Semper (Perez-Gomez, 1998).

22   While I prefer Cross' morphology, there are other ways to think about it. For example, Rittel writes that design research (science of design) has three tasks: (1.) To further develop theories of and to learn more about the reasoning of designers; (2.) To pursue empirical inquiries about how "plans" come about; (3.) To discover new tools to support designers in their work. (Rittel, 1987, p. 9)

1   **People**: designing is a distinctively human activity, there is no evidence that other animals display such behavior,[23] and (so far) machines cannot do it either.[24] As such design research studies designing as a kind of human behavior. This includes examining the nature of designing ability, performance expectations of practice, as well as understanding how people learn to design.

2   **Processes**: designing is an observable behavior that follows predictable patterns or processes, making use of similar tactics and strategies (methodology/methods) that aid the designer in discovering a solution. Much of this research involves careful observation of designers at work in a controlled environment (design/talk aloud protocol).[25] Critical reflection on these observations gives insight into how designers actually work, which tools and methods facilitate the process, when various strategies are applied.

3   **Products**: these are the embodiment of the design solution. Their shapes, forms, materials, textures, functions, applications, references and precedents all embody design attributes. How a product evolves over multiple generations, how new products emerge, and what forms a designer can imagine often depends on the nature of the problem, the needs of the user, the available fabrication and production technologies. The study of the end product provides a wealth of information that can be used to gain deeper insight into designing.

---

23 This not completely true, there is some evidence that animals do engage in deliberate problem solving activities including evaluating aesthetic quality. See Ramachandran (2011); Damasio (1994); de Waal (2016) and Dong (2015). A famous example is that of the bower birds from Australia and New Guinea who build elaborately decorated nests with arrangements of flowers, berries, stones, and even bits of plastic in deliberate patterns. Such is the intention of these arrangements that should the bower bird return to his nest and find even one stone out of place, he will immediately return it to its proper place. (Ramachandran, 2011, p. 194-195)

24 Dreyfus (1992), discussing the limitations of "good old-fashioned AI," argues that due to the disembodied nature of computers, they are (and will always be) incapable of solving certain types of problems (a kind of bounded rationality of computers), architectural design being one of them. As a fundamental characteristic of architectural design is the quality of the aesthetic experience, and both the ability to assess and experience that quality relies on embodied cognition (having a human body), and as computers do not have human bodies (and most likely never will), it is impossible for computers to generate, evaluate and assess the quality of the aesthetic experience of the design solution. This does not however mean that computers are useless in the design process. See Schön (1992) for a discussion on the role of computers in the design process.

25 *Think aloud protocol analysis* emerged as a method of research in the area of problem solving in the 1920's. Both the general availability of tape recorders in the late 40's and video in the 70's aided in increasing the accuracy and verifiability of note-taking and observations. Two landmark studies were by de Groot (1965) on playing chess, and by Newel and Simon (1972) on problem solving. "In essence, protocol analysis relies on the verbal accounts given by subjects of their own cognitive activities" (Cross et al. 1996) as well as documenting sketches and similar externalizations related to the thought process. Cross et al. (1996), Zeisel (2006), and Goldschmidt (2014) recognize the limitations inherent in asking someone to describe their thinking process while actively working (think aloud protocols) but, even so, the empirical data gained from these protocols has led to significant insights, and in fact is the most common data collection method used in design research.

Based on these three sources of design knowledge, Cross (2007) proposes a taxonomy of the field of design research that includes:

— *Design epistemology* – study of designerly ways of knowing (cognition)
— *Design praxiology* – study of the practices and processes of design (methodology)
— *Design phenomenology* – study of the form and configuration of artifacts (criticism)[26]

In addition to the three sources mentioned above, there is an additional source of study related to designing and designer's behavior, and that is Artificial Intelligence (AI), design automation, and computer generated design. Research related to problem-solving, systems and cybernetics, the mechanization of the problem-solving process and AI (cognitive science), has influenced design research as a discipline from the beginning (See Polya,1945; Popper, 1959; Churchman, 1968; Simon, 1996; Rittel, 1984; Schön, 1992). While research into design automation has led to many important insights into designing, designer's behavior, and design mechanization, (see Cross, 1977; Gun, 1982; Coyne et al. 1990; Mitchell, 1990; Ward and Smith, 1992; Tzonis & White, 1994; Davis, 2015; Gero & Maher, 2016), my interest in this research is only insofar as it provides insight into how humans design and how design expertise is acquired by people (students). Computer aided design is considered here as one of multiple design tools (technologies) that facilitate the work of the (human) designer.[27]

---

26   While I am considering aspects of all three: design epistemology (acquisition of design expertise), design praxiology (methodology) and design phenomenology (the special characteristics of architectural design as a particular domain of design research, and the function of aesthesis in the design process), my emphasis is on design epistemology and design praxiology.

27   Schön (1992, p. 131) discusses computer aided design in terms of the "purpose of the exercise." Schön lists four possible purposes: (1.) To achieve a design output, given some input, as well as, or better than, designers ordinarily do it, but without particular reference to the *ways* in which the do it; this is the Turing test, more or less, and it will be called functional equivalence. (2.) To reproduce *how* people actually go about designing; this will be called phenomenological equivalence (3.) To assist designers in their designing (4.) To provide an environment for research aimed at understanding how designers design. It is the latter which I am most interested in.

§ 2.4   Designing in the Most Basic Sense

In the most basic/simplistic sense, designing as an activity (not necessarily design expertise) can be understood as a fundamental (human) activity in which all people engage that leads to "making things to serve a useful goal" (Dorst, 2015, p. vii).[28] Terzidis, (2007) in an article about the etymology of design writes:

[D]esign is a conceptual activity involving formulating an idea intended to be expressed in a visible form or carried into action. Design is about conceptualization, imagination, and interpretation. Design is a vague, ambiguous, and indefinite process of genesis, emergence, or formation of something to be executed, but whose starting point, origin, or process often are uncertain. Design provides the spark of an idea and the formation of a mental image. It is about the primordial stage of capturing, conceiving, and outlining the main features of a plan and, as such, it always precedes the planning stage. (p. 69)[29]

The verb "design"

is derived from the prefix *de* and the Latin verb *signare*, which means to mark, mark out, or sign. The prefix de is used not in the derogatory sense of opposition or reversal, but in the constructive sense of derivation, deduction, or inference. In that context, the word 'design' is about the derivation of something that suggests the presence or existence of a fact, condition, or quality. (p. 69)

---

28   "Everyone can – and does – design. We all design when we plan for something new to happen, whether that might be a new version of a recipe, a new arrangement of the living room furniture, or a new layout of a personal web page. The evidence from different cultures around the world, and from design created by children as well as adults, suggests that everyone is capable of designing... it is a key part of what makes us human" (Cross, 2011).

29   Design is not the same as planning.

The word design in Greek

is σχε'διο (pronounced schedio), which is derived from the root σχεδο'ν (pronounced sche- don), which means 'nearly, almost, about, or approximately.' Thus, from its Greek definition, design is about incompleteness, indefiniteness, or imperfection, yet it also is about likelihood, expectation, or anticipation. In its largest sense, design signifies not only the vague, intangible, or ambiguous, but also the strive to capture the elusive. (Terzidis, 2007, p. 69)

During the Renaissance, Walker (2009) writes, *disegno* "described the inventive, conceptualizing phase which generally preceded the making of paintings, sculptures and so forth" (p. 42). It wasn't until the industrial revolution of the 18ᵗʰcentury that the modern notion of (professional) designers, as such, began to emerge as "the full-time activity undertaken by trained specialists employed or commissioned by manufactures" who were not normally involved in the production of the things they designed (p. 43).[30]

The *Merriam-Webster Learner's Dictionary*[31] definition of design is: "de·sign **verb** \di-'zīn\: to plan and make decisions about (something that is being built or created): to create the plans, drawings, etc., that show how (something) will be made." In this definition designing is understood as an action, a verb, it is not the end product.[32] Further, designing is understood as a creative goal-oriented, teleological activity. An activity that involves planning and making decisions about something that will be made, built or created; where the perfection of the action is determined by its proper end.

The word design can also be used as a noun (as in, "What do you think of my design?"), and as an adjective (as in, "design research"). Both of these forms are derivatives of the verb form. When used as a noun design can refer to the design concept, or the idea that generated the product, thus making a distinction between the object at hand and the design.

---

30   Though the evolution of the architect as a design professional removed from actual building (from craftsman, to master builder, to professional) evolved over centuries, it follows a similar pattern. See Kostof (1977); Cuff (1992) "Metamorphosis of Architecture," and http://www.designingbuildings.co.uk/wiki/The_architectural_ profession for an excellent historical summary of the evolution of the architect as a professional in England.

31   http://www.learnersdictionary.com/definition/design (January 24, 2017)

32   Properly speaking, one does not design for the sake of designing.

Design as a noun can also refer to the proper end or product of the design activity (*qua* verb) as an artifact called 'a design' (*qua* noun) – which is not the thing itself but, as Habraken (1985) calls it, a *functional approximation* of a thing to be made.

Schön (1988, p. 182) writes, "**design is understood as a kind of *making*: an action that results in an artifact**" [for human use]. This is the basic understanding of designing that informs this research.

§ 2.5   The Proper End of Designing

The type of something/artifact that is intended to be made greatly influences how one goes about designing (tacit knowledge) and determines the scope of knowledge necessary (declarative knowledge) in order to design it. While there are broad general principles, methodologies and methods that can be applied to all design disciplines (graphic design, industrial design, architectural design, engineering design, etc.) each discipline (domain) specializes in designing different types of artifacts, that require different areas of specialized knowledge, competencies and skills.[33] The specialized knowledge necessary to design a website is not the same as that which is necessary to design a toaster; is not the same as that which is necessary to design a building; is not the same knowledge necessary to design a sewer system. The criteria for and the way one experiences or uses a website, a toaster, a building and a sewer system are not the same either.

---

[33]   That there are principles, methodologies and characteristics of design thinking/problem solving that are cross-disciplinary is well established. See Jones (1992) Cross (2007), Lawson (2005), Schön (1991), Lawson and Dorst (2009), Buchanan & Margolin (1995). However, due to the significant variation between the (content and expected outcomes of) different domains of design, there is also value in discussing design as it is situated in a particular domain. This research will use many of the concepts and theories from design research that are considered cross-disciplinary, and then look more closely at them as they can be applied to architectural design in particular. The emphasis on design as a cross-disciplinary activity was, and to some extent continues to be, preferred within the design research community. However, as this research is not about design in general, but rather design *expertise* within the domain of architecture, I am emphasizing the *situatedness* of design as a kind of expertise. Gero and Kannengieser (2008) write, "Situatedness is a paradigm that provides a framework for understanding how a designer's interactions affect both what is designed and the designer's experience (Gero 1999), drawing on models of situated cognition (Dewey, 1896; Bartlett, 1932; Clancey, 1997; Ziemke, 1999). It can account for the central role of Schön's reflection-in-action and related phenomena reported in empirical studies of designers (Suwa et al., 1999). Gero and Kannengiesser (2004) have modeled situated designing as the recursive interaction between three different worlds: the external world, the interpreted world and the expected world" (p. 3).

Designing, by its very nature, tends to be situated in a particular domain.[34] One doesn't normally ask an engineer to do graphic design, just as one usually does not ask an architect to design a tea kettle – though I suppose you could.[35]

In the *Nicomachean Ethics* (2004), Chapter 1, book 1, Aristotle argues that every action has an end that is proper to it (a *telos*).

Every art and every inquiry, and similarly every action and pursuit, is thought to aim at some good; and for this reason the good has rightly been declared to be that at which all things aim. But a certain difference is found among ends; some are activities, others are products apart from the activities that produce them. Where there are ends apart from the actions, it is the nature of the products to be better than the activities. Now, as there are many actions, arts, and sciences, their ends also are many; the end of the medical art is health, that of shipbuilding a vessel, that of strategy victory, that of economics wealth. (p. 3)

Designing as a goal oriented (teleological) activity has a goal (*telos*) that is proper to it: the thing to be made/the artifact. As such architectural design also has a *telos* (just as making ships is to ship-building) that is proper to it: the making of buildings.[36]

---

34   There is a general assumption that problem solving/design skills are transferable across disciplines. The research, following McCormick (1997), does not accept this. Decades of research have found that problem-solving skill is highly dependent on considerable domain specific knowledge. See Glaser (1984). Both problem-solving and design (as a kind of problem solving) cannot be reduced (or generalized) to cross-disciplinary procedural heuristics, processes or pure algorithms.

35   Lawson quotes the noted product designer Richard Seymour who observed "Although some architecture and some product designs look very close it is really the extreme end of the bow of the architecture tree rubbing up against a leaf at the extremity of the product design tree. We tend to think that they are very similar, but they are not. Fundamentally their roots are completely different" (1994).

36   While this observation may seem self-evident, it is a surprisingly contentious point. In an informal survey I asked 12 colleagues and grad students at Tsinghua University what they thought the proper end of architectural design was: a concept (idea behind the design or generative idea), a set of plans (model and diagrams), a building (the actual built building), or quality of space (created by the building). Six answered concept, two a set of plans, one answered building, two answered quality of space, and one answered concept and quality of space.

This is not to say that the practice or occupation of architectural design may not have other benefits and produce other ends,[37] but these benefits and other ends are subordinate to the proper end of the action – in the Aristotelian sense.

The quality of the action is determined by the quality of the end that results from the action. This quality is determined by domain specific, *normative*[38] performance expectations. Just as the excellent ship-builder is said to be so because he builds excellent ships, so it is that the level of expertise of the architectural designer is determined by the quality of the (built) buildings/built environments that he designs. **The proper end of architectural design is buildings/built environments.**[39]

§ 2.6   Proximate End of Designing

However, while buildings may be the proper end (*telos*) to architectural design, buildings are not the proximate end. Designers (normatively) do not "make" buildings *per se*. What they do is make *functional approximations* for the purpose of building buildings (Schön, 1988; Habraken, 1985). Its been many centuries since architectural designers were known as "master-builders," or were directly involved with the actual construction/making of buildings.[40] From the outside, many people believe what architectural designers make are drawings, models and renderings.

---

37   See Cuff (1992) for a general overview of architecture practice

38   Normative is this sense is a generally accepted standard or expectation for performance as commonly used in the study of Ethics. It is not meant to be evaluative. It simply refers to a what one usually means by or reasonably expects when describing a particular behavior or practice.

39   Dewey (1938/1987) writes, "Why put it down in black and white that painting cannot exist without color, music without sound, architecture without stone and wood, statuary without marble and bronze, literature without words, dancing without the living body?" Explaining that "in every experience, there is the pervading underlying qualitative whole that corresponds and manifests the whole organism of activities which constitute the mysterious human frame (p. 204)

40   Though there is a growing interest in design/build where the architect is both designer and builder, it is not considered normative. In fact, it was not that long ago that it was considered unprofessional if not unethical by the AIA for architects to be both architect and builder on the same project.

The confusion comes not from the fact that architects do make drawings, and drawings are/can be approximations, but with what the nature and the (intended) function (purpose) of the drawings (or approximations) are.[41]

In the most fundamental sense an approximation can be understood, without reference to physiology or "hardware," as "the way patterns within [a system] mirror, or fail to mirror the patterns without that they represent" (Newell, Shaw, & Simon, 1958, p. 51). In this way,[42] design activity can be understood as being comprised of two (inter-related) meta activities: that of ideation (conceiving of the thing to be produced) – what is normally referred to as the "design process," and that of devising a means for *externalizing*[43] the idea in a manner that sufficiently communicates the design intention so that it can be produced (usually by others), resulting in an artifact (building) that actualizes the design intent (within an acceptable range). The intended purpose of the (proximate) product of designing is to provide a means of communicating (transferring) the information necessary to actualize the design intent.

---

41   It is also of interest how the designer "encodes" his internal representation (design idea that is not, in a cognitive sense, visual, spatial, haptic or auditory) in order to translate the idea into an external representation (verbal description, drawing, model, CAD, etc.) that can be perceived and understood by another. (See Newell et. al., 1958, p. 54 ff.) This problem is further complicated, if one is of the belief that the proper end to architectural design is not a building but spatial experience. Gibson (1986), Bloomer and Moore (1977), Weber (1995), Zumthor (2006) and others, observe that spatial experience involves not just single senses (such as smell, touch, taste, sight, hearing) but rather by *sense systems*, which are informed by past experience (memory), and perceived meaning (cognition). How does one accurately encode such intention in a manner that can be reliably communicated to the builder? Does one make a note: "Room to be light and airy"? And just to make this ever so slightly more complicated, Newell et al. propose the concept of the "mind's eye," or the "mind's ear," asserting that "an internal representation is visual if it is capable of serving as an input to the same information processes as those that operate on the internal representations of immediate visual sensory experiences" (p. 55). Their point is that while in fact the mind does not "see", people do experience the phenomenon of "seeing", (without the use of their eyes) which from an operational point of view is sufficient. Pallasmaa makes a similar point in his *Eyes of the Skin* (2005). The significance of this phenomenon, which is related to the experience of *empathy* and described by *mirror-neurons* for design expertise will be discussed below.

42   In terms of producing the end-product of design. Within the design process drawing/externalizations serve many purposes.

43   The topic of externalizing design ideas is closely related to the question of the role of drawing in the design process. While this is a closely related and fascinating topic, I will not deal with it in detail here. Goldschmidt (2003) and Arnheim (1993) frame the issue well. In the studio, I make a useful distinction for my students. Designers make five different types of drawings: diagrams (used for understanding/exploring relationships), sketches (used for exploring formal/spatial ideas), technical drawings (used for testing and refining ideas as well as communicating detailed information about building assemblies), and finally illustrations (intended to simulate the visual appearance of spatial experience of the finished thing). The cognitive function of drawing is two-fold: the physical act of drawing and seeing provides feedback to the designer allowing him/her to *see* if what he is thinking about is what he intends; and as a means of extending the short-term working memory of the human mind, allowing the designer to extend the mind's capacity to deal with highly complex problems.

To do so the designer makes a *functional approximation* or representation (which may include drawings, models, CAD, prototypes, written documentation, etc.) that is intended to communicate to another how to make the intended thing. For the designer, this representation is *instrumental* or *functional*: it is not the end-in-itself.

Let me explain...

A representation or image of a thing is not the thing itself, it is an approximation. Larkin and Simon (1987) write, "Two representations are computationally equivalent if they are *informationally equivalent* and, in addition, any inference that can be drawn easily and quickly from the information given explicitly in the one can also be drawn easily and quickly in the other, and vice versa" (p. 67). But it is impractical for architects to produce *computationally equivalent* representations of things as complex (and big) as buildings. Instead what architects do is make *representations*, whose purpose it is **to approximate the information necessary to actualize the making of a building with the intended characteristics.** It does not matter what form the representation takes: drawings, diagrams, models (physical or computer generated), BIM, specification manuals, conversation or scratches on a rock. The point is to transfer the information – through whatever means – that effectively facilitates the communication of an accurate representation of the "design" to another who will make the building as per the design approximation.

There are many types of representations (sometimes called externalizations) involved in designing. These serve different functions in the design process.[44] Schön (1988) writes, "Sketches, diagrams, drawings and models function as virtual worlds, representations of the real world of building on a site, within which architects can experiment at relatively low risk and cost" (p. 182). However, finally, the design needs to externalize and reliably transfer the elements of the "virtual world" as a representation so that someone can make it in "the real-world of building on a site."

Polanyi (1974) makes a helpful distinction when he discusses two kinds of *meaning* that a thing (whole) may possess: *existential* and *representative* (or *denotative*). He writes, "anything that functions effectively within an accredited context has a meaning in that context and... any such context will itself be appreciated as meaningful" (p. 58). Within such a context (as design), a thing (the outcome of the design process, i.e.: the functional representation embodied as a set of drawings or model, specifications, BIM, etc.) may have either existential or representative meaning. In the existential sense, a thing has meaning in itself, for example, pure math or "the meaning of music is mainly existential."

---

44   The topic of representations as they function in the design process will be taken up later.

In the representative sense, a thing means, or points to (as a symbol might), or describes (denotative) another thing. The thing, in this sense has no *meaning* in and of itself, its meaning comes from that toward which it is pointing or that which it is describing – it is *instrumental*. The proximate product of designing (the functional representation of the proposed object) is therefore understood not in the existential sense (the drawings or models as products in themselves), but rather in the sense that they (the drawings or models, etc.) point to something else: the intended building/built environment. The functional representation of the object only has meaning insofar as it means "not the building, but at one remove, sets of instructions for building" (Hillier, et al., 1972). The proximate product of designing is better understood as a "data set" or set of instructions, in whatever form, whose primary function is to communicate the information necessary to make (build) the building as intended by the designer(s).

However it is possible for a thing to possess both primary meaning and subsidiary meaning(s), even at the same time. For example, it is possible that technical drawings, though made for the purpose of providing technical information for the purpose of building, can be (at the same time) understood or appreciated as expertly crafted artifacts in themselves.[45] But it must be understood, that in this case, the artifacts (technical drawings) are no longer valued (though they still retain it) for their intended purpose as a *functional approximation* of the thing to be built. Their value in this case is as *objects that were intended for another use*.

The proximate end of architectural designing, then, is the making of a functional approximation for the purpose of building (making). While the proper end is the building (object) that meets certain demonstrable criteria and constraints and possess certain experiential qualities. Insofar as the actual building that results from the interpretation and implementation of the functional approximation produced by the designer satisfies the minimum standard expectations of professional practice it is considered minimally competent. And to the extent that the functional representation produced by the designer significantly exceeds the minimum expectations the work is considered to be that of an expert. So, then what is meant by designing? What is it that designers do?

---

45   Consider the sketches by Gehry, Johnson, Calatrava etc. or the beautifully inked technical drawings displayed in offices and museums. These have become objects in themselves, appreciated for the skill and meaning and/or emotion that they convey, or simply as historical artifacts. But, as objects in themselves they are no longer valued as functional representations. It is not unlike the tourist who, fascinated with the traditional dress of an ancient culture, takes it home, mounts it in a frame, and proudly displays the artifact over his sofa. The artifact is still a piece of clothing, but its value is no longer as a piece of clothing, but rather as a souvenir. One further example is personal. Before my grandfather died he asked me if I wanted anything. I asked if I could have his hammer. The hammer brought me back to childhood days working by his side. The hammer, though designed and intended as a tool for pounding in nails, is not valuable to me as a tool (though it is perfectly useful), but rather as a relic that induces a state of anamnesis.

§ 2.7 Some Attempts as Defining Designing

The way designing is defined by a dictionary and historians, and the way that designing is understood by designers and design theorists is not necessarily the same. Some attempts at defining design by some noted design theorists include:

— A purposeful activity directed toward the goal of fulfilling human need. (Asimow, 1962, p. 150)
— The process of inventing physical things which display new physical order, organization, form, in response to function. (Alexander, 1964, p. 1)
— The performing of a very complicated act of faith. (Jones, 1966, p. 3)
— Design as we know it can be seen as the socially differentiated transformation of the reflexive cognition of the maker in terms of the latent possibilities of his tools, materials and object types. Its object is not the building, but at one remove, sets of instructions for building. (Hillier, Musgrove, & O'Sullivan, 1972, p. 6)
— The area of human experience, skill and understanding that reflects man's concern with the appreciation and adaptation in his surroundings in light of his material and spiritual needs. (Archer, 1979, p. 17)
— Designing is not a profession but an attitude... [design should] be transformed from the notion of a specialist function into a generally valid attitude of resourcefulness and inventiveness. (Moholy-Nagy, 1947, p.42)
— [Design is] an activity, aiming at the production of a plan, which when implemented, yields the desired results, but no undesired and unforeseen side- and aftereffects. (Rittel, 1968, as cited in Protzen and Harris, 2010, p. 14)
— The conscious and intuitive effort to impose meaningful order... both the underlying matrix of order and the tools that creates it. (Papanek, 1984, p. 4)
— Courses of action aimed at changing existing situations into preferred ones. (Simon H. A., 1988, p. 111)
— Design is a form of problem solving where individual decisions are made toward the fulfillment of objectives. (Akin, 1986, p. 20)
— Design is a complex game in which exploration of formal possibilities in some world and critical inference from some knowledge base proceed in parallel and eventually reach a reconciliation. (Mitchell, 1990, p. 81)
— To design is to plan for the making of something new. (Goldschmidt G. , 1991, p. 125)
— Design is the human power of conceiving, planning, and making products that serve human beings in the accomplishment of their individual and collective purposes. (Buchanan, 2001, p. 9)
— The most essential thing that any designer does is to provide, for those who will make the artifact, a description of what the artifact should be like. (Cross, 1990, p. 128)

- We shall describe architectural designing as a kind of experimentation that consists in reflective 'conversation' with the materials of a design situation… an interaction of making and seeing, doing and discovering. (Schön & Wiggins , 1992, p. 135)
- Design is an enactment of a set of operating principles wherein the actors emphasize different aspects of these principles. (Dong, 2009, p. 9)

The above quotes offer a glimpse into the plurality of ways designers and theorists think about designing in general. Dorst, (2015), building on advances made in design studies over the past 50-60 years proposes five statements that challenge some common misconceptions about designing:

- Designing is not just about creating beauty
- Designing not all about ideas
- Designing is not irrational
- Designing is not mysterious
- Not all designing is good

A common misconception is that designers are only concerned with designing beautiful objects and/or that they are willing to sacrifice function for aesthetics. Dorst points to the 18th century industrial revolution that first mass-produced "over decorated monstrosities," as the historical root of this perception from the perspective of his discipline (industrial design).[46] The result of this "flood of curls and patterns on every available surface" was a wake-up call "for the need for a new aesthetic for industrial products." Dorst is not saying that beauty doesn't matter, but that a sense of refined taste was lost in the transition from hand-crafted objects where "ornaments were expensive, and thus were a status symbol owned by very few," to mass-production and manufacturing that "suddenly made ornamentation very cheap" and less refined.[47]

---

46 A similar situation arose in the area of architectural design during the period that lead up to Modernism. Loos et al.

47 Dorst's point is not that a well-designed object should not have refined aesthetic qualities, rather, he is critiquing the simplistic additive technique of "beautification," where objects are "overly decorated," not refined. Dorst references his own discipline where "designers are torn between the requirement to create a product that is technically viable and ergonomically sound and the need to make it visually attractive." His point is that there is a balance between technical viability, ergonomics and aesthetics within his design discipline. Later on, I will make a similar argument from the discipline of architecture.

When Dorst states that designing is not all about ideas, he is critiquing the popular notion amongst novice designers (and non-professionals), "who haven't yet developed the skill and amassed the experience to work in a much more deliberate way," (and unfortunately taught in design schools), that the key to a successful design solution is (principally) the *generative idea* or *concept*: once you have a "concept" everything else magically falls into place.[48] Dorst explains that professional designers do not rely exclusively on the generation of "the idea," rather "they approach problems in a very strategic, deliberate, and thoughtful way" (p. 43). This is what is meant by design methodology – how one approaches the design problem in a systematic, strategic, deliberate and thoughtful way.

There is an impression (by non-designers) that because designing is a "creative," activity and perhaps because it involves drawing (rather word processing or spread sheets), that it is somehow not serious work, that designing is *fun*, [49] that it does not require disciplined reasoning. When Dorst writes that designing is not irrational, he not saying that designing is rational, but that designing is not completely *objectifiable*, that is "design is inherently open-ended" (p. 43). Designing requires exercising judgment based on clear analysis to develop viable "solutions that can be judged on a sliding scale of better or worse relative to the needs of stakeholders" (p. 43). In designing there is no single right answer, that can be justified in a strict "rational" or "scientific" manner.[50]

---

48   The term/concept of the *generative idea* is attributed to Jane Darke (1979). The generative idea works within the "generator – conjecture – analysis" model of design, where the generative idea is understood to be "a broad initial objective or small set of objectives, self-imposed by the [designer]" (Darke, 1979)., p. 40

49   Rittel writes: "The act of designing could be fun: what would be a more rewarding pastime than to think up some future and to speculate how to bring it about? However, what is troublesome is the recognition that the plan may actually be carried out. If so, the designer faces two possible kinds of failure. A *type-1 failure* has occurred if the plan does not accomplish what was intended. A *type-2 failure* has occurred when the execution of the plan causes side and after effects that were unforeseen and unintended, and prove to be undesirable. Normally, mainly the fear of the latter type of failure spoils the fun of design: Have I forgotten something essential? Designers worry" (1987, p. 2).

50   This aspect of design can be particularly frustrating for beginner designers (novices) who are determined to produce and believe that there is a "best" or an optimal solution. The open-ended characteristic of design is very frustrating for them. This is also related to why design cognition is said to be primarily abductive (rather than deductive or inductive).

Designers like to talk about what they do in mysterious ways, they like to suggest that what they do cannot be explained, or relies on some special knowledge. [51] This is related to the *tacit* nature of designing. Dorst argues that in fact designing is not really all that mysterious. Over the past 50 years a great deal has been learned about designing, design cognition, designers and the things that they design. By now, Dorst claims, there is a "core body of knowledge that is largely beyond contention." His point is that while there is still much to be learned, and there is still much room for innovation, there is a body of research and knowledge that has been amassed that forms a generally accepted foundation for design theory.

Finally, Dorst writes that not all designing is good designing. There is an opinion amongst some that if a design is based on reliable research and sound thinking and done by a professional, that the design must then be good. This is simply not true. Not all designers are equally skilled, and as in any profession, "there is also superficiality and mediocrity in designing – and many designs that make up our human-made world are hard to defend, even inexcusably awful" (p. 44). Implied in this observation is the acknowledgment that there are established performance expectations of practice against which the work of a designer is judged and the developmental aspect of design expertise: there is a difference between the competency of a novice and an expert designer. These in turn beg the question of *connoisseurship* (which will be discussed in detail later). How does one know bad design from good design, and a good design from an exceptional design?

---

51   Coyne and Adrian (1991) propose that the *mysteriousness* associated with design has its roots in the "dual knowledge thesis," which is related to *Cartesian dualism* and the mind/body problem. They describe the dual knowledge thesis as positing that there are two ways of thinking: logical, analytical, and rational (science is associated with this kind of thinking); and subjective, idiosyncratic and irrational (design is said to fall into the latter). Coyne and Adrian argue that "the dual knowledge thesis is untenable and unnecessary." Theirs is an argument to return to "the way things appear." Founded on the hermeneutics of Gadamer and the pragmatism of Dewey, the authors argue that the idea that design is mysterious is pervasive because, generally speaking, there is a belief that "there is a kind of thinking that is logical, analytical and rational," and that any kind of thinking "that is not explicable in these terms" is deemed mysterious. Their thesis argues that "understanding is acquired" when expectations are brought to bear on a situation. As expectations are brought to bear "that are derived from our effective historical consciousness" they are constantly renewed as we respond to new situations. As expectations are brought to bear on a situation are renewed, knowledge (understanding) is "accomplished through interpretation" of the situation in light of expectations. By offering this hermeneutic understanding of knowledge they argue that "when mystery is removed then effective dialogue, and hence learning, can ensue." While this explanation is intriguing and insightful (and points to a significant problem in how we understand what *knowing* is), it seems to me that the argument from two different types of knowing, knowing that and knowing how, where knowing that is associated with declarative/conceptual knowledge that is easily transferable, and knowing how is understood as procedural/heuristic knowledge that is tacit, offers a clearer explanation for why design knowledge/ability (like other kinds of expertise) is often described as "mysterious."

Summary

This chapter places architectural design in the context of an occupation. As an activity within an occupation, it is understood that designing is evaluated by normative (explicit and/or implicit) performance expectations of that occupation. Based on my working definition of designing, I have proposed four normative performance expectations. These include producing a solution that: (1.) Solves for the criteria and constraints of the design; (2.) That is technically possible; (3.) Coherent; (4.) And induces intended qualities of aesthetic experience. These components are of two types: demonstrable and experiential. The demonstrable components describe the quantitative, measurable (perhaps objective) aspects of the design solution. The experiential components describe the qualitative (perhaps subjective) aspects of the design solution. By placing designing within a profession with performance expectations I also establish the possibility of discussing design expertise: a designer (recognized by the profession) who consistently produces design solutions that significantly exceed the performance expectations of the practice. While it is true that said expectations, especially the experiential expectations, are difficult to codify, and are in flux, there is an ability amongst practitioners to recognize work that exceeds the normative standard. This ability is related to connoisseurship. Architectural design has both a proper and a proximate end. The proper end of designing is a building (object). The proximate end of designing is a functional approximation for building (making). The degree of expertise possessed by the designer is determine by the degree to which the building exceeds both the demonstrable and experiential components of the performance expectations.

3   Design Cognition

The natural sciences are concerned with how things are. Design on the other hand is concerned with how things ought to be, with devising artifacts to attain its goals. We might question whether the forms of reasoning that are appropriate to natural science are suitable for design. One might well suppose that the introduction of the verb 'should' may require additional rules of inference, or modification of the rules already embedded in declarative logic.

Simon H. , 1996, pp. 58-59

The above quote raises the question of cognition – "the activities of thinking, understanding, learning, and remembering,"[52] More specifically it raises the question of *design cognition*. It suggests that designers may think differently than scientists. It is a question of the mind. [53] While Simon, who coined the term *sciences of the artificial* and is also credited with first considering designing as a *way of thinking* (1996), others such as Rowe (1987) with his *design thinking*, Lawson (2005) with what *designers know*, Dorst (2015) with his *frames of mind*, Jones (1992) with his *systematic approaches*, and Cross (2011) with his *designerly ways of knowing*, have continued to develop the idea of *designing as a way of thinking*.

---

52   "Cognition." *Merriam-Webster.com*. Merriam-Webster, n.d. Web. 14 Jan. 2017.

53   "Mind" is a problematic term. The mind is not understood as a physical thing as it is a word used to identify the function of human cognition and self-awareness. This is how "mind" is used in this research. In ancient and medieval philosophy mind was used to identify the "essential" qualities of a person not unlike the "soul." It had an eternal existence. Its what was left when you died. Mind and brain are not interchangeable. See Damasio (1994), Searle (1994), Lakoff & Johnson (1999). To explain this the analogy of the mind as the software and the brain as the hardware is often suggested. (McCarthy, 1966, p.65) While the analogy does offer a useful distinction (similar to form and matter), it confuses the issue by locating all cognitive functions in the brain. Human cognition is not limited to the brain, but includes the entire body as well as external resources by means of extension, for example tools, or Ryles' blind man's cane. (Dreyfus, 1992) Philosophers and scientists have attempted to locate where the mind/soul resides. Most famous is Descartes who locates it in the pineal gland. In 1907, Duncan MacDougall performed some experiments to identify the weight of the soul the moment that it left the body upon death. He found the soul in six patients to weigh between 0.5 to 1.5 ounces . See Pandya (2011) Clark (2001) describes the mind as a "meat machine." His is both a "rejection of the idea of mind as immaterial spirit-stuff and an affirmation that the mind is best studied as a kind of engineering perspective that reveals the nature of the machine that all that wet, white, gray, and sticky stuff happens to build" (p. 7). Pinker, referencing the computational thinking model (CTM), he presents in his book *How the Mind Works*, (2009, pp. 22-27) writes that the "mental life consists of information- processing or computation. Beliefs are a kind of information, thinking a kind of computation, and emotions, motives, and desires are a kind of feedback mechanism in which an agent senses the difference between a current state and goal state and executes operations designed to reduce the difference" (Pinker, 2005). He describes the "mental life" as consisting of: beliefs, thinking, and emotions.

Others, with a decidedly more cognitive approach include: Gero (2016), Sussman & Hollander (2015), Brawne (2003), Eberhard (2007), Mallgrave (2011), Eastman, Newstettel, and McCracken (2001), Mitchell (1990), Akin (1986), and to name a few. Dong et al. (2015) consider designing from the point of view of evolutionary biology, looking to the thinking of animals for the building blocks of design thinking.

The question of the nature of design cognition is not so much whether there is a physiological difference in the neural structure specific to the scientist's or the designer's brain that makes one more suited to one domain over the other – though there is some evidence that this may be true (Mallgrave, 2011) – it has more to do with how scientists and designers think about and go about solving problems within their domains. The question needs to be considered in light of the nagging belief that scientific thinking, with its inductive reason and logic, is objectively superior to the way designers think, with their reliance on inspiration, intuition, and feelings. Design researchers believed (or at least they wanted to believe) that by reframing what designers do, using more terminology from cognitive science – and by perhaps changing the way that designers work and doing away with inspiration, intuition, and feelings – that designing, designers, and design solutions may achieve the same credibility as science, scientists, and scientific solutions.

The other question that the above quote poses is related to the word "should." Should implies that while there is a way to see things as they are and understand them as such, there is also an alternative to the way to see things, perhaps a better way, and that this alternative way *ought* to be implemented. It is the difference between making the claim that the pencil *is* yellow and the pencil *should* be yellow. The first is a verifiable observation of what is or what seems to be. The second is a proposition of what should or ought be (for some perhaps some unknown or yet-to-be known reason).

This distinction between observing what is and proposing what could/should be encapsulates the epistemological difference between (scientific) problem-solving and designing – it asks how do designers, as opposed to scientists, know what could/should be, on what basis do they know it, and why should we listen to them. [54]

---

[54] A "way of knowing" is a kind of intelligence. Though the terms are often used interchangeably, there is a distinction between information, knowledge and intelligence. MacFarlane (2013) describes **information** as a "meaningful, shared pattern" (¶ 3). Information is encoded and transferred by language. Information understood as data is transferred and measured in *bits, chunks and bytes* and possesses no semantic value. (However, some do claim certain kinds of information can also be found in the semantic, meaning-related aspects of language.) **Knowledge** is "a store of information [data] proven useful for a capacity to act" (¶ 6).

>>>

The question possesses epistemological, ontological and phenomenological dimensions. Answering it requires an examination of how designers know what they know, what designing is as a behavior, and how one experiences it as an activity. For example, when designing is understood as primarily (abstract) thinking, designers rely heavily on analysis, narrative, conceptual ideation to produce a design solution.[55] The product (expected outcome) of such an approach to designing is understood to be an idea – a concept – the Platonic *form* that gives shape to *matter*, the Aristotelian *substance* that gives meaning to *accidence*, the *essence* that enables *existence*.[56]

It is a disembodied (abstract) concept for a building that is only embodied (given shape) should it finally be built.[57] The design solution does not rely on being built to exist, even before it is built, the design already exists in the realm of possibility.

Though some knowledge is innate, "most is gained by interaction with the world" (¶ 6). There are multiple means for gaining information. **Intelligence** unlike belief and knowledge is a process, or "an innate capacity to use information to respond to ever-changing requirements... to acquire, adapt, modify, extend and use information in order to solve problems" (¶ 10). There can be some confusion when talking about knowing versus knowledge. Just as there are different kinds of knowledge, such as explicit or implicit, practical or propositional, conceptual and procedural, there are also different kinds of knowing. *Way of knowing* is akin to intelligence. Though intelligence has often been considered to be of one type, whose quotient is famously measured by psychologist William Stern with his IQ test. Research, such as that by Howard Gardner (1983), proposes that there are more likely multiple intelligences. Garner proposes eight intelligences but acknowledges that there may be more. Nigel Cross (1982) suggested that there may be a "three cultures view" of human knowledge: sciences, humanities and design. Cross calls these "ways of knowing." D'Souza, (2007) building on Gardner's theory of multiple intelligences, considers *design* as an additional (perhaps ninth) kind of intelligence.

55   "Mitrovic (2009) explains that even to this day, "the view, widespread among theorists in the late 20ᵗʰ century, that the only properties of an architectural work that matter (or even that might exist) are those which can be described in words. Everything else, it was assumed, was superficial and unworthy of consideration" (p. 31).

56   These also include philosophical understandings of design, not in terms of the object or in terms of the action, but in terms of how the action of designing transforms or imbues meaning on the object irrespective of its physical form or material properties. Folkman (2013) writes: "A design process may take its point of departure in an idea, that is, before the object, while it is the cultural context after the object that ultimately determines the meaning of the design object. However, it is the object that gives the idea its tangible expression... In the phase of becoming, that is, in the design process, design converts and transforms the possible into forms and appearances. Accordingly, as final objects, some aspects of the possible remain as a structure of meaning afforded by the objects" (p. 3). This ability or phenomenon where design imbues meaning on an object is related to the quality of the aesthetic experience afforded by the object. Folkman describes this ability of design to imbue meaning on an object as the function of the aesthetic in design. I, however, will discuss the function of aesthesis as a motivational factor in the design process.

57   In this line, Aristotle writes in the *Metaphysics*, book 3,"And this itself is also one of the things that must be discussed- whether sensible substances alone should be said to exist or others also besides them, and whether these others are of one kind or there are several classes of substances, as is supposed by those who believe both in Forms and in mathematical objects intermediate between these and sensible things" (2014, ¶ 2). What constitutes existence of a thing?

When designing is primarily understood as a kind of making, designers rely on emotions, sense perception, experience in space, materiality, technical ability, buildability.[58] These designers also make use of generative ideas or concepts (Darke, 1979), but more so as a method, or a vehicle for generating a form or for identifying a way to think about the problem. It is understood that in the end the concept doesn't really matter, in the end it is only the actual building/built environment that matters. The product of such an approach to designing is not the concept or the idea, but the means to make a building, that explain what the artifact is made of and how to make it. The design is not the *form* that gives shape to *matter*, but more an instruction communicated to a builder that is only actualized (finds its true existence) when it is built. It is only then that one can assess the quality of the design. Before it is built, the design exists in an ontological limbo.

While the above example may only describe the extremes, it illustrates that **what the designer considers to be the proper end of architectural design – the concept (idea) or the building (object) – impacts how the designer expects his design will be experienced by others as an intellectual or a haptic experience**.[59] It suggests that the design is the "meaning" of, rather than the experience of the object (Folkman, 2013); where it is the design that transforms the essential being of the materials in a more basic sense by bestowing them with (new) meaning.[60]

Does such a (ontological) transformation, effect the (phenomenological) experience of the object? Or could it be that the product of designing is (just) the artifact, an intentional assemblage of objects that results in the building/built environment; where the only *meaning* comes from the intended quality of the architectural experience or the meaning imposed on it (perceived) by the user?

---

58   A representative example of this approach can be found in Zumthor's, *Thinking Architecture* (2006). He writes, "Architecture is always faced with the challenge of developing a whole out of innumerable details, out of various functions and forms, materials and dimensions. The architect must look for rational constructions and forms for edges and joints. These formal details determine the sensitive transitions within the larger proportions of the building. The details establish the formal rhythm, the building's finely fractionated scale" (p. 15).

59   Heschong's little book, *Thermal Delight* (1989) is a wonderful exposition on how "the thermal function of a building could be used as an effective element of design. Thermal qualities – warm, cool, humid, airy, radiant, cozy – are an important part of our experience of a space; they not only influence what we choose to do there but also how we feel about the space" (p. vii).

60   For example, I, as a designer, stumble across an oak log in the woods. After I stand up and brush the leaves off my cloths I notice the shape and the texture and the color of the log. I think, "this log will make a great stool." I take it home, I clean it, I adjust its shape so that it doesn't wobble in the floor and it's a little more comfortable to sit on. I put a finish coat on it and polish it. I might even put little floor protector feet on it. Now, have I transformed this log into a stool. Has my "designing" a stool from a log changed its being, its meaning? Is it still a log?

Whether the proper end of designing, is thought of as an idea or an object, or as an action, as primarily thinking or making, in all cases designing is a kind of problem-solving, albeit with the "devising of artifacts" as its goal.

How then do we understand the cognitive functions of design as a kind of problem-solving? Is it a primarily a deductive, inductive or abductive process? [61] Is it an explicit, rational, scientific process or a more implicit, tacit, experiential way of knowing?

To solve a design problem, is it necessary to exhaust every possibility and combination of possibilities, eliminating each option until the most optimum solution is had? Or does design as problem-solving involve short cuts that eliminate all but the most likely optimal solutions from the start? And if it does include such short cuts, how does a problem-solver know which short cut to use when. And how does a designer as problem-solver know when he has found the most optimum solution possible? Does the most optimal solution even exist? The answers to these questions will provide the conceptual foundation for what follows.

This chapter will present concepts from cognitive science [62] that have been influential on design research in general and on designing in particular. Influential thinkers include, Popper, Newell, Simon, Ryle, Polanyi, and Rittel, Dreyfus, Damasio, and Lakoff and Johnson. Their work provides a theoretical basis, supported by legitimate authority and research to claim:

---

[61] When discussing problem-solving and human cognition three types of thinking or inference are generally referred to: deduction, induction and abduction. In short, "Deduction proves that something must be; induction shows that something actually is operative; abduction merely suggests that something may be" (Pierce, 1931).

Deductive reasoning can be equated with the rules of logic or logical inference. Deduction results in new facts. Starting with a verifiable premise and using the rules of logic, deductive reasoning almost guarantees a true statement. Deductive reasoning however is *non-amplitative*, it doesn't add to human knowledge because the conclusions are contained within the premise (*tautological*). Deductive conclusions are not predictive.

Inductive reasoning starts with specific observation that form the basis, in light of the evidence, of a likely, but not certain generalized conclusion. Induction leads to the conclusion that the theory in question is likely true. Inductive assertions are fundamental to scientific inquiry.

Abductive reasoning (a term coined by C. P. Peirce) is projective and generally suggests some kind of action or procedure. Pierce defines abduction as "the process of forming an explanatory hypothesis. It is the only logical operation which introduces any new idea" (Douven, 2016). Abduction leads to a new concept or theory that explains observable facts. Abductive thinking is behind many contemporary theories of design thinking, such as Dorst's *Frame Innovation: Creative New Thinking by Design*,(2015).

[62] See Gardner's *The Mind's New Science*, (1985) for a history of the emergence of *cognitive science* as a new discipline. Gardner defines cognitive science as an inter-disciplinary, "contemporary, empirically based effort to answer long-standing epistemological questions – particularly those concerned with the nature of knowledge, its components, its sources, its development, and its deployment" (p. 6). The cognitive sciences include: philosophy, psychology, artificial intelligence, linguistics, anthropology, and neuroscience.

(1.) Our popular understanding of scientific method is flawed, (2.) There are different ways of knowing, (3.) Problem-solving follows a consistent pattern and is sequential, (4.) Due to the limits of human processing ability and memory capacity, short cuts (heuristics) and/or means for extending these resources (paper and pencil) are necessary, (5.) Even with unlimited (brute) processing power, memory capacity and time, an optimal solution may not be possible for certain complex problems, (6.) We can know more than we can say. (7.) Our bodies play a significant role in thinking, (8.) There is no such thing as the "innocent eye," all human problem-solving is influenced (due to our bodies, memories, intellectual ability, experience, language, etc.) by presuppositions, preferences, and biases, and this is a good thing, (9.) The human "mind" is always seeking coherence (*Gestalten*), (10.) Feelings play an important role as a verification system in the problem-solving process.

§ 3.1   A Short History

The history of Design Research as a discipline has been well documented. [63] (See Langrish, 2016; Goldschmidt, 2014; Margolin, 2010; Bayazit, 2004; Archer, 1999; Cross, 1993; Broadbent, 1973/1984). Over the past 50-60 plus years multiple theories and research methodologies have evolved that have led to important insights into what designing is, its practice and products. The evolution of the discipline can be described as taking place over three over-lapping phases. [64] In the early years the primary aims of design research were to scientise/systematize designing and propose prescriptive methods [65]

---

[63]   It is generally accepted that, though efforts have been documented as far back as the 1920's, the (Design Methods) movement began with the 1962 (London) Conference on Systematic and Intuitive Methods in Engineering, Industrial Design, Architecture and Communications, Imperial College, September 1962. (Jones & Thornley, 1963)

[64]   See Cross (Science and Design Methodology: A Review, 1993, p. 63-64) for a description of this important period of evolution from rejection of the movement by the founders to the emergence of the "second generation."

[65]   Dixon (1987) identified three models (taxonomy) of (engineering) design theory. These include: prescriptions, descriptive cognitive theories, and computational theories. Prescriptive "advocate how design should be done in particular circumstances" (p. 151). Descriptive cognitive theories, require "relating the meaningful operationally defined variables from each of the following: the person or persons; the problem; the organizational environment; the design environment; the design environments including (for example) computer tools, analytical and drafting tools, information resources, etc. and; time" (p. 152). Computational theories: A complete design system for a computational theory requires relating the meaningful operationally defined variables from each of the following: the problem; the knowledge; the control (i.e. communication and decision making); and time. (p. 153)

that would produce reliably superior results. In the first phase the discipline was referred to as *Design Methods*. This phase is said to have ended when two of its founding members (Alexander, 1971; Jones, 1977) famously and publicly rejected the movement.[66] The second phase, referred to as *Design Theory and Methodology*, began with a new understanding of the relationship between the design problem and the design solution.[67]

During this phase the emphasis was/is on the use of protocol analysis and cognitive science that suggests descriptive models based on how designers really work.[68] In the present phase, referred to as *Design Research*,[69] the discipline is applying new discoveries in cognitive science and artificial intelligence, proposing new ways of approaching design problems, refining earlier theories and discovering ways that give insight into how designers think that can be applied to other disciplines. The popularization of the term *design thinking*, has grown out of this phase of the research.[70]

---

66   Alexander, when asked in an interview, "In what areas should future work center in design methodology?" He answers, "I would say forget it, forget the whole thing. Period." This is an oft quoted sentence, but its not the end of his answer. He continues, "Until those people who talk about design methods are actually engaged in the problem of creating buildings and actually trying to create buildings, I wouldn't give a penny for their efforts," One presumes that he is talking about Simon, Rittel and Broadbent, none of whom are architects.

67   In response to the crisis that the design methods movement met when some of the early founders publicly disassociated themselves from it, Rittel (1984) suggested that rather than abandon the entire movement, to consider the beginnings of the movement as a first phase of an evolving discipline. He went on to suggest an agenda for the second phase, which was largely ignored.

68   Zeisel writes that research describing what happens when designers think is necessarily "indirect and inferential or introspective." Such evidence includes personal experience, participant observation, stream-of-consciousness reports, and analysis of successive design drawings. Some theorists look to other disciplines such as linguistics, artificial intelligence, evolutionary biology and neurosciences to provide illuminating analogies and insight into designers' mental processes. (2006, p.21)

69   To avoid confusion, I will refer to the discipline throughout using the designation currently in use: Design Research (DR). This designation is the most inclusive.

70   See Brown's "Design Thinking" (2008) Brown defines design thinking "a discipline that uses the designer's sensibility and methods to match people's needs with what is technologically feasible and what a viable business strategy can convert into customer value and market opportunity" (p. 86). See also Razzouk and Shute (2012) for an overview of the development and the ideas related to design thinking.

§ 3.2 The Desire to Scientise (Rationalize) Designing

The desire to *scientise*[71] designing was the driving force behind the first generation of design research (Cross, 2001). And as such (wittingly or unwittingly) set the agenda (framed the problem) for future research.[72] As early as the 1920's there was a rising suspicion and distrust of the idea of design expertise as *special knowledge* (Banham, 1980) and the function of aesthetics in designing (Downton, 2003). As quoted by Cross (1993, p. 66) this mistrust of that which was not "scientific" is captured by the writings of Theo van Doesburg, who wrote:

Our era is inimical to all subjective speculation in art, science, technology, and so on. The new spirit which already governs almost all modern life, is opposed to animal spontaneity (lyricism), to the dominion of nature, to complicated hair-styles and elaborate cooking. In order to construct a new object we need a method, that is to say, an objective system. (Van Doesburg & Van Esteren, 1924/1994)

And Le Corbusier who wrote about a house as an objectively designed "machine for living" in:

The use of the house consists of a regular sequence of definite function. The regular sequence of these functions is a traffic phenomenon. To render that traffic exact, economical and rapid is the key effort of modern architectural science. (CIAM 2nd Congress, 1929)

---

71   See Schön (2009) for a good overview of how the *technical rationality*, by the second half of the twentieth century, in American universities, had become "embedded not only in men's minds, but in the institutions themselves, [as the] dominant view of professional ..." (p. 30-37).

72   Broadbent (1973) writes that the reasons "for approaching design in new ways... are determined by shifts in philosophical attitudes which are not exclusive to architecture, but pervade the whole of our culture and, most specifically, its science and technology" (p. 56).

These comments epitomize a way of thinking about designing that wants to be objective and methodological – rational. There is a distrust of intuition and inspiration and personal expression, preferring a kind of so called *objective rationality*, devaluing the importance of aesthetic experience as well as the function of aesthesis in the design process. The true design solution was thought to lie in the application of the "scientific method" to designing.[73] The belief emerged that if designers could clearly state the problem, follow a prescriptive procedure, anticipate (all of) the intended and unintended outcomes, then they could arrive at better (optimal) design solutions more efficiently without depending on "special knowledge."[74] Or if designers just collected enough data, organized it in a special way, devised a method for optimizing the desired outcome of a complex system, with measurable outcomes, designing could be systematized (and mechanized/computerized). The belief was (and for some continues to be) that the design process **must** be able to be codified and mechanized.

This desire was tied to the positivism of the early 20th century within the scientific community that called for a "unity of science."[75] That is, that all (respectable) sciences, both human and natural, must use the same methodology. The design professions wanted to be included as one of the sciences, believing that by doing so designing would be legitimized, taken more seriously. To do so designers could only lay claim to truth or certainty if they made use of the (verifiable) methods of the natural sciences. Much work was done based on these premises to rethink designing in these terms. Simon's (1996) *The Sciences of the Artificial*, and the early work of Christopher Alexander (1964) in *Notes on the Synthesis of Form* exemplify this effort.[76]

---

73   By scientific method was meant rational empiricism based on logical deduction and inductive inference.

74   It may turn out that it is exactly this so-called "special knowledge" that designers tried to rid themselves of that holds the key to understanding how designers think. Later I will propose that was meant by special knowledge may be nothing more than what is meant by tacit knowledge coupled with insights from embodied cognition. The problem, I will argue is not with how designers think, but rather that the implicit nature of tacit knowledge makes it difficult to describe how they think using scientific vocabulary.

75   "Positivism claimed that 'the laws and concepts of the special sciences must belong to *one* single system... They must constitute a unified science with one conceptual system (a language common to all the sciences) containing the conceptual systems of the individual sciences as members and their languages as sublanguages'" (Kraft, V, 1953, as quoted by Snodgrass & Coyne, 1997, pp. 71-72)

76   Gabriella Goldschmidt (2014) offers a good summary of Alexander's efforts. (pp. 15-18)

Much was learned by these efforts, but there were several problems (and continue to be) with this scientised approach to designing and design research regarding both what designers do and how they do it.[77] First, as observed by Simon (1996, p. xii), designers do not do the same thing as scientists. Designers propose a world that does not yet exist, while scientists propose theories based on the known world. Scientists are concerned with the necessary while designers are concerned with how things might or ought to be. Second, as design research is about understanding how designers design and designing as a human behavior, methods that are successful for producing new knowledge in the natural sciences, where the subject of study is inanimate with predictable properties, are not as effective when applied to human behavior. "The criteria of objectivity demanded by the natural sciences are self-negating when applied to the study of human behavior" (Snodgrass & Coyne, 1997, p. 9). Third, the emphasis on problem-solving and the use of verifiable methods of the natural sciences had so devalued the experiential/aesthetic nature of design[ing] as to "rob it of its soul," destroying "the frame of mind the designer needs to be in if he is to design good architecture" (Alexander, 1984, p. 310)

Still a more fundamental problem with this approach comes from the presuppositions of the scientific method itself. Positivistic/rational theories of scientific knowledge insist that truly scientific knowledge is gained primarily through verifiable observation and inductive conjecture. That is, as Popper (2002) summarized: "the inference of universal laws from particular observed instances as a method by which we are guided to the point whence we can intuit or perceive the essence of the true nature of a thing" (p. 16). Popper, critiquing this definition, argues that this is not what Socrates meant when describing the process of induction in the *Meno*. Rather, what Socrates meant by induction, as understood within his epistemology, is *anamnesis*. For Socrates, all knowledge (truth) is pre-existent, derived from eternal universal laws. Learning and inquiry is a kind of remembering (re-cognition of pre-existent truths observed in nature), not discovery. The truth already exists.

---

[77]   Whether design should be considered as a science or could ever be considered a science was contested within the Design Methods movement from the beginning: "The question of whether design can or will ever be 'scientised' is a point of disagreement in the field of design methods. Rittel makes a powerful argument that it can never be a scientific activity, based on the observation that science attempts to be "value-free" in the sense of not allowing values or prejudices to distort the observations from nature, while design in fact attempts to implement the very values and images of what ought to be that science attempts to keep out of its procedures. In this view design can be studied scientifically, but it is a fundamentally different activity in itself than the activity of science" (Grant, 1972). The science of design is what is meant by design research.

Popper argues that this misunderstanding of the meaning of inductive reasoning (scientific knowledge), that universal truths can be revealed from verifiable observation, is a fundamental flaw that is central to many noted thinkers, including Bacon, Hume and Descartes.[78] For Popper, due to the inherent limits of observation and human cognitive capacity, knowledge gained by induction is at best an educated guess that has the appearance of truth.

Bruce Archer (1999), summarizing Popper's critique of scientific method argues that we should therefore "reject the old [Baconian] principle that the true scientist should arrive at a scientific theory through inductive reasoning" (p. 567). He argued that we must accept, instead, that induction, is fundamentally flawed as a method of scientific inquiry. That in fact most, if not all, scientific discovery is actually an informed guess based on verifiable observation, and then tested, perhaps, using a method that is something like inductive reasoning with the claims to universal truth, but with the understanding "that most, if not all, scientific discovery is based on the positing of an insightful tentative explanation about the meaning of the evidence" (p. 567).

You do not, said Popper, have to prove whence these conceptions came. What you do have to do, is apply every test you can think of to discover any flaws in, or limitations to your proposition. (p. 567)

---

78   Popper (2002) goes on further to say that what Aristotle (and Bacon) meant by induction is "not so much the inferring of universal laws from particular observed instances as a method by which we are guided to the point whence we can intuit or perceive the essence or the true nature of a thing" (p. 16). Rather, he calls it an "optimistic" epistemological "method of systematic doubt" that like Descartes' method is intended as a way of "destroying all false prejudices of the mind, in order to arrive at the unshakable basis of self-evident truth" (p. 19). Self-evident truth is essentially a religious doctrine that is based in divine authority. The knowledge that is arrived at by induction then, is more properly understood as "the natural or the pure state of man, the state of the innocent eye which can see the truth, while ignorance has its source the injury suffered by the innocent eye in man's fall from grace; an injury that can be partially healed by a course of purification" (p. 20). See also *The Logic of Scientific Discovery* (1959), for Popper's argument with Hume. In Popper's final analysis he argues, "My solution of the logical problem of induction was that we may have preferences for certain of the competing conjectures; that is, for those which are highly informative and which so far have stood up to eliminative criticism. These preferred conjectures are the result of selection, of the struggle for survival of the hypotheses under the strain of criticism, which is artificially intensified selection pressure" (Quoted in, Schilpp, 1974, p. 1024). Induction does not result in empirical truth, but rather preferred conjecture.

The challenge then, is to determine where this "insightful tentative explanation" comes from that initiates the inquiry, and on what basis can it be verified. If the insight induced from careful examination of verifiable observations does not necessarily possess the qualities of a universal truth, from where then does it get its claim to legitimacy?

Archer was determined to reconcile the apparent conflict between science and designing, especially regarding the suspicion with which scientists regard "design knowledge." Building on this critical insight offered by Popper, Archer proposes that if real science "proceeds by the postulating of informed conjectures, followed by systematic attempts at the refutation of these conjectures" designing must be a "science" because that "is exactly what designers do!" Thus, Archer observes, in the end, if what Popper says is true then, "Design activity was [already] scientifically respectable" (p. 567). Problem solved. But not really.

§ 3.3 Problem solving: Information-Processing Theory

All problem-solving starts off with the realization that "it could be otherwise."[79] This insight applies to the most mundane situations such as realizing that I am hungry, hunger is unpleasant, if I eat something I can alleviate this unpleasant feeling; To the realization that the unrestrained use of fossil fuels is causing significant damage to the environment, and considering the possibility that there may be alternative means to generate energy that are less destructive to the environment while still having access to enough energy so that we can continue to use the technologies we currently enjoy.;To starting a revolution. This phenomenon can be described as five *states* of being (based on Prochaska & Velicer, 1997):

---

79   For Sartre the knowledge that it could be *otherwise* is fundamental to human freedom and agency. (Sartre, 1946)

(1.) A normative state where things are more or less acceptable; (2.) A feeling of discomfort that causes one to assess the current state; (3.) The awareness that it could be otherwise/the discomfort experienced by the realization that the current state is not necessary; (4.) Exploration of possible alternative states; (5.) A change in the current state that achieves (within an acceptable range) the desired outcome (goal state). How one decides what action to take, within a range of possible actions to achieve the desired state is the problem of problem solving.[80]

Simon (1996) writes "Human problem solving, from the most blundering to the most insightful, involves nothing more than varying mixtures of trial and error and selectivity" (p. 195).[81] Selectivity arises with the emergence of "rules of thumb" (heuristics) that suggest how to approach a (kind of/type of) problem or offers short-cuts through familiar territory. The effective application of these rule-of-thumb comes from experience when using them in a particular situation tested against a trusted verification system. If it leads toward a promising solution or "solution path," then it's useful. If it doesn't, then it's not. This process is usually learned through experience (situated learning). One recognizes a familiar situation, remembers what worked, and tries it again.

Possible solutions are judged within a range of acceptability based on (implicit or explicit) criteria and constraints. The attempt to maximize the expected value of the utility function (demonstrable) of the solution is called optimization (Simon, 1988).[82]

---

80   The classic problem-solving process proposed by Polya in *How to Solve It* (1945) is: understand the problem → devise a plan → carry it out → review/extend. Here I am describing a situation in which a person recognizes a need, desire or possibility for change which precedes problem solving. Polya's process is a meta-heuristic for how to solve a problem. His process will be described in detail below

81   The work of Simon, Newell, Shaw and Chase has been very influential in the area of problem solving (cognitive) theory. There are other theories of problem solving. However, as the purpose of presenting these theories is to form a basis for understanding the underlying concepts that support DR, I have decided to focus on their work. These are the most often quoted/referred to by Cross, Lawson, Dorst, Schön, Alexander, Cross, Hillier, etc. (Roozenburg & Dorst, 1999).

82   Optimization describes the desired goal state of the problem solver. It is the process by which an optimal solution is sought. This involves establishing a large search area within which all possible solution paths are exhausted from which the best possible solution is determined. In problem solving theory there is only one optimal solution. Optimization requires some means of producing a (objectively) measurable outcome. You may notice that optimization is described in terms of "utility factor" not in terms of experience. As *the problem-solver as information processing system model* is intended as a general theory equally applicable to humans and machines, and machines do not have bodies, and you need a body to experience feelings, and the quality of the experience is determined by feelings, it is impossible for the *problem-solver as information processing system model* to assess the quality of an experience.

Search domain defines the boundaries of the search.

The optimal solution (from a functional point of view) is not always the most desirable (satisfactory) solution. Sometimes a solution may be chosen that is simply good enough (sufficient). When a solution is considered to be both satisfactory and sufficient, it is considered to be *satisficing*.

Much of the early research in problem solving came from chess playing, especially from studies by de Groot. (1978) With more than 200 years of study and experimentation, chess is a favorite because it is sufficiently complex, there is a set of rules (operations) that must be mastered, it requires strategy, and there is a definable goal (objective) that signals the end of the game (Simon & Chase, 1972).[83]

Research about chess, in terms of problem solving, involves both (1.) understanding how expert chess players make decisions/solve problems/think (Simon H. , 1977), and (2.) how to design a machine (computer program) that can "do mechanically what man can do naturally" (Newell, Shaw, & Simon, 1958, p. 320). This early research focused on extracting the processes, procedures, sequences and methods that humans use when attempting to solve complex problems and translating them into a computer program to test their theory in order to both *mechanize* and *demystify* problem solving. Testing a problem solving theory by mechanizing it or by writing a computer program was considered the way to *verify* and validate the theory.

De Groot's study, *Thought and Choice in Chess* (1978), provides an analysis of the way people with different degrees of expertise (in chess) approach the same problem. One of his studies involved showing images of chess boards (with the pieces prearranged in mid-play), and asking 5 grand masters and 5 candidate masters (both playing at expert level) to *think aloud* as they tried to find the best next move. Surprisingly, he found that there were no significant differences (statistically) between the grand masters' and the candidates' thought processes (heuristics, depth of search, etc.). However, he did find that the grand masters were better at finding "the 'right' moves for further consideration, whereas weaker players spent considerable time analyzing the consequences of bad moves" (Chase & Simon, 1973, p. 396). He also found that the grand masters were better able to recall the location of pieces when they were not arranged randomly. The candidate masters, lacking the extensive experience (situated knowledge) possessed by the grand masters were less able to recall the proper location of the pieces.

---

83   Interestingly enough, it is exactly these characteristics of chess that makes it poorly suited for understanding design. But, I don't want to get ahead of myself.

Chase and Simon suggest that this has to do with "immediate perceptual processing" which allows the master to see "structure" or patterns[84] rather than individual pieces or *chunks of* information.[85] So while statistically speaking there appeared to be no difference in performance between the grand master and the candidate, there was a difference in how the grand master perceived, evaluated and processed the situation. Thus it was surmised that "thinking depends on acquiring the ability to recognize relationships, patterns and complete situation" (Lawson B. , 2005, p. 133). These experiments led to insights into how problem-solving systems work, in terms of identifying a problem, memory, defining a search area, recognizing patterns, identifying/prioritizing criteria for evaluation/selection of the next move, anticipating the consequences, making choices, evaluating the effectiveness of the solution, and projecting a possible future. As well as the understanding that expert problem-solvers when faced with a new problem tend to try to make sense of a situation first (solution driven), while novices tend to try analyze the problem (research driven). [86]

With a growing base of research describing how experts solve problems, Newell, et al.(1958) sought to propose their own theory for how human problem-solving works. They identified four criteria for such a theory. It should: (1.) Predict the performance of a problem-solver by explaining what processes are used and what mechanisms perform these processes; (2.) Predict incidental phenomena; (3.) Show how attendant conditions alter problem-solving behavior; (4.) Explain how problem-solving skills are learned (acquired).

---

84   Later on this ability to recognize (non-random) patters or perceive order will be discussed in terms of the natural tendency of humans to seek/impose order, perceive a *Gestalt*, experience a sense of coherence.

85   Chunking is a cognitive strategy that allows short term memory to increase the amount of information it can store. Short term memory is said to be limited to approximately seven bits (units) of information. Chunking information into bits allows one to exceed the constraints imposed by this physiological limitation. One can further extend the limits of short term memory by arranging the chunks in to schemata. (Miller, 1956)

86   This has become a generally accepted principle in design theory, See McCormick (1997), Lawson & Dorst (2009); Beilock (2010), Cross (2011), Ericsson (2016). Lawson (2005) writes: "The scientists adopted a technique of trying out a series of designs which used as many different blocks and combinations of blocks as possible as quickly as possible. Thus they tried to maximize the information available to them about the allowed combinations. If they could discover the rule governing which combinations of blocks were allowed they could then search for an arrangement which would optimize the required colour around the layout [problem-focused]. By contrast, the architects selected their blocks in order to achieve the appropriately coloured perimeter. If this proved not to be an acceptable combination, then the next most favourably coloured block combination would be substituted and so on until an acceptable solution was discovered [solution-focused]" (p. 31).

An organism's *problem-solving behavior* is described as an *information processing system*.[87] This system consists of *control systems, effectors*, and *receptors*. A control system consists of a number of memories containing ordered *symbolized* information, where *primitive information processes* operate on the information stored in these memories based on a "definite set of rules" that are combined into processing *programs*. The program processes include: searching, generating and evaluating.[88] To arrive at problem solutions in a similar manner as humans, programs cannot rely solely on "brute processing power,"[89] but rather must make use of heuristic processes (a kind of cognitive shortcut).[90]

To test their theory they developed a program, Logic Theorist (that later developed into General Problem Solver [GPS] which provided the foundations for AI), that they claimed could "solve problems in a manner closely resembling that exhibited by humans" (p. 162). To prove that their program did in fact solve problems in a manner closely resembling that of humans (it could pass the *Turing Test*)[91] they identified six criteria that they considered (based on psychological research) fundamental to human problem solving and that their program satisfied:

---

87   The use of the term "problem-solving behavior" implies a kind of purposefulness (intention) that seems odd to assign to machines. This notion of machines as purposeful or goal oriented has its roots in cybernetics, especially how an organism (system) maintains homeostasis. Norbert Wiener wrote: "The central nervous system no longer appears as a self-contained organ, receiving inputs from senses and discharging into muscles. On the contrary, some of its most characteristic activities are explicable only as circular processes, emerging from the nervous system into the muscles, and re-entering the nervous system through the sense organs, whether they be proprioceptors or organs of the special senses. This seemed to us to mark a new step in the study of that part of neurophysiology which concerns not solely the elementary processes of nerves and synapses but the performance of the nervous system and an integrated whole" (As quoted by Gardner, 1985, p.20).

88   One begins to see how this relates to design as problem-solving behavior: problem → [searching/generating/evaluating] → solution

89   Memory and processing power at some point all reach their limits in terms of capacity and speed. Simon refers to this reality "bounded rationality" (1972). Bounded rationality refers to the limits of human cognition. Human cognitive systems involve several components: sense/perception systems, thinking ability (processing), memory, skill (the where with all to implement the solution). Each of which has special competencies, capacities and limitations. Human cognition is limited within these bounds. When the resources necessary to solve a problem exceed the competency, capacity and limitations of human cognition, humans can extend or enhance these by training and/or making use of tools and machines, such as: paper and pencil, reference books, conversations, calculators (both primitive and advanced), computer simulations, models, etc. Recognizing the limits of human cognitive systems is essential for understanding how human problem-solving and design works.

90   These ideas have since provided the principles for the "symbolic information processing" approach to problem-solving, or the rational problem-solving, traditional, or computational view (Visser, 2010).

91   Turing (1990) devised a test to assess the intelligence of a machine where if the machine could produce a result that was indistinguishable for what one would expect from a human, then the machine was considered intelligent (at least in that instance). The Turing Test is a standard measure for (artificial) intelligence.

(1.) It incorporated a system of processes that could in fact solve complex problems; (2.) Its problem-solving ability depended on the *sequence* in which problems were presented; (3.) The program "behavior" exhibited both *preparatory* and *directional set*; (4.) It exhibited insight; (5.) It employed simple concepts; And (6.) it made use of a complex organized hierarchy of problems and sub-problems. This was considered quite a success. They wrote that such an information processing system should not be understood as merely a metaphor, but as "a precise symbolic model on the basis of which pertinent specific aspects of man's problem-solving behavior can be calculated" (1972, p. 5).

Newell et al. were careful, to separate problem solving processes from "neurological or pseudo-psychological terms." Problem-solving at the level of information processing, they wrote, "has nothing specifically 'neural' about it, but can be performed by a wide class of mechanisms, including both human brains and digital computers" (1958, p. 153). As far as they were concerned, problem-solving is problem-solving is problem-solving, be it done by a human or a machine.

With this understanding of human cognition as an information-processing system, Newell and Simon,[92] describe the system as consisting of four components: *memory*, *processors*, *effectors*, and *receptors*. Memory is made up of symbols and *tokens* that stand for or represent objects, concepts and their relations. Processors are symbol manipulators that encode information gathered by receptors in a manner that is consistent with the symbols structures (architecture) of the system; *transforms* system codes and relations; and transforms system codes so that they can be communicated to the effectors. Effectors manipulate and receptors gather information from the internal and external environment. Taken together this theory of human cognition as an information processing system and its four components provided a new way to understand human problem-solving, artificial intelligence and consequently design. However, this system was only able to deal with well-defined problems where the parameters were clearly defined, and the outcome was predictable, thus verifiable. This system was incapable of producing novel, innovative or creative results. Nor was it able to consider any alternative solution that included variables outside the data-set. These limitations posed a new problem. Could their system be adapted to tolerate ambiguity, unpredictability and novelty within an open framework and thus allow for creativity?

---

92   As summarized by Akin (1986 p. 12)

For Newell et al. (1958) creative thinking is assumed to be "simply a special kind of problem-solving behavior" (p. 5)[93] Creative problem solving is characterized by novelty, unconventionality, high motivation and persistence, and/or by a problem that is ill-defined, that is, a problem for which there is no right or inevitable solution. (1958, p. 4) The process includes (1.) identifying a suitable problem situation and criteria for evaluation, (2.) identifying a strategy for solving the problem, (3.) defining the search field, (4.) producing and testing multiple test paths (creating a maze), (5.) identifying the optimal path, and (6.) producing an acceptable solution. For a problem-solver to generate a creative solution, the problem-solver needs to be able to (1.) [re]assess the problem situation,[94] (2.) introduce random variables, (3.) frame and reframe based on alternative desired outcomes, and (4.) discover multiple (feasible) solution paths[95] that can lead to unexpected results, and an unanticipated goal state that exceeds expectations established by the problem criteria

Problem-solving systems make use of two processes: a solution-generating process and a verifying process. Solution generators function similar to a "trial-and-error" search. "Associated with a problem is a space of possible solutions" (Newell, Shaw, & Simon, 1958, p. 63). As the problem-solver operates in a sequential manner, it is necessary to not only identify possible strategies, but to determine in which order to execute them to arrive a viable solution path. The order in which processes are executed matters. How the problem-solver does this is by resorting to a "solution generator" that provides a means for evaluating possible solution paths and reduce the search time.

---

93   Creativity in design is a big topic, and is beyond the scope of this project. However, it cannot be ignored. When referring to creativity in this study, I do not mean simply novelty or innovation. I prefer how Gardner, Csikszentmihalyi and Gero use the term. In *Creating Minds*, Gardner (1993) discusses creativity in terms of "big C" and "small c" creativity. For Gardner a person who is big C creative is "a person who regularly solves problems, fashions products, or defines new questions in a domain in a way that is initially considered novel but that ultimately becomes accepted practice in a particular cultural setting" (p. 35). Like Csikszentmihalyi (1996), Gardner identifies a big C creative work as possessing several characteristics. Creativity in design is also explored by Gero, where he identifies four kinds of design (which in his language can be understood as problem solving): routine design, non-routine design, innovative design, and creative design. He notes, similar to the above, "for a design to be evaluated as creative the criterion of novelty is insufficient, utility and value are also required." For Gero (2016), value is the distinguishing criterion, because value is related to *transformation* and *concentration*. That is, the "power to transform the constraints of reality" and that "they have an intensity and an intensity and concentration of meaning requiring continued contemplation" (p. 3).

94   The "problem situation" includes the multiple variables, criteria and constraints, seen and unseen, anticipated and unanticipated that make up the environment in which the problem needs to be solved.

95   The "solution path" is the series of decisions made within the problem space (maze) that leads to an acceptable solution. The problem maze is a matrix of choices and alternatives that is generated by how the problem space is framed. Archer (1963) describes designing in terms of a decision-making map.

A solution generator determines how the problem-solver will *think* about the problem. Newell et al.(1958) write "There is likely to be a positive correlation between creativity and the use of trial-and-error generators" (p. 14). The likelihood of producing a creative solution is determined by the way that the solution generator is defined by the problem-solver.[96]

Verifying processes evaluate the problem states, determining the direction the problem-solver takes on the solution path. The verifying process provides feedback, based on the criteria set by the problem-solver, for the solution generator to inform it if it is heading in the right direction, toward generating the desired solution.

Problems requiring creative solutions quickly grow in complexity due to several factors. Complex problems pose two problems for problem-solvers: the size of the search space (maze) of possible solutions; and determining how to identify creative solutions that are likely to satisfy the problem. Possible searches can be increased exponentially by including additional (random) variables, easily exceeding the processing and memory capacity of the information processing system. The possibility of randomly considering additional variables only exacerbates the situation, quickly overwhelming the system. To avoid overwhelming the system it is helpful reduce the search space (maze) the problem-solver makes use of. The problem then is how to choose which variables to eliminate without engaging in an exhaustive trial and error routine? The answer is to make a "best guess," perhaps based on past experience, statistical analysis, predetermined preferences, etc. These "best guess" routines are called heuristics.[97] One such heuristic might be to search the problem maze for the simplest possible solution path first.

---

[96] This problem of creativity is also explained in terms of the opportunistic nature of design. Referring to Cross (1999) writes, "all the relevant information cannot be predicted and established in advance of the design activity. The directions that are taken during the exploration of the design territory are influenced by what is learned along the way, and by the partial glimpses of what might lie ahead. In other words, design is opportunistic, and so the path of exploration cannot be predicted in advance. (p. 29) Cross (2004) describes opportunism in design as "deviations from a structured plan or methodical process into the 'opportunistic' pursuit of issues or partial solutions that catch the designer's attention." He further makes reference to Guindon (1990), Visser (1990), Akin and Lin's (1995) concepts of "novel design decisions" to explain what is meant by the opportunistic aspects of design from different design disciplines.

[97] Newell et al. define a heuristic as "any principle or device that contributes to the reduction in the average search to solution" (1958, p. 22). Heuristics are kinds of "maxims" or as Polanyi calls them "rules of art." The use of heuristics in problem solving is characteristic of experts. "A major function of heuristics is to reduce the size of the problem space so that it can be searched in a reasonable time" (Newell, Shaw, & Simon, 1958, p.61). However, the problem with heuristics or maxims or rules of art is that they "cannot be understood, still less applied by anyone not already possessing a good practical knowledge of the art" (Polanyi, 1974, p. 31). Heuristics are *reasoning strategies* that "do not guarantee the best solution, but often lead to potential solutions by providing a simple cognitive 'short-cut.'" (Yilmaz, Seifert, & Gonzalez, 2010)

The solution-generator functions to optimize the solution path in a manner that maximizes the likelihood of arriving at an acceptable (creative) solution while reducing the demands it makes on available resources (time, processing power, memory). Each time the solution-generator applies processes to a state, it results in a new state that is acted upon by verifying processes and acted upon again, etc. This sequence of *states* constitutes the solution path. When a problem-solver assesses the problem situation and determines a (best) way for traversing the solution maze, perhaps by breaking a complex problem into subtasks, he is applying a heuristic of planning. By this definition, **design methodologies are considered planning heuristics or meta-heuristics**.

As the problem-solver traverses the solution maze, a significant about of data is collected that when seen together produces "patterns of elementary symbols" or a "state description."[98] This pattern of elementary symbols or state description is what is meant by a *representation*.[99] The representation is evaluated insofar as the patterns within the representation "mirror or fail to mirror the patterns without that they represent" (Newell, Shaw, & Simon, 1958, p. 51). That is, that there is a correspondence between the internal and external representation (based on a set of predetermined expectations for what constitutes a successful solution). Evaluating this correspondence provides feedback on two levels: it allows the problem-solver to determine if the solution path he has chosen is leading to an acceptable solution (feedback), and to evaluate the quality of the execution of the final solution (the artifact) against his internal representation (correspondence).[100]

---

[98] Bartlett (1958) refers to these patterns of elementary symbols or internalized mental images as "schema."

[99] A representation is not necessarily visual. It is considered to be visual "if it is capable of serving as an input to the same information processes as those that operate on the internal representations of immediate visual sensory experience... produce the phenomena of visual imagination" (Newell, Shaw, & Simon, 1958, p. 55). This way of understanding a representation as a visualization of a data set (imagination), can also be understood in the reverse as an internalization of the data set. That is, when we think (observe) about something external, we construct an internal visual representation based on the data gathered by the senses and cognitive processes (p. 58). Recent research in the area of neuro-psychology has provided evidence that internal visualizations of internal data (imagination) and those generated by external data stimulate the same parts of the brain (visual cortex) and effect the same pleasure centers. See Searle (2015), Ramachandran (2011), Damasio (1994). This evidence is critical for substantiating the concept of *aesthetic resonance* presented in the final chapter.

[100] This process of evaluating an internal image against an external representation is called *externalization*. It is a primary method designers use to gain *feedback* during the design (problem-solving) process. Methods for externalization included sketching, model-making, conversation, etc. Criteria for assessing the quality of the externalization include both the demonstrable and experiential characteristics.

This understanding of human problem-solving behavior as information processing (by demystifying it and mechanizing it), in part accounts for the reframing of designing as primarily problem-solving behavior, where designing involves little more than finding a satisficing solution for a clearly stated design problem. Or as Akin writes, "Design is a form of problem-solving where individual decisions are made toward the fulfillment of objectives."

But this theory raises other issues that are not satisfactorily addressed: (1.) What motivates the system to make "decisions" to solve a problem, (2.) on what basis does the system define the problem situation, frame the problem, consider random variables to discover a creative solution, and (3.) how the system understands "fulfillment" and "objectives." When we consider the designer as a human problem-solver we can ask the same questions: (1.) What motivates a designer to solve the problem, and (2.) on what basis does a designer define the problem situation, frame and reframe the problem, consider random variables to discover a creative solution? (3.) How does the designer know what to do? (4.) How does a designer know (and on what basis) when the objectives are fulfilled (solution is had).

Rittel (1987) proposes that this happens via a process that he calls *epistemic reasoning*. He writes, the nature of the designer's reasoning is argumentative,

---

the process appears as one *of the formation of judgment*, alternating with the search for ideas. The understanding of the design situation changes with the alternatives seen in pursuit of the plan. Different facts and different ought-to-be questions come up depending on the means to accomplish these ends. (p. 5)

The process (deliberations) is terminated with a judgment (good enough) "which may be based on the deliberations, but are not [necessarily] derived from them." Rittel concludes: "How this happens is beyond reasoning... There are no 'algorithms' to guide the process. It is left up to the designer's judgment how to proceed. There is no – logical or other – necessity to want to do something particular in response to an issue. *Nothing has to be or to remain as it is or as it appears to be*; there are no limits to the conceivable. There is a lack of 'sufficient reason' which would dictate to take a particular course of action and no other" (p. 5).

§ 3.4   Tacit Knowledge

As opposed to Plato who writes "that which we know, we must surely be able to tell" (Laches, 2015), Polanyi (2009) poses an alternative explanation for how we know what we know, called *tacit knowledge*: a kind of knowledge that starts with "the fact that *we know more than we can tell*" (p. 4).[101] Polanyi (1972) holds that human knowledge is of two kinds: "What is usually described as knowledge, as set out in written words or maps, or mathematical formulae, is only one kind of knowledge; while unformulated knowledge, such as we have of something we are in the act of doing, is another form of knowledge" (pp. 12-13). The first kind of knowledge is called explicit knowledge, (articulate knowledge), was described above. The second is called tacit knowledge, (inarticulate knowledge). Tacit knowledge is a kind of inferential, embodied knowledge that seeks coherence, and mostly operates below the radar of consciousness. It is a kind of knowing with characteristics similar to what Badke-Schaub (2014) calls intuition: "[It] is related to unconscious and subconscious processes; it associates to the totality of the situation" (p. 356); it is accompanied by affects, feelings, emotions; it is fast; it uses multi-sensorial stimuli; it develops with experience; it can simulate creative solutions.[102] For Polanyi, tacit knowledge is fundamental to scientific discovery and artistic genius.

From an Aristotelian point of view[103] design knowledge is considered "practical/technical" knowledge, because the proper end of design knowledge is the ability to make something.

---

[101]   Though the concept of tacit knowledge was present in Wittgenstein (1958) with his concept of "seeing-as", it is normally attributed to Polanyi. *Seeing-as* was explained by using the duck-rabbit drawing borrowed from Jastrow (Jastro, 1901). The point being that depending on certain factors related to one's perceptual predisposition, the drawing can (legitimately) be seen as either a duck or a rabbit. This phenomenon poses a serious challenge to the possibility of "verifiable observation" essential to inductive rationality.

[102]   Simon has a similar theory of intuition. See Frantz (2003).

[103]   In Book 6 of the Nicomachean Ethics, Aristotle classifies all knowledge as being of two types: theoretical/propositional knowledge (*episteme*) which aims at contemplation; and practical knowledge which includes *phronesis* (knowledge which aims at action production) and *techné* (which aims at creation). Architectural design ability, for Aristotle, is a kind of technical knowledge.

Ryle (1949) described propositional/theoretical knowledge[104] and practical/procedural knowledge[105] as "knowing that" and "knowing how" respectively.[106] These ways of knowing can be described as both *explicit* and *implicit*. Explicit knowledge is theoretical/declarative or conceptual knowing, sometimes described as intellectual, rational or logical ways of *knowing that*. It is (relatively) easily transferred (encoded/decoded) via language from one subject to another (taught/learned).[107] The ease by which knowledge is transferred (regardless of the mode of transfer) determines the level of implicitness or explicitness. Language, as a mode of transfer is well suited (though not perfect, as data is occasionally lost) for transferring explicit information. Classroom, textbook, lecture, on-line distance methods of learning are good examples of this mode of transfer. Most areas (domains) of expert knowledge/ability involve a great deal of explicit (propositional/declarative) knowledge. Designing is no exception. Consider the cross-section of declarative/propositional knowledge with which architects are expected to be familiar: history, materials and methods of construction, structures, ergonomics, human environment systems, codes and zoning, economics, management, etc. Explicit means of acquiring this kind of information is very effective and easily measured. However, not all ways of knowing (thinking) or acquiring information are of this kind. Knowing **what** is involved in the domain of architectural design is not the same as knowing **how** or being able to design.[108]

---

104   Historical precedents, theories, technical knowledge about structures, systems, materials and methods of construction, and environmental sustainability, professional practice, finance, zoning and building codes, ergonomics, sociology, environmental psychology, etc. are kinds of declarative/conceptual knowledge.

105   Design methods, methodology and procedure are kinds of procedural/heuristic knowledge

106   This distinction between ways (modes) of knowing can be traced back to Confucius in the East who wrote: "I hear and I forget; I see and I remember; I do and I understand."

107   Collins (2010) describes the transfer of knowledge (information/data) in terms of "strings." That is, "bits of stuff inscribed with patterns" that facilitate the transfer of information between two entities. (p. 9) While strings are the "means by which languages are shared," strings are not the language. **Language is not the only means for transferring knowledge between humans.** Collins' point is that in order for the transmission of knowledge between humans (entities) to take place something with "a relatively fixed meaning that carries a degree of technical empowerment has to be transferred" (p. 10).

108   This question of knowing what and knowing how as different ways of knowing was no by any means settled by Polanyi and Ryles. For a more recent discussion of knowing how and how see Noe (2005). Where he agues that Stanley & Williamson (2001), who argue that all *know how* is a species of propositional knowledge, does not offer a sufficient reason to reject Ryle's distinction.

Knowing how is a kind of implicit knowledge that includes procedural/heuristic knowing, strategic knowing, and connoisseurship.[109] Knowing how (skill/being able to do/make something), involves a kind of data set (domain specific situated information/knowledge) that is difficult to encode and transfer from one entity to the other via explicit means, i.e. language.[110] As such, this kind of knowledge is most often acquired through practice (being shown how) and involves knowing/recognizing the difference (connoisseurship) between something well-done and something done poorly or just average.[111] Schön calls this *situated* knowing, that is "knowing-in-action." It is associated with the acquisition of abilities and complex skills. Apprenticeship or *learning by doing*,[112] deliberate instruction (coaching) and mentorship are effective means for transferring this kind of knowledge, as these allow the learner to observe an expert while attempting to learn not only what the master does, but why he does it.[113]

---

109   *Connoisseurship* (a kind of knowing), like skill, is learned through the example of another, "it can be communicated only by example, not by precept. To become an expert wine-taster, to acquire a knowledge of innumerable different blends of tea or to be trained as a medical diagnostician, you must go through a long course of experience under the guidance of a master. Unless a doctor can recognize certain symptoms, e.g., the accentuation of the second sound of the pulmonary artery, there is no use in his reading a description of syndromes of which this symptom forms a part. He must personally know that symptom and can learn this only by repeatedly being given cases for auscultation in which the symptom is authoritatively known to be present, side by side with other cases in which it is authoritatively known to be absent, until he has fully realized the difference between them and can demonstrate his knowledge practically to the satisfaction of an expert" (Polanyi, 1974, p. 55). See also Polanyi, *Personal Knowledge*, 1974, p. 54. Analogously, until a design student has experienced different types of enclosure, appreciates the dynamics and limitations of structural systems, possesses a first hand feeling for materials and their properties and their characteristics, can demonstrate knowledge of them, appreciates them, and understands how these work together to form a building (see for example Pallasmaa (2005) and Zumthor (2006) for how this works in architecture) it is unlikely that he will be able to perform at an expert level as an architect.

110   It's the difference between explaining how to do something to someone or reading about how to do something, versus being able to actually do it. Knowing how/being able to actually do something (be it riding a bike, playing the violin, making furniture, or designing a building) is a different kind of knowledge than know what to do.

111   "The mechanism for transition of tacit knowledge is not telling and understanding, but rather performance and imitation" (Winch, 2010).

112   Schön's work was heavily influenced by John Dewey's pragmatism and his educational theory that emphasized learning by doing (Schön, 1992). See Dewey's *Experience and Education* (1938/2015).

113   The passing on of skills is best done through apprenticeship. "An art which cannot be specified in detail cannot be transmitted by prescription, since no prescription for it exists, It can only be passed on by example from master to apprentice... To learn by example is to submit to authority. You follow your master because you trust his manner of doing things even when you cannot analyze and account in detail for its effectiveness, By watching the master and emulating his efforts in the presence of his example, the apprentice unconsciously picks up the rules of the art, including those which are not explicitly known to the master himself" (Polanyi, 1974, p. 53). See also Gieser (2008) for a phenomenological approach to apprenticeship learning. Gieser describes how learning through apprenticeship works by introducing the concept of empathy to show how the imitation of movements along with their intentions, and especially their emotions, leads to the perception of merging between two beings and thus to the 'discovery' of cultural knowledge" (p. 301). Gieser calls the process by which this occurs *enskilment*.

It is similar to the Japanese apprentice who is said to be "stealing the master's secrets," where the master expects them to be stolen by the apprentice (Singleton, 1998, p. 26).

Collins, (2010, pp. 85-86) as a critique of Polanyi, proposes that there are three types (levels) of tacit knowledge: strong, medium and weak, "referring to the degree of resistance of the tacit knowledge to being made explicit."[114] Strong (resistance) tacit knowledge is what he calls *collective* (CTK), medium (resistance) is called *somatic* (STK), and weak (resistance) is called *relational* (RTK). Collective has to do with the nature of the social (society/culture in general), "knowledge that the individual can acquire only by being embedded in society;" somatic has to do with the nature of the body, "knowledge that is inscribed in the material of the body and brain;" relational is a matter of how particular people relate to each other, having to do "with the relations between people that arise out of the nature of social life."

For Collins, the question is not whether or not tacit knowledge can be transferred, but the degree to which it can and the nature of the intermediary necessary to facilitate transference. He explains, "certain potentially explicable forms of tacit knowledge are so complex that the only practical way to transfer them from human to human is by close personal contact that allows for guiding, showing, imitating, and so forth as a short cut to explaining" (Collins, 2010, p. 87). Other considerations include whether (tacit) knowledge is difficult to transfer because it is *concealed* (as in trade secrets)[115], or because its *ostensive*, that is, the best way to explain something is to point to something else (as in "just watch how I do it.") Other (contingent) reasons why tacit knowledge might be considered difficult to make explicit/transfer is because it is simply too complicated (*logistically*), or not worth the effort (as in its easier to ask the librarian than memorizing where everything is and go looking for the book yourself); the learner lacks the previous (*salient*) knowledge necessary to understand

---

114   All knowledge (both tacit and explicit) is passed on (transferred) through *intermediaries,* or strings. Intermediaries do not possess knowledge *per se,* rather they are vehicles for the passing on of information. For example, a French cookbook does not *possess* knowledge or the ability to cook French food. The cookbook is an intermediary. It is a vehicle for the transfer composed of bits of data in the form of a collection of papers bond together with recognizable ink stained patterns (letters), that when properly transferred and interpreted (received by optic nerves and deciphered/read) facilitate the transfer of information (communicate meaning) about French cooking. This may seem obtuse, but it is an important insight for understanding the nature of tacit knowledge. In this way architecture drawings, models and written specification are understood as intermediaries.

115   This problem of "concealed" knowledge involves both deliberately hiding or keeping secret special knowledge, and only passing it on to the select few; as well as knowledge that is not deliberately withheld due to a lack of awareness by the expert about why what he does actually works. In this case the learner is expected to "figure it out" on his own, while the expert acts as an evaluator of the performance not as teacher or coach. See "Chapter One: The Curse of the Expert" (Beilock, 2010) for an in-depth discussion on why experts often make poor teachers. Beilock writes: "As we get better and better at performing skills such as operating a cell phone or riding a bike, our conscious memory for how we do it gets worse and worse. As we become more expert and our procedural memory grows, but we may not be able to communicate our understanding or help others learn that skill" (p. 16).

(as in "oh I thought you knew how to read a ruler); the person passing on the knowledge does not know how to, is unaware, (*unrecognized*) or is unable to explain what he does (as in "I don't know, I just do it and it usually works").[116] Polanyi (1969) writes "While tacit knowledge can be possessed by itself, explicit knowledge must rely on being tacitly understood and applied. Hence, Polanyi claims, all knowledge is *either tacit* or *rooted in tacit knowledge*. A wholly explicit knowledge in unthinkable" (p. 144).

Polanyi is interested, not only in how knowledge is transferred, but also in describing how tacit knowledge describes how *scientific discovery* (really) occurs (new knowledge is acquired). He describes tacit knowledge as a kind of *knowing* that is made up of a range of conceptual and sensory information, images and ideas that can *be brought to bear* (made use of) when making an attempt to *make sense of* (understand, frame, find order) or perform some task that is typically associated with expert (design) performance (1974). Contrary to commonly held rationalist belief that scientific discovery is (normally) had by an inductive process based on observable evidence, Polanyi (1966) claims that "scientific discovery cannot be achieved by explicit inference."[117] Rather, he claims, scientific discovery "must be arrived at by the tacit powers of the mind" (p. 138). To explain his position he turns to Gestalt theory of perception. (See Wagemans et al., 2012; Wong, 2010; Weber, 1995.)

Polanyi's *basic assumption* is that the ability that scientists possess to perceive/recognize patterns, systems, and relationships in nature differs from "ordinary perception" only in that scientists have a more refined ability[118] to discover patterns, systems and relationships that ordinary perception cannot. They are experts. Polanyi writes, "Scientific knowing consists in discerning *Gestalten* that indicate true coherence in nature."[119]

---

116   Unrecognized knowledge is the type of tacit knowledge most often associated with expert performance and typical of designers who prefer the "black box" theory of design.

117   This will be an recurring theme

118   Related to connoisseurship.

119   In describing Gestalt Psychology, Broadbent describes Kohler's observation that "whenever a form displays insufficient unity it will be transformed, by laws intrinsic to the brain itself, into a satisfactory... 'good' form, simple, well-balanced and symmetrical which, because of this organization, will stand out from its surroundings and will be perceived as a 'figure' against 'ground.'" This became the basis of the concept of gestalten, the (subconscious) tendency for the human mind to seek out order. Broadbent (1973) writes that, this observation was misinterpreted (especially by the Bauhaus) to mean that the brain prefers simple forms. That rather than interpreting the observation as a preference for simple forms, it is equally reasonable to argue that the "brain 'enjoys' the task of simplifying complex forms and is liable to get bored if the challenge is removed" (p. 66). This is how Polanyi uses it.

It is a kind of knowing that seeks out/discovers *coherence*. He describes the *effortless* ability to perceive coherence as being demonstrated by how one can perceive a series of rapidly changing *clues* "some in the field of vision, some in my eye muscles, some deeper in my body, as in the labyrinth of the inner ear" and somehow *integrate* all these various stimuli into one coherent perception of a particular phenomenon. The only real difference between this effortless/ordinary experience of integration (coherence) and scientific discovery is a matter of range and degree, coupled with "sustained effort"[120] and "guided by exceptional gifts."[121]

This ability to integrate disparate clues into a cohesive perception, or the basic structure (*functional relationship*) of tacit knowledge, is facilitated by two kinds of awareness: *subsidiary* (attending from) and *focal* (attending to). Polanyi (2009) writes, "in an act of tacit knowing we *attend from* something for attending *to* something else" (p. 10). These are fundamental to the "tacit apprehension of coherence." Subsidiary is an awareness of the parts. Focal is awareness of the whole. When one apprehends coherence, one's awareness shifts from the subsidiary clues (parts) to a focus on the whole. The parts, which are elements in themselves, once perceived as part of a whole acquire a *functional appearance*: they cease being perceived as elements in themselves to being perceived as (subsidiary) parts of a whole (*Gestalten*).

Scientific discovery involves a kind of "reverse engineering" of this experience. What scientists do is discover the whole (*distal term* of tacit knowing) and seek to define it in terms of its constituent parts (*proximal term* of tacit knowing). Polanyi calls this act of integration (*functional relationship*) "tacit knowing." What designers do is the opposite. Designers take disparate (constituent) parts and "discover"[122] a whole (coherent unity).[123]

---

120   "Sustained effort" has to do with motivation, which is a topic that I will discuss later in regard to the role seeking an intended quality of aesthetic experience plays in the design process.

121   This issue of "exceptional gifts" will be discussed later as it relates to the concept of talent and the physical/ intellectual/psychological attributes and predispositions necessary to acquire the ability to design at the expert level.

122   Of course designers do not "discover a whole." That would imply that there was a (pre-existent) whole to be discovered, which is absurd seeing as a designer is making something that never existed before. Rather, the designer manipulates the disparate constituent parts, making use of various methods and techniques, in a manner that results in a relationship of spaces/form and assembly of parts that is perceived as a whole and that satisfies (demonstrable and experiential) expectations. The perception of "wholeness" resides in the perceiver (which includes the designer).

123   One might also say "impose" coherence via some kind of organizing mechanism (proportion, composition, spatial relationship, etc.) upon the disparate parts.

The ability to switch between proximal term (seeing things in isolation) and distal term (seeing things as a coherent unity) is an important quality of tacit knowing: "This is the *phenomenal* accompaniment of tacit knowing; which tells us that we have a real coherent entity before us" (p. 2). Tacit knowing is a *claim* that there is a reality that has not yet been perceived. It is based on an *indeterminate* range of *anticipations*, which is based on *actual knowledge* that *cannot be explicitly stated*.

The classic example given by Polanyi, to describe the nature of tacit knowledge by analogy is the ability to ride a bike or being able to swim (Polanyi, 1966).

If I know how to ride a bicycle or how to swim, this does not mean that I can tell how I manage to keep my balance on a bicycle, or keep afloat when swimming. I may not have the slightest idea of how I do this, or even an entirely wrong or grossly imperfect idea of it, and yet go on cycling or swimming merrily. Nor can it be said that I know how to bicycle or swim and yet do not know how to coordinate the complex pattern of muscular acts by which I do my cycling or swimming. I both know how to carry out these performances as a whole and also know how to carry them out as elementary acts which constitute them, though I cannot tell what these acts are. This is due to the fact that I am only subsidiarily aware of these things and our subsidiary awareness of a thing may not suffice to make it identifiable. (p. 4)

The analogy suggests two distinctions. First, just because you know how to ride a bike does not mean that you can (explicitly) tell someone else how. For example, you manage to keep your balance. You do it. But you may not have any idea how it happens. Most likely you cannot explain how to coordinate the complex patterns of muscle acts necessary to ride a bike, but still you ride "merrily" along.

Second, even without explicit knowledge (or awareness) of the "elementary acts" (subsidiary) necessary to perform the whole it is still possible to do it. The disparate elementary acts somehow function, without explicit awareness, together as a coherent whole and allow you to ride from here to there. Polanyi writes that this is because subsidiarity awareness of disparate parts does not suffice to complete the action. For example, a human face is made up of subsidiary parts: overall shape, hair, nose, mouth, ears, chin, etc. The distinctive combination of these parts makes up the human face.

Polanyi's point is that though we may not be (explicitly) aware of the distinctive characteristics of the subsidiary parts (precisely state it) we can recognize a person's face though we may not be aware of how.[124] That one can acquire a complex skill, yet not be able to explain how or even be aware of how it happens (in terms of the all the specific subsidiary acts) exemplifies how/that tacit knowledge is "discovered:" *learning without awareness*. As in learning to ride a bike, "we are relying on our awareness of a combination of muscular acts for attending to the performance of a skill. We are attending *from* these elementary movements *to* the achievement of their joint purpose, and hence we are usually unable to specify these elementary acts. We may call this the *functional structure* of tacit knowing" (Polanyi, 2009, p. 10). Polanyi (1966) posits

if there can be learning without awareness, then there must be also discovery without awareness. Discovery comes in stages, and at the beginning the scientist has but a vague and subtle intimation of its prospects. Yet these anticipations, which alert his solitary mind, are precious gifts of his originality. They contain a deepened sense of the nature of things and an awareness of the facts that might serve as clues to a suspected coherence in nature. Such expectations are decisive for the inquiry, yet their content is elusive and the process by which they are reached cannot be specified. It is a typical feat of discovery without awareness. (p. 6)

Polanyi's point is that there is a capability of the mind to recognize (discover) patterns, order, relationships that is not immediately obvious and that we cannot specify (articulate), but which can be learned.[125] These discoveries occur not by explicit inference – indeed these discoveries may be inhibited by explicit inference – but rather by tacit knowledge. The human mind is a coherence craving, pattern seeking, order making, relationship-loving, fleshy, machine. "It is a work-a-day skill for scientific guessing with a chance of guessing right." A heuristic. Humans seek order naturally if we allow ourselves (Beitman, 2009). But, the ability to go beyond what is possible by simply "allowing ourselves," to exceed the ability possessed by most people, requires practice.

---

124   For example, before I went to China a photo of a group of Chinese students was just that. But after seven years teaching in China that same photo is no longer a "group of Chinese students" but I can recognize each individual (and probably describe his projects)

125   See Beitman (2009), who addresses the following concepts: (1.) The brain seeks patterns; (2.) The brain is predisposed to use coincidences to create or discover patterns; (3.) The philosophical basis for interpreting coincidences is provided by fundamental association cortex schemata; (4.) Personally relevant coincidence interpretation is influenced by a person's biases; (5.) Hemispheric lateralization influences coincidence detection and interpretation — the right brain associates while the left brain inhibits; and (6.) Coincidences suggest the possibility that we can look where we cannot see (pp. 256-263).

In reinserting the body into thinking Polanyi defines tacit knowing as a kind of *embodied* or *extended knowing*. Not unlike the way the blind man uses his cane, feeling his way through the world. He loses the feeling of holding a stick in his hand, the stick disappears, and becomes an extension of his hand.[126] Or the craftsman using a plane, who for all practical purposes may as well be feeling the wood with his hand as he varies the pressure and adjusts for the peculiarities of the wood.[127] It is the difference between *looking* at something and *attending from* it at something else. It is a phenomenon described by Merleau-Ponty (1962) who describes the difference between *dwelling* in our body, and experiencing the world as such (without awareness of it), and dwelling from outside our body and experiencing it as an object. This has to do with how our body participates in the act of perception/knowing (which is a direct assault on Cartesian dualism).[128] Polanyi writes:

When we attend from a set of particulars to the whole which they form, we establish a logical relation between the particulars and the whole, similar to that which exists between our body and the things outside it. In view of this, we may be prepared to consider the act of comprehending a whole as an interiorisation of its parts, which makes us dwell in the parts. ...in the same sense as we live in the tools and probes which we use and in the culture in which we are brought up. Such indwelling is not merely formal; **it causes us to participate feelingly in that which we understand.** [Emphasis is mine.] Certain things can puzzle us; a situation may intrigue us—and when our understanding removes out perplexity, we feel relieved. (p. 11)[129]

---

126   This phenomenon is called "extended cognition." See Clark & Chalmers (1998).

127   See Wilson (1998) and Sennet (2009) for a detailed discussion on the relationship between the hand and tools and the concept of *extension*

128   Ryle (1949/2000), seeing tacit knowing as a matter of *philosophy of mind* with roots in the mind/body problem (or *Cartesian dualism*), sought to once and for all. In simple terms mind/body dualism (with its ancient roots in early Greek philosophy) proposes that there are two types of knowing that are possible: that of the mind, which is reliable; and that of the body, which can deceive. The mind is where the *real* self exists. While the body, imprisoned as it is by the laws of physics, has a subservient (secondary) role. The mind is transcendent. The body is corporal. These two have separate existences. A such, the question becomes, how do they communicate. The body is the vehicle through which the mind *inhabits* the earth, and is dependent on the body for sense perception and data collection. A person can only perceive/communicate what is known through the body. So the mind (self) becomes a prisoner in the body. Descartes proposes then that the only way that a person can know he exists is that he *thinks* that he exists. Ryle finds this mind/body dualism unacceptable. He refers to the theory as "the ghost in the machine." His point being that mind/body dualism is untenable. And argues that a person knows he exists through his body, and that this is *real* knowledge (pp. 11-24).

129   Participating in something "feelingly" begins to suggest the important role of the body in the (design) thinking/decision-making/discovery process. It suggests what Schön calls inhabiting the problem space. It is the application of the sense to the situation, and paying attention to the quality of the experience to gain insight or perhaps inform the choice of which step to take along the problem-solving path.

§ 3.5   Embodied Cognition

This idea posed by Polanyi, that the problem-solver[130] comprehends the problem by
indwelling, or participating *feelingly* in the problem situation, reintroduces the human
body into the problem-solving (thinking) process. It suggests that we do use our bodies
to enter into the problem space, to inhabit it, to experience it, to apply our senses, as
a way to both understand the problem and as a means of assessment to *know* what to
do. This idea that cognitive functions are not exclusively the realm of abstract reason
(and located exclusively in the brain *qua* mind), that they are dependent upon the
physical (beyond-the-brain) body of an *agent* for cognitive processing is the central
idea behind *embodied cognition*. (See Searle, 2015; Mallgrave, 2013/2011; Shapiro,
2011; Johnson, 2007; Thagard, 2005; Clark, 2001; Lakoff & Johnson, 1999; Varela,
Thompson & Rosch, 1991).[131]

Embodied cognition challenges the popular belief, philosophically and psychologically,
that there is a necessary separation between a (disembodied) mind that reasons and a
(sentient), non-rational body, by recalling our (human) evolutionary lineage, as evolved
creatures who have inherited our cognitive abilities in a large part for the purpose
of coping with our environment (Brooks, 1991). Lakoff and Johnson (1999) put it
succinctly, coming at the question as philosophers informed by cognitive science:

---

130   The work of Newell and Simon became the basis for what has become the study of artificial intelligence
(AI). Great advances have been made in making machines that appeared to "think" like humans, (pass the
Turing test) based on the belief that cognition can be accounted for in terms of "the manipulation of abstract
representations by explicit formal rules" In the early 90's this theory of cognition came under attack, especially
by Brooks who argued that this approach could not "account for large aspects of what goes into intelligence"
(Brooks, 1991, p. 1). Anderson (2003) explains that the most significant problem with cognitivism has to do
with its dependence on *representations* that stand for a particular *state* that are composed of symbols (*tokens*)
that have no necessary connection with the state of affairs at hand. And the reliance on "explicitly specifiable
rules of thought." Simply put, "having disconnected the form of a symbol from its meaning, cognitivism rules
out the possibility of content sensitive processing, and so requires rules to govern the transformation from
one cognitive state to another" (pp. 93-94). This kind of cognitivism, with its Cartesian roots forms the basis
for what has come to be known as good old fashion artificial intelligence (GOFAI). The resultant disembodied
theory of cognition is the basis of Dreyfus' critique of GOFAI in his book *What Computers Still Can't Do* (1992).
This inability to perform "context sensitive processing" comes from Dreyfus' understanding that the two most
basic forms of human intelligence, learning and skillful action, are dependent on a human body to form a "tight
connection between the agent and the world" (2002).

131   As a topic of cognitive science, this question of embodiment is looked at from psychological (i.e.: Gestalt,
in terms of perception; Gibson, in terms of affordance), philosophical (i.e.: Heidegger, in terms of *being-in-
the-world*; Merleau-Ponty, in terms of perception and representation occurring *in the context of*) and neuro-
and computer science points-of-view. It is also considered from several other points-of-view: physiology,
evolutionary history, practical activity and socio-cultural situatedness. It is a broad and developing area of
research. This section will only introduce general concepts.

"The mind is inherently embodied. Thought is mostly unconscious. Abstract concepts are largely metaphorical" (p. 3). They argue that reason (cognition), contrary to Cartesian dualism, and the Kantian radically autonomous person, who is absolutely free, whose reason transcends the mortal confines of the body, is not disembodied. Rather, "reason arises from the nature of our brains, bodies, and bodily experience... the very structure of reason itself comes from the details of our embodiment" (p. 4). Reason is not that which allows us to transcend our animal nature or necessarily unique to humans, but rather a consequence of evolution.[132] Reason is not transcendent, as in a universal principle, but it is a capacity, to varying degrees, that is shared by all human beings and (to a lesser degree) animals. Most of what we call reason occurs beneath cognitive awareness. It is not "purely literal, but largely metaphorical and imaginative. Reason is not dispassionate, but emotionally charged" (p. 4). Cognition evolved as a means to allow the body to inhabit the earth. Not the other way around. There is no human reason without a human body. Reason is shaped by the body (physiologically), especially by the sensorimotor system.[133] Lakoff and Johnson (1999) claim that the western philosophical tradition (starting with Plato) has so misunderstood human cognition, as to "drastically distort our understanding of what human beings are" (p. 21). The presupposition of embodied cognition theory is: **People are sentient, thinking, feeling beings, whose bodies have evolved with the cognitive capacity to prosper on the earth.**

---

132   Wilson (2008) considers evolutionary factors contributing to the development of human cognition "from situation-bound to a more flexible, abstract, and general purpose form of cognition."(p. 376) In doing so she considers "a cluster of possibly linked capacities that may have driven human embodied cognition, including the ability to exert flexible voluntary control over particular effectors, the ability to see analogies, and the ability to imitate."

133   An example how cognition is inherently embodied, not just because it is made of flesh and depends on bodily systems for survival, but also due to the way our perceptual and motor systems play a basic role in the definition of concepts and rational inference, is the experience of color. Mallgrave (2011) explains Land's discovery of the area V4 in the visual cortex that lead to a precise description of why we actually perceive color, contrary to the popular explanation that we see color due to the variations in light waves reflected off a surface. "[Land] demonstrated that in focusing on an object we assess the wavelength of light in a particular patch of the visual field (V4) with respect to its surroundings, not only for one, but for all the different wave lengths in the surrounding field. Therefore [making] color, far from being something out there in the world (photons have no color), [but] rather a creation of our biological or neurological apparatus" (2011, p.145). There are less technical examples as well, such as, well, we have eyes which facilitate visual perception in a particular manner. Not like a camera. But in thousands of little snippets that enter through the lens that hit the retina upside down. They then pass through nerve cells distributed across the retina made up of about 100 million rods and five million cones, that transmit information, through the optic nerve to opposite sides of the visual cortex where the information is processed in both hemispheres of the brain that segregate details of object recognition into lines, shapes, color and motion. Other bits of information is sorted and sent out to other areas of the brain (i.e. occipital lobe) where functions such as facial recognition take place. Further information is sent to the temporal lobes for form recognition, and still other functional processing which trigger memories and emotions. This system does not only allow us to see, but determines what we can see, what expect we can see, and how we see.

Embodiment theory argues that the mind is not just something that resides in the body, rather the very properties of concepts are created as a result of the way the brain and body are structured and the way they function in intra/interpersonal relations and in the physical world" (Lakoff & Johnson, 1999, p. 37). The basis for these claims comes from advances in neuroscience.[134] Building on Lakoff's previous work *Metaphors We Live By* (2003), Lakoff and Johnson observe that spatial relationship concepts evolved from the human body's relationship to its environment.[135] Spatial relationship terms such as *in, on, over, through, under*; concepts of body movement, like *grasp, pull, lift, tap, punch*; as well as concepts pointing to the structure of action or events like, *starting, stopping, resuming, continuing, finishing*, describe what the body does, and as such can be understood to be shaped by the body. The point being: "The visual systems of our brains are used in characterizing spatial-relations concepts. Our actual motor schemata and motor synergies are involved in what verbs of motor movement mean. And the general form of motor control gives general form to all our actions and the events that we perceive" (p. 39). There is a strong, inescapable relationship between the development of basic concepts and how the body interacts with its environment.

Even a concept as fundamental (to design such) as Gibson's (1986) *affordance*, relies on a human body in order to know how to interact with a given situation.[136]

---

134   Lakoff & Johnson (1999) refer to their appendix, and research by Regier (1995), Bailey (1997), and Narayanan (1997) to substantiate this claim. See also Mallgrave (2011) and Damasio (1994) for similar research.

135   I first encountered this idea in Bloomer & Moore,'s *Body, Memory, and Architecture* (1977). In the first paragraph of the first chapter they write, "At the very beginning of our individual lives we measure and order the world out from our own bodies: the world opens up in front of us and closes behind. Front thus becomes quite different from back, and we give attention to our fronts, as we face the world, which is quite different from the care we give to our backs and what lies behind us. We struggle, as soon as we are able, to stand upright, with our heads atop our spines, in a way different from any other creatures in the world, and *up* derives a set of connotations (including moral ones) opposite from *down*. In our minds left and right soon become distinguished from each other in quality as well as in direction, as words like 'sinister' and 'dexterous' record" (p. 1).

136   Affordances, a term "made-up" by Gibson (1986), are those elements and situations in an environment that *offer*, *provide*, or *furnish*, for good or ill, value or meaning to an agent. For example a flat surface of suitable strength and area may afford support for a human being. The term flat, extended, rigid, horizontal, are properties of a surface that are measured *relative to the agent*. The concept proposes that a physical thing as experienced or perceived by a physical agent offers opportunities relative to the physical body (form, shape, attributes, properties) of the agent. For example a rock in the forest may afford a cozy shelter for a worm, and also afford a convenient place to sit and take a rest for a hiker. (And these can take place simultaneously.) Much of our environment acquires meaning in terms of the value the constituent elements afford us. This includes the physical elements in our immediate environment (a horizontal surface 900mm above the ground, supported by four elements that keep the surface stable affords a work surface suitable to stand at. But rather than going through the trouble of identifying the many affordances that give this assembly of elements meaning or usefulness, we simply call it a table), as well as "substances that afford ingestion" (seem to be good to put in one's mouth). Some of these substances afford poisoning and others afford nutrients.

>>>

As such Gallagher (2005) poses the question, "To what extent, and in what ways are consciousness and cognitive (noetic or mental) processes, which include experiences related to perception, memory, imagination, belief, judgment, and so forth, shaped or structured *prenoetically* by the fact that they are embodied?" (p. 2).

The above question goes right to the dilemma posed by the *rational processor system* approach to problem-solving described by Newell et al. There is a likelihood that, while Newell et al. arrived at significant insights into problem-solving by attempting to abstract the process from human experience, codifying it and mechanizing it, the system they propose does not really describe how human problem-solvers function. Humans do not seem to function the same as (dis-embodied) *information processing systems*. (Though we do make use of them).

Simon's concept of bounded rationality does not only apply to limits of memory and the cognitive capacity of the brain, but also applies to, due to the shape and characteristics of our bodies, the limits of both how we experience and perceive the world. Humans are limited by space and time. Humans have limited hearing and visual ranges. The sense of smell, touch and the range of temperature humans can experience are all determined by the human body. In addition to this, the human mind possesses a particular type of structure that determines what we can experience and how we make sense of what we do experience in a situation. The human mind is limited by the means of encoding and transferring information that are available, especially by language. These limitation are not deficiencies, rather these are simply the bounds within which human cognition takes place.

In the cognitive model, a human problem-solver (agent) possesses a *body schema* and *body image*[137] that inhabit a world. Body schema refer to how a person perceives his body via a mental model, that includes his perceived shape, size, location of limbs, and orientation in space. Straus (1970), identifies the body schema as a "cortical representation, a neurophysiological map of body parts located in the somatosensory cortex, operating below the level of self-referential intentionality: *close to automatic* performances" (Gallagher, 2005, p. 21).

>>>   This applies to animate objects as well. For example the child affords the family dog a playful interaction. The dog brings the ball to the child and waits for the child to throw it. For Gibson, the concept of affordances is a lens through which to see the world. He distinguishes affordances from *values*, in this way tries to avoid the objections of the philosophers in terms of meaning and being, and the psychologists who are concerned with perception, physicality or phenomenal experience. The concept of affordances affords a way to experience elements and situations in an environment *prenoetically*.

137   There is some difference of opinion in the literature about the meaning of these terms. See Gallagher (2005, p. 21)

The body schema is able to extend its identification beyond personal corporal limits to include, say a hammer. While the body image "consists of a system of perception, attitudes and beliefs pertaining to one's body... that involves a form of reflexive or self-referential intentionality... and normally represents the body as *my own body*" (p. 25). The body image influences posture and location in space.

How does the agent know how to interact with the world in the problem-solver as information processor system?[138] Newell et al. (1958) write, "To think about something, that something must have an internal representation of some kind, and the thinking organism must have some processes that are capable of manipulating the representation" (p. 58). Similar to what was discussed earlier, Newell and Simon proposed that the agent constructs *representations*, which are generated from data (proposition-like mental entities) not only of itself (body schema and body image), but also of its (given) physical environment (situation).[139] Insofar as this environment is stable and predictable, the system can build a two or three -dimensional representation (model) that is sufficiently complex, within which it can function and generate a plan of action.[140]

---

138   Perez-Gomez, referring to the work of Eva Thomson (2007) describes *embodied dynamicism* as the concept in cognitive science that "called into question the conception of cognition as disembodied and abstract mental representation. The mind and the world are simply *not* separate and independent of each other; the mind is an embodied dynamic system *in* the world" (p. 223).

139   Peirce (1873), in addition to coining the term *abduction*, is also closely connected with *semiotics*. It is in this context that he explores the question of *representations*. Peirce defines a representation as "an object which stands for another so that an experience of the former affords us a knowledge of the latter." A representation, for Pierce, has three essential conditions to which it must conform: It must have qualities independent of its meaning; it must have real causal connection with its object; it must address itself to a mind. Ideas, in the strictest sense, are all representations. "A representation not only has material qualities but also *imputes* certain qualities to its object." It is the function of representations not only to communicate abstract ideas, but also to communicate concrete and experiential qualities of the idea/concept. According to Bundgaard and Stjernfelt (2010), Peirce, by including iconic signs, logic and perception as the *basic semiotic phenomena* of representations, he "avoids the pitfalls of linguistic imperialism and the ensuing ideas of being trapped in 'the prison house of language'" (p. 69).

140   The cognitive function of representations and even the existence of mental representations is a contentious issue in cognitive science. The less extreme theories settle in on a happy medium, which allows for a kind of mental representation that has an inter-dependent and dialogical relationship with the environment. An example of such a theory is the Representational Theory of the Mind proposed by Fodor (1980, 1985).

This would have to be a world that accounts for gravity and temperature change,[141] where windows suddenly open, where other agents unexpectedly cross your path. Systems that function like this are called a sense-model-plan-act framework (SMPA).[142] The problem with this framework, according to Brooks, is that it is "insufficiently dynamic." For an agent to survive in an environment like this the system must constantly build and re-build an internal representation of the environment, locate itself in the environment and build and re-build an internal representation/ image of itself, as well as be able to function in an almost infinite number of possible situations. Brooks observes that this "SMPA is by its nature too expensive (in terms of cognitive resources), and therefore biologically implausible" (Anderson, 2003, p. 97). Though it may be possible to solve the technical challenges, its not likely that this is an accurate model of human cognition.

Human cognition evolved over millions of years from the primordial soup to an intelligent agent. The problem with the *agent as information processor* is that it is not "physically grounded in animal systems... These [animal] groundings provide the constraints on symbols necessary for them to be truly useful" (Brooks, 1991). The rules of abstract thinking need to be "grounded" not so much in logic and rational inductive reasoning but in "the more evolutionary primitive mechanisms which control perception and action" (Anderson, 2003, p. 100). Dreyfus writes, "Adherents of the psychological and epistemological assumptions that human behavior must be formalizable in terms of heuristic programs for a digital computer are forced to develop a theory of intelligent behavior which makes no appeal to the fact that man has a body, since at this stage at least the computer clearly doesn't have one" (1992. p.235). That is, "the structure of our conceptual schema – is primarily determined by practical criteria, rather than abstract or logical ones" (Anderson, 2003, p. 104).

---

141   Blickhard (2009) argues that while several aspects of biology (mental and normative processes) have been embraced by cognitive science, the thermodynamics of living systems has not. Framing cognition as an information processing system (plus the cultural predisposition to Cartesian dualism) raised the possibility that the mind could be modeled relatively independently from the brain. As cognitive science has evolved this concept of a disembodied mind has been continually challenged. One particular challenge was that of *interactivism*. The theory emerged from discussions related to the relevance (necessity) of representations to cognitive activity and how these representations correspond to the situation they are intended to represent. From this discussion grew the question of how representational models emerge (and re-emerge adjusted) that more accurately correspond to the target situation. This dialogue lead to a dynamic systems approach (feedback seeking homeostasis) interactive model based on biological foundations.

142   These systems have shown great promise in the area of robotics. See Brooks (1991).

The theory of embodiment has many critics.[143] Probably the most significant of which is the claim that "no complex, intelligent creature can actually get by entirely without representations" (Anderson, 2003, p. 115). This appears to me to be a legitimate criticism.[144] It seems reasonable that complex data sets would be organized and experienced as internal (mental) representations, that can be externalized either to test for congruence or to transfer (communicate) with another. It does seem to be true that a certain aspect of "problem solving routines involve intensive cooperation between computations and internal representations on the one side, and repeated environmental interactions on the other" (Anderson M. L., 2003, p. 108). Be that as it may, embodied cognition does provide a way of answering some of the questions posed by Polanyi, especially those concerning (1.) agency, (2.) situatedness, (3.) tacit knowing, and (4.) the role of the body as an assessing mechanism.

1   **Agency (processing system):** The understanding of the agent as a person with cognitive capacities shaped by a particular body dwelling in the world as it is, is itself a useful meta-heuristic which says: *when faced with a problem, approach it as a person with cognitive capacities shaped by a particular body dwelling in the world, rather than as a disembodied information processor.*

2   **Situatedness:** With this meta-heuristic in hand, it gives the agent permission to engage the situatedness of the problem, making use of knowledge accumulated over a lifetime[145] as well as that bestowed on us by our evolutionary inheritance.

3   **Tacit Knowing:** Given that human ways of knowing are not limited to those acquired as a disembodied *information processing system*, but rather, and perhaps more importantly, exist primarily as means for interacting with world, we have the advantage of thinking about the problem making use of all the cognitive resources of our entire body, including sense systems and emotions. Without having to make excuses or apologize for it.[146]

---

143   See Bickard (2008) for a comprehensive review.

144   See for example Takano and Okubo's (2006) study on metal rotation: the cognitive ability to create mental representations of a rotated object and its transformations. See also Shepard (1971).

145   Which includes cultural knowledge understood as "accumulated collective knowledge." (Conversation with Henco Bekkering 2017, 01, 29.)

146   Mitrovic, in his provocative book *Visuality for Architects* (2013) observes, "The expectation that one must justify architectural design by referring to something outside architecture, that formal and visual qualities are of secondary importance in architecture, has not just accidentally happened to dominate thinking about architecture. It has its own history and originates in a number of philosophical and psychological positions that became influential in the 1960's. While these positions have in the meantime ceased to be credible in philosophy and psychology, they have remained enshrined as dogmas in the writings of architects, architectural theorists, and historians" (p. xiii).

4   **Assessing mechanism:** And finally, the theory of embodied cognition demands that one engage the problem in a *feelingly* way.[147] That one gives into one's natural tendency to restructure the situation in a search for coherence (gestalt). That one applies his senses to feel the situation. That one engage multiple systems, including haptic, somatic, hedonic, that are available to him, considering options and alternative way of framing and reframing the problem outside the (black) box.

§ 3.6   Summary

This chapter explained that while inductive/deductive reasoning is often referred to as the foundation of the *scientific method*, Popper, Rittel, Ryles and Polanyi offer convincing arguments that show that its not that simple. I have emphasized three aspects of their arguments: (1.) That while one can arrive at astute observations, recognize patterns and suggest or make an educated guess as to why phenomena occur in a manner that is verifiable, claiming that such an observation, is a universal truth, useful as it might be, is more wishful thinking than fact. (2.) The presupposition that the scientist approaches the problem with an "innocent eye," without bias, and open to any possible result, while perhaps a great ideal way of approaching a problem that is worthwhile, it does not reflect the reality of the situation. All data processing systems have limitations (are bounded). Scientists, problem-solvers, and designers bring on their experiences, memories, feelings, expectations, expertise, as well as presuppositions to every situation. They rely on these for insight and motivation. (3.) In contradiction to popular concepts of knowledge, it is possible to know more than you can say. A good deal of knowledge is per-linguistic. Its embodied knowledge that allows one to know how. This knowledge is acquired not by explicit means, such as reading a book, but rather by being shown how, and by doing. This kind of knowledge is difficult to transfer (encode) in explicit terms. But it is real.

---

147   The role of emotions in problem-solving has become a topic of interest in the cognitive sciences as well as in decision-making theory. Lerner et al. (2015) provide research that supports emotions as being "powerful, pervasive, and predictable drivers of decision making" (p. 799). Thagard & Schröder (2014) explain this function of emotions as a way of explaining cognitive phenomena "from low-level perceptual abilities all the way up to high-level reasoning" (p. 1). defining this function as *semantic pointers*. The concept of semantic pointers is defined by Blouw, et al. (2015) as "symbol-like representations that result from the compression and recursive binding of perceptual, lexical, and motor representations, effectively integrating traditional connectionist and symbolic approaches" (p. 1).

(4.) All problem-solving and scientific inquiry rely on solution-generators and verification systems. These work in tandem. Solution generators scan the problem space looking for solution opportunities, while verification systems assess the value of these opportunities. Verification systems are not limited to logical rational assessment, but include seeking coherence as well as inhabiting the problem situation *feelingly* as a way to know.

This section shows that while human problem-solving is highly dependent on reason and logic, problem solving involves more than reason and logic, it also involves the body, feelings and experiential knowledge. Human cognition is fundamentally embodied. Humans do make use inductive reasoning for scientific discovery. However, claims to universal truth may be over-stated. The Cartesian mind (disembodied reason) does not adequately describe how humans know, Polanyi's account of tacit knowledge (embodied reason), coupled with the theory of embodied cognition, seems to be a more viable approach to problem-solving and design cognition.

Form Follows Feeling

4 The Design Process

Thinking goes on in trains of ideas, but the ideas form a train only because they are much more than what an analytic psychology calls ideas. They are phases, emotionally and practically distinguished, of a developing underlying quality; they are its moving variations, not separate and independent like Locke's and Hume's so-called ideas and impressions, but are subtle shadings of a pervading and developing hue...

(Dewey, 1934/2005, p.39)

Returning to the working definition proposed in Chapter One,[148] and allowing that this may be a reasonable description of architectural design, how then does this "solution-driven problem-solving process" that results in a building/built environment that solves for certain criteria and qualities, and is intended for human use work? How then, in light of the cognitive theory presented in Chapter Two, does a designer get from the problem state to the solution state. Are there identifiable functions, phases and components? How does the expert designer come-up with a solution? How does the designer know which of the many possible solution paths is the right one to take? And how does the designer know when a solution is had?

....

§ 4.1   Designing as Process

....

As discussed above, problem-solving for real-world problems, where there is an expectation for a novel solution and an artifact intended for human use, is not adequately described by theories of inductive reasoning (traditional definitions of the "scientific method), technical rationality, or general problem theory. This is better achieved by what Clark (1997, p. 135) calls *situateduated* reasoning – reasoning by embodied beings acting in a real physical environment.

---

148   Design is "a kind of solution-driven problem-solving process that results in the making of a functional representation for a building/built environment that solves for design criteria and constraints, is technically competent, coherent, and possesses intended aesthetic qualities for human use." See Chapter Two.

Due to the embodied nature of the human problem-solver, not only are problem-solving processes dependent on/bounded by the neurocognitive architecture of the human body (including the brain), but they are also dependent on the human body-environment relationship as a primary means of assessing the effectiveness, quality and feasibility of a design solution. [149] The theories of tacit knowledge and embodied cognition described above offer a more probable description of how designer/problem-solvers think, that works with open-ended problems, allows for novelty and establishes expectations for the qualitative assessment of a solution (building/built environment) intended for human use. With these theories of human cognition in hand, the next problem is to describe how designers apply their cognitive abilities to a problem situation to produce a solution.

Dewey (1934/2005), as quoted above, writes about cognitive processes (thinking) as occurring in "phases, emotionally and practically distinguished, of a developing underlying quality... [with] subtle shadings of a pervading and developing hue" (p. 39). Newell and Simon's description of cognitive processes is far more mechanical, no emotions, no underlying quality, or "pervading and developing hue." But both Dewey and Newell and Simon, consider human cognition as a **process**: a *series of actions or steps taken to achieve a particular end* (English Oxford Living Dictionary, 2017). [150]

To describe designing as a cognitive process it is first necessary to identify the *series of actions or steps taken to achieve a particular end* that constitutes what it means to design. One method of doing this is the application of *functional analysis*. [151]

---

149   A study by Alexiou et al. (2009) on the neurological basis of design cognition suggest that not only are problem-solving and design different, but that "design and problem-solving involve distinct cognitive functions associated with distinct brain networks" (p. 642). The role of the body in assessing the quality of the design solution will be discussed below.

150   Maier, et al. (2012) describe a process in the *cybernetic* sense as a "particular situation as it happened to unfold" (p. 234). They describe five types of process models that provide insight into and support design problem-solving. These include the *prescriptive* (how it should be done) and *descriptive* (how it is actually done) types which have already been discussed above. The other types include, *predictive* (how it will be done), *contingent* (how it could be done), and *historical* (how it was done).

151   Cummins (1983) provides a psychological explanation of how functional analysis works in three-stages: (1.) function is defined; (2.) it is organized into a set of simpler functions; (3.) the rules for how the functions interact with each other is described. Functional analysis is the analysis of a capacity in terms of the functional properties of a system and their organization, that is "...the attempt to explain the properties of complex systems—especially their characteristic effects—by the analysis of a systemic property into organized interaction among other simpler systemic properties or properties of component subsystems" (Roth & Cummins, 2017, p. 11). The functional analysis of design results in a process where design is (1.) understood as a complex system, that is (2.) broken into its constituent functions, and (3.) how these functions inter-relate are described.

Once the functional properties of a system, their organization and inter-relationships are understood, the system can then be described in terms of a series of (cognitive) actions, states or phases of discernable transitional components. For example, a typical five-phase description of the design process that one might use to describe the design process to a novice might be: a problem situation is presented → [define the problem space → frame the problem (discover a way to think about the problem) → seek a solution for both demonstrable criteria and experiential qualities] → arrive at a solution. [152] Each phase represents a different *state* along the problem-framing/solution-seeking path. The series of actions, transitional components, and inter-relationships are then, typically, represented as a linear diagram.[153] However, it should be understood that while describing designing as a process and producing diagrams to represent them is useful and can be helpful for understanding cognitive capacities involved in designing, diagrams, like the processes they represent are *artificial approximations*. Diagrams by nature lack in detail. That is what makes them useful. They are intended to provide a conceptual approximation (visual representation) of how the design process may happen. They are often missing (implicit and explicit) functions, such as feedback loops, motivations, search and decision-making criteria depending on the *grain* (level of detail) of the representation. How actions and steps are identified and categorized may also differ, from one diagram to another, depending on one's perspective, domain of practice, experience and level of expertise.

---

152   Broadbent points out that even at the first *Conference on Design Methods* (1962) where J. K. Page pointed out "the fallacy of believing that a design process consists of a single, simple sequence 'straight through from analysis to synthesis to evaluation' because, as he said, 'in the majority of practical design situations, by the time you have produced this and found out that and made a synthesis, you realize that you have forgotten to analyze something else here, and you have to go round the cycle and produce a modified synthesis, and so on. In practice you go round several times" (1973, p.256). A few pages later he refers to a report produced in 1966 by the Tavistok Institute of Human Relations, which points out that "no design process can be completely linear. It must incorporate feed-back loops of some kind so that new information which is thrown up at any stage may be included in the further recycling of one of the decision sequences" (1973, p.269).

153   Gedenryd (1988) is highly critical of *design methodology* in general and especially the tendency to represent it in linear diagrams, which he sees as being based on rationality, abstraction, and rigorous principles. Referring to Alexander (1964), Asimow (1962), Jones (1970), and Simon (1996), he writes "It portrays, or rather *prescribes*, design as an orderly, stringent procedure which systematically collects information, establishes objectives, and computes the design solution, following principles of logical deduction and mathematical optimization techniques." He even goes further, writing, "Having said this much about design methods, there is but one thing to add: They don't work, and they don't work at all" (p. 59). It is important to note that Gedenryd died (November, 2002) soon after the publication of this book. So while his opinion about design methodology is representative of the time he was writing, it would be interesting to read what he thinks about how the discipline has evolved over the past 25 years. I have no expectation that using any particular design methodology will result in a superior design solution. My understanding and application of design methodology is as a description of how design in general and how some individual designers work, or think they work. Insofar as these methodologies offer an insight into the acquisition of design expertise, I find them very useful. Still, his critique is well thought out and worth considering. See also Coyne et al. (1990, pp. 94-123) for a discussion on issues related to representing design.

However, diagramming the process (as perceived by the designer, or observed by the researchers), does provide a way to describe designing as an evolutionary process, perhaps as a "journey", that approximates the sequence, means, methods and procedures the designer uses to identify a design problem all the way through proposing a solution.[154]

Even though the term process may suggest otherwise, designing is not a simple step-by-step procedure. Designing is a kind of thinking, that involves underlying cognitive mechanisms (Gabora, 2002). It is a complex cognitive process that is directed, open-ended, self-correcting, seeks novelty (creative), and results in an artifact for human use. In this way designing is better described as a **system**: a self-correcting, recursive process aimed at a specific end.

The application of system theory, such as Churchman's *Systems Approach* (1968), as a means for understanding design, lead to the development of design **methodologies**,[155] that is, a system of **methods**[156] used in a particular domain or type of problem aimed at a specific end.

---

154   Journey, as a metaphor, is used widely in various contexts including research and project-based studies, such as "innovation journey" (Van de Ven, 2017). Richard MacCormack, a British architect, uses the journey metaphor to illustrate his design process: "The design process is a journey, an episodic journey towards a destination which you don't know about, which is what life is and what writing and all arts like; a journey (As quoted by Lawson, 1994, p. 62). Cross (2011) also uses this metaphor to describe the design process. He treats the design brief as the starting point and a known part of the journey. Cross cites Rowe (1998), "stand back and adopt a fresh point of departure" (cited in Cross, 2011, p. 36). Similarly, Jones (1992) likens a designer to an explorer looking for a hidden treasure, and sees design methods as navigational tools and maps. To him, a new problem is like an unknown land, of unknown extent, in which the explorer searches by making a network of journeys. Design methods assist in plotting the course of the journey and maintaining some control over where design goes. On the other hand, Lawson and Dorst (2009) use the journey metaphor to describe the overall process of developing expertise: "we see the creation of design expertise as a journey" (p. 21). For them, acquiring expertise is a long journey that commences with graduation."

155   Though related and often used interchangeably, methodology and method are not the same. Methodology is defined as: A system of methods used in a particular area of study or activity. (English Oxford Living Dictionaries, 2017) Bochenski (1965) describes methodology as "the theory of the application of the laws of logic to various fields" (See de Vries 1997). Method is defined as: "a particular procedure for accomplishing or approaching something, especially a systematic or established one" (English Oxford Living Dictionaries, 2017). A method is a way of doing something, or achieving an incremental goal. A method might be a rule-of-thumb, a simple procedure, or useful trick that solves a problem. A method can also be understood as a heuristic. Newell (1980) identifies a method as possessing four characteristics: (1.) It is a specific way to proceed; (2.) It is a rational way to proceed; (3.) It involves sub-goals and sub-plans; (4.) Its occurrence is observable.

156   Throughout the design process, designers make use of multiple methods (heuristics) and strategies that facilitate the overall design process. Methods include diagramming, mapping, brain-storming, sketching, drawing, modeling, critique, testing, etc. Methods can be used to help define the problem, facilitate the process, evaluate the solution. One of the earliest collections of methods is *Universal Traveler: A Soft Systems Guide to Creativity, Problem-solving and the Process of Reaching Goals* (Koberg & Bagnall, 2003). Christian Gänshirt (2007) calls these methods "design tools."

>>>

Design methodologies describe (and sometimes prescribe) what expert designers do, and help to understand how design expertise is acquired. Alexander (1984) writes, that the intent of describing design methodologies is "to try and create well-defined procedures which will enable people to design better buildings" (pp. 3-7). Cross (1984) describes the purpose of studying design methodology as a way to understand "how designers work and think; [by] the establishment of appropriate structures for the design process; the development and application of new design methods, techniques, and procedures; and reflection on the nature and extent of design knowledge and its application to design problems" (p. vii).

Historically, attempts at systematizing designing have not been well received by practitioners, who resist even the suggestion of a systematic approach to designing for fear of prescriptive, formulaic or cook-book methodologies.[157] The fear was well deserved. During the "design methods" phase of design research, it was accepted that proposing a (scientific) design methodology implied that there must be a way to codify what designers do, analyze it, apply new tools offered by systems theory and cognitive science, and propose a more efficient/effective, if not *the* optimal, way of applying cognitive ability to a design problem that guaranteed (or at least made it more likely), if applied properly, would result in a superior design solution. Broadbent (1973) quotes architect Eric Lyons as saying. "Design methods, ah yes. That's where they do all those charts and diagrams instead of designing buildings" (p. 282). Like Newell and Simon seeking to codify the problem-solving process, multiple attempts were made by design theorists to verify these findings by mechanizing (computerizing) the design process. These involved applying the language of inductive reasoning (scientific rationalism) and systems theory to describe how designers think by proposing prescriptive methods, that could produce predictable, reproducible results. It was successful to a degree, but not to the extent that a design machine could pass the Turing Test.

>>> Design tools can be organized into 12 categories: gesture; sketch; language; design drawing; model, projective view; photograph; film video; calculation; computer, program, simulation; criticism; theory. Curedale has assembled an impressive collection of methods in three volumes: *Design Thinking Process & Methods* (Curedale, 2016); *Design Methods 1 & 2* (Curedale, Design Methods 1, 2012). An excellent synthesis between methodology and methods can also be found in *Delft Design Guide* (van Boeijen, Daalhuizen, Zijlstra, & van der Schoor, 2013).

157 Gerkan (1998) writes that "the assertion that design could be explicitly effected in terms of methodology is charlatanism" (p. 39). Kucker, as quoted by Gänshirt (2007), criticizes the "so-called scientific approach to design:" saying that cutting the dimensions of design down to something comprehensible on the basis of rational planning process is bound to fail, as designing is an artistic act (p. 29).

The mainstream of design researchers abandoned this prescriptive approach. Because, while prescribed methods followed a clear logic, that resulted in logically coherent, elegant, rational processes, they were often based on personal reflection and how design researchers *thought* that designers *should* design, rather than how they actually designed (Broadbent, 1973). This approach to theorizing designing was an example where theory preceded practice (Schön, 1991). In reassessing the situation, especially in light of the work of Simon (1996), Broadbent (1973), Rittel (Protzen & Harris, 2010) and Churchman (1968), it was recognized that due to the different nature of design problems, the expectation for novel results, and difficulty in providing accurate means for assessing experiential factors, general problem-solving theory (GPS) was not adequate for accurately describing design problem-solving. This acknowledgment in many ways breathed new life into the Design Methods movement, leading to what came to be known as Design Theory and Methodology period of design research.

Design Theory and Methodology researchers, rather than starting with prescriptive methods of problem-solving derived from cognitive science, turned to the social sciences, making use of *design protocols* that emphasized observing designers (novice, professional and expert) actually designing. These protocols were then codified, diagrammed and mapped, analyzed, and tested using various (verifiable) means and methods (in an effort) to identify patterns of behavior and thinking processes that describe how designers "really" design.[158]

---

158   One of the on-going challenges with protocol analysis is the lack of a consistent method of documenting the results. Goldschmidt (2014) offers a (mapping) model that tracks the design process using a notation method that documents *design moves* she calls *linkography*. The premise underlying the linkography theory is that "the quality and the creativity of a design process depend on the designer's ability to synthesize a solution that exhibits good fit among all its components"(p. 73). Rather than looking at design phases, or "sweeping comprehensive models," linkography documents how designers design making use of a *linkograph* to identify incremental *critical moves* that make up the design process. A linkograph is similar to a decision-making map. A move, is understood as "a step in the [design] process that changes the situation"(p. 42). The linkograph evolved from years of research based on protocol analysis and a recognition of the inadequacy of the tools available to document the activity of the designers. Its intended as a way to standardize design protocol notation.

According to this theory the early part of the design process can be seen as a *synthesis* of a "series of cycles of divergent and convergent thinking... in which ideation and evaluation follow each other in frequent proximity, pertaining to embodiment and rationale"(p. 47). These cycles are documented by identifying and sequentially numbering moves and connecting them via *backlinks* and *forelinks*. There are four types of moves: orphan moves, unidirectional moves, bidirectional moves, and critical moves. Moves that propose are forward looking, resulting in forelinks. Moves that are evaluative are backward looking, resulting in backlinks. The diagrams that result from the moves (nodes) and the links (lines), result in a web-like graphic. Linkography is concerned with the links between moves, as such "it is believed that this is the best way to capture the essence of design cognition and behavior" (p. 52).

The patterns and processes (heuristics and methods) observed by design researchers, after taking into account the distinctive attributes of the design process, often did follow the meta-structure of GPS phases, but with different functions.[159]

The thing to keep in mind, is that **designing is not a process, per se**. Designing is fundamentally a human cognitive ability. A process is an artificial construct used to describe or approximate directed behavior. Structuring certain human behaviors as processes is a product of the architecture (structure) of human cognition.[160] **Design processes and the methodologies are approximations used to describe/understand what designers do.**[161]

§ 4.2 Design as Black Box

A system is a big black box.
Of which we can't unlock the locks,
And all we can find out about
Is what goes in and what comes out.
Perceiving input-output pairs,
Related by parameters,
Permits us, sometimes to relate
An input, output and a state.
If this relation's good and stable
Then to predict we may be able,
But if this fails us – heaven forbid!
We'll be compelled to force the lid!

(Boulding, 1964)

---

159   One of the most influential protocols was the Delft Protocol (Cross, Christiaans, & Dorst, *Analyzing Design Activity*, 1996). Many of the researchers who were involved in this foundational study, such as Cross, Dorst, Eastman, went on to become leaders in the field.

160   Sweller (2008) defines *human cognitive architecture* as, "the manner in which structures and functions required for human cognitive processes are organized" (p. 370).

161   Insofar as design can be described a processes and/or methodology, whether they are aware of it or not, explicitly or implicitly, all designers can be said to make use of a design methodology, or multiple methodologies depending on the situation. Be it a methodology of their own making, borrowed from someone else, yet to be described, or read about in a book.

Since just prior to WWII, when design research and systems theory were coming into their own as individual disciplines it has become more-or-less common (though there are still some who resist the concept), to think of design in terms of process.

In its most basic (meta) form, designing can be described as a kind of problem solving-heuristic that involves three phases or states: the problem phase → [the problem framing/solution-seeking phase] → the solution phase. If we can accept that what a designer does can be described as a process, and we can accept that a process is made up of multiple phases, and that these phases function in a manner that is inter-dependent and directed toward a particular kind of problem-solving situation; and if we can accept that the designing/problem-solving process is initiated by the problem state and is terminated by the solution state, then what we are interested in is the problem framing/solution seeking phase. This is the question for this chapter; to describe what happens between the brackets described in the three-phase heuristic above.

Expert designers, when asked how they arrive at a design solution, resisting getting into too much detail or hesitant to give away trade secrets, seeming to prefer what is called the "black box" theory of designing: define the problem (input) → [something magical happens (designing)] → solution (output).[162] Of course this black box theory of design/problem-solving is not adequate if one wants to understand how designing really happens (how the designer as transformative agent arrives at a solution),[163] or if someone wants to learn how to design. However, the black box theory does provide a simple three-phase model: input, process, output. The assumption is that the black box receives the input, say the project brief; and the output is a design solution.

---

162   Jones (1992) introduces the black box model of design with a "picture" of the brain as "a semi-autonomous device that is capable of resolving incompatibilities between inputs (i.e. solving problems) by assuming a pattern that is compatible not only with current inputs but also with many previous inputs of which the memory is composed" (p. 47). He then offers three alternative ways of thinking about this basic design model as: intuitive (black box thinking), rational (glass box thinking), and procedural (thoughts about thoughts/brain as self-organizing system). These three ways should be not thought of as exclusive of each other, but rather as describing three aspects of the same action (p. 46-570).

163   Having abandoned Newell and Simon's definition of the problem-solving agent as a thinking process for reasons given above, the transformative agent in this research is understood to be a human designer. There have and continue to be efforts to remove the human designer from the design process by codifying what the designer (as transformative agent) does and programming a computer to design. While this idea is intriguing, it is not the subject of this research. I am specifically interested in how *people* learn to design. For a description of how the computer may participate in the design process see Schön (1992, p. 131), where he proposes four possibilities: "(1.) To achieve a design output, given some input, as well as or better than designers ordinarily do it, but without particular reference to the ways in which they do it. This is the Turing test, more or less, and I shall call it "functional equivalence." (2.) To reproduce how we actually go about designing; this I shall call "phenomenological equivalence." (3.) To assist designers in their designing. (4.) To provide an environment for research aimed at understanding how designers design" (p. 131).

But that is not enough. We need to know what is meant by the input phase, the process phase, and the output phase; where the input is understood to be the problem, the output is understood to be the solution, and the process is understood to be what happens in-between. We need to "force the lid."

The black box, as described by Ashby (1956) is posed as way to introduce the concept of a system.[164] The idea is that an "engineer is given a sealed box that has terminals for input, to which he may bring any voltages, shocks, or other disturbances he pleases, and terminals for output, from which he may observe what he can. He is to deduce what he can of its contents" (pp. 86-117). All the engineer knows is that certain inputs consistently produce certain results. He does not know how or why. His job is to figure out what happens in the box, by observing what kind of output is produced when he applies this or that input.

Its not that different from the experience of the novice watching the master. On Monday the master starts with a pile of wood, (input) and by some mysterious process of cutting, planing, chiseling and carving (black box), by Friday the pile of wood is transformed into a beautifully crafted refined cabinet (output). The novice can see the actions but can only guess why the maker did this or that, and if this or that is how the master produced such a beautiful result. The novice wonders, "Is it simply a matter of refined technical skill, a proper sequence of procedures, years of experience, special secret knowledge?" It all seems so mysterious. The novice wonders, "Will the master tell me, or do I have to figure it out myself?" Unfortunately for the novice, there is a likelihood, due to the tacit nature of expert performance, that the master does not know how he does it either.[165]

The black box theory can also describe how some understand starting a car's engine: insert the key into the ignition switch, turn it and (mysteriously) the engine starts, and we can drive merrily away. Of course it is not really all that mysterious. The system (mechanism) that is initiated by turning the key is easily explained. But for many, simply knowing if one turns the key the engine will start is sufficient. Further knowledge is not necessary.

---

164   Meadows (2008) writes, "A system is an interconnected set of elements that is coherently organized in a way that achieves something" (p. 11). A system consists of three components: elements, interconnections, and a function or a purpose. (p. 11)

165   Recall that the mastering of a skill, how to do something, involves tacit knowledge, and that the distinctive characteristic of tacit knowledge is *the ability to know more than you can say.*

However, should a curious child be interested, she could open the hood (bonnet) of the car, peek in; and by following the wires, locate the battery and the starter and discover that the ignition switch completes the circuit between the battery and the starter motor, which turns the engine and initiates ignition. And should the child be even more curious, she might stumble upon a carburetor (if it's a really old car), or a circuit board and sensors, and figure out that this is how the car self-regulates and adjusts to various conditions, and informs the driver when the car needs to be serviced. Unfortunately, understanding how designers work, is not as simple as lifting up the hood and peeking in.

However, expert designers, it seems, would prefer if you just minded your own business and left the hood closed, *thank you very much*.[166] There are four reasons I will offer to explain this preference: (1.) It is a deliberate attempt to mystify technical knowledge as a means of protecting trade secrets;[167] (2.) There is a belief that design expertise is a special, "God-given" talent, which the designer was blessed to receive;[168] (3.) There is no one way that can describe how designers work;[169] (4.) Experts have so internalized (embodied) design knowledge that is becomes *tacit*, and in fact they really do not know (are not explicitly aware) why they do what they do. This fourth reason is most related to this research.

---

166   Regarding this preference for the mysteriousness of the black box, Gulari (2015) writes, "Cross argues that mystification of design can be a deliberate act. Some designers find mystery rather pleasant. For example, Lawson notes that MacCormac 'seems to be fascinated by the mystery of where design ideas originate.' Designers sometimes use magic in a positive sense and associate it with creativity. For instance: "I am a graphic designer who loves creativity and magic, and my aim in life is to share these with you. I believe that we find our truest vision and purpose in the magical world of creativity" (p. 8). Another graphic designer, Garry Emery (2014), writes, "What matters is the outcome. Ideally the outcome will solve all the functional criteria, be beyond the rational and be imbued with a certain 'magic'" (Designboom, 2014, ¶ 6). MacCormac described his practice as "having a repertoire of *tricks*" to exemplify to his original and surprising ideas (Lawson, 1994, p. 66). Lawson (2004) likens designing to the activity of a gambit, a chess player who needs to create a new and unexpected move in a chess game in order to win. Kolko (2011) also suggests that clients may desire magic because "a satisfying magic show means the money being well spent on the magician" (as quoted by Gulari 2015, p. 8 of 16).

167   Not unlike secret knowledge passed on by master to apprentice in craft guilds.

168   The question of "talent" will be discussed below.

169   This seems to be true. Bahrami & Dagli (1993) offer an exhaustive description of multiple models.

§ 4.3 Systems Theory

The most fundamental challenge to conventional ideas on design... has been the growing advocacy of systematic methods of problem solving, borrowed from computer techniques and management theory, for the assessment of design problems and the development of design solutions.

(Archer, 1965, p. 58)

Attempts to describe what designers do by thinking of designing as a process, has its roots in *systems theory* which includes General Systems Theory and cybernetics. Systems theory looks at the behavior of organized, adaptive, complex systems[170] in terms of process, self-regulating mechanisms and homeostasis, and analyzes their adaptability in terms of the theory of *selective information* (Simon H. , 1962). Design Research, General Systems Theory (Bertalanffy, 1968) and Cybernetics (Ashby, 1956) all emerged as disciplines in the period just after WWII. General Systems Theory is concerned with understanding *open* and *closed*, complex, dynamic systems acting as regulatory devices in science. Cybernetics looks at self-correcting, regulatory mechanisms in complex dynamic systems, such as *feedback loops* and control systems (Broadbent, 1973, p. 368).

Bertalanffy (1968) recognized that just as a living organism, as an entity, involves multiple inter-dependent systems and sub-systems which can be identified as distinct parts, there is also "an interrelationship [that] exists between all elements and constituents of society" (p. 4), just as there are multiple systems of microscopic (atoms) and large (cars) of individual elements, mechanical and biological, in the world that interact as a symbiotic system. He observes that there are structural similarities in the way all systems organize themselves and function. Bertalanffy writes that,

there exists models, principles, and laws that apply to generalized systems or their subclasses, irrespective of their particular kind, the nature of their component elements, and the relations or "forces" between them. It seems legitimate to ask for a theory, not of systems of a more or less special kind, but of universal principles applying to systems in general. (p. 32)

---

170   Simon (1962) defines complex systems as "made up of a large number of parts that interact in a non-simple way" (p. 468).

Bertalanffy describes general systems theory as a theory of "wholeness," one which is "purely formal but applicable to the various empirical sciences" (p. 37). From a general systems approach, all systems consist of input, output, throughput or process, feedback, control or cybernation, environment, goal, as well as a tendency toward entropy, that develop order and energy over time. [171] These components can also be found in most design methodologies. Within this framework, Bertalanffy identifies two kinds of systems: closed systems and open systems (pp. 39-41). Closed systems are self-contained and isolated from their environment, such as the study of thermodynamics where the system is always seeking a state of equilibrium. Open systems are those which are in a constant state of metabolism, always emerging and evolving. The theory includes control mechanisms or cybernation, the activities and processes used by the system to evaluate input, throughput and output to regulate the system, or homeostatic mechanisms, such as *feedback* loops (p. 43). Homeostatic mechanisms,[172] as derived from biology, are the *means* by which "body temperature stays constant, and other built-in devices by which the body senses changes in the external environment and adjusts itself accordingly. Homeostatic mechanisms are the "dynamic (self-correcting) processes by which an organism or device maintains a state of equilibrium" (Broadbent, 1973, p. 369). The mechanical example of a homeostatic mechanism is a thermostat which regulates the temperature of a room based on a predetermined range of comfort. When the temperature of a room exceeds the range of comfort, the thermostat signals the furnace to send more heat; when it reaches or exceeds the desired temperature is sends a signal to stop. The system is made up of the furnace, the distribution system (pipes), the heater (radiator), and the control (thermostat). In this way a system is understood as any organized, interacting, self-regulating and interdependent assemblage of parts or body of knowledge working together as an organized whole, which is more than the simple summation of the parts.

---

171   See Cook (1980) for a simple diagram

172   Alexander (1964) makes reference to homeostatic self-organizing cognitive systems when explaining the "nature of the form-making process", that is design. He writes, "To understand the form-making process, it is not enough to give a quick one-word account of unselfconscious form-making: adaptation... Roughly speaking, I shall argue that the unconscious process has a structure that makes it homeostatic (self-organizing), and that it therefore consistently produces well-fitting forms." His argument is that while this is how design takes place in traditional cultures, where design knowledge is mostly implicit (tacit) in nature, attempts in contemporary culture to make it explicit (self-conscious) have broken down the homeostatic structure of the design process, "so that the production of forms which fail to fit their contexts is not only possible, but likely" (p. 38).

Systems are hierarchical, they serve a purpose, and they take place in time (systems are not static).[173] The general schema of a *system environment* includes: input → [system] → output. The "system box" represents a *transformation agent* that "functions to translate or process a stated set of inputs into a defined set of outputs" (Cook, 1980, p. 15). Systems do not exist independently; they normally exist as subsystems of a larger or smaller system (environment/universe). The system box is the basis for what Ashby (1956) described as the *black box*.

General Systems Theory challenged two assumptions that had been accepted as givens of the "scientific method" [174] since Descartes:[175] (1.) A system could be broken down into its individual components and be studied as independent entities. (2.) Individual components of a system should be added linearly when describing a whole system. While these assumptions work well for simple (closed) systems, they do not when considering *complex* (open) systems. General Systems Theory holds, rather, that (1.) a (complex) system is better understood by the relations and hierarchy of interactions between its components and subsystems; and (2.) That the interactions between individual components in a (complex) system do not (necessarily) behave in a linear fashion.

---

173   Cook (1980) describes a system as having four characteristics: a set or assemblage of parts of entities; inter-related and independent yet identifiable that; that operate or interact or in relationship to accomplish a stated function or objective.

174   There is no one, single, definitive "scientific method" or "model of scientific inquiry." Scientific method is a term for the (rational) rules/techniques used for scientific reasoning and investigation. It normally refers to a logical, inductive/deductive, empirical/measurable methodology for gaining knowledge and testing hypotheses and predicting behaviors related to physical/natural world. A generally accepted test for the validity of a scientific method is its repeatability. Technical rationality is sometimes used the same a scientific method. See Schön (2009, p. 31).

175   Descartes' four precepts (heuristics), found in the *Discourse on Method* (1637/1999), when using the scientific (analytic) method are: (1.) Doubt everything: "The first of these was to accept nothing as true which I did not clearly recognize to be so: that is to say, carefully to **avoid haste and prejudice** in judgments, and to accept in them nothing more than what was presented to my mind so clearly and distinctly that I could have no occasion to doubt it. (2.) Break every problem into smaller parts: "The second was to **divide up each of the difficulties** which I examined into as many parts as possible, and as seemed requisite in order that it might be resolved in the best manner possible. (3.) Solve the simplest problem first: "The third was to carry on my reflections in due order, **commencing with objects that were the most simple** and easy to understand, in order to rise little by little, or by degrees, to knowledge of the most complex, assuming an order, even if a fictitious one, among those which do not follow a natural sequence relatively to one another. (4.) Be thorough: "The last was in all cases to make **enumerations so complete and reviews so general** that I should be certain of having omitted nothing."

In explaining how complex systems evolve Simon (1962) offers the following "parable:"

There were once two watch makers, named Hora and Tempus, who manufactured very fine watches. Both of them were highly regarded, and the phones in their workshops rang frequently – new customers were constantly calling them. However, Hora prospered, while Tempus became poorer and poorer and finally lost his shop. What was the reason? (p. 470)

Simon explains that both men made watches consisting of 1,000 parts each. Tempus had designed his so that if he had one partially assembled and had to put it down to, say, answer the phone, it would fall to pieces. Hora, however, designed his watch so that he could assemble it in sub-assemblies which fit together in to larger sub-assemblies, etc. So when the phone rang, he could put down what he was working on, and not lose everything. The issue here is not the quality of the end product, or the individual's craftsmanship, or even the need for customers. The issue is the system of assembly that did not allow for interruptions (by a telephone call). The connection between this parable and building construction is easily made, but there is a connection between this parable and the design process that can be made as well. The design process, rather than being thought of as a sequence of individual and incremental steps, is rather thought of in terms of phases, states, functions, feed-back loops, and heuristics.

Systems theory can be used to understand three aspects of design practice: (1.)the *design problem*, and (2.) the *problem of designing*. Systems theory can be applied to the *design problem*, (3.) as a way to understand buildings, not as simple entities, but as complex systems, composed of interdependent components, involving multiple regulation mechanisms with the goal of providing an environment for human habitation.[176] Systems theory can be applied to the *problem of designing*, as a means for understanding designing as a complex system of cognitive processes, that includes multiple feedback loops, that when applied to a design problem can result in a solution (functional approximation) that solves for demonstrable criteria and experiential qualities in a manner that exceeds performance expectations.

---

[176] Pye (1978), regarding the design of things and their functions, writes "It is fruitless to consider the action of a thing without considering the system of which it is a component" (p. 17).

The ability to reflect on how something is being done, requires being able to consider the behavior or task in terms of a system of procedures; to break it down into its components and be aware of the desired outcome; then to assess if the component actions and procedures are executed in the proper sequence that maximizes the desired outcome. However, this is only useful if one has properly identified the component actions and procedures. And/or should it turns out that the system model is not useful to be able to consider alternative actions and procedures that have a greater likelihood to achieve the desired outcome. **The problem with system models occurs when the system becomes the ends in itself rather a means to facilitate the effective production of the desired outcome.**

Schön, (1991) writing about professional education, and management develops his theory of the *reflective practice*. Reflective practice is when one is not only aware of the methods and strategies that are used in order to solve a problem, but when one is also constantly taking note of what facilitates the effective production of the desired outcome and what does not, and adjusts the system (methodology) accordingly. For Schön the reflective practitioner is one who recognizes patterns of what works and doesn't work, and adjusts his strategy to adapt to novel situations. The reflective practitioner takes a systems approach to designing, assessing and reassessing the sequence of phases, feedback loops, methods, strategies and situations.

When someone reflects-in-action, he becomes a researcher in the practice of content. He is not dependent on the categories of established theory and technique, but constructs a new theory on the unique case. His inquiry is not limited to a deliberation about means which depends on prior agreement about ends. He does not keep means and ends separate, but defines them interactively as he frames a problematic situation. He does not separate thinking from doing, ratiocinating [sic.] his way to a decision which he must later convert to action. Because his experimenting is a kind of action, implementation is built into his inquiry. Thus reflection-in-action can proceed, even in situations of uncertainty or uniqueness, because it is not bound by the dichotomies of Technical Rationality. (1991, pp. 68-69)

However, expert designers do not normally experience designing as a process, or sequence of differentiated phases, or a step-by-step process. They experiences designing as a fluid, tacit, intuitive ability to produce solutions that exceed performance expectations and resists explanation. Expert designers experience designing more as a *Gestalt*, a unified way of thinking, rather than the sum of its parts.

In addition, **designers, when actively engaging (inhabiting) the problem space, are tacitly (without explicit knowledge) seeking a Gestalt, a unified way of thinking about the problem as a whole**[177].

 By understanding/analyzing (1.) how complex systems evolve, (2.) how components and subsystems interact, and (3.) how systems self-correct within a system (feedback loops), one can assess their effectiveness and look for ways to maximize (optimize) their function. Influenced by the advances being made in manufacturing, business management, and organizational development, the pioneers in design methods research sought to apply this new paradigm to understand, evaluate and propose new ways of approaching and thinking about designing and the role of the designer.

§ 4.4 Designer as Transformative Agent

All designers intend to intervene into the expected course of events by premeditated action.

(Rittel H., 1988, p. 1)

Dong (2009), in the chapter "Rethinking the Designer," asks, when a designer gives an account of who is the 'I/we' who is doing the designing, identifies several models of the *designer as* – *designer as* information processor; *designer as* person who receives inputs from the user and produces outputs; *designer as* conceiver where the user is the receiver; *designer as* community activist who facilitates the design process; *designer as* collaborator.[178] His point is that there is something in a name. The model of *designer as* that one uses reveals what one "expect[s] to observe in the designer, which alternatively questions the autonomy of the designer detached from ontological expectations of designing...

---

177   Recall Polanyi (2009) and his references to Gestalt psychology above.

178   Dong's (2009) account of the different models of designing is in the context of a critique of design where "a designer is only a designer to the extent that the person 'realizes' the legitimate act of design," (p. 4) Dong's point is that the expectations that have traditionally "legitimatized" the designer *qua* designer have changed. He writes that "the boundary between being in/within the process of design and outside of what is considered designing is artificial," (p. 7)

The rationale, intent, influences, and ideas provided in a designer's account of designing should be seen as linguistically enacting the designed work, not just describing it" (pp. 9-10). The way one understands *designer as* also influences how one understands the normative expectations for performance.

In this account of design expertise, I am proposing *designer as transformative agent*. But, unlike Dong, who is reframing the identity of the designer from a multi-disciplinary (even anti-disciplinary) perspective, I am specifically focusing on designing within the domain of architecture, where the designer, as architect, as licensed professional, has fiduciary and civic responsibility, and is bound to a professional code of conduct that (minimally) presumes technical competency. **The model of designer as transformative agent that is being developed here understands the designer (as individual, group, collaborative effort) to be the one who identifies a situation that could be otherwise, engages in problem-framing/solution-seeking activity, and produces a solution for human use that meets or exceeds both demonstrable criteria and experiential qualities**. In this way the design process is the opposite of the process of evolution, in that the designer does not adapt (primarily) to the conditions that nature presents,[179] but rather adapts (transforms) nature for a human purpose. The designer is an agent of change. The designer's method for *changing* is described by the design process. The designer (not the design process) is the *transformative agent*.

§ 4.5   Designing as Heuristic

Designing, understood as a kind of problem-solving process, follows a similar pattern as George Polya's familiar problem-solving methodology outlined in his classic book *How to Solve It* (1945). The meta-structure of his methodology (meta-heuristic) is structured in four phases: understand the problem → devise a plan → carry it out → review/extend, along with recommended heuristics (methods) appropriate for each phase. In Polya's model, the problem is a given, and the optimal solution is the product of the problem-solving process. His model was intended as a learning tool to help students, and as an aid to help teachers to be better able to teach problem-solving.

---

179   Though one would hope that he takes the conditions nature presents us with into account in a way that is respectful and conscientious.

His is a *how to* method that formulates a series of phases in the form of brief questions or *heuristics*. His methodology (purpose-driven system of methods) is one way to describe what happens between the brackets in the black box theory: Problem → [Polya's problem-solving methodology] → Solution.

Newell (1980) assesses the advantages and disadvantages Polya's problem-solving methodology offers in terms of human intelligence vs. artificial intelligence (AI). In Polya's methodology, as in Newell's GPS, the *problem-solver* is the *transformative agent* who functions as an *information processing system*. The *transformative agent*, as problem-solver, whether she/he/it is a human, computer, animal, or some yet to be discovered being, acquires a problem from a *task environment* by "encoding it in an internal data structure [cognitive architecture[180]] and which solves the problem by processing these structures by (a sequence of) internally available methods, making use of 'bodies of encoded knowledge'" (p. 6). The transformative agent functions within the black box, insofar as the black box is understood as the information processing system. **The information processing system is composed of three components: (1.) Basic processing system architecture (methodology), which structures (the problem space of) the overall process; (2.) The methods, which provide specific strategic heuristics for solving various problem situations; and (3.) Knowledge which provides the (domain) information and concepts necessary to solve the particular type of problem.** [181] The same methods and knowledge can be used within different basic processing systems depending on the problem situation and type.

Newell (1980) notes that while Polya's heuristic can be applied to any *problem solver*, it is better suited to problem-solving situations where the transformative agent is human. For Newell, the strength of Polya is that, like the theories of embodied cognition presented above, his heuristic takes into account physiological, cognitive and psychological (bounded) aspects of human cognition. Newell identifies three factors that make Polya's heuristic better suited for a human problem-solver: **Attention needs to be focused**: Attention in humans does not occur automatically. Our sense systems are constantly seeking new information and competing for the attention of our consciousness.[182] Attention in this sense acts as a cognitive filter which allows one to focus (attend to) on the problem at hand and make sense of the situation.

---

180 In AI the basic processing system (methodology) is called the *architecture*.

181 These three components are analogous to: strategic knowledge (basic processing system); declarative/conceptual knowledge; procedural/heuristic knowledge (methods).

182 This concept of "attending to" in order to "make sense of" a situation is supported by research from cognitive science. See Passingham (2016), Ramachandran (2011), Damasio (1994).

It is the ability to attend to one thing while to "blocking out" another that is what allows us decipher what a friend is trying to say in a crowded room. **Human memory needs to be "tickled"**: Human memory is not always directly accessible. Memory is generally understood as short-term working memory and long-term memory. Short-term memory is immediately available, but the mind has limited working memory capacity; while the capacity for long-term memory seems to be limitless, it is often difficult to access (Miller, 1956). Heuristics are necessary to facilitate access to information stored in long-term memory (memory *loci*), such as mnemonic devices. **Problem solvers need to be motivated**: Motivation involves stimulating a "desire to earnestly obtain a solution," the "will" to do it, and a social context that supports the effort.[183]

What is notable in this critique is that not all systems are well-suited to all problem-solvers. Problem-solvers possess characteristics, or "bounded-ness." An effective problem solving methodology takes into account the characteristics, strengths and limitations (physical, psychological, cognitive) of the problem-solver. Problem-solving systems that work well for computers are necessarily not well-suited for humans, and *visa-versa*.[184]

As Polya was primarily a mathematician his methodology is best suited for solving problems where the problem can be clearly defined and there is an optimal solution, or a *closed* system. His is a methodology that a designer might use when facing technical issues, where there are demonstrable criteria, for instance determining efficient space relationships or maximizing floor area usage. This methodology does not work well with *wicked* or open-ended problems, which are a defining characteristic of design problems.

The usefulness of a methodology tends to be domain and situation specific. A methodology (with its associated epistemology)[185] does not only describe how to complete a task but it also explains how the methodology facilities achieving the goals and objectives of the particular task. These goals and objectives of a problem situation can be stated as criteria, constraints, and qualities. However, it should be noted that while design methodologies are by nature teleological (goal oriented), using this or that methodology itself does not necessarily guarantee an optimal solution, or even the most efficient means of arriving at a minimally acceptable solution even though it may have been effective in the past.

---

183   This question of *motivation* will come up again as it is central to my thesis.

184   This is also applicable to degrees of expertise. Methods that are well suited to the abilities and experience of experts, are not necessarily helpful or appropriate for novices. This topic will be taken up in more detail in the following chapter.

185   The function of the epistemological aspects of this or that methodology will be discussed in the section below on the "design problem"

A methodology describes the *procedures* a problem-solver might use, or has used, to solve a similar problem. It is a framework or a tool. But **a methodology does not solve the problem**. Nor does it (nor is it able to) make judgments regarding the quality of human experience and perception.[186] This is the responsibility/work of the designer as human transformative agent. Cross, (2011) when making this point, refers to Simon's "ant" and Jones's "explorer" (p. 124).

Simon (1996) describes the opportunistic behaviors of an ant returning to its nest, encountering all kinds of challenges along the way, and "designing" a way to meet them.[187] However, if one where to take an aerial view of the route the ant took, one might not be convinced that the ant was all that efficient.

Jones's (1992) explorer is in search for a hidden treasure. Like the ant, the explorer has a definite goal and knows what it is; but the way to find the treasure is not yet known. In retrospect after completing the task, it is possible that the explorer may realize there may have been a more direct route to finding the treasure.

Cross observes that while these are somewhat useful metaphors, their use is limited, in that in both metaphors the goal is already known. In designing the goal is not known. **The designer is not searching for something that is lost but rather seeking to discover something that does not yet exist**. So while a design methodology may describe how a designer goes about the search, and may even suggest a procedure to help along the way, the designer is searching for something of which he knows not, but which he will recognize when he "sees it."

It is this aspect of design methodology that is the subject of this research. Not the promise that if one follows a procedure step-by-step (the so called "cookbook" approach) one will produce an acceptable solution: **This research is interested in design methodology's descriptive value**, especially as it is framed in terms of embodied cognition and is related to tacit knowledge – how designers immerse themselves in this intense, focused and disciplined process that requires a broad domain of

---

186   To make judgments about the quality of an experience as a human might, one needs to have a human body or a close facsimile of one. How we make sense of and experience the world is dependent on embodied cognition. For example, how a dog experiences the world, with its body covered with hair, walking on four feet, having greater range of hearing and smell; is different that how a human wearing cloths, walking on two feet, and with a lesser range of hearing and smell, experiences the world. And, as a result, a dog makes sense of the world, using a different set of parameters than a human, simply because of how its relationship with the world is facilitated by its body.

187   I would prefer to say that the ant was "planning" rather than "designing" a way to meet al the kinds of challenges along the way. For Simon, design results in a plan. I hold that designing results in an artifact for human use. Simon was not a designer.

interdisciplinary knowledge, generating a solution for a problem whose definition is only fully understood when he designs something that has never existed before. And finally understanding how it is that expert designers *feelingly* know that they have found the right solution when they see it.[188] Methodologies provide a framework that offer insight into the design process in general, and more specifically in terms of the acquisition of expertise, offer cognitive *scaffolding*[189] that beginner designers can use to build upon.

§ 4.6   Designing as Methodology

... there is no escape for the designer from the task of getting his own creative ideas. After all, if the solution to a problem arises automatically and inevitably from the interaction of the data, then the problem is not, by definition, a design problem... An abundance of artists starving in garrets is the surest guarantee of an artistic breakthrough.

(Archer, 1981, p. 58)

Archer's point is an important one to keep in mind as we go deeper into trying to understand the structure of designing. The purpose of this effort is not to codify designing, to fit it into neat categories, or force it into a prescribed process. The purpose is to understand how the expert designer arrives at a design solution that exceeds performance expectations, and to attempt to describe how a designer does it, as a tool for acquiring design expertise.

Referring to the basic process described above, the act of designing can be described as being composed of three phases: **problem, design process, solution.** Simply stated: a problem is posed, the designer works on it, a solution is had. In this way, the designer – either an individual, a group/collaborative effort, a machine or a combination of the three – acts as the transformative agent on the problem situation to produce a solution. It is a simple model, similar to the black box, and compatible with Polya's problem-solving methodology. However it is not as simple as it seems. Systems, processes, methodologies, and heuristics all occur at different scales and/or hierarchies.

---

188   Later I will call attention the importance of this *feelingly* way of knowing when explain what I mean by *aesthetic resonance*.

189   Cognitive scaffolding, a concept attributed to Lev Vygotsky (1896–1934), functions to provide a framework that facilitates the acquisition of complex abilities within the students zone of proximal development.

Systems do not exist in isolation. Systems seek wholeness. Systems are interdependent. Systems exist within systems. The same is true for processes, methodologies and heuristics. As a complex system, the overall design process can be understood as a meta-heuristic, where a system of sub-heuristics (methods) interact and are regulated as subsystems.

The problem, as will be seen below, occurs when the design process is no longer understood as *only* what happens in the black box, represented by: problem → [design process] → solution. Where the design process is understood primarily as what happens between the brackets experienced as a *dialectic* between the possible interpretations of the problem and the possible solutions (Snodgrass & Coyne, 1997). In this model, design is understood as a cognitive process that receives a specific input and results in a predictable output. As has been demonstrated above, this model of designing/problem-solving is inadequate, primarily because design problems are by definition open-ended and ill-defined. A closed-system problem-solving process is ill-equipped to solve these kinds of problems. These models presume that the phases mostly occur sequentially, but research has shown that this is not the case (at least for architects).[190]

On the other hand, if the design process is described in an all-inclusive manner, that includes problem, problem-framing/solution-seeking, solution, then rather than defining the design process in terms of three phases, it should be defined as three *states*, where the *problem state* is where a problem is identified, the *problem space* is defined (to include determining criteria, constraints and qualities), and a way of *framing* the problem space is decided upon. The *problem-framing/solution-seeking state* is understood as a space where the active search for a solution, exploration of alternatives and testing of possibilities occurs. This state is best described as what happens between the *brackets* as described above. There is general agreement that this state includes three components: analysis, synthesis and evaluation.[191]

---

190   See Cross & Roozenburg (1992).

191   Jones (1992) writes, "One of the simplest and most common observations about designing and one upon which many writers agree, is that [the design process] includes three essential stages: analysis, synthesis and evaluation" (p. 63). Coyne (1990), Asimow (1962) and Bahrami & Dagli (1993) hold this position as well. However, they do not all use the same terms to describe these "three essential phases." In fact just a few sentences after Jones writes the above, he goes on to rename the three phases as *divergence, transformation, convergence*. (p. 64)

The *solution state* is where the solution is externalized as a functional approximation, of a building/built environment to be built, and assessed against criteria, constraints and qualities.[192] The state model presumes that all three states are simultaneously active and interdependent (including feedback loops, framing and reframing, defining and redefining the problem space), to varying degrees over time.[193] This state model can be represented as: problem → [analysis/synthesis/evaluation] → solution.

There are numerous design process/methodology models out there.[194] Most design processes are *phase* model processes. Phase model processes describe procedural approaches to a design problem. Polya's methodology is a good example of a phase model. Another example of a phase model is Asimow (1962). Intended for engineering students, his model includes six phases: (1.)Analysis, (2.) Synthesis, (3.) Evaluation and decision, (4.) Optimization, (5.) Revision, (6.) Implementation.

State models of designing, rely on concepts derived from systems theory. These tend to be systematic approaches to designing, or methodologies. These approaches are not strictly procedural. Jones (1992) writes "Methodology should not be a fixed track to a fixed destination but a conversation about everything that could be made to happen." Two examples of the *state* model are Cross and Lawson. In Cross's (2001) model, he describes these three components as: problem formulation; process strategy; solution generation. Lawson (2005) describes these three components as "discreet properties," (not phases) with the following characteristics: **Design problems** cannot be comprehensively stated, they require subjective interpretation, and tend to be organized hierarchically. **Design processes** are endless, none are infallible.

---

192   Depending on one's model of designer as, the design process ends with the production of the functional approximation. However, as I have argued that the proper end to architectural design is the building/built environment, I hold that the design process is only consummated when the building/built environment is complete.

193   Design states are not distinct. For example the problem state typically involves some level of solution seeking. Just as the solution state involves some level of problem setting. While ever design process is instantiated by the recognition of a problem and ends with a some approximation of a solution, it would be a mistake to describe these states as sequential. Identifying exactly when the designer moves from one state to another poses the same kind of problem posed by Occam's razor. Just as human perception systems make use of multiple parallel cognitive systems in disparate regions of the brain to make-sense of make sense of the various inputs, so it is with the designing.

194   See Broadbent (1973), Jones (1992), Lawson and Dorst (2009), Adams (2015), Delft Design Guide (van Boeijen, Daalhuizen, Zijlstra, & van der Schoor, 2013), Design Thinking Methods (Curedale, 2016). See also, Braha & Maimon (1997), for a comprehensive examination of engineering design methodology including a good overview of many of the theories, models and methodologies that are included in this research.

They involve finding problems as well as solving them, inevitably leading to subjective value judgments. The process looks to the future,[195] and occurs in a "need for action" context. **Design solutions** are inexhaustible in their possibilities, they are optimal and holistic, they make a contribution to knowledge, and exist as part of other design problems.

Recall there is no one (correct) prescriptive design process that guarantees a successful solution. And, there is no one (correct) descriptive design process that describes how all designers work. However, though expert designers do tend to develop their own approach to design problems (methodologies) and preferred strategies (methods), they also follow a predictable pattern. **Methodologies are systems-based models that describe various ways of approaching the design process, an ongoing process with the application of various strategies along the way (methods) intended to result in a solution to a design problem that falls within an acceptable range.**

Returning to the above basic components of the designing, (problem, problem-framing/solution-seeking, solution), the next three sections will take each component one at a time, in an effort to gain a deeper appreciation for how each contributes to the design process. As designing is generally understood to be what happens between the problem state and the solution state, I will start with the problem. And follow with the solution, and finally describe some representative processes/methodologies.

---

195   Here, I am using "looks to the future" rather than "prescriptive" to avoid confusion. Lawson uses *prescriptive* to contrast design with what scientists do: "While scientists may help us to understand the present and predict the future, designers may be seen to *prescribe* and to create the future" (2005, p.125).

5 Problem

Learning what the problem is IS the problem.

(Rittel H. , 1988, p. 2)

If learning what the problem is *is* the problem, how do we know when we know what the problem is, and how do we go about learning what it is?

The problem state is initiated when someone has "the realization that it could be otherwise." The problem can come from anywhere and take many forms. A design problem can be a *what-if* scenario. It can be a list of criteria and constraints. It can be list of requirements and preferences. It can be a narrative. Whatever form a design problem takes, the it needs to be interpreted. Designing begins with the recognition of a situation that should/could be changed.

Design problems have two components: content and structure. Designers work with others to: (1.) Define the content, which includes, criteria, constraints and intended qualities of a design problem (some call this defining or *setting the problem space*); and (2.) Structure the design problem so that it can be solved with the resources available (some call this *framing the problem*). Together these define the problem.

§ 5.1 Who Defines the Problem?

In standard architectural professional practice, it is typically assumed that it is the owner's responsibility to define the problem, also known as the "project brief." It is the architect's responsibility to design a building that satisfies those criteria (as well as others related to responsible professional practice, building codes, and building standards).[196]

---

[196] The normal scope of services as outlined by AIA Contract B141, "Standard Form of Agreement Between Owner and Architect with Standard Form of Architect's Services," lists design, contract, and project administration under *the standard form of architect's service*s that are normally considered to be the responsibility of the architect. (AIA Document B141-1997, 1997) Article 2.1 describes project administration services, design, and (construction) contract administration. Article 1.2.2.1 reads, "Unless otherwise provided under this Agreement, the Owner shall provide full information in a timely manner regarding requirements for and limitations on the Project." Providing the "requirements for and limitations" to "program criteria" is normally considered to be the responsibility of the "owner."

In this way, it is understood that the problem of designing is to solve for the requirements and criteria as defined by the client. And it is upon this understanding that the scope of services, schedule and fees are based. This approach has many characteristics of a closed system approach.

The American Institute of Architects (AIA) list of standard design services, follows almost identically, phase by phase, the problem-solving methodology that Polya identified in *How to Solve It* (1945): problem [evaluate and planning → schematic design → design development → construction documents] → solution. And like the Polya methodology, there are associated methods that are useful to achieve the goals of each phase in question. The AIA phase model may be useful for identifying services, determining a schedule and setting a fee structure. But when tested against the research presented above, it does not reflect the way designers actually work. It is more like older prescriptive models of design that were based on some ideal about how it should be.

In real life, who defines the design problem is not so clear. As described in the section, "Designer as Transformative Agent," Dong (2009) claims that who gets to define the design problem is directly connected to what model (or epistemology) of *designer as* is operative.[197] If one understands the designer as a *cognitive process, information-processor* or the person who receives inputs and generates an output, then the problem is something that is fed into the designer system, and formulated outside it. However, as I have previously suggested, if the model of *designer as* is more inclusive, *designer as transformative agent* that includes the owner/client, end user, fabricator, etc., as well as design professional, not as stakeholders but as integral participants within the design process, the *designer* then is *the group of people involved in identifying the problem (problem-setting), problem-framing/solution-seeking, and solution setting.*

Dong, asking what "is the extent to which we can ascribe design to the perspectival account (testimony) of the designer," writes, "increasingly, design is held in the multitudes rather than in a designer or designers..." (p. 5). From this point of view of the design process, identifying the problem is just as important as solving it, perhaps more so, because until someone recognizes that *it can be otherwise,* there is no opportunity for innovation, novelty or creativity.

---

197   Mitchell discusses this (epistemological) phenomenon by introducing the concept of *inferences*, that is how one derives conclusions (*predicates*) from *premises*. Before a designer can understand a design problem he needs to interpret the presuppositions of the problem statement, its premises: what are the assumptions, the knowledge base, expectations, etc. He also needs to assess, or at least understand, on what basis a conclusion was inferred from the premises. He defines a design problem as one that "is represented by predicates stated in a critical language, a design world which depicts some construction world, a knowledge base about that construction world, and procedures for deriving inferences" (1990, p.79).

Designing begins not when the design brief is given to the designer, but rather, when someone sitting in a café looks out the window at a vacant parking lot and wonders if it would be possible to build a farmers market there.

§ 5.2   Defining the Problem

Embedded in a design problem are criteria and constraints – some explicit and some implicit and some yet to be discovered – of varying degrees of importance. Rittel (1988) writes that "[design] constraints are decided, selected, and self-imposed, and not implied, derived or logical necessities" (p. 5). Rittel is writing against those who believe that somehow – if for example they approach the problem in terms of functional efficiency and cost effectiveness and follow a purely logical problem-solving process – the process will *inevitably* result in the best solution. In designing there is no inevitability or logical necessity or even *best* solution.

All design problems need to be interpreted. Alexander, (1964) in the *Synthesis of Form*, calls this the problem of *fit*.[198] For example, an owner tells her architect that she wants to build a new house on a fairly large site on a lake. She wants the house to have a kitchen, dining room, living room, family room, study, 4 bedrooms, adequate storage area, and 4.5 bathrooms. She is on a limited budget, but wants good quality. There is no rush in getting it built.

---

[198] The concept of *fit* is central to Alexander's theory presented in *Notes on the Synthesis of Form,*"(1964) For Alexander "the ultimate object of design is form" (p. 15). By form, Alexander is not referring to abstract Platonic form, but rather the physical form (shape) of an artifact. The *functional origin* of the form comes from *programmatic clarity*. That is the "earliest functional origins" and the patterns that the design fond in them. It is from this point that the designer begins the effort to "achieve fitness between the two entities: the form in question and its context. In other words, when we speak of design , the real object of discussion is not the form alone, but the ensemble compromising the form and its context. Goof fit is a desired property of this ensemble which relates to some particular division of ensemble into form and context" (p. 16). There are two (extreme) ways of approaching this *fitness between two entities*. One can make an effort to devise an object that is well-suited ("good designers") to the environment. Or one can adapt the environment ("the impractical idealism of designers") to *fit* the form of the object. The *good designer*, "if he knows what he is doing, is able to deal with "several layers of form-context boundaries in concert" and he seeks to achieve "internal coherence of an ensemble." "In a perfectly coherent ensemble we should expect the two halves of every possible division of the ensemble to fit one another" (p. 18). However, one must always keep in mind that the "highly inter-laced and complex phenomenon" we call the *division* between the form and its environment should be considered "arbitrary" at any one time, and that it is only the form, over which we really have any control. For Alexander, the process of achieving good fit (design) is "a negative process of neutralizing the incongruities, or irritants, or forces, which cause misfit" (p. 24).

The designer is already applying the *cost = area/time/quality heuristic*.[199] At first glance it seems like a simple design problem. But upon second glance the problem is filled with premises, assumptions, presuppositions, and cultural preferences. When interpreting the problem, Alexander writes, "It is not possible to set up premises, trace through a series of deductions, and arrive at a form which is logically determined by premises... There is no legitimate sense in which deductive logic can prescribe physical form for us" (p. 8).

Dorst (2004) observes that most design problems appear to have a "three-fold nature": they are partly *determined*; they are partly *under-determined*, and they are partly *undetermined*. Determined problems are those that the AIA B141 contract presupposes that the owner will provide for the architect. These problems allow the designers to quickly unearth "'hard facts,' by information gathering and analysis, and live with these specifications" (Dorst, 2004). Determined problems are well suited to Newell and Simon's rational problem solving paradigm as described above. Under-determined problems, are those where critical elements of the problem can only be discovered and clarified in the process of trying to solve it. These are the kinds of problems where one might say, "I'm not really sure what I mean, but I will know it when I see it." Undetermined problems are those "where the designer is to a large extent free to design according to his own taste, style and abilities" (Dorst, 2004), where the owner/client defers to the judgment of the designer. Dorst observes that all design problems possess, to some degree, characteristics of all these types of design problems.

Take for example, the four bedrooms from the above example. The designer quickly discovers that the owner is married with 3 children (though it is not clear it she is married to a man or a woman, or if the children are biological or adopted). Two of the children are off in college (their sex/gender identity is not known). The presupposition in the West may be that the bedroom should be big enough to accommodate standard bedroom furniture: a bed, small desk, book selves, chair, closet, chest of drawers, night stands, maybe a TV as well (there is no indication of the ethnic/cultural identity of the spouse or the children). The designer may refer to any number of *design standards*, such as *Architectural Graphic Standards* (American Institute of Architects, 2016); *Neufert* (Baiche & Williman, 2000); *Time-Saver Standards* (Watson & Crosbie, 2005). But this assumes the standard for a *bedroom* is both what the owner has in mind, and that these standards are suitable for this particular design situation.[200]

---

199   Assuming time and area are constraints, the higher the quality the higher the cost. Assuming time and quality are constants, the bigger the bigger the area, the higher the cost, etc.

200   Referring to design standards or to previously successful solutions to save time, is a kind of heuristic for problem definition.

The designer may need to ask the owner, exactly what these rooms are for: sleeping, getting dressed, studying, privacy, etc.? For example, if the bedrooms are thought to be primarily for sleeping, and two of the children are off at college, and the other one prefers to study in the living space, basing the size and shape on a standard bedroom may prove to be a less than effective allocation of resources. Perhaps the there is an alternative.

If there is no clear understanding of what the *bedroom* is for, there is little likelihood that the designer will be able to achieve *good fit*. Alexander (1964) writes:

There is a tendency of designers, when faced with difficulty, to change the definition of the problem: 1.) There are the 'impractical idealists' who loosen the difficulty of constraints by stretching the form-context boundary; and 2.) The 'good designer' who 'keeps an eye on the possible changes at every point of the ensemble. He is sensitive to fit at several boundaries at once. His sense of organization leads to the 'internal coherence' of the ensemble. (p. 17)

The challenge for the *good designer* is not to change (interpret) the problem in a manner that fits his presuppositions or convenience, but to engage the situation, challenge his presuppositions and biases, and strive for the best fit possible considering the situation.

With all these variables, spoken and unspoken, explicit and implied, preferred and required criteria and constraints, it can be challenging to gain enough clarity about what the design problem is, before one feels confident enough to start designing, though in reality, once the designer begins considering the problem he has already begun designing. One method that designers use to clarify the design problem so that they can get "started designing," is to make use of a heuristic called *conjectured solutions*. Cross (1990) describes how this heuristic works by quoting Marples:

The nature of the problem can only be found by examining it through proposed solutions, and it seems likely that its examination through one, and only one, proposal gives a very biased view. It seems probable that at least two radically different solutions need to be attempted in order to get, through comparisons or sub-problems, a clear picture of the 'real nature' of the problem. (Marples, 1960)

This quote illustrates the distinctive reciprocal/dialectical relationship that design problems have with their solutions, which distinguishes them from other kinds of problems. See also Akin, 1979 and Darke, 1979.

§ 5.3   Design Problems Have a Structure

What becomes clearer and clearer is just how problematic design problems can be. However, it should be noted that design problems are not *problematic* in themselves, they are what they are. They are considered problematic because they do not *fit* easily into the abstract framework of problem-solving theory. As discussed above, the problem with design problems, is that while typical (well-structured) problems – those that can be solved using the so called "scientific method" – are clearly defined and closed; design problems are described as open, *ill-structured* (Simon , 1973), *wicked* (Rittel & Webber, 1973) or *ill-defined* (Rowe, 1987). Schön (1985) just calls them *real world* problems (p. 15).

For Simon, the structuring of a problem is fundamental to solving it.[201]
That is, solving a problem is essentially a matter of adequately representing it,"so as to make the solution transparent" (1996, p. 153).[202]

---

[201] Dorst (2004) writes that "a fundamental distinction between different kinds of design problems can... be constructed on the basis of the paradigms of [the] design methodology..." being used. These paradigms provide a "basis for further exploration of the structures of design problems." As an example, Dorst describes the *rational problem solving paradigm*, described above, as a positivistic epistemology; while Schön's *reflection in action paradigm* is a phenomenological epistemology. He writes: "Positivism claims that a person lives in an objective world which can be known through his senses; the sensory data is then structured by an internal processing system. This structuring system interprets the data by using basic a *priori* categories. To know the objective world, a person should study it carefully and dispassionately, preferably with scientific methods. While from the epistemological perspective of phenomenology the person is not static, but a dynamic, emotive social being with a history and an environment which heavily influences the person's construction of reality. And the subject is influenced (and in the end 'formed') by what he/she perceives. Therefore, person and object are inextricably connected." His point is that how one thinks about designing/problem-solving will influence how the problem is structured.

[202] Suggesting the kind of "inevitableness" that Rittel (1988) denies above, "Nothing has to be or remain as it is or as it appears to be... which would dictate to take a particular course of action and no other" (p. 5). While I appreciate Rittel's exuberance, as he was not a designer (though he was a planner) and embodied cognition was in its infancy while he was writing. However, while there may indeed be no "limits to the conceivable," there are limits to the possible. Having an appreciation for these limits, and knowing how to work *with* them, is part of the difference between an expert designer and a naive dreamer. Which is not to say that the world does not need naive dreamers. But they are not properly understood as designers, prophets perhaps, but not designers.

Or, structuring the problem so that it fits well into a scientific problem-solving framework. Well-structured problems can be represented (stated) and processed in one or more problem spaces in accordance with identifiable performance criteria, and knowledge and states of the problem can be represented in a complete, accurate and manageable way. In well-structured problems the problem is clearly stated, and can be processed using a specific method producing a repeatable result. This approach is "scientific." Ill-structured problems are characterized by reference to *residuals*, or what is lacking as compared to well-structured problems. As such, these kinds of problems resist being well-structured in the manner described above (Murty, 2006). Rittel (1988), describing design problems in terms of their initial state, operations and goal state, refers to these as "wicked problems." Rittel who writes that "from the beginning the designer has an idea of the whole resolution" (1988, p. 2), like Polanyi accepts that the designer pre-structures the design problem.

From the beginning the designer has an idea of the 'whole' resolution of his problem which changes with increasing understanding of the problem, and the image of its resolution develops from blurry to shard and back again, frequently being revised, altered, detailed and modified. His focus alternates continually from small component parts, back to the whole problem, and back to other details. (1988, pp. 2-3)

Wicked problems as described by Rittel and Webber (1973) are not so much understood as single problems, but problem complexes with multiple interdependencies. In their *initial state* every problem is a symptom of another problem and is essentially unique, with no definite formulation and may pose multiple reasonable interpretations. Every formulation or interpretation of the problem corresponds to a statement of a solution and determines the resolution. In terms of operations, as a result of their initial state, **one cannot understand the problem without solving it.** Each initiative is an irreversible one-shot *operation* "with an indeterminate range of potential solutions, strategies or moves, with no scope for trial and error and with the problem solver being responsible for the consequences"[203] (Murty, 2006, p. 21).

---

203   This speaks to the *opportunistic* nature of designing. As there is an indeterminate range of potential solutions, the designer needs to vigilant to identify and limit the more likely solutions, to reduce his search area, and make better use of his cognitive resources and time. Newell and Simon (1958) explain that limiting the potential solutions is achieved by the application of heuristics, that eliminate certain variables, or impose additional criteria upon the search space to limit the number of potential solutions. Even so, say that the application of these heuristics reduces the possible solution paths from 6000 to six. There are still six perfectly reasonable paths to a solution to pursue. How does a designer know what path to choose, recognizing that as quoted above, "there are no logical or epistemological constraints or rules which would prescribe which of the various meaningful steps to take next" (Rittel 1988). (Though, Lawson (2005) does acknowledge "external criteria" as a type that does function as a constraint.) What then is the basis of a designer's preference for one path over the other? Is it "beyond reason," as Rittel suggests above?

In the *goal state* there is no definite completion of the problem, or "ultimate test, or criterion to judge a solution to be true or false. Outcomes are merely good or bad, or better or worse and any additional effort may be beneficial" (p. 21). The solution is never the *best*, it is only one of many possible solutions, that satisfies the criteria and constraints within an acceptable range, based on the interpretation of the problem and available resources.

Ill-defined problems as defined by Peter Rowe (1987) are problems where "both the ends and the means are unknown at the outset of the problem-solving exercise" (p. 40). As a result, a large part of the problem-solving activity (designing) consists of defining the problem and redefining it as new knowledge and insight is gained.

§ 5.4 Lawson's Comprehensive Model

Lawson (2005) provides a comprehensive model that identifies three characteristics of design problems: (1.) They cannot be comprehensively stated; (2.) They require subjective interpretation; and (3.) They tend to be organized hierarchically.[204] His first point speaks to the way that design problems are formulated. With many uncertainties, multiple stakeholders, and competing priorities, specific criteria and limitations of the design problem typically emerge during the design process. Similar to Simon, Rittel, and Rowe, Lawson holds that is not really until an acceptable solution is had that a design problem is fully defined. Even if it were possible to give a designer a comprehensive list of criteria and limitations, these criteria and limitations would still need to be understood, prioritized and interpreted. Finally, it must be understood that **the solution to a design problem is not always embedded in the design problem.** Design problems always exist in a larger context. Often times the perceived (given) design problem (as defined by the design brief) is a symptom of an underlying unarticulated cause that must be discovered.

---

[204] Some of Lawson's model will repeat points made above. But, as it is a comprehensive model, it is worth presenting it in its entirety.

Lawson's model describes the components of a design problem and how they interact. His model includes three categories: *generators of design problems*; the *domain of constraints*; the *function of design constraints*.[205] The generators of a design problem include the designer, client, user and legislator. The four groups are then organized by the type of constraint they propose – flexible optional (designer/client); and rigid mandatory (user/legislator). Designer/client generated constraints are comparatively flexible, while user/legislator generated constraints tend to be fixed and absolute. Further, Lawson identifies levels of flexibility that constraints possess by categorizing them terms of their domain: internal or external. Internal constraints are those that are normally included in the design brief, such as a program of spaces, intended use, user load, etc. External constraints are those that are outside the designer's control. These might include site conditions, climate, availability of materials, building codes, etc. The significance of these constraints is found in having an awareness of what can (easily) be changed and what cannot. Finally, based on models proposed by Hillier and Leaman (1972), Markus (1969), Rand (1970), Portillo and Dohr (1994) Lawson categorizes constraints by their function: radical, practical, formal, and symbolic. Radical constraints deal with fundamental requirements based on the primary purpose of the object being designed. Practical constraints are those that are related to the fabrication, construction or technical requirements of the design solution. Formal constraints have to do with the organizational and compositional aspects of the design solution. And symbolic constraints have to do with the expressive qualities of the design and aspects that are implemented in order to create a specific quality of experience.

---

205   Lawson, for the clarity of argument, does not make the distinction between design *criteria* and *constraints*, preferring the term constraint. However, he does make reference to Portillo & Dohr (1994) who do make this distinction. For Portillo & Dohr constraints "organize internal relationships of objectives within a design problem and equally establish relationships between the design problems and its larger setting" (p. 408) "usually characterized as restrictive and more closely aligned with specific solution requirements" (p. 409). While "criteria appear to offer a larger context for problem solving and evaluations solutions than do constraints. Criteria consistently reference design functions and evaluative processes based on purpose" (p. 409). Heath (2010), answering the question of where constraints come from, writes that constraints can come from: authority, needs, facts and values. The distinction between "criteria/constraints" is used throughout this research.

§ 5.5   Not all Design Problems are Solvable

Finally, it must be noted, not all design problems are solvable. This can be due to limited resources, because the solution relies on technology that is not yet (or will never be) available, or because of how the problem was defined (structured) in terms of problem space and/or how the problem was framed. Sometimes a key element was over-looked or not considered important to include in the problem space. Or, sometimes the way the problem was framed (interpreted) was not leading anywhere. Or sometimes, how the problem space was defined and how the problem was framed was leading to solution possibilities that were not satisfactory, in terms of demonstrable criteria, experiential qualities or personal preference. Adjusting these variables may lead to a new *way of thinking about the problem* which may lead to, suggest new possible solution paths. Another reason a design problem may not be solvable, is due, simply, to the lack of ability/expertise of the designer.

6 Solution

Every block of stone has a statue inside it and it is the task of the sculptor to discover it.

(Michelangelo)

The solution to a design problem is an artifact, and in the case of architectural design is a building/built environment. The solution is not an idea or a plan or a concept. This does not mean that all design problems that are solved by architect's must be, or even should be buildings/built environments. Often times the best solution to an architectural problem is not a building at all. The point here is that, normatively speaking, the solution to an architectural design problem is a building/built environment.[206]

The Michelangelo quote above speaks to two problems faced by all designers. How does a designer know, out of all the possible solutions one encounters along the *solution path*, that the solution he is pursuing is the right one? And how **can** the designer know that he has arrived at a solution, when the solution is something has never existed before? Recall the working definition of design presented in Chapter Two which claims the proper end of design is a *coherent, and satisficing solution that solves for given and anticipated design criteria and constraints that is technically competent, buildable and induces an intended aesthetic experience.* This description identifies four performance expectations which identify demonstrable criteria and experiential qualities. The quality (level of expertise) of the solution is determined by the extent to which the solution satisfies demonstrable criteria and induces desired experiential qualities. Ultimately this will be determined by assessing the building itself (the proper end of designing).

---

206   This is the basic presupposition of this research. As this research proceeds, the reader can see that the presupposition that a design solution (where the solution is understood as the proper end to the act of designing) is, by definition, an artifact (object, thing), has consequences. The most significant consequence is that, if the product of design is an artifact that possess certain qualities, one needs to have a body to assess those qualities. If the product of the action is a policy, or a plan, a disembodied solution, one can assess how well that product solves for abstract criteria and theoretical constraints. One can even assess the level of coherence of the solution. However, one cannot assess the physical properties of the object, because it doesn't have any. It is disembodied. But, if the product is intended to be embodied, physical solution, then, it is necessary to possess a way of assessing the physical (not only structural, thermal, mechanical, but also experiential) qualities of the product, not when it is completed (by then it might be too late), but while it is still experienced as an evolving idea or approximation in the mind of the designer.

However, and this gets to a central problem of this research, **the designer needs, somehow, to determine that the building he has in mind, has externalized as a functional approximation, with the expectation that it will result in a building/built environment, will both satisfy demonstrable criteria and induce the desired experiential qualities.** The trial-and-error method, while effective, is simply not practical for the design of objects as large and complex (and expensive) as buildings. And the method of incremental improvement, such as multiple releases of software (verson.1.0, 1.2, - 1.7 - 2.0, etc. – my computer is using OSX version 10.12.03 – is not practical, as buildings are typically "one-off." **How can a designer determine the likelihood that the functional approximation** (the proximate end of design)**, he produces will result in a building solution** (proper end of design) **with the intended characteristics?** This is the question that this section will explore.

§ 6.1   Who Determines the Quality of a Solution?

The artist embodies in himself the attitude of the perceiver while he works.

(Dewey, 1934/2005, p. 50)

Dewey's quote above describes the posture of the designer as he is designing, as embodied in the attitude of the perceiver. The designer does this because he is intent of inducing a particular quality of experience in the user. An effective means for achieving this is to enter into the experience of the user, to walk in his shoes. From this perspective one may ask, who determines the quality of the design solution? **Finally it is the user as the perceiver. In the end it is the one who encounters/experiences the building/built environment who determines the quality of the design solution.** As an occupation, the designer's work is assessed by the extrinsic performance expectations established and maintained by the professional associations, historical precedent, and civic expectations. It is the designer, however who defines, who sets the intrinsic expectations for his performance. The designer, embodied in the attitude of the perceiver, is aware that finally he is not designing for himself. The designer is aware that he is not designing for professional, government or civic organizations. The designer knows that he is designing a building/built environment for those who will perceive it and those who will use it, whomever they might be.

Cuff (1992) writes that there are three "principle evaluators of any building's quality, and these are the consumers or public at large, the participants in the design process, and the architectural profession. ...[A]n excellent building is one perceived to be excellent by all three of these groups" (p. 196). These groups participate in generating the criteria and constraints of the design problem that define and frame the problem. Each of these parties have their own interests and agendas. It is the goal of designing to produce a solution that satisfies these within an acceptable range agreed upon by the participants, and which conforms to the performance expectations of the profession.

Recall the working definition of designing described in Chapter Two. It identifies two categories of performance expectations: (1.) Demonstrable criteria and constraints, and (2.) Experiential qualities. Demonstrable criteria have to do with the functional and technical aspects of the building, in terms of plan/section, tectonics, and performance criteria.[207] Experiential qualities have to do with the quality of the design solution in terms of coherence and aesthetic experience. These identify the reasonable expectations that anyone might expect from a competent design solution.

Referring back to Ryles and his description of how an expert pre-structures a problem in Chapter Three, Archer's argument (above) recommending the postulating of informed conjectures as a means of understanding the problem, and Rittel's observation that "from the beginning the designer has an idea of the 'whole' resolution of his problem," a strong case for claiming that **the way one pre-structures the problem has a direct relationship with the anticipated outcome**. By pre-structuring one establishes expectations and biases the possible solution paths. The designer (group or individual) comes with, if not a preconceived solution, at least a sense for how she/he wants to approach the problem (informed conjectures). Pre-structuring a problem can be an effective designing/problem-solving heuristic. The client may have his vision of a building he has be dreaming about for years. The end user, say the tenant, once a pre-agreement has been made about the required area, has already been planning how they are going to use the space. Building officials have their own ideas about the proper way to provide means of egress and other building code requirements. And, then there are the builders, who have their own ideas, friends and family. **The problem is not that designers, owners and users pre-structure the problem; the problem is that they are often not even aware that they are doing it.** And as a result they may unwittingly eliminate or overlook possibilities that may have led to a more acceptable design solution.

---

207   See *Studies in Tectonic Culture*; (1995); *Materials, Form and Architecture* (2003); *Architect's Handbook of Professional Practice* (2005); *Architecture: Form, Space and Order* (2007); *Neufert Architect's Data* (2000); *Architectural; Graphic Standards* (2016) for performance expectations and theory regarding demonstrable criteria.

Imagine that as a group, in a fictional, ideal situation, after some discussion (and a miracle), designers, owners, and users all come to share the *same* interpretation (definition and structure) of the problem. Now that the problem has been clarified and there is some consensus as to what it means, the designer(s) enters the problem-framing/solution-seeking phase, with the understanding that as the design process proceeds and solutions are considered, the problem itself will evolve. Multiple solution paths are identified. Some are taken, some are not. After time a solution begins to emerge and a way of thinking about the problem has solidified. Will the *generator* group be able to come to an agreement, as to whether or not the solution is *satisficing*? This will depend on many variables, both implicit and explicit, including how well the building satisfies the pre-conceived ideas everyone started with. As well as the willingness of the generator group to challenge their presuppositions and biases for the sake of a more acceptable solution. But in order for this to occur the generator group needs to be cognizant that they in fact do pre-structure the problem.

Once the building is built, the designer, client, user and legislator can walk around the building, determine if it functions as planned, if it satisfies legal requirements, if it earns desired energy/ecological sustainability performance expectations, the quality of construction, building environment systems, lighting, etc. As they walk around and walk through the building they are making assessments, about both the demonstrable criteria and constraints, as well as the experiential qualities. Assessing if the demonstrable criteria and constraints have been satisfied is relatively easy. One can easily check the width of a hallway, examine the quality of finishes, check to see if the furniture fits, confirm that the means of egress is unobstructed, etc.

The designer/client/owner/user and legislator can also walk around and through the building, to determine if it induces intended experiential qualities. There is admittedly a certain level of *subjective relativism* involved in assessing the experiential qualities, but as everyone is walking through the same building at the same time, there is a reasonable expectation that they can come to some level of *inter-subjective agreement*.[208] The question is not if one "likes" the quality of atmosphere that the building/built environment induces. This has to do with personal taste. The question is if the building/built environment induces the **intended** quality of experience. Much like if we all take a bite out of the same apple we can come to a consensus about the quality of its crunch, texture, sweetness, tartness. A discussion about the quality of the shared experience is possible. Once the building is built, assessing its demonstrable criteria and experiential quality is more-or-less straight forward. There is an actual building to assess.

---

208   Both the concept of *subjective relativity and inter-subjective agreement* will be discussed in the chapter on aesthetic experience

In this fictional example, the four participants (generator group) have the advantage of being able to assess an actual building. One may argue whether or not there should be a toilet in the lobby (in terms of functional efficiency, building codes or cultural preference), if the color of the entrance is appropriate (in terms of reflective quality of light, symbolic meaning, personal preference), if the materials will resist local weather conditions (in terms of porosity, strength of materials, availability) if the details communicate the desired level of quality (in terms of anticipated building movement, daily use, level of available craftsmanship), if the furniture fits properly in the rooms (in terms of ergonomics, anticipated and unanticipated use). One may even agree/disagree on how coherent the overall design feels (how easy is it to figure out how to get around), and if the quality aesthetic experience is satisfactory (does it look/feel like it was supposed to). Whether one is satisfied with the demonstrable criteria and the experiential qualities is another question. The group can participate in this common assessment because they are faced with a *situation at hand* (experience of an actual building) where there is a reasonable expectation that everyone in the group (more-or-less) shared the same experience. This is what is meant by inter-subjectivity. The problem arises when there is no physical building at hand, but only an emerging idea in the mind of the designer.

Throughout the design process, the designer assesses the quality of the emerging design solution by inhabiting the design world (a mental/internal approximation of the design solution) feelingly. He inhabits the design world *qua* the designer. He inhabits the design world *qua* the client/owner/developer. And he inhabits the design world *qua* the user. And he inhabits the design world *qua* the designer, client/owner/developer and the user. In each instance, he is anticipating how the designer, client/owner/developer and the user will experience the building/built environment by applying his senses to the mental approximation of the building he holds in his mind. In the end the distal assessment of the design *qua* building is by the client/owner/developer and the user. But the proximate assessment of the design solution *qua* internal approximation is (necessarily) by the designer, as up to now there is no way to see what another sees/experiences in his mind's eye.

§ 6.2   Making Representations

Both composers and performers are said to hear with the "inner ear," but that immaterial metaphor is misleading – famously for composers like Arnold Schoenberg, shocked by the actual sounds of what they've written on the page, equally the performer whose study of the scores in necessary but not sufficient preparation for putting bow to string, or lip to reed. The sound itself is the moment of truth.

(Sennett, 2009, p. 159)

While the proper end of architectural design is a building, the proximate end (product), that is what designers normally produce are externalized approximations (representations) of a thing to be built.[209]

These external representations provide the basis for assessing the likelihood that the design will satisfy demonstrable criteria and experiential qualities. Designers envision a possible future and then produce (externalize) a functional representation that results in a building that has never existed before. But, predicting the future is a risky endeavor. There are so many variables to plan for and anticipate. One soon realizes, and perhaps begrudgingly accepts, that just because one can imagine a possible future building, doesn't mean that it is possible to build it.

The world of thought and cognition is a world where one can (if one chooses) overlook inconvenient complexities (like gravity) if they challenge one's big idea.[210]

---

209   This issue of internal/external representations can be, and often is connected to theories of perception and knowing. As a point of clarification this research takes a decidedly *embodied* approach to representation and how it functions in human cognition. It is outside the scope of this research to engage in and in-depth discussion on this complex topic. However, a few comments and references may help the reader. While an embodied approach to representation and perception has psychological roots in Gestalt psychology (Weber, 1995), the *ecological model* of Gibson (1986), as well as philosophical roots in Husserl (1970) and especially Merleau-Ponty (1962), this research relies heavily on theories of embodiment as found in Lakoff and Johnson (1999), Damasio (1994) and Ramachandran (2011). For a phenomenological approach to inner-state/external-state, and cognitive functions of representations see Merleau-Ponty (1962), and for a somewhat more technical treatise see Peirce, *On Representations* (1873); and Pape's (1990) critique of Peire's theory.

210   Pylyshyn (2004), regarding the phenomenal properties of internal images that are products of imagination, writes, "They are our images and we can make them have very nearly any property we wish– and we generally make them have the properties we believe would actually obtain if we were to see the real situation" (p. 2). But, as qualitative properties associated with mental imagery result from linking these attributes through experience, unless one has experienced the properties and characteristics of real materials (tacit knowledge), it is difficult to experience a mental representation *feelingly*, in a manner that induces an experience that correlates with the real world.

As the Gestalt psychologist have demonstrated, the mind has a tendency to fill in the missing parts suggesting the appearance/illusion of a whole. What seemed like a good idea at the time, often enough, disappoints in the end. Like Sennett observes in the above quote, even though a composition may have sounded good to the "inner ear," it is very difficult to anticipate how it is going to sound before it is performed: that is *the moment of truth*. The same is true for building design, or for that matter, any action that involves imagining a possible future. Even though an emerging design solution looked good to the "inner-eye," or felt good to the "inner-body," it is the externalization of the internal representation that is the *moment of truth*. Anyone can come up with a novel idea for a building and a possible future. Coming up with a novel idea or imagining a possible future is the easy and fun part. The real work of designing is looking at the novel idea and possible future, listening to it, feeling it, testing it, developing it, figuring out how it can be built; externalizing the internal representation and communicating it as a functional approximation, with as fine a grain and fidelity as necessary, so that someone else can use it to make it an actual building. This then is the *moment of truth* for the designer, when the building is built and is experienced by the intended user. Depending on his level of skill, and a bit of luck, there should reasonably good correspondence between the designer's "inner-eye" (mental representation) and what we see/experience in the world (the building at hand). How is this possible?

§ 6.3   **Metal Representations**

Mental representations that are produced during the design process as a means of *visualizing* the emerging design solution, though having much in common, are not the same as the internal representations originated from our eyes. That is to say, there are "very significant differences between retinal/cortical images and mental images" (Pylyshyn, Z., 2003, p. 115). They are not representations in the visual sense (though they may be experienced as such).

To appreciate the significance of these differences it is first important to understand that we don't actually *see* with our eyes. Or as Ramachandran (2011) puts it, "vision does not occur in the eye. It occurs in the brain" (p. 41). Pinker (2009) provides an excellent explanation of how visual stimulus from the eyes are filtered, processed, interpreted, assembled in the visual cortex, resulting in the images of the world we perceive. He notes that seeing involves solving problems that are literally unsolvable (not unlike design problems). In an effort to provide reliable, actionable and accurate information and considering limited cognitive processing and memory capacity or "bounded-ness," the visual system needs to deduce – making efficient use of available resources – "an object's shape and substance from its projection, making use of inverse optics." The problem is that, like design problems, the projections that are perceived by the eye are "ill-posed" problems, that is, "a problem that, as stated, has no unique solution" (p. 212). **There are multiple reasonable ways to visually interpret a situation in a manner that makes sense.** The way the visual system makes sense out of these ill-posed problems of perception, is by making some assumptions (heuristics) about the world. For example, similar to the theory the Gestalt psychologists developed over 125 years ago, Pinker writes, "the human visual system 'assumes' that matter is cohesive, surfaces are uniformly colored, and objects don't go out of their way to line up in confusing arrangements" (p. 212). These assumptions are normally learned by experiencing the world. All sense systems work in a more-or-less similar way. Limbeck-Lilienau (2016) writes, "The sensory receptor [be it eyes, nose, ears, skin, etc.] 'transduces' the stimulus into an electrical impulse of the nerves. Different stages of cognitive processing in the sensory areas of the brain lead finally to a perceptual state, which is generally described as a conscious perceptual experience" (p. 1). What we perceive as the real world, with all its attributes, qualities, and meaning, is a cognitive construction. Visual images, colors, smells, taste, are all experiential qualities that are the product of cognition.[211] Cognition is how we know the world.

Mental representations have similar characteristics as visual representations, except that they do not originate as electrical impulses caused by sense percepts being transduced to initiate cognitive processing. Mental representations are constructs of the mind/imagination. Limbeck-Lilenau (2016) explain that a distinction can be made regarding perception between the "phenomenal experience and the larger perceptual processing in our sensory systems which describe how that experience is caused and how it is used in further cognitive processing." Most perceptual processing is not conscious, we are aware of only certain aspects of it, these are what are referred to as (conscious) *phenomenal experiences*. "Phenomenal experience is defined by the qualitative character of our conscious state" (p. 2). A phenomenal experience (state) is best described by *qualia*, or "what it feels like to..."

---

211   Backhaus & Menzel (1992) write, "[W]e know from psychophysical and neurophysiological investigations that color is created somewhere in the brain, although the exact location of this process is still unknown, and we even have no idea what entities the sensations called color are . . . In short, colors appear only at a first naive glance to be located in objects" (p. 28).

A distinction is made between the phenomenal content of the perception and the representational content of perception. While it is possible to separate the phenomenal content of the perception from the representational, for example one can see a red light and recognize it as such without feeling an impulse to stop, or feel anxiety as one speeds through it. Another distinction is that perceptual states can be distinguished from perceptual judgments and beliefs (p. 5). This distinction is somewhat related to Gombrich's concept (1960/2000, p. 14) of the *innocent eye*. Or, in moral philosophy it is similar to the pre-ontic, that is the experience of a phenomenon that has no intention (good or otherwise) associated with it.[212]

There is a debate regarding the quality of mental representations that is relevant to this research: do mental representations possess the same phenomenal qualities as sensory representations? There are two side to the debate. Kosslyn et al. claim, that mental representations function as depictions of an idea, like the cathode ray tube used in television sets back in the 70's that produce "images [that] are temporary spatial displays in active memory" resulting in a *quasi-pictoral* (analog) representation (p. 536). Pylyshyn (2004) critiques this idea arguing that it confuses images of the imagination with representations of ideas. He writes, "imagery and vision are dissociable, that images are not visually reinterpreted, and that the pattern of cortical activity does not spatially (homeomorphically) map properties such as the size of imagined objects" (p. 111). Pylyshyn explains that people when asked to imagine something "ask themselves what it would be like to see it, and the then simulate as many aspects of this staged event as they can as seem relevant"(p. 113). He refers to this as the "null hypothesis," or an "appeal to format," because it only appeals to "the tacit knowledge that people have about how things tend to happen in the world, together with certain psychological skills" (p. 113). Pylyshyn, argues that the defense for the theory of images being projected in the visual cortex is based on misunderstanding recent discoveries in neuroscience. He sites two findings: (1.) When a visual pattern is presented to the eye, a homeomorphic (continuously deformed) mapping of retinal activity occurs in the visual cortex. (2) Although it remains controversial, it has also been reported that there is increased activity in retinotopically-organized areas of visual cortex during mental imagery.[213]

---

212   For example the difference between killing and murder. Killing is simply the termination of a life. While murder is the termination of a life with intent to kill.

213   See, Tootell, (1982); Roland (1995); Roland & Gulyas (1994).

From these findings it appears that "cortical images occur in both vision and imagery, the difference being that the former is caused by light on the retina while the latter is caused by top-down projections from higher cognitive systems" (p. 115). But Pylyshyn goes on to argue that these findings do not prove anything about the form of the representation. His point is that **"imagery and vision might involve the very same form of representation without being pictoral in either case"** (p. 115).

There are two ramifications of this way of thinking about mental representations that are critical to this research. (1.) The argument is that the electrical impulses that stimulate the images generated in the visual cortex, can either come from retinal activity or from within the mind itself (imagination). These images that are generated in the visual cortex have similar characteristics, whether they are stimulated by visual percepts or percepts of the imagination. (2.) The images generated in the visual cortex that are stimulated by retinal activity are perceived as possessing associated phenomenal qualities: color, weight, distance, texture (what Böhme (1993) calls *atmosphere)*, "where perception is understood as the experience of the presence of persons, objects and environments" (p. 116).

This means that the **images generated by the imagination can also be experienced as possessing associated qualities and atmosphere**.[214] That is, it is possible to imagine a thing and experience its qualia in a similar way as one experiences a thing in the real world.

---

214   In his doctoral thesis, Ostman (2013) presents a case for the phenomenal qualities of mental images and how they are related to *qualia* and *phenomenal* character supported by recent research in brain theory. His argument is that phenomenal qualities are instantiated by the brain. To defend this position he points to hallucinations, arguing that the phenomenal qualities experienced when a person is experiencing a hallucination (as real as it feels) are instantiated by internal cognitive functions. He uses this evidence to argue for the verifiability of veridical perception, that is the direct perception of stimuli as they exist. He calls this his *instantiation thesis* (p. 4).

§ 6.4 Representations in Architectural Design

Representations in architectural design are of two kinds: inner-state representations (cognitive approximations generated by imagination), or outer-state representations (externalizations of the cognitive approximation). Most working design representations occur somewhere between the two states. Representations also serve two primary purposes: as a way of thinking about something, and as a means to communicate an emerging design solution to another agent. Like states, the purpose (intended use) of the representation is also fluid.[215]

As discussed above in the section on problem solving, Newel and Simon (1958) wrote that: to think about something, that something must have an internal representation of some kind... As the problem-solver traverses the solution maze, a significant amount of data is collected that when seen together produces "patterns of elementary symbols" or a "state description." This pattern of elementary symbols or state description is what is meant by a *representation*. The thinking organism, in order to deal with complex problems... must have some processes that are capable of manipulating the representation... which is generated from data (proposition-like mental entities) not only of itself (body schema and body image), but also of its (given) physical environment (situation). The representation is evaluated insofar as the patterns within the representation "mirror or fail to mirror the patterns without that they represent.[216]

Throughout the design process, there are typically multiple instances, at various states, where the designer/client/user/legislator, need to assess/re-assess the likelihood that the building being designed will satisfy the criteria and induce the experiential quality as intended *before* it is built.

---

[215] There is also some confusion in the literature regarding the terms *representation*, *image*, and *approximation*. None of these terms should be thought of as pictures or projections in the mind. These are not *visual* phenomenon. For clarity's sake, assume an image is a kind of representation and a representation is a kind of approximation, and an approximation is an attempt to make sense of or delimit a situation. Limbeck-Lilenau (2016, p. 12) describes three different uses of the term *representation*: (1) a mental representation is a mental state which indicates or informs about properties of the external distal stimulus. (2) Representation as an *inner mental model* or picture, (3) representation as *information storage* in the mind or more specifically in memory. The first description is closest to how representation is being used in this research. The *inner mental model*, *picture*, and *image*, can be problematic, as they suggest that there is a little guy inside the mind who is looking at the internal representation (similar to Kosslyn above); and as such he looks at the representation in a similar way that we look at the chair or the painting over the couch in the living room. Internal representations are obviously not physical things, but rather the result of neuro-chemical, physiological cognitive processes.

[216] For the purpose of simplicity, and brevity I composed this paragraph using quotes from several sources in the study. All sentences and fragments are referenced elsewhere.

Assessing a representation of a building is far more complicated than assessing an actual building. The representational data transfer can be achieved by any medium, be it spoken or written language, diagrams, renderings, plans, models, digital representations.[217] The designer is expected to make representations that effectively transfer (so that others can understand) data that describes the current *state* of the evolving design solution, for the purpose of getting input (such as approvals) from others (the owner for example). The purpose of this type of representation is primarily to communicate/externalize so that another agent can understand the idea, and imagine the experience with some degree of inter-subjectivity. For many this is the primary reason for making drawings, models, renderings, and digital representations. There is however another way that both internal and external representations of the emerging design solution, in its many states, functions; that is to inform, provide feedback for the designer, and to motivate the design process as one **seeks** a particular quality of aesthetic experience within the design world. These externalized representations take on a much more personal, sometime expressive, spontaneous character. These externalizations provide the basis for the conversation with the design situation that is the designing/problem-solving/creative process.

---

217 Typically, except for the making of scale models and on-site assembly "mock-ups," most externalized representations in architecture are visual, and in two dimensions. This applies just as well to so-called 3-d computer models. The 3-d models, insofar as the a visualized on a flat computer screen, are not actually 3-d, but only 2-d images that trick the mind into considering it as a 3-d model. This is true of video as well. This poses a cognitive challenge for both the designer who is seeking a solution and the owner/user who needs to evaluate the design proposal prior to it being built. This difficulty is discussed in detail by Mitrovic (2013), *Visuality for Architects*. Mitrovic argues that considering the significant advances made in the cognitive sciences, the "lack of awareness of these changes is a remarkable aspect of contemporary thinking about architecture" especially the continued insistence on "the primacy of language in human thinking" (p. 3). Through an excellent review of contemporary theories of perception and human cognition, as well as concrete observations from his experience teaching design, he provides an articulate and convincing critique of the underlying theory beneath how architectural design is taught. He writes, "The expectation that one must justify architectural designs by referring to something outside architecture, that formal and visual qualities are of secondary importance in architecture, has not just accidentally happened to dominate contemporary thinking about architecture. It has its own history and originates in a number of philosophical and psychological positions that became influential in the 1960's. While these positions have in the meantime ceased to be credible in philosophy and psychology, they have remained enshrined as dogmas in the writing of architects, architectural historians, and historians... moat of contemporary architectural thinking is based on assumptions that have lost their credibility in the disciples from which they were originally imported into architectural theory" (p. xiii).

For a designer, the *representation* takes the form of (*visualized as*) the thing being designed. It is an internal means of visualizing, that makes use of the same neurocircuitry and regions of the brain that are used when seeing/experiencing the outside world (Ramachandran, 2011). As an inner-representation evolves in complexity it is experienced by the designer as what Schön (1992) calls a *design world*. To use Polanyi's (1974) idea, the designer inhabits this design world *feelingly*.[218] That is, using the same sense systems he uses to navigate a busy street, and that induces a sense of awe at the magnificence of the Grand Canyon, to assess the experiential quality of the emerging design solution, except in this case the origin of the image is not cortical, but imaginary. In this design world the designer can *view* the emerging design solution, walk around it, and test it. While most people possess the basic ability to apply the senses to an internal representation, like other "natural" abilities, this ability also requires training to develop.[219] Through a related ability called *Einfühlung* (translated as *empathy*)[220] and *mirror-neurons*[221] the designer can imbue the emerging design solution with experiential qualities. This ability to enter into the design world feelingly is made possible because of the embodied nature of human cognition.

---

218   Pallasmaa (2009) writes, "While drawing, a mature designer and architect is not focused on the lines of the drawing, as he is envisioning the object itself, and in his mind holding the object in his hand or occupying the space being designed. During the design process, the architect occupies the very structure that the lines of the drawing represent" (p. 59).

219   This ability to visual, manipulate, rotate and inhabit internal mental representations is a fundamental skill for acquiring architectural design expertise. While, it is an ability that most people have to some degree, expert designer's skills are more advanced than most. An often referenced experiment by Shepard and Metzler (1988) factors that influence estimated rates of mental rotation, including previous exposure, the existence of a physical model, memory, eye-movement, 2-d vs. 3-d dimensionality, and a comparative study of previous research. Another noted experiment is in Hollard & Delius (1982) where a comparative study between pigeons and humans test the cognitive ability to manipulate, rotate and recognize images.

220   The concept of *Einfühlung* a "process by which we endow the object of our vision – whether human or non-human – with life, or with a soul" (Bridge, 2010, p. 3), emerged as a key concept among early 20th century German aesthetic philosophers, including F. and R. Vischer, Lipps, Wölfflin, Worringer. Introduced into the English language by Titchener as "empathy" term *Einfühlung* described the projection of a sense of the inward feeling of our bodily state onto inanimate objects. See Pionotti (2010) for a general overview; Bridge (2011) for a description of Wölfflin; and (Jahoda, 2005) for a description of Lipps.

221   *Mirror-neurons* were discovered by Rizzolatti in the ventral pre-motor area of monkeys, in the early 1990's at the University of Parma (Rizzolatti & Craighero, 2004). Mirror-neurons, found in both primates and humans, fire when one acts and when one observes another performing the same action. Anytime one observes another doing something, the corresponding mirror neuron might fire in the observers mind allowing him/her to empathize with the other's feelings by mirroring his actions and thereby constructing an implicit model through which the other can anticipate the other's intentions (Ramachandran, 2011).

The capacity of human (embodied) cognition has its limits (recall Simon's concept of *bounded rationality*), in terms of processing capacity as well as short term (working) memory. There is a limited amount of data (according to Miller [1956] the limit is +/- seven bits), that the mind can actively work with simultaneously. The mind does, however, have some tricks that allow cognitive processes to deal with increasingly complex ideas in working memory. These include: *clumping*, *schema*, and *scaffolding*. An immense amount of processing capacity and data (*cognitive load*) [222] is required to maintain, assess, rotate and inhabit an internal representation in working memory of something as complex as a building design. The cognitive load involved in processing a complex internal representation often exceeds the mind's processing capacity, even after applying all the tricks and load-reducing heuristics available to it. However, the mind has one more trick: *extended cognition*. Extended cognition is the ability humans possess to make use of the external world as a means for increasing cognitive capacity.

As discussed above, human cognition is not limited to what goes on in the brain or as Clark and Chalmers (1998) refer to it, the "skin/skull boundary." Cognition engages the whole body, both as a way to interact with the world, as well as a way to extend cognitive capacities.[223] Some simple examples of how this happens are: writing something down so as not to forget it; counting fingers (and toes) as a way to simplify a math problem; making and use of tools is another example.[224] Above, Polanyi explained extended cognition by describing how a blind man explores the world, not with his hand, but with the tip of his cane. The cane becomes an extension of his body. Clark and Chalmers (1998) describe *these extended* cognitive abilities as

---

the basic package of cognitive resources I bring to bear on the everyday world... The biological brain has in fact evolved and matured in ways which factor in the reliable presence of a manipulatable external environment... that has favored on-board capacities which are especially geared to parasitizing the local environment so as to reduce [cognitive] load. (p. 645)

---

222   For a description of *clumping*, *schema*, and *scaffolding* and See Paas, Renkl & Sweller (2004).

223   Damasio & Damasio (2006) write, "...the body and the brain are engaged in a continuous interaction that unfolds in time, within different regions of the body and within mental spaces as well. Metal states cause brain states; body states are then mapped to the brain and incorporated into the ongoing mental states" (p. 19).

224   Wilson (1999) provides an excellent description of the inter-dependency between the evolution of the mind and the hand.

The function that allows the mind to extend itself into the external environment is called *coupling*. This is what allows the blind man to know the world through the tip of his cane. Polanyi (1974) call it "focal awareness."[225] It is a way we have of knowing and increasing cognitive capacity by extending ourselves into the world.

Designers have a favorite way of extending the capabilities of their cognitive ability into the world – that is through *sketching*. When the designer sketches, he is thinking with pencil and paper, not unlike an accountant trying making sense of complex financial transaction by working with spreadsheets. It is impossible to keep track of all the figures and interaction is his mind. When the designer sketches he is externalizing thought, exploring opportunities, testing possibilities.

Sketching assists in examining the internal emerging representation, and to provide feedback. Goldschmidt (2003) refers to the feedback gained from self-generated sketches as *backtalk*.[226] Goldschmidt writes that sketching facilitates some basic functions involved in solving novel problems and creative problem-solving, such as *restructuring of the problem* and *productive thinking*, and "that it is the sketch's backtalk, and the plausible interpretations of it, that make this possible" (p. 84). The purpose of the sketch, is not only as a means to test an idea by externalizing the representation and seeing how well it approximates (correlates with) the internal representation,[227] but also as a means for discovering new ways of thinking about the problem. Goldschmidt continues, "The self-generated sketch talks back, and its backtalk reflects some of the sketcher's innermost, tacit, otherwise untapped knowledge, biases, and preferences" (p. 87). Arnheim (1993) writes, "By making a sketch, the designer supplies the mental image with the assistance of an optical image, which has all the properties of such visual percepts" (p. 17).

---

225   Polanyi (1974) writes, "When we use a hammer to drive in a nail, we attend to both nail and hammer, but in a different way. We watch the effect of our strokes on the nail and try to wield the hammer so as to hit the nail most effectively. When we bring down the hammer we do not feel that its handle has struck our palm but that its head has struck the nail. Yet in a sense we are certainly alert to the feelings in our palm and the fingers that hold the hammer. They guide us in handling it effectively, and the degree of attention that we give to the nail is given to the same extent but in a different way to those feelings. The difference may be stated by saying that the latter are not, like the nail, objects of our attention, but instruments of it. They are not watched in themselves; we watch something else while keeping intensely aware of them. I have a subsidiary awareness of the feeling in the palm of my hand which is merged into a focal awareness of my driving the nail" (p. 55).

226   See also Arnheim (1993) written in response to Goldschmidt (1991).

227   The mind, often "fills in the blanks" as a means to reduce cognitive load, and increase speed, causing us to sometimes discover that what worked in the fuzzy logic of the mind does not work when put on paper.

Sketching forces the designer to apply the constraints of the visual (external) world, to the approximate representations of the (inner) mind. It is a dialogical process, or as Goldschmidt (1991) calls it a *dialectic*, that allows the designer to *enter into a conversation*, explore, test and discover ways of *seeing* the emerging solution.

§ 6.6 Criteria and Constraints

The two great rules for design are these: 1st, that there should be no features about a building which are not necessary for convenience, construction, or propriety; 2nd, that all ornament should consist of enrichment of the essential construction of the building. The neglect of these two rules is the cause of all the bad architecture of the present time.
(Pugin, 2006, p. 385)

The normative expectation that a design solution should solve for demonstrable design criteria and constraints is self-evident and does not need much explanation. This is the most basic expectation/requirement of a design solution, sometimes encapsulated by an erroneous reference to the dictum, "form follows function." A building design is expected to serve its intended purpose (function) in a sufficient and satisfactory manner. For those with a functional bias, this is the primary expected outcome of the design process. This bias has its roots in theories associated with modernism (Banham, 1980), and some of the same theories that influenced the first generation of design research and methodology (Broadbent, 1973). The emphasis on "functionalism," the devaluation of decoration, the fascination with advanced technology, radical changes in building technology, the commodification of housing, the financial structure of real estate development, etc.,[228] all led to a radical shift in the expectations for what a building should do, and how the (architecture) profession functions within the building development process.

The desire for/belief in the possibility of *objective* criteria for the assessment/judgment of a design solution has also given weight to this normative expectation.

---

[228] See Perez-Gomez (1992, 2016) for an insightful assessment theory and an overview of how social/cultural/civic expectations of architecture and architects has evolved and changed since and after the "crisis of modern science."

As discussed above, early problem solving theory models, such as that proposed by Simon, requires that a (design) problem be well-behaved: a clearly defined problem that can be solved with an observable, repeatable process, that leads to an optimized/ sufficient/satisfactory solution. And if it was not "well-behaved," the design problem/ process could be broken down into its constituent parts so that it "operates within a closed abstract system, that is controlled and manipulated by a professional problem-solver and free from human judgment and experience" (Huppatz, 2015).

There is no doubt that a design solution must solve for (and anticipate) design criteria and constraints. There is no question that a building design should result in a building/built environment that serves the "function" for which it is intended in an efficient and effective manner. However, this is not the only normative performance expectation, nor is it the most important, rather it is one of several **incommensurable** performance expectations.

§ 6.7 Technical Competency

In addition to the tool and the hand that guides it, there is the material to be treated, the formless mass to be transposed into form. Every work of art should reflect in its appearance the material as physical matter... In this way, we may speak of a wood style, a brick style, and ashlar style, and so forth.

(Semper, 1989, p. 269)

The expectation that the design solution must be able to be built seems to be a self-evident. A built building/built environment is the proper end of architectural design. If a building design (approximation) cannot be built (implemented), it fails. This is the meaning of the term *functional approximation*; that the design documents provide a representation of a building such that it can be built. The above quote from Semper calls to mind that buildings are made by hands and tools in the hands of craftsman, who form the materials, that result in the building. Buildings are made of the stuff of the earth. And the stuff of the earth has physical properties that must be taken account of.

It has been observed[229] (and is confirmed by my experience) that it is less and less the normative expectation that a designer actually knows how a building is made, is familiar with materials, or that the (normative) outcome of the design process should be a *functional approximation*, that is that a design solution should be able to be built.[230] More and more, it seems that design students (and professionals) only need to provide a *representative* approximation of how the building should (could) look. Figuring out how and if it can be built is someone else's problem. Designers are only expected to generate an approximate representation of a novel form (not unlike a stylist), others are expected to find a way to fabricate/build it. The problem with not thinking about buildings in terms of their materials and how to build them is well said by Pallasmaa (2009), who writes "Fully computer-generated designs may well project a seductive surface appeal, but in fact they take place in a world in which the observer has no skin, hands or body" (p. 99).

One possible explanation (referring back to the section on making representations), for this disconnect between the design solution as plan/form/section, and the material/structural aspects of the design solution may be attributed to a general lack of direct experience (and internalized knowledge) of the characteristics and properties of materials. So that when novice designers are generating internal/external representations they are unable to couple the phenomenal qualities of the materials with the representational images that induces the experience of inhabiting the design world feelingly.

Another explanation is that architectural designers no longer consider the building as the proper end to design, but rather consider the representation of an idea for a building to be the proper end of design.

---

229   See Mallgrave, who writes, "When one devotes an inordinate amount of one's attention to compositional or novel form, for example, one tends to ignore materiality and detailing" (Mallgrave H. F., loc. 261-262).

230   See Mitrovic (2013), Zumthor (2006),Pallasmaa (2005), Frampton (1995), Pye, (1978) for the importance of thinking about a building in terms of built object that possesses material, environmental and structural properties. This trend of focusing on the conceptual aspects of architectural design does seem however to be shifting, as can be witnessed by the renewed interest in design-building projects and the proliferation of fab-labs in architecture schools around the world. See Carpenter (1997), ACSA Design Build Award honors program (www.acsa-arch.org); as well as TU Delft Bucky Lab (http://buckylab.blogspot.nl). Spiller & Clear (2014) collected 40 essays from educators and practitioners around the world that together offers a good, current overview of the state of architectural design education.

§ 6.8 Coherence

Pattern pleases us, rewards a mind seduced and yet exhausted by complexity. We crave pattern, and find it all around us, in pedals, sand dunes, pine cones, contrails. Our buildings, our symphonies, our clothing, our societies – all declare patterns. Even our actions: habits, rules, codes of honor, sports, traditions – we have many names for patterns of conduct. They reassure us that life is orderly.

(Ackerman, 2004)

There is a normative expectation that a design solution both possess and communicate a sense of coherence. However, what is meant by a sense of coherence as a performance expectation is not as *self-evident* as the previous two. To begin with, coherence here is being used as a quality of an experience. That is, it is a feeling that is induced in the beholder by the object. It is a *mental construction*.

Just as one can think of designing buildings as problem-solving/satisfying demonstrable criteria and constraints, and technical requirements; it is also possible to think of the *design* of a building, as the imposition of order, composition, intentional arrangement on the materials of the earth. The painting by William Blake (1757-1827) of God as the architect wielding a compass circumscribing the surface of the earth, inspired by Milton's *Paradise Lost* (Milton, 1667/2016) comes to mind:

Then stay'd the fervid wheels and in his hand
He took the golden compasses, prepared
In God's eternal store, to circumscribe
This Universe, and all created things.
One foot he centred, and the other turned
Round through the vast profundity obscure,
And said, "Thus far extend, thus far thy bounds;
This be thy just circumference, O World!"
Thus God the Heaven created, thus the Earth,
Matter unform'd and void.

In circumscribing the "vast profundity obscure" (chaos) God is said to have imposed order (cosmos) on the stuff of the earth, the place we inhabit, and from which we all evolved, with all its complexity and vast inter-connected ecosystems. An open, self-correcting, opportunistic, adaptive world comes into being. This is designing.

From the Judeo-Christian tradition being a designer involves participating in creation as co-creator, actively participating in this process of bringing something that never existed into being. To have the power to impose order, and the ability to perceive order.[231] Coherence is a quality that is perceived through order-making and sense-making. It is a *quality* of perception (not unlike aesthetic quality). The perception of coherence suggests deliberate actions and the involvement of a rational being.

The question of coherence, sense-making, [232] meaning, the perception of patterns and order in designing can be approached from theology, philosophy, psychology, cognitive science, and/or evolutionary biology. The approach in this section with be primarily from cognitive neuroscience science and evolutionary biology. The aspect of coherence that is most relevant to this study has to do with the quality of the experience induced by the design solution in the beholder and the quality of experience induced the designer as he immerses (looses) himself in the design process,[233] where seeking coherence is a function of the design process.

All design solutions, even if they fail to satisfy demonstrable criteria and constraints must minimally appear to be coherent, make sense, have some kind of perceivable order or organizational system. As Ackerman points out in the above quote, "we crave patterns." The perception of patterns suggests predictable order, predictable order allows us to anticipate impending doom, surviving impending doom allows us to anticipate the future, being able to anticipate the future gives us a feeling of coherence. A feeling of coherence is reassuring, puts us at ease, allowing us to consider more than the immediate concerns of basic survival and reproduction.

---

231   Not unlike the Gestalt concept of *pragnänz*: "pregnant with meaning" A basic principle in Gestalt Psychology: the brain imposes a "psychological organization" on the phenomena of experience (not entirely dissimilar to Kant's "forms of sensibility"), one that "will always be as 'good' as the prevailing conditions will allow" (Kurt Koffka, *Principles of Gestalt Psychology*, 1935).

232   Klein, Moon & Hoffman (2006) describing sense-making write "By sense-making, modern researchers seem to mean something different from creativity, comprehension, curiosity, mental modeling, explanation, or situational awareness, although all these factors or phenomena can be involved in or related to sense-making. Sense-making is a motivated, continuous effort to understand connections (which can be among people, places, and events) in order to anticipate their trajectories and act effectively" (p. 71).

233   The experience of loosing oneself in a creative act is called *Flow*. A term coined by Csikszentmihalyi (1996), Flow is described as an *optimal experience* that involves a kind of loss of self and focused immersion into the creative act. It is an *autotelic* experience where a kind of exhilaration comes from the pursuit of beauty. It is a fragile experience, easily interrupted by distractions. It's a state of being that requires great discipline to achieve (pp. 110-111).

Humans need to make sense of their environment. On a primitive level, making sense of one's environment is involuntary (though focused attention may reveal additional information missed by non-conscious cognitive operations). Just as one does not choose to feel cold, choose to feel hungry, choose to know which way is up and which side is back (if not there is a feeling of disorientation and confusion), assessing a situation and making-sense of it is an ability that has its roots in evolutionary biology that allows us to effectively interact with the environment. It is an involuntary, physiological impulse. Dervin (1997) writes, the term sense-making "is a label for a coherent set of concepts and methods used ... to study how people construct sense of their worlds and, in particular, how they construct information needs and uses for information in the process of sense-making" (p. 2). In an article entitled "Human Perception: Making Sense of the World", Lipari writes:

During the second half of the twentieth century, neuroscientists and cognitive scientists began to identify the actual physical processes that transform sensations into perceptions. According to this new scientific paradigm, everything we perceive, including "external reality," "is a construction of the brain. Our senses are confronted by a chaotic, constantly changing world that has no labels, and the brain must make sense of that chaos. It is the brain's correlations of sensory information that create the knowledge we have about our surroundings... (2015, ¶4)

Coherence, order, meaning do not exist in the world, these are constructions of human cognition. Lipari's *correlations of sensory information that create knowledge*, is what Godfrey-Smith (2001) calls *cognition*, what he defines as "a collection of capabilities which, in combination, allow organisms to achieve certain kinds of coordination between their actions and the world... a biological tool-kit used to direct behavior" (p. 5). In describing *Environmental Complexity Thesis* (ECT), Godfrey-Smith (2001) poses as a first principle that, the functional capacity of human cognitive abilities evolved to enable the agent to deal with environmental complexity (heterogeneity). That is to say, the only reason we have cognitive abilities at all is to allow us to function in-the-world. It is a claim similar to those made above by promoters of embodied cognition, such as Lakoff & Johnson (1999), Searle (1994), Damasio (1994).

Perceptual mechanisms "all respond, with some degree of sensitivity or discrimination, to some physical or chemical variables that impinge causally on the organism, in such a way as to enable the organism to make sense of the information about the world that is carried by these variables" (Godfrey-Smith, 2001, p. 4). The world is complex. Environmental complexity both poses problems and opportunities – for example reproductive advantage, as well as adapting to and adapting the agent's environment for survival advantages.

These cognitive abilities do not evolve independent of other bodily functions and environmental factors, but rather, like systems theory described above, they evolve as inter-dependent systems and sub-systems, adapting to and adapting the world in which they inhabit to maximize the likelihood of survival.[234]

The ability to make use of multiple sense-systems together, is what allows us to create a conception of the world as a dynamic whole that makes sense.[235] This is no small ability. Ogilvie (1999) writes that "in spite of the multiplicity of sensory inputs" and the lack of a 'master' area where all signals converge: we usually perceive the world as a unified whole" (p. 171). To support this claim they describe an experiment (Rodriguez, 1999) that suggests that the perception of the world as a unified whole is due to the "transient synchronization of neural discharges act[ing] as an integrative mechanism to bind widely distributed neurons into a coherent ensemble underlying a given percept or cognitive task" (Ogilvie, p. 171). Gamma band synchronization is found to be consistently present in "the visual cortex and the region of the somatosensory cortex in subjects who had learned an association between a visual stimulus and a tactile stimulus" (p. 171). The theory that coherence has to do with the synchronization of brain waves is not a new idea, but experiments like these are offering empirical evidence that this may in fact be how it works. Like all systems, this sense-making/coherence-seeking system involves a complex, multi-modal dialectic, between the agent's *metal map* (Tolman, 1948), the world as it is (as perceived by the senses), the world as it is expected to be (based on beliefs), and the world as the agent wants it to be (projection).

Thagard (2002) calls this seeking coherence: when we attempt to make sense of a situation, text, picture, built environment, we "construct an interpretation that fits with the available information, better than alternative interpretations" (p. 16). That *construct* is a kind of *knowledge* about the world that produces **maximal satisfaction of multiple constraints**. The presupposition of Thagard's theory, supported by research in evolutionary biology and neuroscience, is that there exists in all humans a basic need to make sense of the world. Coherence can be understood as a kind of *fit*: a fit between the experience at hand, and a perceivable system of relations and inter-relations that induces a sense of well-being or pleasure (satisfaction). He writes, "various perceptual processes such as stereoscopic vision and interpreting ambiguous figures are naturally interpreted in terms of coherence and constraints... computing coherence is a matter of constraint satisfaction" (p. 40).

---

234   Wilson (1999) provides an excellent example of the inter-dependent evolution between the unique structure of the hand and its intimate communication with the brain through the impact this has had on areas such as neurology, psychology and human creativity.

235   Recall Bertalanffy (1968, p.37) from above holds that all systems are oriented toward wholeness.

Knowing, Thagard (2002) writes "involves at least five different kinds of coherence – explanatory, analogical, deductive, perceptual, and conceptual" (p. 41). Perceptual knowledge includes visual, auditory, olfactory, and tactile representations of what we see, hear, smell, and feel. The world is not experienced directly through these sense experiences, but through *inference* and *constraint satisfaction*. As discussed elsewhere, perception of the world is not assembled one sense at a time, but via the parallel processing of multiple sense systems that our cognitive systems use to make sense of the world. Thagard explains, relying heavily on Gestalt theory, that the brain constructs a coherent, nonverbal representation of the world via interpretations which follow certain principles: symmetry, interpretation, sensory priority, incompatibility, and acceptance. *Symmetry*, does not mean the mirror image of a thing divided in half along at least one axis. Instead what is meant by symmetry as it relates to perception is balance: all the parts appear to fit well together as a composition.[236] *Interpretation* has to do with how well sensory input fits are governed by "innate perceptual principles." Thagard refers to Gestalt principles of *proximity* and *similarity* as examples of such an innate principle. *Sensory priority* and *incompatibility* have to do with the cognitive processes that filter information (sense data) in an effort to make sense of the situation. Some sense information jumps to the foreground as deemed essential to sense-making, while other information is passed over, as it does not *seem* relevant to the perception of a whole.[237] Finally, *acceptance* has to do with the acceptability of an interpretation "depending on its coherence with sensory inputs, other... interpretations, and background knowledge" (p. 58). **It is this state of acceptance that is both sought by the designer as a function and motivating factor of the design process; and the state that the designer anticipates that the building/ built environment will induce in the user.** Sense-making and seeking coherence mostly concern *inference* making. And the only rule of inference is that we "accept a conclusion if it maximizes coherence" (p. 66). Fundamentally coherence is the cognitive need that humans display for "constraint-satisfaction." Or satisfying, "mentally balancing many complementary and conflicting pieces of information until they all fit in a satisfying way" (Thagard, p. 3).

Given this description of seeking coherence in terms of *inference making*, one could easily replace *sense-making and seeking coherence* with designing, where *inference* and *constraint satisfaction* are understood to be biases or heuristics.

---

236   Vitruvius (1998, p. 27) defines symmetry as "the appropriate harmony arising out of the details of the work itself; the correspondence of each given detail among the separate details in the form of the design as a whole. As in the human body, from cubit, foot, palm, inch and other small parts comes the symmetric quality of eurhythmy" (Book 1, c. II. 4).

237   This functions in a similar fashion as the two of the three factors observed by Newell (1980) that make Polya's heuristic better suited for a human problem-solver.

It is this *cognitive need* that drives (motivates) us to seek order, or impose it when necessary, as a way of *balancing complementary and conflicting pieces of information until they all fit in a satisfying way*, such that when a way is found that *maximizes coherence* we accept it as a *conclusion*. Coherence is the quality of feeling experienced when order is perceived and the situation makes sense.

Designing is a process of *constraint satisfaction*; where the constraints are understood to be demonstrable criteria and constraints of the design problem; and where a solution is achieved when *they all fit in a satisfying way*.[238] The expectation that a design solution should (1.) function as intended, (2.) be technically feasible and (3.) *make sense*, describes the qualities that most design methodologies identify as essential. Indeed both Alexander (1964) and Papanek (1984) above both describe designing in terms of imposing order. The only performance expectation that is missing is inducing an intended quality of aesthetic experience.

As I reflect on the work of students, participating on design juries, and discussions with colleagues, it does seem that after a design solution is shown to solve the problem in a somewhat novel way, it appears to function well, and it seems reasonable to assume that it could be built; the only experiential quality of the design that is explicitly discussed is whether the solution seems coherent or not, does it make sense, is there order, proper hierarchy of form, scale, meaning. The quality of the experience induced by the design solution as building/built environment is rarely discussed. And when it is, the discussion is typically ended with an assent to subjective relativism: *de gustibus non est disputandum*.[239]

---

238   Thagard (1998) describes the seeking of coherence as *constraint satisfaction* (sense seeking function/making sense of) that operates over the set representational elements which can be made to fit together (cohere/feeling of satisfaction) or resist fitting together (incohere/feeling of dis-satisfaction). Recently Thagard has further developed this idea proposing a theory of *emotional cognition*, a theory that describes the how emotions function both in the cognitive process and as a means for seeking *emotional coherence*. There is a psychological reward for seeking coherence, a sense of satisfaction or well-being. That emotions (feelings) play a significant role in cognition is not a new idea in psychology. Gottfried (2011, p. 62) writes, "In psychology, a reward is defined operationally as anything that increases the behavior that leads to obtaining it. When reward acts in this way, psychologists call it a positive reinforce because it reinforces or strengthens the underlying associations in the brain that are said to 'control' the reward-seeking behavior. The concept of reward can be divided into primary and secondary rewards, with primary rewards being those that directly meet biological needs (e.g., food, water, salt, sex) and secondary rewards [also known as condition reinforces] being stimuli that have acquired rewarding properties through their association with primary rewards."

239   "There is no accounting for taste."

Even when working on professional projects, the question of experiential quality is normally relegated to being a question of style, personal preference, taste. It is considered to be one of many design criteria; alongside environmental sustainability, code compliance, life-cycle costs, parking capacity. Experiential quality is negotiated, and is often the subject of so called *value-engineering*. It is as if the building functions well, is technically feasible, and seems coherent, then it will result in building/built environment that induces intended experiential qualities, somehow... And this may be true for a disembodied, rational mind. But then one wonders why would a disembodied rational mind would need a building anyway. We need buildings, because we have bodies. It is through our bodies that we assess the quality of the experience of a built environment.

The quality of the experience induced by a building/built environment is more than the satisfaction gained by making-sense or imposing order to satisfy the need for coherence, it possesses has *hedonic* (body sense experience) qualities as well. **An embodied understanding of both the proper end and the proximate end of designing takes into account the embodied (hedonic) quality of the architectural experience (atmosphere) induced in the intended user as an incommensurable, determinative quality.** This quality is best described as *aesthetic*.[240] It is my claim that expert designers are those who not only know how to make a functional approximation that will result in a building that satisfies demonstrable criteria and constraints, is technically feasible, and coherent, but are those whom possess the knowledge, skill and ability to make use of plan, shape, form, materials, structure, systems, in a manner that induces an intended (not accidental) quality of aesthetic experience that engages the body and inspires the mind.

---

240   Hekkert (2006) points out that the aesthetic experience of an object is only one part of the whole experience of the designed object. He limits aesthetic experience to the "(dis)pleasure that results from sensory perception" (p. 157). (This limitation of aesthetic experience to sensory perception is challenged by Chatterjee [2014] below.) Hekkert's argument, relying heavily on evolutionary psychology, is that we have evolved to aesthetically prefer "environmental feature that are beneficial for the development of the senses' functioning and our survival in general" (p. 157). He identifies four general principles for his aesthetics: maximum effect for minimum means, unity in variety, most advanced, yet acceptable, and optimal match. To make his argument Hekkert refers to evolutionary psychologists (and others who incorporate aspects of evolutionary psychology into their work) such as Hildebrand (1999), Orians & Heerwagen (1992), Pinker (2002), Ramachandran & Hirstein (1999), as well as Dissanayake (1999) and Tooby & Cosmides (2001). Hekkert observes that the one thing these authors have in common is "the notion of adaptation." This is true, but many of them also build on the concept of exaptation. Gould & Vrba (1982) signifying the importance of this phenomenon for the emergence of many of the traits, characteristics and preferences that make up what we think of as human prefer the term exaptation, that "arose as by-products of other evolutionary processes, or were originally selected for some function unrelated to their apparent use" (Larson & Tehrani, 2013, p. 497). See also Ramachandran (2011) p. 166, and Pinker (2009) pp. 36-37. This concept of exaptation is fundamental for understanding how experiential qualities (such as aesthetic experience) evolved to function within the design process.

7 Aesthetic

Physical forms possess a character only because we ourselves possess a body.
If we were purely visual beings, we would always be denied an aesthetic judgment
of the physical world.

(Wölfflin [1886] in Vischer, 1994, p. 151)

Finally, there is a normative expectation that a building should possess intended aesthetic qualities. Aesthetic quality is understood as, the quality of the hedonic experience induced by a building/built environment. This normative expectation is typically more implicit than explicit, related to tacit knowledge. However, it is often also the *elephant in the room*, that everyone sees, but no one wants to admit seeing or talking about. This chapter will consider the aesthetic quality of the design solution as an intention of the designer, as well as aesthesis as it functions throughout the design process; how what is meant by aesthetic has evolved over history, and their implications for how we understand aesthetic today; as well as how one's understanding of the aesthetic influences how one designs.

Aesthetic experience as it is being used here is not synonymous with "Beauty" (the Beautiful, as in a Platonic universal ideal state), or beauty (as in a quality possessed by an object).[241] Rather, what is meant here is **a kind (type) of hedonic experience that is evoked in a beholder by making use of various architectural elements, materials and techniques.** Chatterjee (2014) describes aesthetic as a quality of experience that is,

---

[241] There has been a long-time association between aesthetic theory and art, as art is often made with the specific intention of inducing a reaction in the beholder it is thought to be the proper subject of aesthetic theory. However, there is not a necessary connection between aesthetics and art. An aesthetic experience can be had anywhere, though this research is only concerned with the quality of an intended (fabricated) aesthetic experience). We are constantly experiencing multiple sensory experiences that are constantly being processed by our cognitive systems. Therefore it is reasonable to consider that an aesthetic experience does not need to be limited to museums, concert halls, and theaters, though it may be more likely that an aesthetic experience will be induced in those places. Neuroaesthetics is interested in understanding how an aesthetic experience is induced and what an aesthetic experience is from the perspective of neuroscience. See Best (2005) who makes a sharp distinction between artistic and aesthetic, writing "[t]here are, then, *two, quite distinct,* although sometimes related, concepts. To put it as starkly as possible, a central feature of an object of *artistic* as opposed to *aesthetic* interest is, to put it roughly at this stage, that it can have subject matter" (p. 68). While, "[a]esthetic quality is an intrinsic aspect of the appreciation and evaluation of the movements involved in sporting activities such as gymnastics, diving, skating, and many others" (p. 67). See also Danto (2002),"The Abuse of Beauty" for a discussion on how beauty and art came to no longer be necessarily associated with art in the West.

rooted in but not restricted to basic appetites. The pleasure of gazing at a beautiful person or an enthralling painting is not the same as the pleasure of sugar on our tongues. Aesthetic pleasures stretch beyond appetitive pleasures in at least three ways. First, they extend past desires by tapping into neural systems that are biased toward liking without necessarily wanting. Second, aesthetic pleasures are nuanced and encompass admixtures of emotions more complex than simple liking. Third, aesthetic pleasures are influenced profoundly by our cognitive systems. They are colored by the experiences and knowledge we bring to the aesthetic encounters. (pp. 111-112)

The aesthetic is an *embodied* way of experiencing/knowing the world through the body. The ability that allows us to experience/know the world through our bodies is aesthesis.

Due to the subjective nature of experiential knowledge, there may be an objection to claiming aesthetic experience as a normative expectation of practice. There is no doubt that any problem situation that does not have an objectively necessary solution (such as a well-structured problem); one that relies on bias heuristics to reduce the possible solution paths; and that relies on the interpretation and re-interpretation of the problem in search of a sufficient, satisfying, somewhat novel solution; is going to involve **multiple reasonable ways of seeing the problem and seeking a solution**. As noted earlier, Pinker observes that even the act of seeing poses a complex problem state "that has no unique solution" (p. 212). Due to the limited cognitive processing capacity and memory, we only take in information necessary to provide a comprehensive and coherent picture of a situation. That is to say that there are multiple legitimate ways of seeing the same thing, it all depends on what one is looking for.

The challenge is determining which reasonable way of thinking about a problem is preferred. And which way of thinking about a problem has the greatest likelihood of resulting in a solution that is acceptable to the designer, client, owner, user group. As discussed above, this is complicated, due to the many people with different agendas who participate in defining and framing the design problem. It is ultimately a question of preference. This of course also applies to a sense of coherence as well. What seems to be coherent to one person make not appear coherent to another. The term for this problem is *subjective-relativism*. But relativism is not limited to individual preference, it can be extended to cultural relativism, gender relativism, regional relativism, age relativism, etc. However, subjective relativism is not always the un-crossable chasm it appears to be. Moreover, the fact that different people have divergent opinions about the desired quality of a space (atmosphere), and perhaps even about how to achieve it, does not mean that it is a topic that should be avoided, or about which one should pretend does not matter.

Describing intended quality of aesthetic experience as a normative performance expectation of a design solution should not be confused with the imposition of a normative standard for aesthetic experience. This normative expectation simply claims that it is reasonable to expect that a designer should possess the skills necessary to produce a design solution that possesses *intended* aesthetic experience. The question is not whether or not aesthetic experience is an essential aspect of architectural design; that is a given. The question in this section is to understand what is meant by aesthetic experience, and how it functions in the design process.

Böhme (1993) uses the term *atmosphere* as a way of talking about the *aesthetic experience* of a built environment. The concept of atmosphere describes a "quality of feeling [that] can be produced through the choice of objects, colours, sounds, etc." (p. 123). Böhme understands "the production of atmospheres" (p. 116) and the quality of experience (feeling) that they induce as the work of architectural aesthetics. Atmosphere, refers to the quality of the experience between subject and object. One may use expressions such as, "this is a peaceful place," or "there's a lot of tension in that room," or "I felt overwhelmed when we went there," or "there is something familiar about this place." Böhme, argues that the quality of feeling that is experienced by a person when he encounters a place or a thing is what is meant by aesthetic. The qualities of a thing or a place (color, volume, materials, temperature, smell, light, etc.), are the *determinations* that taken together induce a quality of experience. These qualities of the object determine the *perceivability* of the thing. To be effective the qualities of an object must be such that they *can* be perceived by the perceiver, that is within his range or ability (or boundedness). For example, the range of hearing and smell of a dog is different than that of a human. As such, there are certain sounds or scenes that when perceived by a dog (not to mention the difference in the range of cognitive abilities between dogs and humans) will result in a quality of experience (atmosphere) quite different from that which a human would perceived in the same situation. It is the role of the designer to both anticipate the quality of the intended experience (atmosphere), and to have the skill to know which materials to use, how to arrange architectural elements, etc. that will likely induce the desired atmosphere, or as McCormick (1997) puts it, of "how-to-decide-what-to-do-and-when knowledge" (p. 145).

A helpful example, used with my students, that describes what is involved in/what it means to design an environment that induces an intended quality of atmosphere, is the romantic meal. From a functional point of view one may argue that the basic purpose the romantic meal is to facilitate eating. The *romantic* aspect of the meal is extra (an un-essential experiential quality), nice, but unnecessary. Though, it is true that eating is a *desired outcome* (proximate), it is not the *primary* (distal) function. The *primary function* of the romantic meal is to create an environment that is likely to induce a feeling of intimacy.

One may even argue that if the design of the meal is really good, it will induce such an experience of intimacy and pleasure that the couple will perhaps even forget to eat.

In this case the designer is faced with many choices that will result in a *scene* that will evoke an atmosphere, that *feels* romantic. Start with a table: round or square, and what size? Consider its size. It should be big enough to comfortably fit plates, eating utensils, a bottle of wine, flowers, etc. But not so big that one cannot easily reach across. How about the shape? The corners of the square establish boundaries, while the round table makes the boundaries ambiguous. Perhaps a square table on the first date. What about the lighting: bright, dim; fluorescent, incandescent; general ambient lighting, focused task lighting, candle light? So many choices. The design *bias* or heuristic used to limit the solution path (designing possibilities) is: *make design choices that facilitate the eating of a meal such that the elements induce a romantic atmosphere.* (What I like about this thought exercise, is that I can see the students' eyes going back and forth as they imagine the space, as they enter the design world feelingly.) Florescent light is on the cold side of the spectrum, having a tendency to make everyone look gray. Ambient light lights the entire room: Too many distractions. Candle light, has several advantages: Its light is on the warm side of the spectrum, so it makes everyone look better. Its range of luminosity (foot-candles) is quite limited, forcing one to lean forward slightly to see with whom one is dining. Plus, there is the added advantage of the smell of a candle burning, and the culturally significant symbolic value of a round table, with a white table cloth, set for two, with wine glasses, a flower in the middle and candle light that triggers a memory and an associated emotion. All these choices are made with the intention to induce a particular quality of experience. Making use of Chatterjjee's *core triad* that are involved in an aesthetic experience: sensations, emotions and meaning.[242]

The designer of the romantic meal starts off with a feeling – or using the vocabulary of Hillier discussed in the section on design cognition – he *pre-structures* the design problem as: *a meal that involves a particular quality of atmosphere.* Assuming that the designer is working in a familiar culture, there is no need to engage in extensive research to gain a deep understanding of the psychology of intimacy, or the courting rituals of peoples of Western-European descent. The designer when faced with the problem, immediately *knows* how the solution should feel. Still, how does the designer know which elements to use and how to arrange them? Perhaps, he considers precedent. What worked and what did not work in the past? What was the criteria for evaluation of those past experiences? The quality of the food? The type of music? The color of the table cloth?

---

[242] These refer to the qualities of an aesthetic experience described in the quote by Chatterjee (2014) above. The elements of the core triad will be described in detail below, in the section on neuroaesthetics.

Yes, but no, not really... The resultant experience was not the sum of individual elements. To use a foundational concept from Gestalt psychology, (Koffka, 1935) all those elements, including many more, add up to an experience *that is other than the sum of the parts*.[243] The designer, pre-structures the problem situation not only by identifying key elements, but by self-inducing a feeling of what he intends the experience to feel like and measures the success of the design by testing the quality of the experience he intends to *feel if it resonates* (is congruent) with the experience he has self-induced.

Like coherence, aesthetic quality both functions as motivation (feeling that is being sought internally) within the design process, and as an intended quality induced by the solution in the user. Entering into the design world *feelingly* involves being able to assess the quality of the feeling (phenomenal experience) of both internal and external representations during the various states of the design process: this is the function of aesthesis. Like learning to see, aesthesis is a learned ability.[244] And, also like coherence, there is a need to produce external representations of the emerging solution for both the purpose of gaining input from others, and as a means to extend the designer's cognitive capacity, enabling the dialectic that seeks congruence of the intended aesthetic experience between internal and external representations, through the application of the senses.

How does the designer know which solution path to take, and when the solution is finished? He knows which one to take when it feels right, when there is (emerging) congruence between what he intended and the situation at hand. This kind of knowing (aesthesis) through the application of the senses – like declarative and propositional knowledge – is an acquired and highly developed of kind of embodied knowledge, something like what might be called a "sense of design." Certainly the designer needs to satisfy criteria and constraints, and he must possess the technical competence to design a building that can be built.

---

243   Koffka is often misquoted as writing "the whole is *greater* than the sum of its parts" when what he actually wrote is "the whole is *other* than the sum of its parts." Koffka took issue with that translation. He firmly corrected students who substituted "greater" for "other" (cited by Heider, 1977, p. 383). "'This is not a principle of addition,' he said. The statement as originally worded was intended to mean that the whole had an *independent existence* in the perceptual system." Dewey (2007) explains, "When the perceptual system forms a percept or gestalt, the whole thing has a reality of its own, independent of the parts."

244   Das (2014) in his research on how infants acquire the ability to "see" explains "that neural responses at even the earliest stage of visual cortex get reshaped in a way that faithfully reflects ongoing learning" (p. 129). It seems that even seeing is an acquired ability.

But, once all the site analysis, space relationship diagrams, use programing, size of spaces, means of egress, schematic plan, overall form, location on the site, structural, mechanical, electrical, plumbing, communications, and fire suppression systems have been worked out; the designer is still faced with how to assemble all of these elements into a cohesive whole (something that is perceived as *other than the sum of its parts*); and find a way to induce the intended quality of aesthetic experience (that possesses *atmosphere*). It is the seeking of these experiential qualities that motivates the process and leads to a solution that engages the whole person. **The internal self-induced quality of aesthetic experience, functions to pre-structure the problem space and as a heuristic device that seeks congruence between internal/external representations of the emerging design solution influencing the direction of the solution path with the expectation that a similar quality of experience will be induced by the building/built environment in the user.**

§ 7.1   Approaches to Aesthetics

There are many ways of approaching aesthetics – from philosophy, psychology, evolutionary biology, neurosciences, and from the inter-disciplinary perspective of cognitive science. The way of approaching aesthetic experience here relies heavily on cognitive science. Even so, it is necessary to acknowledge that many contemporary ideas about aesthetic experience have their roots in how aesthetic experience was understood in Classical Greek philosophy. It was not until after Hume and Kant that Baumgarten, Lipps, Fetchner, Wölfflin and the *Gestalt* psychologists would begin developing an empirical aesthetics that was more heavily influenced by observable phenomenon, rather than seeking universal truths. As aesthetic experience came to be understood as a kind of knowledge of the world by perception induced by feeling, Clay, Dutton, and Miller and Dissanayake identify the evolutionary advantages that our delight with this quality of experience might have. More recently, there is growing interest in understanding aesthetic experience from neuroscience, that includes Mallgrave, Damasio, Ramachandran and Chatterjee.

To this day we are burdened with reconciling early definitions of what Plato, Aristotle, Augustine, Aquinas, and others meant by beauty, and how their ideas influence how we understand aesthetic experience in the 21st century. Plato writes, "How, if you please, do you know, Socrates, what sort of things are beautiful and ugly ...Could you tell me what the beautiful is?"[245] The question is not what is beauty, but what is "the Beautiful."

---

245   See Plato (2014), *Philebus*.

The Beautiful in Plato is akin to the Truth and/or the Good: the three transcendentals that point to the One. [246] In ancient Western philosophy, aesthetics was the study of Beauty. Beauty, or the aesthetic, was not understood to describe the quality of an experience as it is being used here. Rather it was understood to be an *intrinsic* good, or transcendent characteristic: a *form*.

In ancient Greek philosophy there are, generally speaking, two conceptions of beauty: the idealist (Platonic) and the classical (Aristotelean). The idealist conception of beauty and the classical conception of beauty have several things in common: they both conceive of beauty as an objective reality (not localized in the beholder); the beholder, insofar as he has access to the concept of *the Beautiful*, experiences the Beautiful in the object, and thus is lead to a deeper knowledge of the *One*; Beauty is a kind of knowledge in which one takes delight in as one takes delight in the Truth. The ancient philosophers held that there is one Beauty whose existence is inevitably tied to the Good, Truth, and ultimately God (the One). Beauty in creation, and the pursuit of Beauty in the arts, as well as the profound effect that being in the presence of a thing of beauty has on the beholder, are all understood as evidence of God's presence.

§ 7.2 Plato

For Plato (427-447 BCE), Beauty is a transcendental (ideal) form, along with Justice and Truth. It has an existence independent of the object. His argument is that if different things can possess the quality of beauty to various degrees of perfection, then it follows that there must be the possibility of the perfection of beauty, or complete Beauty: the Beautiful. Plato writes "Now if a man believes in the existence of beautiful things, but not of Beauty itself, and cannot follow a guide who would lead him to a knowledge of it, is he not living in a dream?" (*Republic*, 1956, p. 276).

---

246   In the *Symposium* (2014), Diotima instructs Socrates, "But what if man had eyes to see the true beauty — the divine beauty, I mean, pure and clear and unalloyed, not clogged with the pollutions of mortality and all the colours and vanities of human life — hither looking, and holding converse with the true beauty simple and divine? Remember how in that communion only, beholding beauty with the eye of the mind, he will be enabled to bring forth, not images of beauty, but realities (for he has hold not of an image but of a reality), and bringing forth and nourishing true virtue to become the friend of God and be immortal, if mortal man may. Would that be an ignoble life?"

That things are in the world, and that things are perceived, and that some things appear to have different qualities (*qualia*) than others and that some things give pleasure and some do not is a given. The question is why and how? This why and how does not only extend to the phenomenology of perception, but also includes metaphysical and epistemological considerations. A concept (thing, quality, experience) as important as beauty is not taken lightly. So when Plato discusses the perception (knowledge) of things and their proper place in the order of the *cosmos* he approaches it with great care. The things that are seen (perceived), *mimic* the *form*. The perfection of a thing or its ideal (or universal) state exists in the world of the *forms*.[247] The (ideal) form is manifest in *matter*, which gives it physical properties. But this manifestation of the form in matter is a mere shadow of the form, that is less than perfect (an approximation). As such it follows, that if the (physical) manifestation in matter of the ideal form is a mere shadow of the ideal form, then an image of the physical manifestation (representation) of the ideal form is even less perfect, similar to a second generation photo copy: two steps away from the ideal. For Plato the *really real* is the ideal (disembodied/abstract) world of the forms, which is eternal, where things are perfect, where one does not worry about corruptibility or materiality.[248] So, it is not hard to understand why, for Plato, artists are considered "unworthy rivals of philosophers" – who deal exclusively in the world of ideas – because they try to reveal truth but only manage to create poor imitations (*mimêsis*) of reality (Shimamura, 2012, p. 5).

To further explain how art functions as an imperfect embodiment, or revelation of the form of Beauty, Plato introduces terms such as: imitation and inspiration (*mimêsis*) and (most importantly) he defines beauty as a transcendent characteristic (form). Within the world of forms, there are also ideas, (transcendent) universal truths that hold the most distinguished place in human civilization, that describe the ultimate *Good*.[249] As such the theory of forms guarantees stable referents for evaluative terms. In this way Beauty comes to have its own existence as a universal value that points to the Good. The Beautiful is an intrinsic good. And the artist, who has knowledge, insofar as he has access to beauty, is an "imitator of the Beautiful."

---

247   While architects use the term form to refer to the shape and volume of a thing in design, architects are familiar (analogously) with the idea behind platonic form in terms of the *generative idea*: the idea (concept) that generates the building. This is what Plato means when he talks about forms.

248   This is an idea that leads to the mind/body dualism found in Descartes discussed above.

249   The Good in Plato is the Absolute (One), Eternal, Truth (God).

The artist, through special knowledge and technical skill, makes use of certain characteristics of the object, that include the qualities of measure (*metron*) and proportion (*symmetron*) which invariably ...constitute beauty and excellence.[250] The artist may also make use of pure tone or hue, a straight line or regular polyhedron which also possess the characteristics of absolute and eternal beauty. It is not the individual characteristics that point toward the Beautiful but rather their unity, regularity and simplicity that gives them their ideal character and allies them with the One, the True and the Eternal, supporting and sustaining their beauty" (Beardsley, 1966, p. 43).

For Plato, the Beautiful has its own existence. It is not a quality of an object, but rather a universal, transcendent, eternal, inherent good, that an object points to, depending on its level of perfection. The artist, insofar as he has knowledge of the Beautiful, can make things that point toward the Good.

§ 7.3 Aristotle

For Aristotle (384-322 BCE), the Beautiful is much the same as the Good, as they possess the same metaphysical root, "the good and the beautiful are the beginning both of knowledge and the movement of things" (Marshall, 1953, p. 229). The Beautiful is the "appropriate" (in right proportion) whose chief forms are order, symmetry, and definiteness. Beauty, in its highest form is a fixed and eternal concept, that is recognized in objects, and can be applied to God (the Good). Aristotle's aesthetic theory – insofar as he had one – in many ways is a response to Plato. However, for Aristotle, Beauty, as found in the arts, exists in the present. It is a kind of knowledge that we desire and satisfy through the arts.

Art belongs to a particular type of knowledge. As discussed above in the section on cognition, Aristotle identifies three types: knowing (*theoria*), doing (*praxis*), and making (*poiesis*).[251] Art is a kind of making. Making, as an imitative art has two further distinctions: imitating through visual appearances (painting, sculpture) and imitating human actions (theater, poetry).[252]

---

250   Socrates says to Philebus, "And now we are at the vestibule of the good, in which there are three chief elements — truth, symmetry, and beauty" (Plato, 2008).

251   See Aristotle (2014), *Metaphysics*.

252   See Aristotle (2015) *Poetics*.

Making has four causes: (1.) The material cause (the medium, such as marble, wood or bronze for the statue); (2.) The formal cause (the essence or concept for the object); (3.) The efficient cause (the craftsman or sculptor and their activity); and (4.) The final cause (the "end" or the sake for which a thing is made).[253] Imitation finds its perfection insofar as it fully actualizes its potential. Potentiality is the intent behind an action, and actuality is the action, or the manifestation of the intent.[254]

The formal cause is defined by an object's *essence* ("the what it is to be" such as "chair-ness" or the disembodied idea of a thing); and its accidence ("the what it is," or the actual chair or the embodied existence of a thing). The essence of a thing is that which makes a particular thing what it is. In terms of accidence, Aristotle identifies nine types: quality, quantity, relation, *habitus*, time, location, situation (or position), action, and passion (being acted upon). Art in Aristotle is a form of *mimesis* (imitation) that provides a natural kind of pleasure or delight. Art is a good (a value) that requires extensive knowledge and technical skill (*techne*). Its value, or the pleasure/delight that it offers, is found in the way that it makes use of extensive knowledge and technical skill to imitate reality.

Beauty in Aristotle is a quality of objects: "to be beautiful, a living creature, and every whole made up of parts, must ... present a certain order in its arrangement of parts" (*Poetics*, 2009). Beauty resides in the thing. Aristotle (2015) in the *Metaphysics* writes: "The chief forms of beauty are order and symmetry and definiteness, which the mathematical sciences demonstrate in a special degree." Beauty has to do with *right relationship*; relationship that is in proper proportion. Right relationship can be described by a mathematical formula (such as the golden section), or exemplified in the Parthenon or the *Canon* of the sculptor Polykleitos.[255] Beauty in Aristotle is a quality of an object that can be described and exists independent of the object.[256]

---

253   See Aristotle, (2015) *Physics*: Translated by R.P. Hardie & R.K. Gaye.

254   In Aristotle, a thing can exist in a state of potential (without being actualized).

255   The Canon of Polykleitos is a lost work that is believed to have provided the basis for the unit and proper proportions for Greek sculpture, similar to Le Corbusier's *Le Modular*. See Tobin (1975) for an extensive discussion on the unit, measure and proportion system of the Canon of Polykleitos.

256   Aristotle (2014) writes, in Book III of the *Metaphysics*, "Now since the good and the beautiful are different (for the former always implies conduct as its subject, while the beautiful is found also in motionless things), those who assert that the mathematical sciences say nothing of the beautiful or the good are in error. For these sciences say and prove a great deal about them; if they do not expressly mention them, but prove attributes which are their results or their definitions, it is not true to say that they tell us nothing about them. The chief forms of beauty are order and symmetry and definiteness, which the mathematical sciences demonstrate in a special degree. And since these (e.g. order and definiteness) are obviously causes of many things, evidently these sciences must treat this sort of causative principle also (i.e. the beautiful) as in some sense a cause. But we shall speak more plainly elsewhere about these matters."

§ 7.4   Vitruvius

For much of ancient history, and even to some extent up to the present, the presupposition that beauty was to be found in the object remained a given. Vitruvius (80-15 BCE),[257] provides a good characterization of the classical conception of beauty with his description the three components of architecture as consisting in order (*taxis*), arrangement (*diathesis*), and proportion (*oeconomia*):

- Order is the balanced adjustment of the details of the work separately and as to the whole; the arrangement of the composition with a view to a symmetrical result.
- Proportion implies a graceful semblance; the suitable display of details in their context. This is attained when the details of the work are of a height suitable to their breadth, of a breadth suitable to their length; in a word, when everything has a symmetrical correspondence.
- Symmetry is the appropriate harmony arising out of the details of the work itself; the correspondence of each given detail to the form of the design as a whole. As in the human body, from cubit, foot, palm, inch and other small parts come the symmetric quality of *eurhythmy*.

§ 7.5   Hume, Locke, Kant

However, by the 18th century beauty had begun to migrate from an objective reality outside the beholder (a property of the object) to become a type/quality of pleasure experienced by the beholder (Sartwell & Crispin, 2014). For those who hold this position, such as Hume, Locke and Kant, the issue in not so much the object itself, as it is the quality of the effect the object/experience elicits (induces) in the beholder. The arguments here emphasize perception, physiology, psychology and epistemology.

---

257   Vitruvius (1998) Bk. I, Ch. 2.1.

Hume writes:

Beauty is no quality in things themselves: It exists merely in the mind which contemplates them; and each mind perceives a different beauty. One person may even perceive deformity, where another is sensible of beauty; and every individual ought to acquiesce in his own sentiment, without pretending to regulate those of others. (Korsmeyer, 1998, p 139)

In considering beauty as the quality of a personal experience, Hume seems to be suggesting an extreme degree of subjective relativism. But then, as if to contradict himself Hume writes:

But though this axiom, by passing into proverb, seems to have attained the sanction of common sense; there is certainly a species of common sense, which opposes it, at least serves to modify and refrain it. (Korsmeyer, 1998, p 139)

Acknowledging that though it is possible for two people to have such extreme opposite of perception of the same thing, there are "species of common sense" that make this unlikely. To illustrate this observation Hume offers the example of someone who might suggest that the (17th Century) authors Ogilby and Milton, or Bunyan and Addison, should be considered of equal genius. "Such a person who might hold such a ludicrous position may as well maintain 'a mole-hill to be as high as Teneriffe, or a pond as extensive as the ocean.' Such a conclusion should be considered 'absurd and ridiculous.' No one pays attention to such a taste" (Korsmeyer, 1998, p 139).

Hume then goes on to describe the importance of refined taste.[258]

In a word, the same address and dexterity, which practice gives to the execution of any work, is also acquired by the same means, in the judging of it. The principle of natural equality of tastes is then totally forgot, and while we admit it on some occasions, where the objects seem near an equality, it appears an extravagant paradox, or rather a palpable absurdity, where objects so disproportioned are compared together. (Korsmeyer 1998, p. 139)

---

[258]   Similar to Ericsson (see acquisition of expert performance), Hume recognizes that refined taste is not simply natural, but that it is an acquired skill that requires deliberate practice.

Hume denies that beauty exists in the object to be beheld, rather, beauty is a quality that is perceived by the beholder. However, he does hold that certain compositions, materials and effects, when assembled properly, "by the structure of the mind, be naturally calculated to give pleasure," do elicit a pleasant effect. This pleasant effect can be enhanced by developing its *delicacy*. "Where the organs are so fine, as to allow nothing to escape them; and at the same time so exact, as to perceive every ingredient in the composition: This we call delicacy of taste..." (Korsmeyer, 1998, p. 143).

Locke makes a distinction between secondary and primary qualities of the aesthetic experience: qualities that are dependent on a subjective response, located in the mind of the perceiver, (such as color);[259] and qualities that are independent (such as shape and volume). Dependent qualities (like phenomenal qualities) are by nature subjective, as they exist only in the mind of the beholder and have no independent existence outside the beholder's experience of the object. While independent qualities are by nature objective. These are qualities that are observable and have an existence independent of being perceived. See Jackson, 1929.

In the *Critique of Judgment*, Kant holds on the one hand, not unlike Hume, that beauty is not a real quality of objects – aesthetic judgments are not matters of cognition. Kant writes:

[The aesthetic judgment], ...refers the representation, by which an object is given, solely to the subject, and brings to our notice no quality of the object, but only the final form in the determination of the powers of representation engaged upon it. The judgment is called aesthetic for the very reason that its determining ground cannot be a concept, but is rather the feeling (of the internal sense) of the concert in the play of the mental powers as a thing only capable of being felt. (Hofstadter & Kuhns, 1964, p. 300)

This is because the judgment of beauty is based on a feeling of pleasure induced by the object, not on reasoning, or on a perception where the object is experienced as having some cognizable feature.

In *The Critique of Judgment*, Bk. 1.1 "The Judgment of Taste in Aesthetic", Kant (1790) concedes that every aesthetic judgment is, to some extent, based on personal experience, that varies from person to person.

---

259   Color is a particular problem, in that while it appears to be so, it is not a physiological quality of an object, but rather, is totally dependent on the context in which it is observed. See Pinker (2009) Chapter 4, "The Mind's Eye."

The judgment of taste is therefore not a judgment of cognition, and is consequently not logical but aesthetical, by which we understand that whose determining ground can be no other than subjective. Every reference of representations, even that of sensations, may be objective (and then it signifies the real in an empirical representation); save only the reference to the feeling of pleasure and pain, by which nothing in the Object is signified, but through which there is a feeling in the subject, as it is affected by the representation. (Hofstadter & Kuhns, 1964, p. 300)

But it is not only subjective. For Kant, it is necessary to distinguish between the pleasure an object provides in terms of its usefulness (or one's interest in the object) and the pleasure gained by the mere presentation of the object to my senses (disinterested-ness). This is a very important point in Kant's argument. Kant writes

... if the question is whether something is beautiful, what we want to know is not whether we or anyone cares, or so much as might care, in any way about the thing's existence, but rather how we judge it in our mere contemplation of it (intuition or reflection). (Gage, 2011, p. 83)

Kant argues that the aesthetic qualities of an object have nothing to do with the practical usefulness or value of the object, or even *enjoyment*. These all imply interest. A pure judgment of taste must be completely distinguished from an assessment of the utility or other perceived value of the object, having only to do with the quality of the presentation of the object one feels within one's self. That is to say,

We can easily see that, in order for me to say that an object is beautiful, and to prove that I have taste, what matters is what I do with this presentation within myself, and not the [respect] in which I depend on the object's existence. (Hofstadter & Kuhns, 1964, p. 281)

To further develop this idea, Kant makes some distinctions regarding what is meant by *agreeable sensations* versus *feelings*. For Kant agreeable sensations are objective experiences of sense that refer solely to the subject and entail no cognition. Whereas feeling refers to the subjective experience of the object. For example, the green color of the meadow belongs to the objective sensation, while the delight that the color green induces belongs to the subjective sensation.

Even though Kant argues that a judgment of taste is necessarily subjective, both Hume and Kant, and to some extent Locke, also propose means for inter-subjective agreement or as Kant puts it: *sensus communis*. The presupposition is that the object presenting itself has an objective reality that is perceived by the beholder – similar to Locke's primary qualities. That is, each beholder sees the same object. Secondly, each beholder shares the same basic human nature, and as such perceives the object in a similar manner via the same sense, perception and cognitive systems.

With these fundamental concepts in hand it is now possible to discuss how aesthetic experience is induce in the beholder and (building on Kant's *sensus communis*) what characteristics of human perception facilitate the possibility of intersubjective agreement. It is here that aesthetic theory takes a decisive turn toward more empirical approaches such as psychology and cognitive sciences.

§ 7.6 Connoisseurship

Contrary to popular belief, aesthetic judgment can be learned.

(Osborne 1979)

Connoisseurship has to do with the refinement of the ability to distinguish the quality of an experience, skill or ability. In aesthetics, connoisseurship is often referred to as *taste*. Generally speaking, taste has to do with a person's personal or cultural patterns of choice that allow him to make distinctions between the qualities of things according to his own preference or by the performance expectations of a particular domain. That is: the acquired ability to make evaluative distinctions between the quality of sense/perception experiences within a discipline.[260]

We learn to love beauty, so to speak, in diluted form to start with – the physical beauty of man or woman – but having acquired the taste, or developed the perceptual skill to discern it clearly, we can go to higher and better beauties – with the promise, or at least the hope, that we may again behold Beauty in itself. (Beardsley, 1966, p. 41)

260   Such as architectural design

It is a form of *intentional belief acquisition* or *adaptive preference formation*, as opposed to ordinary or discovered taste, or what Burke (1756) called "natural relish" (p. 14). See Melchionne (2007). Natural relish requires no discipline. There is a naive simplicity to it. It is not acquired, its discovered. It's a kind of a "I know what I like" personal preference where there is no expectation that another would or should enjoy it.[261] The acquisition of taste within a particular domain however, requires a deliberate effort to appreciate subtle variations, references and precedents within a particular domain and the ability to recognize performance expectations of excellence.

The cultivation of taste, or the refinement of aesthetic judgment is a decidedly deliberate action. One decides to cultivate taste for/or refine aesthetic judgment of an object or experience because one desires to reach out for new experiences, deliberately desire to appreciate something one does not understand, or because one desires to immerse oneself into a particular discipline (Nimkulrat, Niedderer, & Evans, 2015).

According to Melchionne (2007) – whose argument while insightful is also arguably novel – the cultivation of taste normally starts by pretending that one already has the desired taste. One puts aside or detaches from one's ordinary preferences in order to enter into the experience seeking to discover something new. This *pretending* is a pretending with intent (deliberate); the intent to acquire an appreciation for a thing or an experience.[262] It is not the same as pretending to like something for the sake of someone's feelings or to conform to an external belief system for the sake of fitting in. In the case of adaptive belief acquisition the change of belief is real, and made for a purpose. An acquired taste must be deliberately chosen or desired in order to be authentic.[263]

Related to the refinement of taste, and familiarity with the performance expectations within a domain, aesthetic qualities are attributed (in part) in accordance with the category of that specific work of art (Walton, 1970; Mitrovic, 2013, p. 83). For example, if one assesses the taste of an apple with the categories of normative expectations of an orange, the apple will always be wanting.

---

[261] Later "natural relish" will be referred to as "personal taste."

[262] "But though there be naturally a wide difference in point of delicacy between one person and another, nothing tends further to increase and improve this talent, than practice in a particular art, and the frequent survey or contemplation of a particular species of beauty" (Hume, 1757/2015, *Of the Standard of Taste*).

[263] There is a connection between the deliberate refinement of taste within a domain and the immersion of the novice seeking expertise into the culture of the domain.

If one is not familiar with the standards for judging a refined art work within its domain, then it will be difficult to assess its aesthetic value, except in terms of personal preference, and perhaps as a sympathetic outsider. This question of attributed qualities is also related to the idea that concepts or prior knowledge are necessary in order to experience the aesthetic qualities of a work of art. Zangwill (2014) refutes this position by arguing that "some aesthetic properties depend exclusively on formal properties of objects, while others depend on non-formal properties as well" (Mitrovic, 2013, p. 83).

Berlyne (1970), argues that one's aesthetic experience is driven by novelty, surprise, and incongruity, all of which increases arousal. His argument relies on the properties of the Wundt Curve, which was originally used to describe how increases in stimulus intensity, such as sweetness, is pleasurable up to a point but as intensity moves beyond that point our enjoyment drops and can even become negative.[264] Berlyne argues that we find pleasure (i.e., positive hedonic value) when an artwork (an object whose proper end is to induce aesthetic experience) arouses our sense of novelty, surprise, or incongruity, but as the Wundt curve describes, when arousal moves past an optimal point it leads to a negative response. Importantly, the flip side of novelty is familiarity, and thus what appears new or surprising is a moving window, as the more you know, the more things become familiar and the greater chance a new work will lie within your "sweet spot" of *optimal hedonic value*. Producing a design solution that lies within the sweet spot of the intended users is fundamental to a successful design.

Hume (some two centuries earlier) seems to agree with Berlyne. He writes,

---

It appears then, that amidst all the variety and caprice of taste, there are certain general principles of approbation or blame, whose influence a careful eye may trace in all operations of the mind. Some particular forms or qualities, from the original structure of the internal fabric, are calculated to please, and others to displease; and if they fail of their effect in any particular instance, it is from some apparent defect or imperfection in the organ. (Korsmeyer, 1998, p. 141)

It is the objective of good design to be able to manipulate the general principles, forms and qualities to elicit an optimal experience calculated to please, assuming that there is no defect or imperfection in the beholder. But, if the beholder's performance expectations are incongruent with the domain in question, uninformed, and poorly developed it becomes exceedingly difficult for the designer to induce an optimal aesthetic experience.

---

264   See York (2013) for an explanation of how the Wundt curve works in aesthetics and the development of taste.

If someone is expecting an apple and is given an orange, there is little likelihood, no matter how one well one explains the quality of the orange are tries to apply the performance expectations of the orange to the apple, that he is going to be satisfied.

§ 7.7 Alexander Baumgarten

It is Baumgarten (1750) who introduces the term aesthetics, to designate what up to now had been the study of beauty, in his book *Aethetica*. This book is said to mark the beginning of modern aesthetics. [265]

While Baumgarten was principally known as a rationalist philosopher, it is in his psychology, where he discusses *the nature of sensible experience*. Psychology, for Baumgarten, is the study of the "soul," that which is conscious. The objects of consciousness are *representations of the world as they present themselves to the soul*. These representations fall under two categories: the *superior faculty* and the *inferior faculty*. The superior faculty perceives/knows a thing distinctly, that is intellectually. The inferior faculty perceives/knows a thing indistinctly, as a *sensitive representation*. The study of aesthetics has to do with the inferior faculty (sense knowledge): "The end of aesthetics is the perfection of sensitive cognition as such" (Wessell, 1972, p. 337). That is, it is the study of things perceived (the science of perception), as opposed to the study of things known (logic). "'Things known' (i.e., conceptually intuited) are the proper objects of logic and 'things perceived' (i.e., sensitively experienced) are objects for the science of perception which is called 'aesthetic'" (Wessell, 1972, p. 338). Baumgarten is interested in knowledge about the *form*[266] that determines the order of perceptual or sensate experience (or as he called it, confused experience). The appreciation of beauty is produce by "sensitive cognition" (Chatterjee, 2014, p. 117). Aesthetics for Baumgarten is the science of perception.[267]

---

[265] Unfortunately there is no complete translation of *Aethetica*, in English. All quotes and citations come from other's work.

[266] By *form* Baumgarten is referring to order or the way a thing presents itself.

[267] "The Greek philosophers and the Church fathers have always carefully distinguished between the *aistheta* and the *noeta*," that is, between objects of sense and objects of thought, and while the latter, that is, "what can be cognized through the higher faculty" of the mind, are "the object of logic, the *aistheta* are the subject of episteme *aisthetika* or AESTHETICS," the science of perception (*Meditationes*, CXVI, p. 86). As quoted by Guyer (2013).

Baumgarten writes: "The science of sensitively knowing and proposing is aesthetics, the logic of the inferior faculty of knowing, the philosophy of the graces and the muses, the inferior knowledge, the art of thinking beautifully, the art of analogy and reason" (Wessell, 1972, p. 338). As a type of knowing, aesthetics follows an ordering process (discourse) not unlike logical ordering. As a type of discourse, aesthetics involves "a series of different representations apprehended by the mind in some sort of unity" (Wessell, 1972, p. 339). This involves identifying the elements (sensations) that are perceived, and how they are ordered together to form the (aesthetic) discourse/experience. Further, as not all (sense) experiences are of equal value, the type of sensation proper to aesthetic experience must be further understood. The aesthetic experience arises when several representations are ordered that form a sensate discourse. It is *from the unity* that is perceived in the sensate discourse that the aesthetic experience evolves.[268]

§ 7.8   Empathy

Baumgarten writes that aesthetics is *sensitively knowing*. Above Polanyi describes tacit knowing as *inhabiting the problem space feelingly*. As it became generally accepted that the aesthetic experience is induced and experienced as a sensation of the body, how this actually happens became a topic of research. It is in this context that the concept of *Einfühlung* – feeling into – emerged as a key concept among early 20th century German aesthetic philosophers, including, Vischer, Lipps, Wölfflin, and Worringer. Introduced into the English language by Edward Titchener as "empathy" the term *Einfühlung* describes the projection of a sense of the inward feeling of our bodily state onto inanimate objects (Jahoda, 2005).

For Lipps, *Einfühlung* is not only important for understanding aesthetic experience, but as the primary basis for recognizing each other as minded creatures (Stueber, 2017). Bridge (2011), referring to the aesthetic theory of Lipps, writes that for him "empathy does not primarily concern our ability to feel sympathy or compassion for other human beings, but refers, more generally, to a process by which we endow the object of our vision – whether human or non- human – with life, or with a soul" (p. 3). For Vischer (1873/1994) *Einfühlung* is the ability to project a bodily form and personality into inanimate objects.

---

268   For a related understanding of aesthetic experience see Thagard's discussion the emotional dynamics of the human pursuit of a sense of coherence in, *Coherence in Thought and Action* (2002); and *Hot Thought: mechanisms and applications of emotional cognition* (2006).

It is a kind of merging that he ascribes to "the pantheistic urge for union with the world" (p. 109). Taking another perspective, Wölfflin (1884/1994) in his dissertation, is concerned with "how it is possible that architectural forms are able to express emotion and mood?"

Wölfflin (1884/1994) also refers to Goethe's idea that one should be able to feel the effect of a beautiful space even when blind folded, because the architectural impression is not about seeing, but rather "essentially based on a direct body feeling" (pp. 149-162). **It is our body which makes it possible for us to have an aesthetic experience of architecture form**s.[269]

The concept of *Einfühlung* in its fundamental sense has a remarkable resemblance to the function of mirror-neurons discovered by Giacomo Rizzolatti in the ventral pre-motor area of monkeys, in the early 1990's at the University of Parma (Cinzia & Vittorio, 2009). Mirror-neurons, found in both primates and humans, fire when one acts and when one observes another performing the same action. Anytime one observes another doing something, the corresponding mirror neuron might fire in the observers mind allowing him/her to empathize with the other's feelings by mirroring higher actions and thereby constructing an implicit model through which the other can anticipate the other's intentions. Ramachandran (2011) and Damasio (1994), referring to Freeberg & Gallese (2007), suggests that mirror-neurons induce a kind of *embodied simulation* which may be the basis for empathic "responses to images in general and to works of art in particular" (p. 197). Embodied simulation not only induces a response to figurative works of art, but surprisingly with non-figurative abstract art and architecture as well. Freeberg & Gallese (2007) write that there is a growing body of "neuroscientific evidence clarifying the nature of empathy and the role of sensorimotor activity in empathy and emotion" establishing a definable and measurable basis for aesthetic judgment in the brain.[270]

---

[269] Unfortunately Wölfflin never developed this idea of how the body facilitates aesthetic experience. See Bridge (2011) pp. 10-12. However many of his intuitions as well as those of Lipps and Vischer have been validated by research in neuroaesthetics (Gallese & Gattara, 2015).

[270] See also Eberhard (2007) for a review of how neuroscience is influencing architecture practice in particular. Nicholson (1998) wrote an interesting article for *Harvard Business Review* that provides a good introduction to how evolutionary psychology can offer useful insights for understanding human behavior.

§ 7.9 Evolutionary Aesthetics

Two disciplines that have had a profound influence in the area of empirical aesthetics are evolutionary psychology and neuroaesthetics. Evolutionary psychology considers how humans evolved to experience aesthetic pleasure; neuroaesthetics considers it from the inner workings of the brain and body. These empirical approaches avoid some of the traditional problems of (philosophical) aesthetic theory, most notably the problem of subjectivism, and in terms of a transcendental (disembodied) universal truth. This approach to aesthetic experience is less concerned with defining what is considered beautiful, or even judging the quality of aesthetic experience. Rather the empirical approach starts off with observable evidence that humans have evolved in such a manner that physical environments induce feelings, that these feelings have qualities, with subtle variations, that result in knowledge, that with practice one can become more attuned to. Further as humans evolved there were some environmental experiences that began to be sought primarily for the pleasure they provided – as opposed for the survival or reproductive advantages they afforded – and that humans learned to intentionally manipulate the environment with the specific intention to induce those feelings.

Ramachandran (2011) writes,

Just as we consume gourmet food to generate complex, multidimensional taste and texture experiences that titillate our palate, we appreciate art as gourmet for the visual centers in the brain (as opposed to junk food which is analogous to kitsch). Even though the rules that artists exploit originally evolved because of their survival value, the production of art itself does not have survival value. **We do it because it's fun and that's all the justification it needs**. (p. 241)

Rusch and Voland (2013) write, "Humans are an aesthetic species. We react with aesthetic pleasure to a diverse array of phenomena" (p. 1). Why did humans evolve certain types of aesthetical preferences? Evolutionary aesthetics seeks to understand how human aesthetic preferences evolved and what their usefulness may have been in the evolution of the species.[271] See also Consoli (2014).

---

[271] The argument goes, if we accept that the discovery (not invention) of fire affected human biological evolution: teeth, digestion, etc.; why couldn't the (cultural) invention (not discovery) of some art forms (i.e. music, poetry, painting, sculpture) also have affected human biology: co-evolution.

Within the discipline of evolutionary psychology, aesthetic pleasure is understood as an *adaptive trait*, that is, "a cognitive system that produces aesthetical preferences" (Rusch & Voland, 2013, p. 1). Tinbergen (2005) proposes that this system comprises four main parts: (1.) An understanding of the ontogenetic development, i.e., the changes the trait undergoes and the regulations of these changes from conception through the various stages of life until the death of an individual. (2.) The phylogenetic development of the trait, i.e. its evolutionary history. (3.) Its proximate mechanisms, e.g. the neural circuitry and emotions controlling mental representations and behavior. (4.) Its ultimate function, i.e. the reason why the trait was promoted or at least conserved by natural selection (as quoted in Rusch & Voland, 2013, p. 113).

It is this last trait that is most often the topic for discussion in aesthetic theory. As discussed above in the section on Kant, aesthetic qualities and the pleasure that they induce were thought to require a posture of disinterestedness – that is, aesthetic qualities (properly understood) were thought to be devoid of function. By explicitly investigating the function of aesthetic pleasure in the evolutionary development of humans, evolutionary aesthetics seemed to be undermining this principle. However, this apparent discrepancy has been avoided by recognizing that the traditional (Kantian) view of the disinterested (immediate) quality of aesthetic pleasure is intended to describe the *proximate phenomenology of aesthetics*, while evolutionary aesthetics deals with the ultimate function of human aesthetic experience as a biological trait and its role in the evolution of cognitive systems. That is, how "the basic aesthetic preferences of homo sapiens[272] are argued to have evolved in order to enhance survival and reproductive success" (Dutton, 2003).[273]

---

[272] Human beings, however, are not the only species that has acquired aesthetic preferences in order to enhance survival and reproductive success. Other species also engage in deliberate behaviors that involve arranging objects, choosing colors and/or making patterns with the specific intent of eliciting an emotional response. The most famous of these is the male bower bird from Australia and New Guinea who build these elaborately decorated, individual and unique "bachelor pads" to attract mates. The bower bird collects clusters of flowers, berries, bits of bone, eggshell and pieces of plastic, foil and shards of glass, which he dutifully arranges in specific patterns to create a composition to his liking. It is not unusual for competing males to come by to rearrange his composition or steal individual objects to use in his composition. Interestingly enough, when the bower bird returns and sees that his composition has been tampered with, he immediately replaces misplaced objects and tidies up the arrangement. Individual females come to check out the males' compositions, and choose their mates accordingly. (See http://www.pbs.org/wnet/nature/bower-bird-blues-introduction/2109/)

[273] Clay (1908), writing on the origin of aesthetic emotion, writes, "The usual view indeed is to regard [aesthetic experience] as an adjunct to the serious business of survival, and yet its deep emotional influence, its soul affecting power seem to force upon us the conclusion that it too, as in love, hate, or fear, must draw its strength from some old instinct deeply planted and firmly fixed, as only the long fight for life has power to do; this it must be possible to trace back the aesthetic emotion to some instinctive necessary function or activity, that subsequently, when refined and raised into the ideal regions by the intellect, becomes artistic spirit (p. 282-283).

Dutton posits a *universalist* conception of human nature which regards the making of art as a *natural* human activity and experience. When considering aesthetic theories as diverse as Tolstoy, Schiller and Bell, Dutton identifies an element held in common – "they presuppose or posit the existence of a fundamental human nature, a set of characteristics, including interests and desires, and uniformity cross-culturally present in the constitution of human persons" (p. 267). As further evidence for a natural inclination to seek aesthetic pleasure he refers to Aristotle's mimetic naturalism – the pleasure people get from imitation.[274] Kant and Hume, he argues, also rely on this universality of aesthetic pleasure – Kant by his assent to *sensus communitas*; and Hume by claiming that "the general principles of taste are uniform in human nature." Further he argues, based on research by Martindale (1990)[275] that the (universal human) craving for novelty or the principle of *habituation*, is the "single force that has pushed art always in a consistent direction ever since the first work of art was made" (p. 11). This pleasure and instinctive delight in imitation and fascination with novelty that all humans seem to enjoy points to the likelihood that aesthetic pleasure is *natural* to (all) humans. This *universalist* conception, holds that there exists a human nature, which is stable, and posits that (1.) art is a predictable component of society and that (2.) art will have predictable content – insofar as the quality of an aesthetic experience can be predicted based on the likelihood that this or that stimulus will evoke similar feelings in one person to the next.[276]

The universal preference for certain kinds of aesthetic experiences has been documented through numerous experiments. One such notable experiment involved showing a series of photographs to children and adults of different landscapes. Children showed a demonstrable preference for open savannas, even when they had never seen such landscapes before (Orians & Heerwagen, 1992). A similar study was done where a systematic poll of the art preferences of people from 10 different countries in Europe, Asia, and the Americas recorded a uniform interests in the pictorial content of art worldwide (Komar & Melamid, 1997). Other cross-cultural studies have been done in literature and performance.

---

274   "For it is an instinct of human beings from childhood to engage in imitation (indeed, this distinguishes them from other animals: man is the most imitative of all and it is through imitation that he develops his earliest understanding); and it is equally natural that everyone enjoys imitative objects. A common occurrence indicates this: we enjoy contemplating the most precise images of things whose actual sight is painful to us, such as forms of the vilest animals and corpses" (Aristotle, *Poetics*).

275   Martindale (1990) argues that there is a *primordial content* in art that seeks to make use of emotion, greater complexity, and ornamentation, to increase the *arousal potential* of a style or genre until its potential for aesthetic arousal has been exhausted. This cycle repeats itself as new styles are explored though incremental development until audiences become satiated and new styles emerge.

276   For example see Jacobsen, Schubotz, Höfel, & Cramon (2006) see also Di Dio, Macaluso, Rizzolatti (2007)

From these kinds of studies Dutton (2003) proposes that there are certain *signal* characteristics of art that can be considered universal and cross-cultural. These include expertise or virtuosity, non-utilitarian pleasure, style, criticism, imitation, special focus, and imaginative experience. It is Dutton's conviction that the (cultural) relativism that has become "dominant orthodoxy" in recent years has resulted in a "dismissive attitude toward universal values in art," and has resulted in a "general denial of the possibility of universal aesthetic values" (p. 275).[277]

Dissanayake (1999) looks to our propensity for "making special" as an indicator of evolutionary genesis of aesthetic emotion.

Artists in all media deliberately perform operations described by ethologists[278] as they occur instinctively during ritualized behavior: they simplify or formalize, repeat (sometimes with variation), exaggerate, and elaborate ordinary materials, bodies, surroundings, times, beats, body movements, semantics and syntax, motifs, ideas – thereby making these things more than ordinary. (p. 148)

Dissanayake calls this "making things more than ordinary" *artification*. Artification is "the deliberate use of the proto-aesthetic operations that evolved... as mechanisms used unconsciously by ancestral human mothers in the highly adaptive context of reinforcing emotional bonds with ever more helpless infants" (p. 156). She argues, children, due to various evolutionary and physiological adaptations, are born in a highly vulnerable state.[279] As such they require a great deal of care and nurturing before they can survive on their own. To facilitate this, certain behaviors evolved both from the infant's side (such as a sustained gaze, smiles, cooing, etc.) and from the mother's or care-giver's side (such as baby talk, bouncing, facial expressions) that provided emotional pleasure and deepened the bond. The reward that reinforced these behaviors was (emotional) pleasure, not unlike other critical survival behaviors such as sex, eating, and sleep.

---

277   See Gombrich (1987) and Crowley (1958) for an overview of aesthetic judgment and cultural relativism.

278   The naturalistic study of behavior from an evolutionary perspective. (Burghart, 2005)

279   It has been observed that the human preference for upright walking required multiple adaptations to the physiology of humans, including a shortened and narrower birth canal than early primates. Meanwhile the human brain was growing in size. In order to make it possible for the infant to pass through the birth canal, it was necessary to give birth to an infant with a skull that was somewhat flexible and a brain that was not yet fully developed. As a result human infants are helpless after birth, requiring considerable brain development outside the womb and significant care and vigilance (Gould, 1977).

These *behavioral* adaptations, or *adapted innate affinitive expressions*, assured that mothers would be "emotionally bounded to their immature offspring and thus willing to provide the necessary extended care over months and years" (p. 154).[280]

The hunger for this kind of pleasure (emotional state), that provided a sense of comfort and well-being, became ritualized as the human brain increasingly became a sense making organ, resulting in the practice of *deliberate artification* which contributed to socialization and cooperation among ancestral humans. As humans evolved we learned that certain ritualized behavior (rhythms, colors, special arrangements, patterns, textures, etc.) in the right combination, had the ability to induce a desired/desirable emotional state. For Dissanayake, its is not so much the making of art as it is an evolutionary adaptation, that fed the hunger for the emotional benefits that "making special" (artification) and led to the evolutionary adaptation.

Gould and Vrba (1982) introduced the concept of *exaptation*. This concept has made a particularly significant contribution understanding **how we evolved to seek out aesthetic experience, no longer for evolutionary advantage, but for the sake of the pleasure itself**. As discussed above, adaptations are characteristics "currently enhancing fitness and that were constructed by natural selection to function in that particular role; thus, their selection context has not varied historically" (Lieberman & Vrba, 2005, p. 119). However, there are some characteristics that we now have that were not initially determined by natural selection or evolved for a different role. These are exaptations. Chatterjee (2014) describes exaptations as "evolutionary by-products that become useful as the environment changes" (p. 162). Ramachandran (2011) describes them as "a mechanism that originally evolved for one function and then provided the opportunity for something very different to evolve. i.e. language" (p. 166). There is some evidence that exaptation may help to explain how it happened that we came to simply enjoy some more refined experiences for the sake of the subtle experience that they provide.[281]

---

[280]   Adaptation, in evolutionary theory, is understood as an anatomical structure, physiological process, or behavior pattern that adds to ancestral individual's ability to survive and reproduce in competition with other members of their species (Crawford, 1998).

[281]   Consoli (2015) writes, "[the] neuropsychological approach is increasingly framing aesthetic experience as a complex and multifaceted experience of knowledge—more precisely, as a specific implementation of the epistemic goal of knowing that becomes active when people experience objects (and not only artworks) adopting an aesthetic viewing orientation."

§ 7.10   Neuroaesthetics

Rather, there are indeed universal patterns of appreciation of beauty – aesthetic
preferences valid for humans in every culture. All humans evaluate objects that
correspond to these patterns as beautiful... Analogously, recent brain research also
teaches that the experience of the beautiful is determined by the internal architecture
of the brain, that our subjective neural disposition is decisive for beauty – that beauty is
indeed brain happiness.

(Wolfgang Welsch, 2008, p. 7 & 29)

Neuroaesthetics seeks to understand aesthetic experience from the point of view of
neuroscience, cognitive science and evolutionary psychology. Neuroaesthetics starts
with two presuppositions: (1.) All human behavior has a neural counterpart, that is
to say that there is "no thought, no desire, no emotion, no dream, no flight of fancy
that is not tethered to the activity of our nervous system." (2.) Evolution has played a
significant role in shaping the human brain and behaviors (Chatterjee, 2014, p. xi).

Neuroaesthetics is a branch of empirical aesthetics, "a branch of psychology dedicated
to studying the nature of beauty, aesthetics, art, artistic production, aesthetic
experience, and audience responses to artworks in a broad range of media" (Seeley,
2014). Empirical Aesthetics has its roots in the work of Fechner. In *Vorschule der
Äesthetik*, Fechner (1876) makes a distinction between *speculative aesthetics* (from
above) and *empirical aesthetics* (from below). His was not so much an aesthetics *per se*
as it was a methodology (from below), that relied on (objective) research methods that
sought to understand people's preferences. As such, **the goal of empirical aesthetics is
not to define what is beautiful, but rather to identify empirical evidence that helps us
to understand the nature of aesthetic experience** – why and how certain arrangements
of objects, colors, proportional relationships, produce/induce certain qualities of
experience. The fundamental presupposition of empirical aesthetics is that as people
all experience the same world as embodied beings with fundamentally the same
bodies, there is a likelihood that what induces an aesthetic experience in one person,
will induce a similar experience in another.

Chatterjee (2014), referring to Shimamura (2012), writes, "**aesthetic experiences have
the core triad of sensations, meaning, and emotion**" (p. 138). Each component of the *core
triad* has different neural underpinnings that vary depending on which sensory system is
being stimulated, as each has a different entrance point to the brain. By sensations they
mean "the multi-sensory experience of vivid colors, bold lines, meter and melody." By
emotions they mean pleasure evoked by art, disgust and other more subtle emotions.

Meaning could include political, intellectual, religious, or subversive. Aesthetic pleasure extends beyond "basic appetitive pleasures in three ways."(p. 111) (1.) They tap into neural systems that are biased toward liking but not wanting. (2.) They are nuance, with admixtures of complex emotions. (3.) They are influenced by experience, memory, knowledge. **Aesthetic pleasure is kind of optimum combination of sensations, meaning and emotion**. Its hard to say exactly what the mixture is, but you know it when you are experiencing it.

Initially, neuroresearchers relied heavily on single cases of patients suffering from brain damage, lesions or neurodegenerative diseases (Chatterjee, 2014). These cases allowed neuroscientists to identify areas of the brain that served specific functions, and how damage to these parts effect or do not effect the cognitive capabilities of the patient. More recently a good deal of the research in neuroaesthetics relies on neuro-imaging studies, such as DOI, MRI, fMRI, PET and others. These studies provide the data necessary to construct a "basic picture of the neural correlates of visual aesthetic appreciation" (Cela-Conde, Agnati, Huston, Mora, & Nadal, 2011). The introduction of non-invasive means for studying the brain has had a significant impact on the discipline.

In their article "Toward A Brain-Based Theory of Beauty," Ishizu & Zeki (2011) introduce neuroaesthetics with a quote from Burke (1756): "Beauty is, for the greater part, some quality in bodies acting mechanically upon the human mind by the intervention of the senses" (p. 1). The quote suggests that there is some neuro-mechanism that perceives "qualities acting upon the human mind" involved in experiencing beauty. The objective of Ishizu & Zeki's research is to find out if in fact such a [neuro]mechanism exists – one that correlates information from various sense systems. And if so, how does such a mechanism correlate information from different sense systems to simulate a sense of beauty. There were two principle results of their study: (1.) Through the use of brain imaging studies activity was identified in a single region of the brain that correlated with both visual and musical beauty, (2.) thus establishing that there is a linear relationship between a particular neural signal and the intensity of the experience declared by the subject. In very simple terms, these results provided them with a basis for a *brain-based definition of beauty*, where beauty is understood as a particular quality of aesthetic experience.

Neuroaesthetics "engages in scientific investigation of the brain-body physiological correlates of the aesthetic experience of particular human symbolic expressions, such as works of art and architecture" (Gallese & Gattara, 2015, p. 162). Gallese & Gattara propose that there are four reasons why neuroscience matters to architecture:

— Relationship between perception and empathy: As the of concepts of empathy, as described above, have been validated new insight has been gained into the cognitive function of art and how we experience architectural space (p. 162).

— Embodied simulation: That the neuromechanisms we use when encountering the world, are similar to those that we use when exploring a fictional (imagined) world (p. 164).

— Embodied simulation allows us to enter into the design word feelingly, to be aware of the *qualia* of a mental image (p. 164).[282]

— Intercorporeality: Research into the function of mirror-neurons has demonstrated that the cortical motor system functions not only as a movement machine, but it is an integral part of our cognitive system, allowing "direct apprehension of the relational quality linking space, objects, and others' actions to our body." Mirror neurons also facilitate *intercorporeality* – "the mutual resonance of intentionally meaningful sensorimotor behaviors" (p. 166).

Just as designers are expected to know how to make an efficient and effective use of space; a stable but soaring structure, and a building facade where everything looks just right, so they are expected to design a built environment that induces the (right mix of) optimal hedonic value that results in an intended quality of aesthetic experience.

The above overview of aesthetic theory provides a context in which to appreciate the complexities surrounding the discussion of aesthetic qualities. The empirical theories provide a somewhat more objective way of understanding aesthetic experience than the more philosophical approach. The above gives substantial evidence that all humans experience aesthetic qualities in their environment. In addition, the above also identifies several ways of understanding the cognitive mechanisms that make these aesthetic experiences possible. Also evidence has been cited that supports the claim that the same cognitive mechanisms that are stimulated by our environments and trigger the feelings that together result in an aesthetic experience, are the very same that we make use of when inhabiting an imaginary space.

---

282   See also Xenakis, Argyris, & Darzentas (2012), "The Functional Role of Emotions in Aesthetic Judgment"; and Wilson and Foglia (2011), who observe, "Electrophysiological results have shown that observing the action executed by another individual blocks the *mu rhythm* (as opposed to the *alpha* rhythm) of the observer, thus providing evidence for a *resonance system*, which links the observed action to the action of the subject's own motor repertoire " (sec. 5.4).

Thus supporting the idea mentioned earlier, based on Polanyi and Schön, that when designing, the designer possesses the possibility to inhabit the design world feelingly, and thereby assess the aesthetic quality of the emerging design solution both as an external representation. Aesthetic experience is kind of embodied knowing. Embodied knowing is aesthesis.

The following are a representative sampling of some standard design methodologies. None of them is of a particularly fine grain. They are intended to describe, in broad strokes, how some designers think that designing occurs. This will be followed by a synthesis of the methodologies discussed and a proposal for a methodology that includes how experiential performance expectations, especially aesthetic experience, influences and drives the design process.

8 Methodologies

The act of producing that is directed by intent to produce something that is enjoyed in the immediate experience of perceiving has qualities that a spontaneous or uncontrolled activity does not have.

(Dewey, 1934/2005, p.50)

The design process, is what happens between (and including) defining the problem and generating the solution. There are numerous ways of describing the design process, as well as numerous design processes. [283] Design processes are descriptions of how designers design. Methodologies are ways designers go about or strategies they use to generate design solutions. Methodologies are a kind of meta-heuristic (not an algorithm), or purpose-driven system of methods, that describes a way of approaching a design problem that has a likelihood of leading to an acceptable (satisficing) solution. Methodologies can be general purpose or situational. The distinction between design processes (descriptive) and methodologies (strategic) is subtle. In many cases there may be no practical difference between a process and a methodology. Nonetheless it is important to keep in mind that the design process or the design methodology is *not* designing; both are artificial constructs intended to offer insight into how this human cognitive ability called designing occurs. [284]

---

283   For an overview of multiple design theories from an engineering perspective see Tomiyama et al. (2009) who present a vigorous evaluation and means of categorization. They explain that the ultimate goal of design research is to identify general and abstract (that is universal) laws. Design research theories, take many forms, including the observation of phenomena, attempts at universal laws and mathematical formulas. Tomiyama et al.categorize these theories into four general categories along two axes: one is "concrete vs. abstract and the other is "individual vs. general." This results in a matrix that categorizes design theories as: concrete and individual; concrete and general; abstract and individual; and abstract and general. See also Jormakka (2008) who describes methods that include: nature and geometry as authorities, music and mathematics as models, accident and the unconscious as sources, rationalist approaches, precedent, responses to site, generative processes. Pressman (2012), from years of teaching design proposes processes that to "help students and young professionals in creating excellent designs, even magical buildings..." (p. 8). All of the methods follow the same basic structure described above.

284   Coyne et al. (1990) write, "In modeling design we do not attempt to say what design or how human designers do what they do, but rather provide models by which we can explain and perhaps replicate certain aspects of design behavior" (p. 11).

Cross and Roozenburg (1992, p. 33) write:

There is no well-formulated consensus model of the design process in architecture (nor any longer in industrial design) but we may conclude that there has emerged a 'type model' with the following features: It has essentially a spiral structure; It recognizes the importance of pre-structures, presuppositions or protomodels as the origins of solution concepts; It emphasizes a conjecture-analysis cycle in which the designer and the other participants refine their understanding of both the solution and the problem in parallel; It assumes design problems, by definition, to be ill-defined problems.

In retrospect, we might say that in architecture and industrial design the attention of the design researchers and theorists shifted from the vertical (linear, procedural) dimension of the design process to the horizontal (iterative, problem-solving) dimension. (p. 331)

Describing how designers work based on evidence from design protocols, Cross (2004) observes,

designers start by exploring the [problem space], and find, discover, or recognize a partial structure. That partial structure is then used to provide them also with a partial structuring of the [solution space]. They consider the implications of the partial structure within the [solution space], use it to generate some initial ideas for the form of a design concept, and so extend and develop the partial structuring. . . They transfer the developed partial structure back into the [problem space], and again consider implications and extend the structuring of the [problem space]. Their goal . . . is to create a matching problem-solution pair. (p. 434)

Cross identifies the tendency of (expert) designers to first look for coherence (partial structure). This sense of coherence provides them with an inclination – a bias heuristic – to pursue one solution path over another as he defines the problem space. As the partial structure initially discovered/recognized and used to structure the problem space begins to structure the solution space, this sense of coherence (feeling) motivates/drives the design process, resulting is congruence between the problem-solution pair.

§ 8.1　There is no All-encompassing Model of Designing

Lawson & Dorst (2009), in an effort to describe how designers work, describe designing – not unlike Dong, 2009 – from several points of view in terms of *design as*: designing as a mixture of creativity and analysis; designing as problem solving; designing as learning; designing as evolution; designing as the creation of solutions to problems; designing as integrating into a coherent whole; designing as a fundamental human activity. Their point is that even after picking a design solution up, rotating it around, and looking at it from several different perspectives they "still cannot find a single all-encompassing model of designing" (p. 46). The insight gained from this exercise is that the design methodology that best describes how anyone designs is first determined by how he thinks of *design as*. However, how one thinks of design as, is not static. One's understanding, experience, and ability, all influence how one thinks of *design as*.[285] What a beginner thinks of *design as* and what an expert thinks of *design as*, are not the same. As such the methodologies appropriate for a beginner vs. an expert are not the same. There are methodologies that are developmentally more appropriate for beginners and methodologies that are developmentally better suited for experts (Curry, 2014).

§ 8.2　Teaching Devices

The usefulness of design methodologies is not limited to describing how designers work, or as a means of analysis to improve the quality of the design product, but they can also be helpful as teaching devices. This was the intended purpose of the methodology developed by Thornley. Thornley returning to teaching from professional practice was appalled at the state of architecture education. To him the student designs *looked* like modern architecture

---

but there was little functional analysis, and appearance (both of the building itself and, most particularly, of the drawing) accounted for nearly all. All the tutor could do was to compare his prejudices with the students; there was no rational basis for criticism. (Broadbent, 1973, p. 264)

---

[285]　In a previously published article (Curry, 2014) I made use of these categories as a means for describing design acquisition as a developmental process.

Thornley developed a process that was both a systematic basis for teaching and for his own theory of architecture, as a reflection on "what an architect actually does when he is designing something" (p. 265). The process he proposes is organized into four *stages*, each with their related heuristics: accumulation of data → isolation of a general concept or *form* → development of the *form* into the final scheme → presentation of the final scheme. This process, with its associated heuristics, like Polanyi's methodology, assisted the design tutor as he taught the student how to design providing *cognitive scaffolding* (as defined earlier).

§ 8.3   Classification Schemes

Wynn and Clarkson (2005) propose three *classification schemes* for models of designing based on *practical relevance*: "stage vs. activity-based models; problem vs. solution-oriented literature; and abstract vs. analytical vs. procedural approaches" (p. 35). Stage vs. activity-based models, follow the distinction made above between *phase-based* and state-*based processes* where stage-based models are primarily linear, and activity-based models are more spiral.

Their problem vs. solution classification builds on the observation that design strategies can be either problem or solution driven, depending on the level of expertise or the discipline of the designer. This classification describes a meta-approach to design problems observed by Jones (1992), Cross (1992), Lawson (2005), Dorst (2010), Badke-Schaub et al. (2011), and others, that distinguishes the difference between how an expert and a beginner approaches a design problem. As the may be recalled from above, Hillier et al. (1972) argue, against the rationalist position that holds a problem-solver must approach a problem from a posture of disinterested-ness, that designers "must, and do, pre-structure their problems in order to solve them." The argument is that expert designers, relying on tacit (embodied) knowledge and with years of experience, pre-structure a design problem in a manner that anticipates how he will solve it (solution-oriented). While beginners, with little experience and limit knowledge of the domain, tend to rely on research, analysis and procedure to solve the problem (problem-oriented). The problem-oriented approach is rooted in an approach to problem solving similar to Polya' methodology, and calls to mind Rittel with his claim that defining the problem IS the problem. The implication being that once a designer truly understands the problem, the solution will be self-evident. Wynn and Clarkson describe Darke (1979) and Jones (1992) as examples of solution-oriented models.

Their final classification is abstract vs. analytical vs. procedural classification is more a typology of the types of literature related to design methodology. Analytical approaches are used to evaluate the process for the purpose of improving designing in a particular instance. Procedural approaches are generally distinguished as being descriptive or prescriptive. A further distinction Wynn and Clarkson (2005) make is in the scope of the procedural approaches, described as: models and methods. Models "refer to a description or prescription of the morphological form of scope in procedural approaches" (p. 40). This is similar with the meaning of *methodology* used in this research. Methods prescribe systematic procedures to support stages within a model. Further both models (methodologies) and methods often "fall between two extremes." These are either designing focused, which are intended as (prescriptive) means for generating better products; or these are project focused which are intended as means to improve the management of a design project.

As the primary focus of this research architectural design expertise, the Wynn and Clarkson classification that best describes the model of interest here is the stage-based, solution-oriented, descriptive, procedural model with its associated methods. There are many other classifications schemes. The usefulness of these schemes is that they provide a framework within which to compare and contrast multiple design methodologies.

§ 8.4 Ways of Thinking about Designing

Broadbent proposed a normative model (methodology) of how architects work that follows the pattern described above: problem → [analysis/synthesis/evaluation] → solution. His is a more-or-less information driven, rationalist approach. Perhaps more insightful than his methodology, Broadbent (1973), coming to designing as a sociologist, brings two important perspectives to this overview of methodology, these are (1.) four *ways* of thinking about designing (pragmatic, iconic, analogical, and canonic); and (2.) an assessment of the changing situation of, and the identification of performance expectations for architectural design. His *ways* of thinking about designing, have to do with what the expected outcome of designing is to be. Lawson (2005, pp. 203-205) summarizes these four *ways* succinctly: (1.) Pragmatic designing is essentially a traditional and conservative making use of available materials methods of construction, generally without innovation. (2.) Iconic designing – perhaps even more conservative – is where a designer might make use of existing design solutions (styles) and modify them to meet new conditions. (3.) Canonic designing looks to the use of rules such as planning grids, proportioning systems, classic orders, Corbu's modular and the like.

(4.) Analogical designing looks to other fields and disciplines to find new ways of structuring the problem. This this last way is currently very popular in design schools. No one of these ways of design is really sufficient. One would think that an expert designer, while perhaps emphasizing one way over another, would make use of all the ways. Certainly a concern for how a building is built, a willingness to make use of existing successful solutions, an appreciation for proportion, and the pursuit of new ways of thinking about a design problem are all of value. What is revealing, and relevant to this research, is Lawson's clear preference for the analogical way evidenced by his enthusiastic description, writing "Broadbent himself seems to suggest that the 'analogical' methods are the most promising of these four for form generation" (p. 205). He considers the use of human form, organic form, metaphor and narrative all as outgrowths of this idea. But, like Broadbent said, it all depends of what you expect of designing.

In terms of expectations for the product of designing, Broadbent (1973) observes that "the new maths, with a certain amount of statistics, has been almost as influential in the development of new design methods as all the other sources and disciplines put together… raising design to the highest level of abstraction" (p. 272). This desire for "the abstract purity of a concept" did not stop at designing, but led to a "tendency to think of people as abstractions… rather than as persons, and the same unwillingness to think of a building (or anything else in design) as a concrete physical thing" (p. 272). Still, Broadbent writes, there are those (empiricists) who find these views unacceptable, who insist on seeing "the building as a real, tangible thing which modifies the physical environment, and in doing so impinges on the user's senses" (p. 272). Their ideal would be, if it were possible "to work again pragmatically – manipulating real materials to full size on the actual site" (p. 272).

His design thinking will tend to be analogic or repetitive, and his approach to design will depend as far as possible on comparing his experience of things which he has observed in the real world. His own sketches, drawings and models fall into this category; these will be comparable, in perceptual transaction, with his ever-changing visual aura, thermal and other sensory experience of real buildings. Some of the finest designers in history have worked in these ways… (Broadbent, 1973, p. 272)

Still, there is a rationalist, "parallel tradition, in which the abstract geometry of the designing analogue seemed even more important to the architect than the sensory stimulus which the building would afford its users" (Broadbent, 1973, p. 273). It is this *empiricist* vs. *rationalist* dichotomy, that this research is challenging, in light of new research in the area of embodied cognition and the embedded ways that design expertise is thought to be acquired.

§ 8.5   Divergence, Transformation, Convergence

On one level the normative model of designing (problem → [analysis/synthesis/
evaluation] → solution) described by Broadbent is sufficient. Jones (1992) taking a
systems approach to the design process "disintegrates" the design process to "make
public the thinking that a designer traditionally keeps to himself" (p. 69).

While disintegrating the "design act" Jones focuses on the dynamics of the design
process, recognizing that "the way in which this mixing of judgment and calculation…
is not settled" (p. 63). His process, like Broadbent's is based on what he calls the
"simplest and most common" three essential stages: [analysis → synthesis →
evaluation], except that in the process of disintegrating designing he redefines
the stages from analysis to divergence; from to transformation; from evaluation to
convergence. Jones also makes note of the on-going interrelationship and feedback
between the three stages, making it a less linear model of designing. His model is
summarized as: problem → [divergence/transformation/convergence] → solution,
where the problem and solution are both outside the brackets.

— Divergence involves expanding the problem space (boundary of the situation) large
   enough to seek a fruitful solution
— Transformation involves pattern-making, seeking cohesion, fun, flash of insight, how to
   think about the problem
— Convergence involves reducing variables and options until a final solution begins
   to emerge

While these terms are analogous with the procedures traditionally used to describe the
design process, they are meant to describe *means* that facilitate the discovery of new
methods that are needed to face new kinds of problems. Jones then uses these terms to
both describe existing methodologies and to explore new ones. While Jones does refer
to divergence/transformation/convergence as stages in the design process, he does
not hold that these stages occur sequentially.

§ 8.6 Pre-structuring the Design Problem

The description of the design process proposed by Hillier et al. (1972) is a more integrated, than a procedural, process or linear model. Theirs is a break with the rationalist, analysis-synthesis "notion of design" that was popular with design theorists at the time. One of their main critiques of the trend at the time to adopt a rationalist approach to designing was the claim that a designer approach a problem with no presuppositions (an *innocent eye*).[286] They argue that this rationalist claim of "disinterestedness," is a myth and that its time to simply accept that expert designers do approach design problems with presuppositions, that is that they *pre-structure* design problems. Being able to pre-structure a problem in light of previous experience, mastery of the domain, and vast situated strategic knowledge, is in fact what distinguishes an expert from a novice. From Hillier's perspective, the rationalist approach is an illusion that has failed. They argue that if this rationalistic approach is so good then why is it that "designers do not produce better buildings out of the information [design] research provides, and why, with expanding technological means and user requirements the theoretical open ended-ness of architectural problems lead to so little fundamental variety in solutions proposed." Hillier (1972) asks, why not just embrace the reality, along with Ryle (1949) and Polanyi (2009), that **"the cognitive schemes by which we interpret the world and pre-structure our observations" are a precondition to doing science and design** (p. 3).[287]

Free of the prohibition to pre-structure a design problem, they propose an alternative theory. To explain how their theory works, and the consequences of accepting that designers really do pre-structure their design problems, they offer a simple scenario:

---

286   This argument is reminiscent of Gombrich's critique of the myth of the "innocent eye," a term to which Ruskin gave currency, and the importance of *schemata* in perception. Gombrich (1960/2000) writes, "it is so hard for us all to disentangle what we really see from what we merely know and thus to recover the innocent eye" (p. 223). It speaks to the cognitive ability to shift focus from what one thinks one sees (informed by pre-existing schemata) and what one actually sees (trying to just see what is there), to be aware that one is doing it and the difference between the two.

287   Polanyi (1966) calls this *tacit inference*, writing that "no rules can account for the way a good idea is found for starting an inquiry; and there are no firm rules either for the verification or the refutation of the proposed solution of a problem" (p. 1). His argument is that scientists because of their training and years of practice, have acquired a "way" of seeing things (making sense of the world), that their perception (way of scientific knowing) has developed the capacity to perceive in nature certain patterns and systems that non-scientists (typically) do not: "Scientific knowing consists in discerning gestalten that indicate a true coherence in nature" (p. 1). Gestalten here is used in the sense of perceived order (*the tacit apprehension of coherence*), when we apprehend something as a whole, we "see its parts differently from the way we see them in isolation" (p. 3) as differentiated from a simple aggregation of parts. For a concise description of how gestalten works in perception see Arnheim (1987).

We can imagine a man and an object he will create as though separated by a space which is filled, on the one hand, with tools and raw materials which we can call his 'instrumental set' (or perhaps technological means) and on the other a productive sequence or process by which an object can be realized. If time is excluded from the space, we can conceive of the 'instrumental set' as though laid out on a table, and constituting a field of latencies and pre-constraints. If time is in the space, then the instrumental set is, as it were, arranged in a procedure or process. (Hillier, Musgrove, & O'Sullivan, 1972, p. 6)

The *instrumental set* (technological means) is the "stuff" of architectural design, including design criteria/ constraints, codes/zoning ordinance, site considerations, functional requirements, structure systems, mechanical/electrical/HVAC systems, materials and methods of construction, social/cultural/economic/environmental consideration, etc. These are all laid out on a table. All of this stuff possesses *latencies* – characteristics and properties (potentialities) or affordances (Gibson, 1986) – that offer designing opportunities.[288] Rather than thinking of materials, codes, functional requirements and structure as "constraints" that limit the "creativity" of the designer, these are thought of as designing opportunities. These opportunities that emerge from discovering latencies (gleaned from the properties and characteristics of the instrumental set) then need to be integrated somehow into a cohesive whole.

On the other table, "our man" is faced with multiple *productive sequences* (methodologies, strategies, procedures) – ways of thinking about (processing) the instrumental set that will lead to any number of solutions of which he needs to pursue one that will work within an acceptable range. All productive sequences (strategies) are of three types. This fictitious man then is faced with choosing between one of the three. He can follow some predetermined process (for example, a step-by-step linear design methodology) which will lead to a definite design/plan of a preconceived object (building type/form/personal obsession) or one based on pure imagination (impose a form with little consideration of the instrumental set).

---

288   Not unlike the possibilities offered by asking a brick what it wants to be.

Or he can "interrogate his instrumental set, by an understanding of its latencies in relation to general object [building] types" (p. 7) to generate a form from which a design solution may be developed. For example, ask the brick what it wants to be and see where that goes.[289]

In other words, the instrumental set is understood as the *problem space* which is *framed*[290] by the designer's (intrinsic/extrinsic) pre-structuring of the problem (setting expectations/conjecture) be they be based on a knowledge of the solution types or by knowledge of the latencies of the instrumental set. The designer then (having already pre-structured or framed the problem) considers the instrumental set (engages in a dialectic between what is on the table and the objects that are possible to produce from them (in light of an expected outcome). Then by engaging in a tacit productive sequence he explores multiple possible solutions (solution paths). The designer needs to engage in some process of *variety reduction* (bias heuristic) so that the possible solutions can be reduced to one that will result in "not the building, but at one remove, sets of instructions for building." For Hillier et al. (1972) the product of designing (proximate goal) is not a building, but rather "a set of descriptive documents of increasing refinement and specificity," not unlike Habraken's *functional approximation* (p. 10). These are "sets of instruction for building," not a set of documents that describe/represent a possible building.

This concept of *variety reduction* is essential. Up until now, most of the methodologies, described the various phases, stages or states of a design process. But, there has been little mention regarding how the designer proceeds through the process. Newell and Simon's process was motivated by searching for the optimal combination of variables that would result in a satisfying solution. Polanyi's methods provided a meta-heuristic that promised to increase the likelihood that the problem-solver would find the optimal solution. The decision-making criteria for these processes is dependent on verifiable deductive logic.

---

289   This second approach described by Hillier is not unlike the great architect and educator Luis Kahn's suggestion to his students, when they lacked inspiration, and when analysis and functionalism failed them, to ask the materials what they want to be: "You say to a brick, 'What do you want, brick?' And brick says to you, 'I like an arch.' And you say to brick, 'Look, I want one, too, but arches are expensive and I can use a concrete lintel.' And then you say: 'What do you think of that, brick?' Brick says: 'I like an arch.'" https://www.theguardian.com/artanddesign/2013/feb/26/louis-kahn-brick-whisperer-architect

290   A frame is "an active perspective that both describes and perceptually changes a given situation" (Kolko, 2011, p.13).

Heuristics that are effective in reducing the search area, and eliminating solution paths have already been discussed that are effective when faced with well-defined problems. But there are aspects of the design process that have already been observed that make the need for variation reduction more complicated.

§ 8.7 Design Abduction

As discussed above, cognition (thinking) is often described three ways: deductive, inductive and abductive. Kees Dorst (2010) writing about the nature of design thinking (Rowe, 1987), offers an accessible way of describing the differences between these three ways of thinking.

Dorst (2010) recommends a return to the basics, back to "the formal logic behind design reasoning." Dorst's model, similar to the basic components given above (problem → [problem-framing/solution-seeking] → solution), involves three components that make up the basic equation: **what** is the problem, **how** to solve it (where methodology is understood as problem-framing/solution-seeking), to achieve the desired **outcome** (solution). In deductive thinking "we know 'what' the players in a situation will need to attend to, and we know 'how' they will operate together," thus allowing us to "safely predict the results" (p. 132). In inductive thinking "we know the 'what' in the situation, and we can observe the results. But we do not know the 'how'" (p. 132). Both deductive and inductive thinking help to predict "phenomena that already exist in the world," the outcome is a *result*. Abductive thinking helps to create new things, where the outcome is a value. Dorst makes a distinction between *normal* abduction and *design* abduction. Normal abduction, is typically associated with problem-solving, where we know what the methodology (working principle) is and we know the desired outcome (value), what we don't know is what (thing) will produce this value. For design abduction we know what the desired outcome (value) is, but we don't know what the problem (thing) is and we don't know *how* we will solve it. For Dorst, the problem of designing is the problem of how to solve it.

§ 8.8   Reflective Conversation with the Situation

Schön proposes a comprehensive theory of how designer's work that is fundamentally a critique, of the (positivist) understanding of professional education founded on *technical rationalism*.[291] His is a theory of "reflection-on-action, reflection-in-action, responding to problematic situations, problem-framing, problem-solving, and the priority of practical knowledge over abstract theory" that finds its roots in the writings of Dewey (Shapiro H. , 2010, p. 311).[292] Schön is not writing about architecture *per se*, but rather proposing an epistemological alternative (similar to the critique of prescriptive methodologies above), where the actual practices of professionals rather than science or theory (only) constitute the core of professional *knowledge*.

Schön was neither an architect, nor involved directly in any design profession. He was a philosopher (a pragmatist in the line of Dewey), a policy maker, scholar and teacher. Schön turned to university-based architectural studio design education as an alternative model for professional education. In so doing, Schön – making use of design protocols and direct observation – studied the studio as a model teaching method for professional education. His studies, critiques and insights have resulted in not only a theory of how the studio works as a teaching tool, but also how designers design.

Schön, like Ryle and Polanyi, recognizes **the limitations of a positivistic philosophy of science293 and technical rationality as a basis for real life problem-solving.**

---

291   "A view of professional knowledge [where] professional activity consists in instrumental problem solving made rigorous by the application of scientific theory and technique" (Schön, 2009, p.21).

292   Dewey, along with the technical rationalists, accepted science as a valid method of reflection. However he takes issue with science as the primary (only valid) method of reflection (real knowledge) because science does not require verification and often is disconnected with the actual experiences of practitioners and clients, claiming that "scientific inquiry is merely an intermediate stage, a kind of 'time out' in a process which begins when practice becomes unsettled or problematic" (Waks, 2001, p.40). The result is that problems encountered in practice are studied outside of their context, where inquiry guided by scientific method result in theories that are to be applied in practice before they can be verified or proved to be relevant. The process ends there. However, for Dewey, the process only really ends when the results of the scientific inquiry are carried back into practice and conformed in the experience of practitioners.

293   Schön (1985 p.19) refers to a quote by Bernstein, "There is not a single major thesis advanced by nineteenth century Positivists or the Vienna Circle that has not been devastatingly criticized when measured by the Positivist's own standards for philosophical argument. The original formulation of the analytic-synthetic dichotomy and the verifiability criterion on meaning have been abandoned. It has been effectively shown that the Positivist's understanding of the natural sciences and the formal discipline is grossly oversimplified. Whatever one's final judgment about the current disputes in the post-empiricist philosophy and history of science... there is rational agreement about the inadequacy of the original Positivist understanding on science, knowledge, and meaning" (1976, p. 207).

Referencing Glazer (1974), Schön (1985) identifies three characteristics of a problem that is well-suited to be solved by traditionally trained "technical experts": the problem is clearly defined, goals are relatively fixed, and phenomena lend themselves to the categories of available theory and technique (p. 17). Unlike Simon, Rittel, Rowe and Lawson, Schön does not define a new category for design problems (i.e.: ill-structured, wicked, ill-defined, etc.) as a *special* kind of problem. Rather, Schön (1985) observes that the structure of *real world problems* makes them difficult to solve for "technical experts" who due to their professional education, rely too heavily on the methods and theories of technical rationality, leading to what he calls the "dilemma of rigor or relevance" (p. 15). Expectations of practice came to hold that professional rigor was only to be found in "well-formed problems of instrumental choice whose solution [relies on] research-based theory and technique" (p. 15). As such, the professional who limits his practice to the application of *rigorous research-based technique* soon finds himself with only three options: choose the high ground by narrowly limiting his practice to purely technical problems; be selectively inattentive to data that does not fit within their theories; or use junk categories, to explain away variables that do not fit within their theories (1991, pp. 240-241).[294] The other option is to "choose the swampy lowland;" jump into the messy, murky sometimes confusing reality of the situation. The "swampy lowland" is what Schön means by the "intermediate zones of practice – the situations of complexity and uncertainty, the unique cases that require artistry, the elusive task of problem setting, the multiplicity of professional identities..." (1985, p. 12) – **where the rigorous methods of the technical expert fail, the embodied, tacit knowledge of the expert practitioner takes over**. But this choice of relevance over rigor, soft science over hard science, tends to leave the practitioner with "a nagging sense of inferiority." To validate his position as an expert, he needs a science that validates his ability.[295]

Schön, like Hillier, accepts that the (expert) practitioner/designer approaches the problem with a bias that comes from years of practice and situational knowledge.[296]

---

294   These *options* are ways of dealing with *real world* (ill-defined, wicked) problems typical of novice designers who tend to be problem-oriented and have limited mastery of the domain's declarative/conceptual and procedural/heuristic knowledge. See below.

295   For example, "engineering is an application of engineering science; rigorous management depends of the use of management science; and policy-making can become rigorous when based on policy-science" (1985, p. 14).

296   Novices also approach problems with a *bias*, or a preconceived idea as to what the solution will be. However, the pre-structuring of the problem that typical of experts should not to be confused with the naive and uninformed pre-suppositions of the novice. The novice needs to learn how to put his initial (uninformed) bias aside, and learn to test it against newly acquired domain specific knowledge/concepts and normative procedural heuristics and apply these to various situation as he engages in the *deliberate practice* the essential for the acquisition of expertise. See section on expertise below.

There is no innocent eye or purely deductive reasoning. He writes, "when the practitioner sets the problem, he chooses what he will treat as the "things" of the situation... what he will attend to and what he will ignore." In *The Design Studio* (1985) Schön provides a description of the process or "schema" that he is proposing:[297]

To begin with, the starting condition of reflection-in-action is the repertoire of routinized responses that skillful practitioners bring to their practice.[298] This is what I call the practitioner's knowing-in-action. It can be seen as consisting of strategies of action, understanding of phenomena, ways of framing the problematic situations encountered in day-to-day experience. It is usually tacit, and it is delivered spontaneously, without conscious deliberation. It works, in the sense of yielding intended consequences, so long as practice situations fall within the boundaries of the normal and routine. It is a dynamic knowing process,[299] rather than a static body of knowledge, in the sense that it takes the form of continuing detection and correction of error,[300] on-line fine-tuning, all within the framework of a relatively unchanging system of understanding.[301] A process of continual adjustment in the service of maintaining a sense of constancy[302]... Sometimes, however, there are surprises. These take the form of unanticipated events which do not fit[303] existing understandings, fall outside the categories of knowing-in-action. They are anomalous, and if they are noticed, they yield uncertainty – meaning not merely that one cannot predict for sure what will happen but that, at least for a time, one cannot make sense of the situation. Often, such surprises appear as unique events – things one has never seen before and may never see again. Often, they are associated with conflicting values, conflicting ways of framing the problematic situation, even conflicting paradigms of practice.

---

297   It is a lengthy quote, but it is the most concise account I can find that describes what he means by "reflection-in-action" that I can find, and fundamental to this research.

298   In other places this "repertoire of routinized responses that skillful practitioners bring to their practice" is what is meant by procedural/heuristic knowledge.

299   Similar to *dialectic* used above.

300   Similar to *feed-back* used above.

301   Similar to a way of thinking about the problem used above.

302   Similar to the experience of *coherence* used above.

303   A reference to Alexander's concept of *fit* used above.

These are tensions or contradictions in what Geoffrey Vickers[304] called the appreciative system of the practitioner. Together, uncertainty, uniqueness, value-conflict, make up what I call the indeterminate zones of practice. In these zones, competence takes on a new meaning. There is a demand for reflection, through turning to the surprising phenomena and, at the same time, back on itself to the spontaneous knowing-in-action that triggered surprise. It is as though the practitioner asked himself, "What is this?" and at the same time, "How have I been thinking about this." Such reflection must at least be in some degree conscious. It converts tacit knowing-in-action to explicit knowledge for action. It must take place in the action present – the period of time in which thinking can still make a difference to the outcomes of the action. It has a critical function, questioning and challenging the assumptional basis of action, and a restructuring function, reshaping strategies, understanding phenomena, and ways of framing the problems. Thinking gives rise to experimenting – but to a particular kind of experimenting, unique to practice, like and unlike the experimenting of laboratory science. It occurs on-the-spot, in the practice situation. It consists in actions that function in three ways to test new understandings ("what is going on here?"), to explore new phenomena ("What else looks odd here?"), and to affirm or negate the moves by which the practitioner tries to change things for the better ("How can we get this under control?") On-the-spot experiment may "work", in the sense that you get what you intend and/or like what you get. Or it may yield further surprises, pleasant or unpleasant. In these instances, we can think of the inquirer moving in the situation and the situation "talking back" to the inquirer, triggering a reframing of the problem, a re-understanding of what is going on. The entire process then has the quality of a reflective conversation with the situation. (pp. 24-26)

---

304   Vickers (1983), coming out of systems theory, and influenced by writers such as Wiener, von Bertalanffy, and Ross (as mentioned above), argued that the making of judgments is a necessary element of all human action. Vickers was highly critical of Simon, referring to his "unbounded" enthusiasm for computerized models of decision-making, and his principles of management as "proverbs masquerading as science" (p. xvi). Vickers' theory of appreciative judgment has three components: reality judgments – what is and is not the case; value judgments – what ought and ought not be; instrumental judgments – concerning the best means available to reduce the mismatch between what is and what ought (p. xix). Human action inextricably includes all three forms of judgment. Three other components of the appreciative systems include: the ability to find pattern in complexity, and the ability to shift focus and find other patterns; artful selectivity in deciding what features of a situation are most important, in keeping with shifting interests, values and concerns; the ability to read the situation, including how to simplify the complexity of an environment. John Forrester comments on the back cover, "Sir Geoffrey Vickers taught us that a value-free judgment would be literally worthless. Human systems become recognizable as more than machines only as they honor (or betray) valued norms like impartiality or responsiveness, respect or productivity, or combinations of these. So all management and administration, all planning political action, depend not just on mechanical rule-following, but on practical goal-setting too: on appreciative judgments constructed in the face of ambiguity and uncertainty about what a rule, obligation, or goal really means" (Vickers, 1995).

In general terms, Schön observes that professional designers: recognize a problem → [define the problem space/frame the problem] →[(move/see/move) → reframe →(move/see/move)] → produce a solution. It is a complex process that functions like a system with multiple feedback loops, involving defining/redefining the problem space, framing/reframing the problem, challenging assumptional biases, a willingness (courage to) confront the *indeterminate zones of practice* as the designer both builds and inhabits (feelingly) a design world that is directed toward a goal.

As the designer engages in the frame/re-frame → move/see/move → refine (*iterative*) process, a *design world* begins to emerge in which he inhabits.[305] This world has – normative, external and self-imposed – rules and variables.[306] The more the designer works in this world the more detailed and complex it becomes.[307] **The designer inhabits this design world feelingly, making use of embodied cognitive abilities, experiencing its spatial qualities, looking around, feeling, moving around, testing it against design criteria, and looking for opportunities.**

The *problem space* is derived from the *problematic situation*. It is the space where all the design, performance, economic, environmental, technical, legal, etc., criteria/constraints as understood by the client, users, stakeholders, architects, engineers, etc. are identified. Analysis/structuring of the problem space allows the designer to gain an understanding of the design problem.[308]

In the process of defining and understanding the problem space the designer begins to *frame* the problem. Criteria are prioritized. Particular interests are discovered. Client, user-group, stakeholder priorities are taken into consideration. Vague patterns and relationships are suggested. Personal preferences and interests are considered (explicitly and/or implicitly). There is an attempt to *make sense* (seek coherence) of the problem space. In doing so, a *way of thinking about the problem* emerges, that includes a sense of coherence and a feeling for the quality of aesthetic experience that is desired (intended).

---

305   It is important to keep in mind that Schön is trying to describe how architect's design from what he has observed watching designers (professionals/studio masters/students) design.

306   These rules and variables are similar to Lawson's *criteria*.

307   There comes a point where the design world has become so complex and detailed that it exceeds the memory/processing capacity of the human mind, at which point it needs to be externalized or represented in a manner that will retain necessary information and allow for further manipulation and development of the data set. This is related to Simon's concept of "bounded rationality."

308   Unlike Hillier's *instrumental set*, Schön's *problem space* does not explicitly include building materials, components and systems. The problem space can be understood as consisting of a pre-ontic consideration of all the criteria and constraints related to the project. Building materials, components and systems emerge as part of the *design world*.

Once the designer has framed the problem (discovered a way of thinking about the problem) he "jumps in" and begins, with pencil in hand (computer, models, etc.), to explore possibilities. To do so, the designer engages in an exploratory/iterative process of discovery that involves assessing the situation (seeing), trying out ways of responding to the situation (move), and then evaluating whether the response had the desired effect (see). Schön call this iterative, problem framing/solution seeking process *see-move-see*.[309]

Move: A move is a conjecture: "Given this situation, and these objectives, let's try this and see what happens." It is similar with what Akin calls inference-making, where "the designer takes a piece of information, adds to it what he knows, and arrives at new or modified information" (Akin, 1986, p. 49).

See: Schön refers to the evaluation of moves as *seeing*. Seeing involves generating/ assessing internal/external representations. After the designer makes a *move* he steps back and *sees*, that is evaluates his move: "OK, I tried this, it seems to have solved this problem, but in doing so I caused another problem over there. Maybe that's not such a big problem, or maybe it can be solved easily if I try something else. Still I do like how that last move solve this." Schön (1985) writes, "the designer evaluates his moves in a three-fold way: in terms of the desirability drawn from the normative design domains, in terms of their conformity to or violation of implications set up by earlier moves, and in terms of his appreciation of the new problems or potentials the have created" (p. 49). The evaluative meta-heuristics being applied in seeing involve the application of demonstrative criteria and testing for experiential qualities: a feeling of *coherence* and *resonance* with the intended quality of aesthetic experience.

Building on insights from Simon and Rittel, as well as Ryle and Polanyi, Schön, recognizes, and observes, that in the dialectic process of problem-setting/solution-seeking, the designer gains a deeper understanding of what the actual problem is. As such, Schön describes move-see-move not as a linear step-by-step process. Rather he observes that at times the designer is faced with an *irreconcilable situation* where the way the problem is framed, how he is thinking about the problem, the way the problem space is defined, and the direction that the design solution is going cannot be resolved in a satisfactory manner: something needs to change.

---

309   Move-see-move as described by Schön is a kind of verification process where the designer tests his ideas through some kind of externalization. The idea being that complex spatial ideas that are held in the mind are ambiguous and need to be tested. The brain (neural systems) compensate for complexity beyond its capacity for the necessary level of detail, by glossing over the details (not unlike fuzzy logic). When a designer forces his self to *externalize* (draw or make a model) he is forced to figure out the details that his mental image may have glossed over, to see if it actually works. Additionally, by externalizing the move, the designer may discover new, previously not considered, moves (options) that may prove to be excellent design opportunities.

Schön refers to this as the "intermediate zone." In this zone the designer assesses the situation and adjusts either the problem space (adding or subtracting some variable), how the problem is framed (changing priorities, discovering a new/better way of thinking about the problem), or makes a radical change in how he is approaching the design solution. The (creative) ability to reframe a problem space (situation) that leads to new insight, acting as a key or *re-ordering principle*, is analogous to a *paradigm shift* (Kuhn, 1962). It is precisely in this zone that creative and novel insight often takes place.

The *indeterminate zone* is analogous to the "Rashomon effect,"[310] a realization that the way the problematic situation was/or is being framed (one of any number of legitimate ways of framing the problematic situation) has led to a problem-solving situation that is resulting in conflicting values or paradigms of practice. Multiple solution paths can be followed with no active heuristic bias. The designer does not know (explicitly or implicitly) what to do next. A sense of coherence is lost. "It is not turning out the way I thought/wanted." It is at this point that the designer needs to reassess, take account of where he is in the process; to stop as ask his self "what do I know, and how I have been thinking about this?" **This is the point when the designer realizes (or not) that the way he has been thinking about the problem (how the problematic situation has been framed or what kind of solution was hoped for), the assumptional bias and/or the appreciative system, is not working; insofar as it is not producing kind of solution that resonates with the designer's expectations. It is in this intermediate zone that design innovation/creativity is most likely to occur.**

---

[310] Anderson (2016) observes the dual phenomenon associated with the Rashomon effect. The first is the disorienting effect the observer feels that comes from the experience of never really knowing what happened, as is Kurosawa's 1950 film, *Rashomon*. The second refers to "the naming of an epistemological framework – or ways of thinking, knowing and remembering – required for understanding complex and ambiguous situation." It is a way of making sense and imposing structure in an ambiguous situation.

§ 8.9 The Design Problem and the Problem of Designing

Designing is an interaction of making and seeing, doing and discovering.

(Schön & Wiggins, 1992, p. 135)

Kolko (2011) writes about designing as a synthesis that "involves the combination of two complicated entities: the designer and the design problem" (p. 3). Schön calls it a *reflective conversation with the situation*. From the above it can be seen that this conversation involves more than the designer (as an individual person). Following Wong and Lawson, the *designer* includes those who identify and structure the problem, as well as those who participate in the iterative process of externalizing the emerging representation of the solution. As discussed above, all of the persons who make up who we call the designer each come to the problem situation with their own presuppositions and expectations, and biases, and experiences, and expertise. This conversation with the problem situation is very complex indeed.

Though the focus of this research is about design expertise, and explicitly not about how to design a building, the two are nonetheless incommensurably inter-connected. Designing, as an object of study, is difficult to understand separate from the domain within which it functions. This research starts with the presupposition that the proper end of designing is an artifact, and so it follows that the proper end of architectural design is buildings/built environments. The end of designing in not an idea or a concept. Though the *generative idea* (Darke, 1979) can be a powerful tool for framing the problem, achieving coherence and identifying the intended aesthetic experience, and even variation reduction. The generative idea is not the design solution, it's a heuristic, a design strategy. Neither is a narrative, an algorithm or whatever other conceptual device the designer uses as a heuristic to frame the problem and/or generate conceptual form.[311] **As critical a function that it might play for generating form, making sense of the problem, or even as a motivational factor, in the end, concept, the narrative, the generative idea does not matter**. The owner, client, user, government official, do not care how or why you designed what you did. The only thing that matters is if whatever and however you designed it, it resulted in a building/built environment that satisfies demonstrable criteria and the induces the intended quality of experience. It is critical for the reader to appreciate this.

---

311   See Jormakka (2012) for an overview of alternative methods for generating architectural form.

Related to this presupposition is the distinction between the *proper end* and the *proximate end* of designing. This distinction is necessary in order to preserve the understanding that designing results in artifacts not an idea for or representation of an artifact. The act of designing is only consummated in the making of the artifact. As such, the proximate end of designing is a functional approximation, whose *raison d'etre* is to result in a building.

While it may be argued, that what the designer produces is nothing more than an external representation of the building concept (be it drawings, models, animations, written documents), the argument presented here is that this distinction is not a simple question of semantics. The argument is that if the designer understands the *proper end* of designing as an external representation whose *raison d'etre* is to effectively communicate the *idea* or *concept* for a building design, then the way he engages the design problem is (can be) more abstract, and disembodied. But, if the designer thinks of the proper end of designing to be a building that will be built, he always has a physical object before him. It is the difference between appreciating a piece of furniture in a catalogue and trying to figure out how it was possible to make such an exquisite object. Both appreciate the form, how well it functions, the materials, and perhaps the craftsmanship. But after that, the appreciation of the furniture takes a decidedly theoretical turn, while trying to figure out how it was made takes a decidedly tectonic turn.

When the designer thinks of designing as making an artifact, he must find a way to engage the object throughout the design process, from structuring, defining and setting the problem space, to framing the problem; through move/see/move; through efforts at variety reduction, assessing and reassessing assumptional biases based on the quality of the design world as he inhabits it feelingly; through determining the most effective way to externalize the approximate representation; through on-site modifications; through experiencing the building/built environment and assessing how well it correlates with how he anticipated it would feel.

§ 8.10   Designing as Making a Functional Approximation of a Thing to be Built

Our job is to give the client, on time and on cost, not what he wants, but what he never dreamed he wanted, and when he gets it, he recognizes it as something that he wanted all the time.

(Denys Ladson in Cross, 2011)

I propose a description of the design process that is a synthesis of the above. My primary references are Schön, Hillier and Dorst. The overall design process is one that involves setting the problem space, framing the problem (way of thinking about the problem), engaging in the dialectic of see/move/see (testing/discovering), refining the problem space, reframing the problem, further engaging in the dialectic of see/move/see until a solution beings to emerge that begins to satisfy the design criteria and constraints, and induces a sense of coherence and intended aesthetic experience.

The expert designer comes to the problem with years of situated knowledge, an understanding of materials/structure/systems, various techniques for achieving architectural experience, mean and methods for achieving coherence, analytic abilities to understand the problem and the expectation of the client, etc. with which he engages the problem situation. He enters the world of the problem space, with the expectations of the intended-user in mind, seeking a way to "think about the problem" that suggests possible solution paths with associated internal representations. The designer makes a preliminary assessment the possible solution paths, identifying a preference for a solution path that seems likely to satisfy demonstrable criteria and induce intended experiential qualities. A "design world" begins to emerge. This design world begins not unlike a vague memory or a sense of *déja-vu*. He inhabits the world. Sees it. Moves things around. Sees it again. Externalizes (sketch, makes a quick model) Looks at the externalization. Inhabits it. Considers the possibilities, as well as the intended and unintended consequences. Its beginning to work, but something isn't quite right. He feels lost. He has entered into and intermediate zone. Reassess. Look for opportunities (opportunism) outside the problem space or heretofore unrecognized relationships. Test it. Feel it again. Does it feel right? Is it working yet? Move things around again. See/move/see. Externalize (a more detailed drawing, perhaps a computer model). Things are beginning to fall into place. He likes it. It feels like it is working. He is immersed in the design world (flow). There are too many variables. Its hard to keep the entire design world in active memory. Externalize again. Take some parts to a higher level of detail. Look. Does it look (feel) the way it looked (felt) in my mind (congruence)? What's working? What's not? Ask someone else to look. Does what he says make sense? Does it feel right? Does he "get it?" Revisit the problem.

What do I know. Is the way I am thinking about the problem (framing) working? See/move/see. Externalize. Get more input from others (they can see what I cannot, because I see what I want to see, not necessarily what is there). See/move/see...

The above should sound familiar to a designer, at least in a meta-fashion. The basic structure of the above narrative is consistent with problem → [problem-framing/solution-seeking] → solution. The primary differences with this model of the design process is that coherence and aesthetic experience have been moved from being one of several prioritized design criteria to functioning as meta-heuristics – motivating factors and points of reference, and means of assessing the emerging internal/external design representation throughout the design process. In addition to critical thinking, and technical knowledge, the designer is described as inhabiting (bodily) the design world, and using his body and associated sense systems as a means for limiting possible solution paths, reassessing *assumptional biases* and/or the *appreciative systems*. The designer inhabits the design world not only in the first person as I/we, he also inhabits the design world in the second person as "you," also in the third person as "him/them," attempting to anticipate how the building/built environment will be experienced by the user. The model presupposes that there is no "innocent eye," an expert designer comes to the problem with certain (refined and developed) biases, presuppositions, and previous experience, these are what makes him an expert.

You must have a starting point, a standard of comparison, to begin that process of making and matching and remaking which finally becomes embodied in the finished image. The artist cannot start from scratch, but he can criticize his forerunners. (Gombrich, 1972, pp.271-272)

This description also presumes that the designer is human (bounded) with full use of the embodied/extended cognitive abilities and capacities that evolved and developed over so many centuries to allow us to engage with the world and each other.

The following chapters will explain how these happen.

9 Expertise

Generally, in acquiring a skill – in learning to drive, dance, or pronounce a foreign language, for example – at first we must slowly, awkwardly, and consciously follow the rules. But then there comes a moment when we finally can perform automatically. At this point we do not seem to be simply dropping these same rigid rules into unconsciousness; rather we seem to have picked up the muscular gestalt which gives our behavior a new flexibility and smoothness. The same hold for acquiring the skill of perception.

(Dreyfus H. L., 1992, p. 249)

This chapter is concerned with factors (cognitive and psychological) related to the acquisition of design expertise.[312] It is not about the process of becoming a practicing architect, though many of the principles do apply.[313]

The previous chapter described ways to understand and think about design expertise as processes and methodologies. It provided a simple framework of design as a series of states that include: [problem-setting → (problem-framing/solution-seeking) → solution-making]. After describing what these three states mean, some theories and ways of thinking about designing were presented. Special attention was given to Hillier, Dorst and Schön. The chapter was concluded with a synthesis of design expertise that included the function of experiential qualities in the design process, the multiple ways that the designer inhabits the design world, and emphasis on designing as an embodied/extended cognitive ability.

Above, design as practiced within the context of an occupation that exceeds performance expectations, was describe as what is meant by designing expertise. Obviously no one is born an expert. Though there is the belief that some are born with *natural talent*, and without natural talent one can never be an expert.

---

312 See Badke-Schaub, Roozenburg, and Cardoso (2010) for a critique on the negative effects an overestimation of a designer's expertise may have.

313 For an excellent study of the process of "becoming-an-architect" see Cuff (1992) where she describes "the more tacit, more intricate evolution of an individual through a sequence of distinct periods: as an architectural student, an entry-level architect, a project architect or associate, and finally as principal" (p. 116). Cuff describes the evolution of a professional architect in 5 phases which are analogous to AIA definitions: Entry (Technical III), Late Entry/Early Middle [Technical II], Middle and Late Middle [Technical I], Late Middle [Supervisory], Full-Fledged [Principal] (p. 139).

When considered together, no one is born an expert abut natural talent in necessary to be an expert, it seems reasonable to ask how then does one become an expert designer? In the broadest strokes this question seems to simply comes down to nature vs. nurture. However, recent research into the acquisition of expert ability, theories of technical knowledge, and cognitive theory, provide another way of discussing this question that goes beyond the nature vs. nurture conundrum. There are few observations this research offers to start with. First, talent is over-rated. While being able to excel in any activity that has established expectations of excellent performance requires some natural pre-disposition, there is no such thing as a *natural talent*. Some studies suggest that certain personality types are pre-disposed toward designing while other types are not. Other studies suggest otherwise. Efforts at testing for *design aptitude* have not produced consistent results. There is however strong evidence that expertise (in any area) requires thousands of hours of *deliberate practice*. However, there is no evidence that thousands of hours of deliberate practice *guarantees* the acquisition of expert performance.

Designing, like other occupations where the proper end of the action is making something, is considered a technical ability. Technical ability involves the mastery of three different types of knowledge: declarative/conceptual, procedural/heuristic, strategic/situational (McCormick 2004). Mastering these does not happen all at once. Rather, the acquisition of expert ability follows a sequential, developmental process, where beginners spend much of their energy mastering declarative/conceptual thinking, advanced beginners develop procedural/heuristic knowledge, while experts rely on embodied/tacit knowledge to assess a situation (Dreyfus 2002). Feelings and a lack of self-consciousness play an important role in expert performance, developing a *sense* of what to do. Not everyone who tries will achieve a level of expertise. Some will become satisfied once they reach a level of functional competence. Others will find that they do not have the aptitude, pre-disposition, personal motivation (grit) or ability to achieve expertise. And others will simply loose interest. Not everyone who wants to be an expert can be an expert.

What the following will demonstrate is that **while, natural predispositions, physical ability, better than average intelligence, and the *grit* to spend thousands of hours of deliberate practice are certainly important, in the end, it is the development of the ability to *inhabit the design world feelingly,* so fundamental to tacit (embodied cognition), that determines who will become an expert designer and who will not. The ability to inhabit the design world feelingly is what is meant by a *sense of design*.**

The chapter begins with the question: Who can be an architect? This will be followed by a review of recent research from the relatively new disciple of expertise theory. Having established that expertise is acquired, I will review cognitive theory related to technical expertise and a developmental model for the acquisition of expert performance.

§ 9.1 Who can be a designer?

Wherefore a man who is to follow the architecture profession manifestly needs to...
have both a natural gift and also a readiness to learn. (For neither talent without
instruction nor instructions without talent can produce the perfect craftsman.)
He should be a man of letters, a skillful draughtsman, a mathematician, familiar
with scientific inquiries, a diligent student of philosophy, acquainted with music;
not ignorant of medicine, learned in the responses of jurisconsults, familiar with
astronomy and astronomical calculations.

(Vitruvius)

If the prerequisites that Vitruvius lists above were included in qualifying exams
for professional practice (such at the ARE in the USA), it seems likely that there
would be far fewer men and women licensed to practice architecture. Perhaps
this paragraph – which is more a description of an impossible ideal than a
useful list of characteristics, abilities and aptitudes – was Leonardo da Vinci's
inspiration for his iconic "Vitruvian man" who is the measure of all things.
[314] The answer to who can be a designer depends on how designing and what
designers do is described,[315] and if one who wants to be a designer possesses
the characteristics, abilities and aptitudes necessary to acquire some level of
competence if not expertise at designing.

---

314   It is doubtful that Vitruvius even considered the possibility that women could be architects, which is
        interesting when one considered that 40% of architecture students in the USA are woman today (ACSA 2015,
        http://www.acsa-arch.org/images/default-source/data/acsa-atlas-2015-03.jpg?sfvrsn=0).

315   See Box (2007), Krupinska (2014), Spiller and Clear (2014) for recent descriptions of who can be an
        architect. The internet is full of sites on who can/can't be an architect. Shelley Little (2015) writes that
        there are "10 signs that you should be an architect:" You are smart, you are willing to work hard, you are
        a problem solver, you have killer negotiation skills, learning is fun for you, you are a creative thinker, you
        have a scientific mind, you still like to play with blocks, you are a fount of knowledge, you have a love of
        nature. Michael Riscica's (2017) published two complimentary articles "10 Reasons why you should not
        become and architect," and "10 reasons why you should become an architect. A brief overview of these
        sites suggests that what Vitruvius thought important may still ring true for many architects.

The above, theories of what designing is includes from "everyone designs"[316] (Papanek, 1984) to Dong's (2009) theory that "design is an enactment of a set of operating principles wherein the actors emphasize different aspects of these principles," with others in between. There are those who believe, such as Vitruvius above, that like other areas of expertise, design requires some kind of natural (perhaps genetic) talent;[317] while others are convinced that it is an acquired ability. So, for some, who can become a designer is a matter of determining if he possesses natural talent. For others, becoming a designer is mostly about the acquisition of a complex skill set, competencies and abilities.

For some design expertise is akin to engineering; for others, it is a form of artistic self-expression. For some design expertise is primarily about growing a successful professional practice; while others consider design expertise as a way to engage in community service. With all these different ways of thinking about design, are there identifiable markers, traits, aptitudes or characteristics that suggest who is well-suited to be a designer?

---

316   The claim that "everyone designs" is a sentiment that reminds me of the rat in the Pixar animation, "Ratatouille" (2007) who is inspired by a famous (fictitious) French chef's proclamation that "everyone can cook," The rat (building on his highly developed, innate sense of taste/smell, and constant experimentation and practice) acquires such great skill at cooking that even the famous French food critic (not knowing that the food was cooked by a rat) writes a review of the food prepared by the rat declaring it the "best in Paris," It's a fun movie. I recommend it. Though light-hearted, there is a kind of truth in the movie – just like the famous chef claims "everyone can cook", it could be argued that "everyone can design"; but everyone cannot be a great cook, nor can everyone be a great designer. To be great requires something else. Insofar as designing is a fundamentally human behavior, akin to problem solving and decision-making, everyone can and probably does design. But this is not the sense of designing that I am concerned about. I want to know what is that "something else" that distinguishes the expert designer from the novice, and how does one acquire that "something else"? How one is able to, learn to, acquire the skills and competencies necessary to significantly exceed the performance expectations. How does one acquire design expertise?

317   The cult of the gifted genius and natural talent has many believers and apocryphal stories to support their beliefs. There's the story, reported by his sister, of Mozart writing his first symphony when he was five years old that can be found in Deutsch (1965, p. 455). The awe at the natural ability of athletes Tiger Woods. And then there is the favorite of architects, who love to tell the story of how Wright "designed" Falling Water (arguable one of the most significant building of the 20th century) in two hours. The story goes, as can be found in Edgar (1979), that Mr. Kaufmann Sr. was in Milwaukee nine months after his initial meeting with Wright. He called Wright at home at breakfast time to *surprise* him with his plan to take the train that same day to come check on the progress he has made on his house. Though Wright had only been to the site to visit and had a survey, he had told Kaufman that he had been working on the design since they first met nine months earlier. In fact, to date, he had not drawn anything on paper. So, it is said, in preparation for Kaufman's surprise visit, Wright walks calmly into the studio, surrounded by interns (witnesses), lays out a piece of paper, picks up his pencil, and proceeds to draw the plans for Falling Water in the two hours it took Kaufman to take the train from Milwaukee. Done! Good story. But completely unbelievable. For an excellent study on the topic on the myth of creative genius see Gardner (1993) *Creating Minds: An Anatomy of Creativity Seen Through the Lives of Freud, Einstein, Picasso, Stravinsky, Eliot, Graham, and Ghandi*; and Colvin (2008) *Talent is Over-rated: What Really Separates World-class Performers from Everybody Else*.

This section asks this question in terms of personality, characteristics, aptitude, and intelligence, in an effort to identify at least some characteristics and aptitudes that describe the kind of person who may be well-suited to be a designer.

There is some evidence that designers have similar personality attributes. Broadbent (1973) describes several studies that sought to describe the psychological/personality traits of successful *creative* architects. For example, the seven items in a collated list from a study referred to as *Block's 100-item Q-sort* (1961) included:

— Enjoys aesthetic impressions; is aesthetically reactive
— Has high aspiration level for self
— Values own independence and autonomy
— Is productive; gets things done
— Appears to have a high degree of intellectual capacity
— Genuinely values intellectual and cognitive matters
— Concerned with own adequacy as a person, either at conscious or unconscious level

Broadbent notes that many of these early personality profiles, including those of Allport (1954) and MacKinnon (1962) describe the architect as "a thoroughly pleasant individual and able, above all, to see the other's point of view." But referring to a study by Blake where he describes F. L. Wright as "arrogant, strident, full of conceit;" Le Corbusier as "cold, suspicious, pugnacious, sarcastic (but quite humorous about himself), and arrogant;" and Mies van der Rohe as "massive, granite faced, elegantly dressed, gentle, fantastically self-disciplined, taciturn and shy to the extent that he found speech-making painful" (1973, p. 9). Broadbent suspects that these descriptions may not be reliable. Broadbent makes reference to another study by Smith (1964) who claims that good architects are likely to be "unsociable, humorless, severe, aloof, suspicious, cool, reticent, misanthropic, calm, cold, calculating, self-centered, shut-in, and fanatical" (p. 9). Smith claims that this is characteristic of people who possess high special ability, which is typical of people with *schizothymic* personality, that is, people with schizoid tendencies. So, at least up to the time when Broadbent was writing, it seems that the personality of the creative architect covers the whole spectrum.

Owen (2006), in "Design Thinking: Notes on Its Nature and Use," recognizes that even with "considerable speculation over many years, the nature of creativity, what makes one person creative and another not, and the creative process itself, remains elusive" (p. 26). While the creative process is not the same as the design process, and while creativity is not the same as designing, they do have enough similarities that an overview of what is thought to be the *characteristics of creative thinking* will be helpful. Owen offers three lists from educators, practitioners and theorists: Fabun, Arieti, Csikszentmihalyi, plus his own list of characteristics for design thinking.

Fabun lists: Sensitivity; Questioning attitude; Broad education; Asymmetrical thinking; Personal courage; Sustained curiosity; Time control; Dedication; Willingness to work (p. 22). Arieti added to Fabun's list: Fluency in thinking; Flexibility, Originality; Redefinition; Elaboration; Tolerance for ambiguity (p. 23). Csikszentmihalyi sees creative people in terms of "pairs of apparently antithetical traits that are often both present in such individuals and integrated with each other in a dialectical tension." They include: Generalized libidinal energy and restraint; Convergent and divergent thinking; Playfulness and discipline – or irresponsibility and responsibility; Fantasy and reality; Extroversion and introversion; Humility and pride; Masculinity and femininity; Traditional conservatism and rebellious iconoclasm; Passion and objectivity; Suffering and enjoyment (p. 23). Finally Owen's characteristics of design thinking are: Conditioned inventiveness; Human-centered focus; Environment-centered concern; Ability to visualize; Tempered optimism; Bias for adaptively; Predisposition toward multi-functionality; Systemic vision; View of the generalist; Ability to use language as a tool; Affinity for teamwork; Facility for avoiding the necessity of choice; Self-governing practicality; Ability to work systematically with qualitative information (pp. 24-25). As can be seen from Owen's lists of characteristics, it is hard to say who can be a designer.

An alternative to personality studies of successful architects, and lists of characteristics produced by practitioners, educators and theorists, is to look to the criteria design schools use as a basis for admittance to their programs. The presupposition being that the purpose of the criteria is to identify students who are likely to successfully complete the program. In their study "Who Should be a Designer?" (2002), Goldschmidt, Sebba, Oren, and Cohen discuss criteria for admission into schools of architecture as well as a historical review of the admissions practices of various schools. They observe that the history of university-level professional education is relatively recent, with most pre-WWI schools of architecture being modeled after *École Nationale et Spéciale des Beaux Arts*. In the 1920's an alternative model was founded in Europe. The most famous are the *Bauhaus* (in Germany) and *Vkhutemas* (in Russia). The second half of the 20th century saw a surge in the number of university based schools of architecture. Despite their number, geographical distribution and cultural contexts, "almost all of them share similar goals and the programs they offer are based on training principles that were, to a significant extent, inherited from the *Beaux Arts* and the *Bauhaus-Vkhutemas* traditions" (Goldschmidt, et al., 2002). Central to all these programs is the *design studio*, the teaching method that so fascinated Schön (1985).

Admission to *École des Beaux Arts* involved joining an Atelier headed by a *Patron* – usually an accomplished architect – where students were prepared to participate in the *entrance competition*. The competition had three parts: two sketch problems, the first being a simple structure making use of classical motifs, while the second problem involved producing a full-scale drawing of an architectural detail. The third part of the test was a comprehensive exam focusing primarily on scientific knowledge.

The *Bauhaus* had a different philosophy. Gropius's admissions policy was, "Any person of good repute, without regard to age or sex, whose previous education is deemed adequate by the Council of Masters, will be admitted, as far as space permits" (Wingler 1969, p.33). In addition to previous education that was deemed adequate, novice applicants were expected to provide a portfolio. More advanced applicants were expected to provide "certificates of previously completed training in the crafts" (p. 44). All successful applicants were then required to take the *primary course*. Successful completion of this course gained them admission into the workshop of their choice.

Goldschmidt et al. (2002) surveyed 69 schools of architecture from 21 countries, "requesting information about practices, policies and procedures pertaining to admission of students" (p. 69). Eight different forms of criteria were identified, with all schools making use of more than two forms on average. These criteria are: high school records, psychometric/general scholastic aptitude tests, special architecture aptitude test, interview, portfolio, essay, written statement, letters of recommendation. Most schools require high school records. About half required psychometric/scholastic aptitude tests and/or portfolios. Though there is belief in their predictive power, there seems to be little correlation between previous school performance and later success. The value of aptitude tests is highly contested, as it is argued that they generally test non-curriculum based knowledge, and it is thought that students from private preparatory schools have an unfair advantage.

Special aptitude-for-architecture tests look for evidence of non-verbal or visio/spatial intelligence. In Denmark this test has been considered effective in predicting student future success. Schools in other parts of the world have not found it effective. The portfolio functions in a similar manner as the architecture aptitude test, with several schools finding it effective. Other schools, find that, like the general aptitude tests, the quality of the high school program gives some students an unfair advantage. It is interesting to note that the same schools that prefer the general aptitude test, tend not to require portfolios, using concern for the quality of the high school program for each. The study concludes that not much is known about the success of prevalent admissions criteria and even less is known of the impact such criteria have on the built environment. More study is needed.

Most of these admissions criteria are intended to test interest, aptitude and ability. Interest has to do with motivation, or as will be discussed below *grit*. Aptitude is defined as an innate, learned or acquired ability of an individual to perform certain tasks. Aptitude tests inculcate many factors such as numerical reasoning, verbal reasoning, abstract reasoning, speed, accuracy, and other such abilities. Cross (1990) claims that "design ability is, in fact, one of several forms of fundamental aspects of human intelligence" (p. 128). Further, Cross (2011; 2007), recognizing how multiple aspects of practical problem-solving ability are spread out among the multiple intelligence theory of Gardner (1983), proposes that in addition to Gardner's six forms of intelligence (linguistic, logical mathematical, spatial, musical, bodily-kinesthetic, personal) "it seems reasonable, therefore, to try to separate out design ability as a form of intelligence in its own right" (2011, p. 136). Cross goes on to identify some of the aspects of "design intelligence." He writes, "good designers have a way of thinking that involves operating seamlessly across different levels of detail, from high level systemic goals to low-level physical principles;" designers have "cognitive skills of problem framing, of gathering and structuring problem data and creating coherent patterns from the data that indicate ways of resolving the issues and suggest possible solution concepts"; designers can engage a problem with intensity and "reflective interaction with representations of problems and solutions, and an ability to shift easily and rapidly between concrete representations and abstract thought." Finally, good designers "apply constructive thinking not only in their individual work but also in collaboration in teamwork" (p. 136).

From the research that Broadbent presented, there does not seem to be one particular *personality type* that is predictive of the likelihood of succeeding at designing. The lists of characteristics of designers, while being illustrative, is not of particular use. From the research that Goldschmidt et al. presented we know that there have not yet been any exams or aptitude tests that reliably predict the likelihood of succeeding at designing. There is some anecdotal evidence that ability to draw and above average intelligence do seem to indicate the likelihood of succeeding at designing. But there is one aptitude that does seem to be commonly held and is supported by research; that **an aptitude for spatial thinking and problem solving.** See Nazidizaji, Tome, and Regateiro (2015), Sutton and Williams (2010), Kvan & Jia (2005).

From the above review, who can be a designer seems to be inconclusive. Certainly the Vitruvian man would likely be successful as a designer, but only if he was motivated to learn to design. The one thing that does continue to be generally accepted is that success in design is made more likely if one possesses non-verbal or visio/spatial intelligence, which is more an aptitude than a natural talent.

Expertise Theory

If people knew how hard I worked to get my mastery, it wouldn't seem so wonderful at all.

(Michelangelo)

To acquire the complex cognitive abilities involved in designing as described above, one needs more than predispositions, aptitudes, and formative childhood experiences. One needs years of deliberate practice, (intrinsic) motivation to avoid being satisfied with mere competence and resist complacency, and the mastery domain related declarative, procedural and strategic knowledge. In addition one needs the resources, opportunities and support required to immerse ones self in the pursuit of mastery of designing as an occupation.

Expertise theory, having roots that date back to the learning theories of Pavlov, Watson, Thorndike, Tolman, Hull, and Skinner, has evolved in to a cognitive science that, studies the acquisition of skills through learning and practice. According to expertise theory,**the expert is the one who consistently exceeds the performance expectations of a particular occupation at a level that is considered exceptional.** Recall, expertise is domain specific, an expert in one field, even a closely related field, is not necessarily an expert in another field. Each domain of practice, has its own, skills and related fields of knowledge, as well as performance expectations.

Traditional theories of skill acquisition identify three phases of development (Ericsson, 2003): (1.) The "cognitive" phase, when the underlying structure and special aspects of the activity need to be attended to are learned; (2.) The "associative" phase, when a level of *functional* performance is attained; (3.) The "autonomous" phase, when performance of the activity is possible without thinking about it (p. 989). An acceptable standard of performance for everyday and recreational activities can be achieved in less than 50 hours, already possessing many characteristics of *automated performance*. Once this level of automation is achieved and a *functional* (cognitive) *representation* of the activity has emerge, everyday and recreational activities require a minimum of effort to perform and enjoy. However, this level of skill acquisition (autonomous), should not be confused with expertise. Once the skills necessary to perform a task or activity at an acceptable level are acquired, further development is not necessary. Its deemed good enough. Further development is arrested.

Skills development can be arrested at any level. However, for some, skills acquisition at an acceptable (functional) level is not enough. They, for whatever reason, desire to exceed the minimum level of skills acquisition necessary to perform at an acceptable level. To do so they choose to resist the complacency "associated with generalized automaticity of skill by deliberately acquiring and refining cognitive mechanisms to support continued learning and improvement" (Davidson & Sternberg, 2003, p. 63).

Based on years of research and observation into the acquisition of superior expert performance among athletes, musicians, chess players, scientists and artists, Ericsson (2016 & 2008) challenges the general belief that the underlying reason why some people are able to perform at such high levels, are considered prodigies, or seem to have super-human abilities, is fundamentally based on "natural talent," or having the "right genes" to start off with (genetic predestination), and no amount of practice, discipline or motivation would made a difference. Expertise theory posits that "**no matter what innate genetic endowment may play in the achievement of 'gifted' people, the main gift that these people have is the same one that we all have – the adaptability of the human brain and body, which they have taken advantage of more than the rest of us**" (Ericsson & Pool, 2016, p. xvii).

The argument is that even if you accept that certain people are genetically pre-disposed to certain abilities, what really matters is the potential to exploit the incredible cognitive/physical adaptability possessed by every human being to achieve new heights in expert performance. With this in mind, expertise theory claims that **the acquisition of superior expert performance is not so much about the actualization of potential (abilities), but rather creating "abilities that may not have existed before"** (Ericsson & Pool, 2016, p. xxi). This research is somewhat counter intuitive, when considering the almost cult-like prevalence of the idea of "talent" and "gifted-ness" that is so deeply ingrained in common culture. However, current research into the structure and plasticity of the brain, experiments and case studies have begun to demystify what is meant by talent and debunk the whole notion of "natural gifted-ness," or genetic predestination (Hill & Schneider, 2006).

There are several factors that influence the level of expert performance one can achieve. Most importantly, and perhaps least surprisingly, extensive experience within a particular domain is required to reach expert levels of performance.[318]

---

318 While many would like to believe that expertise is possible in multiple domains, the research has not supported this. In fact it seems that choosing a particular domain or discovering a kind of activity that gives one pleasure is a prerequisite for the acquisition of expert performance.

However it should be noted that extensive experience in a particular domain does not necessarily lead to expert levels of achievement.[319] Normally, after someone is first introduced to a profession and after completing basic training and related formal education, he works under the direct supervision of an accomplished professional. After a period of time actively engaged in related activities and accepting some level of responsibility, he achieves an acceptable level of proficiency in his field. With more extensive experience leading to an acceptable level of mastery within his field he is able to work as an independent professional. This is a critical moment in determining the level of achievement he will finally attain. Most professionals reach a level of performance that is acceptable and satisfactory, and maintain this level of *acceptable* performance for the rest of their careers.[320] They have reached a level of professional performance that is good enough. However, some professionals are motivated to continue to improve, reaching the highest levels of professional performance. Why?

In the mid-19th century Galton (1869), [321] provided a description of the generally accepted view of why this happens. According to Galton, every healthy person improves through experience at first. But these improvements gradually decrease due to "innate factors that cannot be changed through training; hence attainable performance is constrained by one's basic endowments, such as abilities, mental capacities, and innate talents" (as quoted by Ericsson, 2004, p. 685). His point is that while most healthy people can acquire the basics in an area of expertise, only those with "innate talent" will succeed in becoming experts. This view also explains declines in professional achievement as one gets older and "the inevitable degradation of general capacities and processes with age" (Krampe & Charness, 2006).

---

319   Gladwell (2008), in his book *Outliers: The Story of Success*, implies that 10,000 hours of deliberate practice is all that is needed to acquire expert ability. There is no evidence that this is true. Gladwell, makes this claim based on broad generalizations of Ericsson (1993). See also Daniels (2015).

320   "Research has shown that generally speaking, once a person reaches [a] level of 'acceptable' performance and automaticity... additional years of 'practice' does not lead to improvement" (Ericsson, 2016, p.12).

321   Galton (1869) proposed one of the earliest theories exploring why some people succeed and why others fail. A half cousin of Charles Darwin, his theory presupposed what we might call genetic determinism (*eugenics*) based on observable inherited physical characteristics and abilities (Galton, 1883, pp. 24–25), and is credited with first posing the question, *nurture vs. nature* (Galton, 1874). Based analysis of a list of notable figures in the sciences, arts and athletics Galton concluded that there are three ways in which these (presumably) men were remarkable: "they demonstrated 'ability' [natural talent] in combination with exceptional 'zeal' and 'the capacity for hard labor'" (1869, p. 38). "Exceptional zeal and the capacity for hard labor" is what is meant by "grit."

Ericsson (2004), challenging this view, found that in fact there are many types of experience related to both the acquisition and maintenance of expert performance, and "that these different types have qualitatively and quantitatively different effects on the continued acquisition and maintenance of an individual's performance" (p. 685). The framework he proposes claims that "some types of experience, such as merely executing proficiently during routine work, may not lead to further improvement, and that further improvements depend on deliberate efforts to change particular aspects of performance" (p. 683). What makes the difference between people who achieve mediocre, or minimal levels of competence, and those who achieve high levels of expert performance in their chosen domain, is their ability to harness the innate cognitive/physical adaptability to refine their skill.

Ericsson and Pool (2016) argue that the most efficient and effective way to benefit – achieve expert level of performance – from the cognitive and physical adaptability of the human mind/body is through *deliberate practice*. Ericsson makes a distinction between *naive*, *purposeful* and *deliberate* practice. Naive practice is essentially just "doing something repeatedly, and expecting that the repetition alone will improve one's performance." While, he adds, purposeful practice "has well defined, specific goals." It is focused, involves meaningful feedback, and requires one to get out of one's "comfort zone." Maintaining the focus and motivation necessary for purposeful practice "is hard work, and generally not fun."[322] Generally speaking, the motivation for persisting in purposeful practice comes from "the 'feel good' experience of being able to do something you here-to-fore could not" (pp. 14-22).

---

322   This often misunderstood point made by Ericsson observed that a distinctive characteristic of deliberate practice is that "it is not fun." Duckworth in her recent book, *Grit* (2016) contrasts this idea of deliberate practice (which is not fun) with Csikszentmihaly's (2008) concept of *flow*, which top performers all agree that they seek "primarily because it's fun." She suggests that these two concepts are in conflict with each other. This is a misunderstanding. Ericsson's point is that actively seeking the acquisition of expertise (training) requires more than the simple repetition of an enjoyable activity such as one might engage in on a Saturday afternoon with one's friends in a friendly game of basketball. Without the requisite intensity, repetition and focus on particular skills (deliberate practice), and meaningful feedback (coaching), one is not likely to improve. Systematic repetition, hours of intense practice, being constantly pushed outside one's comfort zone, is not usually fun. Csikszentmihaly's concept of *flow*, on the other hand, describes a state "focused immersion" in the creative/discovery process that "feels" like it is leading to a solution. This intense experience of losing oneself in the creative process is associated with pleasure, or what Csikszentmihaly calls *optimal experience*. *Flow* is normally only experienced once one has achieved a certain level of expertise.

Deliberate practice, while similar to purposeful practice, is specifically intended to harness the brain/body's adaptability. Previously it was believed that once a person reached adulthood, the wiring of his brain was pretty much fixed, that individual differences in abilities were mainly due to fixed genetically determined differences in the brain's wiring and abilities, and as mentioned above learning was little more than a way of fulfilling/actualizing one's potential. [323] However, research has shown that the plasticity of the brain, that is the brain's capacity to reroute neurons to compensate and achieve homeostasis exceeds levels previously imagined (Ericsson & Pool, 2016, pp. 31-38). Deliberate practice is different from other kinds of purposeful practice in that it requires (1.) a domain of expertise that is relatively well-defined, where training methods and of practice are well-established; and (2.) an accomplished experienced teacher who can suggest specific practice activities designed to help a student to (incrementally) improve his performance. These practice activities (drills) are focused on helping a student to improve specific skills, often requiring hours of repetition and regular feedback leading to subtle adjustments with incremental goals.

One study suggested that for some domains (specifically learning to play the violin) this can take up to 10,000 hours (Ericsson, Krampe, & Tesch-Romer, 1993). [324] Their intention is not to say that 10,000 hours of deliberate practice is all that is necessary to become a virtuoso. What Ericsson and others are arguing is that the highest level of expert performance is accessible to anyone with a basic predisposition,[325] motivation and years of intense and deliberate practice. The the body and mind can be reshape, it doesn't come easily. It is Ericcson's argument that this is what it takes to harness and reshape the amazing plasticity of the body and mind so that one can perform at an exceptional level.

---

323   Seung (2012), proposes a theory of how the wiring of the brain influences who we are called the *connectome*. His theory is that there are three things that influence the development of the brain: genetics, environment, and how the brain develops throughout one's life. He argues that there is good evidence that, "reweighting, reconnection, rewiring, and regeneration" (p. XV) of neurons, influenced by genes and environment is what makes us unique individuals.

324   This nice round number was picked up by Gladwell (2008) who proposed the "10,000 hour rule," in his book *Outliers*, suggesting that with 10,000 hours of deliberate practice anyone can master anything. Ericsson has challenged this misinterpretation of his research (Ericsson & Pool, 2016). Previously Simon and Chase (1973) suggested the so called "10 year rule." Which held that the minimum necessary to acquire expertise (in chess) was a period of 10 years.

325   This idea of a "basic predisposition" is not well developed in Ericsson and Pool (2016). It can refer to physical characteristics, childhood fascination, innate sense of curiosity, or certain genetic traits that increase the likelihood of succeeding in a particular area of expertise. What is clear in Ericsson is that "basic predisposition" is not the same as natural talent.

An additional characteristic that is typical of experts is the qualitative difference in the organization of their (domain related) knowledge and representations thereof. This has to do with how experts' knowledge is encoded (scaffolding) around foundational domain-related concepts (conceptual/declarative knowledge) and solution procedures (procedural/heuristic knowledge) that allows for the rapid and reliable retrieval of stored information whenever it is relevant.[326] The process of encoding and mastering conceptual and procedural knowledge leads to the acquisition of domain-specific memory and skills allowing experts "to rapidly access relevant information in an extended working memory that relies on storage in long-term memory" (Ericsson et al., 1993, p. 397). This is the value of reflective practice and the identification of methodologies.

The superior quality of expert's mental representations[327] is what allows them to adapt rapidly to changing circumstances and anticipate future events in advance (Ericsson K. A., 1995). Mental representations are similar to the patterns of play that de Groot's grand master chess players made use of (discussed in the section on problem-solving), that allowed them to quickly assess the situation and choose the next move and to be able to remember the arrangement and strategic relationship of pieces from multiple games (de Groot, 1978). These mental representations appear to be essential for experts' ability in providing a self-monitoring feedback loop of their own performance (Ericsson K. A., 1996; Glaser R. , 1996) that facilitates ongoing improvement by designing their own training and assimilating new knowledge.[328] What Schön calls reflective practice.

This question of what motivates some people to exceed performance expectations and push themselves beyond their limits has also been considered by Csikszentmihalyi (2008) and Duckworth, Peterson, Matthews and Kelly (2007). Csikszentmihalyi argues that the (intrinsic) motivation for exceeding normative performance is the pursuit of a kind of pleasure he calls *optimal experience*. The key element of an optimal experience, Csikszentmihalyi writes, is "that it is an end in itself" (2008, p. 67). He calls this an *autotelic* experience.[329] That is, it is a self-contained activity that is done with without expectation of reward. These experiences are contrasted with *exotelic* experience -- activities done for external reasons.

---

326   What is meant by and the function of declarative/conceptual knowledge, procedural/heuristic knowledge, mental scaffolding is discussed in the next section.

327   What is meant by mental representations is discussed at length in the section "Making Representations" above. As used here it is similar to Schön's *design world*.

328   Schön refers to this as *reflective practice*.

329   Csikszentmihalyi (2008) derived the *autotelic* from the Greek *auto* (meaning self), and *telos* (meaning goal).

This distinction between types of activities hinges on what in ethics is called *intrinsic motivation* (where the motivation comes from inside the agent, such a personal and religious belief) and *extrinsic* motivation (such as for reward, to avoid punishment, to gain advantage). Most activities are not one or the other. For example, there are somethings we do because we have to, but then in the midst of doing whatever it is, something about it becomes intrinsically rewarding. As an activity becomes intrinsically rewarding (autotelic), it takes on a life of its own. One loses oneself in the activity. The autotelic experience (or *flow*) lifts the experience to a different level. "Alienation gives way to involvement, enjoyment replaces boredom, helplessness turns into a feeling of control, and psychic energy works to reinforce the sense of self, instead of being lost in the service of external goals." Flow is "an almost automatic, effortless, yet highly focused state of consciousness" (Csikszentmihalyi, 1996, p. 110).

Csikszentmihalyi discovered that the flow experience, whether it was experienced by athletes, artists, religious mystics, scientists, or ordinary working people, was described in almost identical terms. Nine elements of the flow experience were identified: (1.) There are clear goals every step of the way; (2.) There is immediate feedback to one's actions; (3.) There is balance between challenges and skills; (4.) Action and awareness merge; (5.) Distractions are excluded from consciousness; (6.) There is no worry of failure; (7.) Self-consciousness disappears; (8.) The sense of time becomes distorted; (9.) The activity becomes autotelic. Csikszentmihalyi writes that those who he has interviewed often talk about the "autotelic aspects of their work as the exhilaration that comes with the pursuit of truth and beauty" (p. 122). It is the way that focused, intense, engaging work induces this state of flow that motivates people to exceed the norm. It seems once you have experienced it, you cannot get enough of it.

Duckworth, et al. (2007) take a different approach to the question of motivation. They observe that while "we know a great deal about intelligence, or mental ability... we know comparatively little about why... most individuals make use of only a small part of their resources, whereas a few exceptional individuals push themselves to their limits" (p. 1087). They observe, "In addition to cognitive ability, a list of attributes of high-achieving individuals would likely include creativity, vigor, emotional intelligence, charisma, self-confidence, emotional stability, physical attractiveness, and other positive qualities." But, there is one personal quality that they have found was shared by "the most prominent leaders in every field: grit" (p. 1087). They define *grit* as perseverance and passion for long-term goals, "the ability to work strenuously toward challenges, maintaining effort and interest over years despite failure, adversity, and plateaus in progress" (p. 1088). They contend that "grit, more than self-control or consciousness, may set apart the exceptional individuals [who] make maximum use of their abilities." Bloom (1985) writes, in his qualitative study of world class musicians, athletes, scientists and artists, that "only a few of [the 120 in the sample] were regarded as prodigies by teachers, parents or experts" (p. 533).

Instead, what he learned was that most high achieving individuals worked every day for a minimum of 10 – 15 years to attain their level of expertise. Duckworth et al. attribute this capacity to invest oneself so heavily, and commit so much time and energy, to make maximized use of their resources in pursuit of excellence, to grit.

The point is that "natural ability" and desire are not enough. **Though the likelihood of acquiring design expertise may be enhanced by the possession of certain physical, psychological and intellectual predispositions, design expertise is not an innate skill, a gift, or a God-given talent.** Design expertise is acquired, and possesses characteristics that are similar to other areas of expertise. Due to the complex nature of problem solving and the demands it makes on memory and cognitive functioning, mastery is greatly facilitated by making use of *cognitive scaffolding*. Making use of various models of design methodology aid in providing cognitive scaffolding during the process of acquiring design expertise.

§ 9.3 The Acquisition of Expert Performance[330]

Tell me and I will forget. Show me and I may remember. Involve me and I will understand.[331]

(Confucius)

Above, Ericsson (2003) described the traditional three phases to achieve a competent level of *new skill automation*; the "cognitive" phase, the "associative" phase, and the "autonomous" phase. But, as Ericsson observes, this level of automated performance – while sufficient for everyday ability and enjoyment of a task – should not be confused with *expertise*. Expertise is highly dependent on and the expectations of practice as determined by an occupation. These establish the base-line acceptable level of performance. To achieve even this level of performance in a complex occupation such as architectural design involves different kinds knowledge and ways of structuring the knowledge that develops over time.

---

330 § 9.3 -"The Acquisition of Expert Performance," and § 9.4 - "Dreyfus Model" rely heavily on previously published research (with permission), Curry (2014).

331 不闻不若闻之，闻之不若见之，见之不若知之，知之不若行之，学至于行之而止矣

To review, there are three types of knowledge involved in the acquisition of technical ability, the ability to do/make something: conceptual/declarative, procedural/ heuristic, strategic knowledge. These three types of knowledge can be understood as "know what," "know how," and "know when." This was discussed above at length. McCormick (1997) observes that these distinctions are "remarkably close to the idea of 'know how' as procedural knowledge and the 'know that' as conceptual knowledge.[332] The third kind of knowledge is "know when." Know when is a kind of *strategic* knowledge that "in effect controls the procedural and declarative knowledge as a 'how-to-decide-what-to-do-and-when' knowledge" (p. 145).

But even mastery of these three types of knowledge is not enough in themselves. Mastery needs to be acquired in a *situated learning environment* – one needs not only to learn the what and the how of the domain of the occupation, one needs to *learn while doing* in a suitable environment.

This section will describe the types of knowledge related to the acquisition of technical expertise, how they are acquired, and how they function. To do so I will refer to McCormick's theory of learning and knowledge in technology education (1997, 2004, 2006), Sweller's theory, the theory of cognitive load (2016), Pass et al. theory of scaffolding (2004, 1998), and Dreyfus' developmental stages of expert performance (2004).

Conceptual/declarative knowledge is traditionally thought to be the foundation upon which expert performance in built. In the popular imagination one assumes that before someone can do something, he should know as much as possible about what is involved. The is the kind of technical rationalism that was critique by Schön above. The thought is the more one knows, the more likely one is to succeed. And in a certain theoretical way, this makes sense. Even so, however logical this theory is, we know that this is not really how it works. (Recall the section on tacit knowledge.) Learning how to do something does not occur the same way as learning abstract ideas. One needs to be clear about what the learning objectives are. Is the objective to master conceptual/ declarative knowledge about how something is done? Or is the objective to become an expert performer? Because, if the objective is to become an expert performer, it is necessary to get the body involved right from the beginning.

---

332   There is some debate as to whether or not the distinction between conceptual and procedural knowledge is genuine or an artificial construct. There are several alternative theories offered, including Dillon, Scribner, Lave, Vygotsky (see McCormick, 1997). The value of the distinction is found in trying to understand how the two kinds of knowledge work together. In this way the distinction is useful. I will continue to use this distinction as a part of this working model.

Declarative/conceptual knowledge is the explicit knowledge of facts and concepts and the relationships among items of knowledge related to the domain of expertise that leads to *understanding*. Understanding is the forming of links between discreet ideas, concepts and facts. There are two theories for how this kind of knowledge occurs: constructivism and schemata. Constructivism relies on the building up of (mental) representations (conceptual models) that one tests against one's reality or experience. When a new concept is introduced or discovered, there is an attempt to fit that concept within the structure of one's mental representation.[333] Learning only takes place if/ when the new idea or concept is integrated into the pre-existing representation. Or occasionally the pre-existing representation needs to be adjusted to allow for the new concept or idea. Pre-existing conceptual models are difficult to change/ challenge as they are built upon prior knowledge. Concepts from other disciplines, misunderstanding, cultural issues, and alternative meanings can make integrating new knowledge (constructing) into a coherent model challenging.

Conceptual knowledge frameworks – including knowledge structures that exist in memory – are known as *schemata*. Schemata are ways that complex concepts are held in memory.[334] Such as knowledge about the look, feel, smell, characteristics and properties of materials. Or the proper way to assemble and name the components of a Doric column. Schemata are also known as *device knowledge*. It is knowledge of how all the parts work together to produce a particular outcome. Easy access to these schemata is how experts in a domain are able to solve problems quickly.

In this case the domain of expertise is architectural design. The conceptual/declarative knowledge that a designer needs to master includes: history and theory, materials and methods of construction, statics and principles of structure, mechanical systems, codes and zoning, etc. Students come to architectural design with pre-existing mental representations (models) that include concepts and ideas related to the domain of architecture – that may or may not be correct or useful. This is similar to how a designer pre-structures a problem discussed above.

---

333   The structure of the representation into which new knowledge needs to be incorporated to become learning, is similar to the concept of *scaffolding below*.

334   Human memory is limited. To compensate for the limitations of memory 2 types of memory have evolved: long-term and short-term or working memory. The smallest unit of memory is a bit. It is said (Miller, 1956) that the human mind can process a maximum of 7 bits of memory (+/- 7) at a time. This limitation can be surpassed by *clumping* several bits of information into a group (clump). Clumps are multiple bits of related information help together in memory. So now it is possible to hold 7 clumps of information in working memory. This limitation can also be exceeded by connecting multiple clumps of information with a concept or idea. These groups of related clumps are called schemata. Further, schemata are organized in memory through a complex system of relationships that is called a *mental representation, mode* or a framework.

Many of these concepts and ideas may need to be changed or at least challenged. Others do not. An early challenge for many students is to adapt or re-structure their mental representations – related preconceptions about what architectural design entails – in a manner that can support the new concepts and ideas, that will sustain and allow for new links, and that can provide an adequate framework to support the diverse, inter-disciplinary concepts and ideas that make up the domain of architecture.

Procedural/heuristic knowledge, described above in detail, is most closely associated with tacit knowledge, or how to do something. This kind of knowledge involves making use of the conceptual/declarative knowledge to solve problems. Sometimes referred to as *metacognition* or *self-regulation*, it includes rules-of-thumb, and situation specific methods of solving design problems and details. Procedural/heuristic knowledge has an obvious connection with design methods and methodology.

Strategic knowledge is situated knowledge. It is knowledge that a designer uses to know when, how and what to. This kind of knowledge, allows a designer to draw upon the vast amount of conceptual/declarative knowledge and procedural/heuristic knowledge at his or her disposal, to assess the situation, and then decide how best to use his resources to solve the problem (McCormick, 1997). Strategic knowledge is most closely associated with expertise. At it highest level, strategic knowledge functions as *embodied* knowledge – implicit knowledge that relies on feeling and intuition. How this works is described by Dreyfus's (2004) developmental model below.

McCormick (2004) considers technical learning as situated learning. Similar to Dewey (1938/2015) and Glaser (1992), McCormick (2009) identifies three aspects to situated learning: (1.)"Not only do cognitive processes differ according to the domain of thinking, but also to the specifics of the task. Knowledge in this sense is embedded in the context and not in abstractions" (pp. 22-23). Knowing and doing have a reciprocal relationship. (2.) Research provides evidence that "action affects thinking and thinking affects action" (pp. 22-23). This is crucial to understand. A foundational skill that students learning to design need to develop is "to think through their doing, and for the feedback from this doing to affect their thinking" (pp. 22-23). Schön (1992) calls this "the reflective conversation with the materials of a design situation" (p. 131).

Situated learning also includes enculturation and participation in the domain. That is to say "When we learn, we learn to become something (McCormick, 2004, p. 23). Learning how to design is not just a matter of mastering a body of knowledge, procedures and strategies, it also includes learning how designers work. The final aspect of situated learning (3.) learning experiences need to be authentic. That is the problems that the student is working on needs to be meaningful, and related to the domain. As discussed above, deliberate practice requires a level of intensity.

If the project a student is working on seems irrelevant personally and professionally, it will be difficult for her or him to motivate himself (intrinsically) – be emotionally engaged – thus relying on external motivation to complete the task at hand. Being able to immerse oneself into the task at hand is critical to situated learning, and a prerequisite to experiencing flow.

McCormick (2006) points out that "concepts in technology may differ from those in science" (p. 24). This is related to Schön's (1991) critique of professional education that emphasizes technical rationality and concepts of *how it should be*, rather than what actual expert designers know. Scientific concepts "deal with generalities (abstractions), whereas technology [deals] with how these concepts are manifest in particular contexts" (p. 24). This observation raises two points. (1.) The frustration that recent graduates face when they in good faith attempt to apply the conceptual knowledge they learned in school to a real problem, and find out that those theories and case studies did not take into account the realities of actual practice. For example the challenge of finding a way to communicate one's internal representation of an emerging idea to a client who is not trained in design. One quickly learns that designers do not see the world the same way as non-designers. (2.) When students learn design problem-solving as a series of steps (cookbook method), without engaging in a real-life problem situation, it quickly becomes a blind ritual where the student does what he thinks is expected, because that what they thought they were supposed to. Or, they do in fact solve the problem, finding their own methods. But then make-up a story the follows the narrative that they thinks the teacher wants to hear.[335]

---

[335]   Mitrovic (2013) provides and excellent anecdote that describes this situation. "A short silence follows her presentation. The guest critic, who feels obliged to say something, comes up with a question: "Well, what is your theoretical position? I mean architectural question?" – one of those formulations that guest critics use when they feel obliged to help the student. Yet, for the student, the question is unexpected: it does not pertain to visual issues, the kind of problem that motivated her work. A theoretical position ultimately consists of statements one believe to be true or false – it does not pertain to what the building looks like. Although well intended, the critic's question redirects discussion away from her *spatial* and *visual* interests. Noticing the student's perplexity (she's got excellent grades in her theory courses, but how can reading Derrida help you decide about the color of the facade, or the shape of the window), another crit tries to save the situation by providing guidance: "What is the meaning of your building?" (p. 9-10). And so it goes. Rather than talking about what she did, the visiting crits wanted her to make up a story, a narrative, or refer to theory.

Cognitive Load Theory: Cognitive Scaffolding

As mentioned above, novice designers are often overwhelmed by the amount of declarative/conceptual knowledge and heuristics they need to master before they are able to produce (successful) design solutions. Cognitive load theory, which grew out of research related to the acquisition of expert performance, provides a framework and some strategies for understanding and responding to this situation.

Mastering architectural design, requires what is generally referred to in education circles as competency-based learning, that is: "the ability to operate in ill-defined and ever-changing environments, to deal with non-routine and abstract work processes, to handle decisions and responsibilities, to work in groups, to understand dynamic systems, and to operate within expanding geographical and time horizons" (Keen, 1992; cited in Kirschner, 2002, p. 2). The acquisition of complex skills occurs within a specific domain of expertise and presumes the mastery of the foundational declarative/conceptual knowledge related to the field. Architectural design as a specific domain of expertise assumes familiarity with a sometimes overwhelming amount of cross-disciplinary information (declarative knowledge). The mind has a way of dealing with this.

Developed by Sweller (1988), Cognitive Load Theory, begins with Simon's concept of *bounded rationality* as a starting point. Humans have limited cognitive ability and capacity. The theory proposes strategies for working with the bounded-ness of human cognition. As mentioned above, it is generally accepted that human cognition involves three types of memory: working memory, which is limited; and long term memory which is practically limitless; and general-purpose working memory which has a limited capacity of about seven chunks of information (Miller, 1956) when just holding information, and not more than two or three chunks when processing information. (This does not include the numerous other way access to information is increased via extended cognition, i.e.: writing, books, internet, photos, etc.) The way long-term memory achieves its virtually unlimited capacity, is by storing information as *schemata*. Schemata can also reduce working memory load, because once they have been acquired and automated, they can be handled in working memory with very little conscious effort making use minimal cognitive resources. In addition, no matter how extensive a schema is, it will be treated as one chunk of information, thereby increasing the amount of information that can be held and processed in working memory without requiring more conscious effort. This ensures that there is enough cognitive capacity available to solve very complex problems.

However, when schemata have not yet been acquired, all information elements (bits and/or chunks) of the problem have to be kept in working memory as separate items, which can lead to excessive demand on working memory capacity, resulting in a feeling of being overwhelmed. Consequently, there is not enough capacity left for the formation of problem schema, and learning is hampered (Gog, T., Ericsson, K. A., Rikers, R.; Paas, F., 2005). The demand made on cognitive processing and memory resources is called *cognitive load*. Paas, Renkl and Sweller (2004) explain that cognitive load (i.e.: for novices) can be greatly reduced with the introduction of *procedural frameworks* that offer a more effective way of structuring complex cognitive tasks than conventional problem solving. Procedural models of designing (methodology) function as such frameworks during the early stages of learning to design; providing scaffolding to facilitate the development of schemata, reducing cognitive load on the student who is seeking to master the complex cognitive task that designing is.[336] The frameworks function as a kind of training wheels for a beginner designer recommending a systematic way to approach a design problem. The point is that the our cognitive architecture – with all its amazing abilities *and* limited capacities – has a significant influence not only on what we can learn but on how we are able to acquire complex skills. Making use of design methodologies or referring to descriptive processes during the early stages of learning design builds upon this cognitive architecture, taking into account its strengths and limitations, reducing the stress associated with cognitive load, and greatly facilitating the acquisition of design ability.

---

336   A common mistake, made by well-intentioned design instructors, is to overload the students' working memory before they have had a chance to develop chunks that lead to the emergence of schemata essential for complex problem solving, thus limiting their ability to discover generative concepts upon which to develop a design solution. This overload impedes learning. This is not intentional. The design competency of design instructors is typically quite high. They are usually actively engaged in professional practice performing at the level of expertise, and highly motivated teachers. However, most design instructors are not consciously aware of how they arrived at such a high level of competency and what factors where critical in their development. Once one embodies the knowledge necessary to be an expert, the designer loses awareness of what he had to do to acquire it. He relies on tacit knowledge.

A Designer's Brain

Research related to expert performance has shown that acquisition of expert ability occurs developmentally, not all at once. In explaining how this occurs, Ericsson et. al. (2007), refer to the seminal theory of expertise posed by Simon and Chase (1973), that observed "extended experience led experts to acquire a gradually increasing number of more complex patterns" (p. 59). By *extended experience* Simon and Chase meant more than longevity. They meant deliberate, focused experience that was immersed in the domain, similar to Ericsson's deliberate practice described above. The difference between the ability of a novice and an expert is not simply that the expert has more years of extensive practice and accumulated knowledge (Ericsson, 2008). The difference is the result a demanding process of moving from data driven, fact based, heuristically programmed problem-solving to an intuitive, feeling driven, effortless, tacit ability, that informs the designer what to do without explicit recourse to rules.

Expert performance involves the acquisition of knowledge and the appropriation of schemata, as well as the internalization and embodiment of knowledge and action that allows an expert to have a *feel* for what to do: a sense of design. Long years of study, deliberate practice and on-going experience (training) taking advantage of the plasticity and adaptability of the body and brain, results in physiological changes in brain structure.

Research has shown that as one progresses on the long road from beginner to expert performer, many fundamental changes in the structure of the mechanisms mediating performance as well as the conditions of learning and practice take place, as well as biological changes in brain structure (Hill & Schneider, 2006). As discussed above in relation to the *connectome*, the structure of the brain is not fixed as previously thought. As it turns out, the repetitive actions associated with deliberate practice reinforce synaptic connections across different regions of the brain results in a literal restructuring of the brain: One acquires a designer's brain.[337] This restructuring occurs incrementally, with much effort, over time and is highly adaptive (see Seung, 2012). The acquisition of expert design ability is not simply about working in a studio environment solving incrementally more complex design problems over a specified number of years under the guidance of an expert designer/tutor. It involves an actual restructuring of the brain.

---

[337]   See Mallgrave (2011) *The Architect's Brain*, for a detailed description of what this involves.

§ 9.6   Dreyfus Model

Over the past 25 years Dreyfus and Dreyfus (1980) have developed a developmental model of skills acquisition that describes how expert performance is acquired. Their model is based on the insight that anyone seeking to acquire a new skill has two options: he can try the less efficient (and perhaps more dangerous) method of learning on his own by trial-and-error; or the more efficient method of seeking out an instructor and/or instruction manual. By observing how experts acquire skill in several disciplines Dreyfus and Dreyfus have developed a model that provides a framework for increasing the efficiency of the learning process.

Their developmental model of skills acquisition "consists in analyzing and systematizing descriptions of changes in the perception of the task environment in the course of acquiring complex skills" (Dreyfus & Dreyfus, 1980, p. 1). They claim that rather than simply extended experience (like Simon and Chase, and Ericcson), the acquisition of expert performance occurs in stages. And that the nature of the problem being considered, how it is framed and reframed, is dependent on the level of expertise of the problem solver. "The tradition has given an accurate description of the beginner and of the expert facing an unfamiliar situation, but normally an expert does not calculate. He or she does not solve problems. He or she does not even think. He or she just does what normally works and, of course, it normally works" (2004, p. 180). Over the years the number of and the names given to each phase by Dreyfus has changed. The phases I will use here are: novice, advanced beginner, competent, proficient, and expert.

Dreyfus (2004, pp. 179-180) describes how one learns to drive a car to illustrate his model: A **novice** student driver learns to recognize and understand domain independent variables such as speed, rules for shifting, braking and accelerating, rules of the road, safety precautions, etc. He begins by attempting to follow all the rules. But this results in poor performance in the real world. As an **advanced beginner**, the student driver gains experience with real situations and begins to make connections, master basic tasks, learns to make situational decisions, such as "shift-up when the motor sounds like its racing." At the level of **competence**, the student benefits from more experience, and begins to be aware of the potentially overwhelming number of variables. It can be exhausting. To deal with this possible overload, he becomes more selective about which variables to attend to. For example, when leaving the freeway off ramp he learns to be attentive to the speed of the car and not to whether to shift gears. He becomes emotionally involved in choosing what to do rather than being driven by rules. At the level of **proficiency** the student is becoming more emotionally involved in the task. He is developing a "feel" for what to do.

At this level, the student might, approaching a curve on a rainy day, feel that he is going too fast and decide to either apply the breaks or to down shift or to ease off the accelerator. His experience of different types of situations and the various possible, viable responses have increased and he has developed some reliable strategies for how to choose the right option in this particular situation. At the **expert** level, the student is completely immersed in the situation. He sees the situation and knows how to respond in a seemingly intuitive manner. He no longer needs to consider all the options, he just sees the curve, feels the gravitational pull and knows what to do.

Below I propose a version of the Dreyfus model (Dreyfus, 2004) adapted for learning to design, based on and in consideration of the principles and insights described above:

STAGE 1   Novice:
Acquisition of (non-situated) domain specific factual knowledge and heuristics.
....

Novices are generally presented with decomposed tasks in context-free environments that require minimal skill to complete. Performance tends to be rule-based and data/ research driven with little need to interpret the situation [Problems appropriate for this stage include abstract, disembodied form and space exercises: emphasis on plan form and functional considerations].

STAGE 2   Advanced Beginner:
Appropriation of frameworks for understanding/interpreting the situation
....

As novices gain experience, acquire increased domain specific conceptual/declarative knowledge and begin applying new skills in real situations, they begin to adapt to the relevant contexts and recognize aspects of new situations. Maxims or *heuristics* for dealing with varying situational contexts emerge [Problems appropriate for this stage include emphasis on plan, section, elevation, form and site: minimal concern for technical issues such as structure, materials and systems: relatively simple program requirements].

STAGE 3   Competence:
Assimilated ability to "see" (read) the situation

With increasing skill and this new awareness of the increasing number of potentially relevant elements and procedures can be overwhelming. To deal with this students seek means and methods (heurisitcs) to limit relevant variables for consideration and to identify opportunities that speak to his or her interests. Accountability for strategic choices and emotional involvement (sense of design) emerge. Here the student is beginning to be able to *see* the problem and test new skills and strategies to solve it. Design solutions tend to be "concept" driven. [Problems appropriate for this stage include complex program requirements and use types, consideration of structure, systems and materials: producing a whole idea for a building].

STAGE 4   Proficiency:
Appropriation of strategies for responding to the situation (scenarios)

This stage is distinguished by *emotional involvement with the problem-solving activity* that reduces the need to apply detached, rule-based strategies. A seemingly intuitive, "feeling" driven, tacit sensibility begins to emerge. Successful approaches produce positive emotional responses ("It *feels* right") and unsuccessful approaches produce negative emotional reactions ("Hmm, that doesn't *feel* right"), resulting in the embodiment and assimilation of successful strategies. "At this stage, the involved, experienced performer sees goals and salient aspects but not [necessarily] what to do to achieve these goals." [Problems appropriate for this stage include highly complex building types/program requirements, integrating structure, systems, materials, environmental, and other issues].

STAGE 5   Expertise:
Assimilated ability to respond to the situation

What distinguishes expertise is the ability to, seemingly without effort, see the situation and to see (among a large repertoire) a way to solve it that is most likely to produce the desired outcome, and then to choose the solution that *feels* right (and usually is). To know more that you can say. The expert relies heavily on a broad based, domain specific tacit knowledge, and experience with diverse situations and strategies, to solve the design problem. The expert sees "immediately how to achieve this goal." This is when a fully developed *sense of design* has been acquired. [Problems appropriate for this stage include self-directed learning: exploring architectural ideas].

This chapter after considering what designing is, how designers think, and what designers do, examined who can be a designer, how expertise is acquired and theoretical considerations related to the cognitive processes involved in acquiring design expertise. Several observations have emerged. There does not seem to be any particular personality type, or aptitude test that is effective in determining who is likely to be a successful designer. However, there is evidence that suggests that there are some predispositions, and competencies that increase the likelihood of success – especially an aptitude for visio-spatial thinking and problem solving. Ericsson's research provides a convincing argument supporting the counter-intuitive idea that the likelihood of achieving exceptional performance in any domain has more to do with taking advantage of the adaptability of the human brain and body, and years of deliberate practice than natural talent. Duckworth et al., recognizing that very few people seem to be motivated to achieve levels of exceptional performance, even if they have the intellectual and physical potential, proposes a motivational theory she calls *grit*: "[The] ability to work strenuously toward challenges, maintaining effort and interest over years despite failure, adversity, and plateaus in progress" (p. 1087). Then, assuming a highly motivated person, with grit, and an aptitude for visio-spatial thinking and problem solving, who is willing to invest the time and effort into years of deliberate practice; the cognitive processes related to acquiring design expertise were considered. These included the three types of domain related knowledge, declarative/conceptual, procedural/heuristic and strategic, that need to be mastered. It was observed that acquiring expert performance ability requires situated learning, that facilitates the development of structure or scaffolding that assists learning complex skill. Finally, the Dreyfus five stage developmental model was presented as a way to make sense of how the novice develops from an (explicit) problem-oriented design approach to the expert's (implicit) solution-oriented, tacit approach to design that is driven by a feeling for what to do.

What becomes apparent, when seen as a whole, is that while design expertise is highly dependent on explicit, declarative knowledge and conceptual methods for solving problems, it relies just as heavily (perhaps more so) on implicit, tacit, embodied knowledge that is highly influenced by body knowledge and feeling (aesthesis). It is this feeling knowledge that is the foundation for a sense of design.

The next chapter will introduce the concept of aesthetic resonance. Aesthetic resonance describes the feeling that expert designers experience (aesthesis), that *tells designers what to do.*

10 Aesthetic Resonance

The artist embodies in himself the attitude of the perceiver while he works...

(Dewey, 1934/2005)

§ 10.1   The Theoretical Foundation for Aesthetic Resonance

This chapter introduces the concept of *aesthetic resonance*, which describes the function *aesthesis* plays in design cognition. The above provides a theoretical foundation for understanding the way this concept is used in this research.

§ 10.1.1   The Body Knowing

The above argument is based on the presupposition that while the proximate end of design is a functional approximation, the proper end of design is a building/built environment. Without this, this thesis cannot be defended. If one supposes that the proper end to design is a plan or a design concept or a representation, even a representation that describes a building that could be built, then designing can be satisfied with abstractions and "pure form" – without a body. But abstract concepts, as useful as they are, and pure forms, as interesting as it is to contemplate them, do not exist; except as abstract ideas in the realm of a disembodied mind. But, as was argued above (and seems self-evident), people are not disembodied minds. Indeed it was proposed above that there is no such thing as a mind (vs. body). Rather, *mind* is a word (a convention) used to describe human cognition, which is not independent from the body, but quite the opposite; it is absolutely dependent on the body.

Some scholars, referring to the above, propose that the body did not evolve as a physical means of gaining sense information, nourishment, and locomotion in the world; but rather, rather, they argue the mind evolved to increase the ability of the body to interact with the world. Or as Ryles might quip, *to allow the man-in-the-machine to get around*. This thesis presupposes, and has argued that there is no *mind-body dualism*.

The body came first, and there is no such thing as the Cartesian mind. This is difficult for some to accept, as the idea of a mind/body dualism is so deeply ingrained not only in popular Western culture but popular Eastern culture as well.[338] The point is that if the proper end to designing is a design object for the purpose of human use, one then needs a body to experience the functional and aesthetic qualities of the object. Our bodies are quite good at this. Without a body one cannot open a door, one cannot enjoy the cozy feeling of sitting in front of a fireplace (atmosphere), one cannot look out the window, one cannot smell fresh bread baking in the kitchen, one cannot complain about a draft. Of course one might argue that one does not need a body to imagine all those things, but one might need to consider if one doesn't need a body, then one does not actually need all those things either. Above, research has been presented that offers a reasonable argument that the human body and cognitive abilities evolved simultaneously. That how we experience, perceive and make sense of the world is a function of embodied cognition.

It was also shown that the theory of tacit knowledge, as proposed by Ryles and Polanyi, offers a convincing explanation of how experts from scientists to master carpenters are able to do what they do – by feelingly inhabiting the situation – establishing the importance of body knowledge over Newell and Simon's disembodied general problem solving theory. Ryles, describes two types of knowledge: knowing that and knowing how. Knowing how, or how-to, is normally associated with procedural, heuristic, tacit, implicit knowledge. Polanyi (1974) describes tacit knowledge as a *kind of knowing that is made up of a range of conceptual and sensory information, images and ideas that can be brought to bear (made use of) when making an attempt to make sense of (understand, frame, find order) or perform some task that is typically associated with expert (design) performance.*

The concept of *Einfühlung* (empathy), proposed by German empirical psychologists of the 19th century was introduced as well. *Einfühlung* is the embodied experience of *feeling into* that induces an aesthetic experience. More recently, the discovery by Rizzolatti of mirror-neurons gives evidence that the cognitive functions (sense perception) that we use to interact with the world, are the same as that which allow us to experience a full range of sense experiences in our imagination. From the discipline of neuroaesthetics the concept of *embodied simulation* was described by Gallese & Gattara, as how one can experience an internal representation using the same sense systems that one uses to know the world. Chatterjee proposed the *core triad* – sensations, meaning, and emotion – that are the components of aesthetic experience.

---

338   As mind and soul are often used interchangeably, this resistance may be ascribed to fear of losing the existence of the *soul*. But, however interesting is would be to muse on this, questions of the soul are outside the scope of this research.

These provide a way to talk about the quality of the aesthetic experience, and what mix of stimuli and cognitive functions may be at work that produce the various and subtle variations of quality in such experiences. The implications for design, or at least for providing empirical evidence that describes what designers do is exciting. These theories not only provide empirical evidence that inter-subjective experience is probable, but they pose a challenge to designers, that cannot not be ignored: **feelings matter**.

Ericsson's theory of expertise can be described as the process of acquiring tacit knowledge. His theory holds that it is the ability to take advantage of the body's and mind's amazing plasticity and adaptability, and years of deliberate practice, more than "natural talent," that leads to expert performance. He too pointed to the primacy of the ability to *feel* the situation and respond in a seemingly effortless manner as the hallmark of exceptional performance. Finally there is the Dreyfus developmental model that gives structure to Ericsson's theory, and describes how mastery of multiple types of knowledge in the domain, evolve into a situated, highly automated ability to perform complex tasks and the ability to assess a situation with one's feelings rather than relying upon the rule-based procedural heuristics associated with beginners. The acquired ability to rely on one's feelings seems to be the hallmark of expert performance. This ability to rely on one's feelings, as the hallmark of expertise suggests that it is also what is meant by a sense of design.

§ 10.1.2   **Resonance**

Another theme that was explored above had to do with the cognitive mechanisms (perception/representation) that facilitate the way we interact, experience, and learn about the world. Above, Anderson (2003) is cited in the section on embodied cognition, holding that it is probable that *complex data sets are experienced as internal (mental) representations that can be externalized either to test for correlation or to transfer (communicate) with another.* Lipari (2015) was also cited in the section on coherence, writing about correlation in reference to sense-making, *It is the brain's correlations of sensory information that create the knowledge we have about our surroundings.* Regarding representations Newell et al. (1958) write about the *correspondence between the internal and external representation* in human problem solving as a way to test the veracity of the solution. These terms, *correlation* and *correspondence*, both describe a situation where two phenomena are being internally compared – not to see if they are identical -- but to test if certain properties work as intended or needed.

The terms suggest that one is looking not for *fit* as Alexander uses it, but rather for congruence, *right relationship* – harmonious relationship as Aristotle uses it: *appropriate (in right proportion) whose chief forms are order, symmetry, and definiteness*. Schön (1992) describes this activity within the design process as *appreciation*, "by which is meant both their active, sensory apprehension of the stuff in question, and their construction on an order in that stuff that includes the naming and framing of things, qualities and relationships" (p. 9). The word that comes to mind is *resonance*.

Resonance in physics means, "the reinforcement or prolongation of sound by reflection from a surface or by the synchronous vibration of a neighboring object" (Oxford Dictionary of English, 2016). Resonance is a *synchronous vibration*. When one says that an idea *resonates*, it implies not only that one understands the meaning, but that there is kind of knowing that is hard to explain; it is as if one *feels* the meaning. Resonance refers to knowing something feelingly. It is more than making sense of a situation – a sense of coherence; it is feeling the mood, the vibe, the atmosphere of a situation (aesthesis). Synchronous means "existing or occurring at the same time" (Oxford Dictionary of English, 2016). To resonate is to vibrate at the same time.

§ 10.2   Inhabiting the Design World Feelingly

The hybrid idea of *inhabiting the design world feelingly*, adapted from Polanyi (1966) and Schön (1992), is proposed to describe this feeling/experience of resonance in the design process. But, instead of describing the resonance one might experience between two abstract ideas when they feel like they are working together as hoped for, resonance is being used here to describe the experience of the designer actively seeking a particular quality of atmosphere that requires a level of connoisseurship of spatial experience. A feeling the designer knows, cannot really describe, but only recognizes when he experiences it. Combined, aesthetic resonance refers to the application of aesthesis to assess the quality of the atmosphere of the design solution as it emerges as both internal and external representations against the anticipated feeling the designer is seeking. When using the phrase aesthetic resonance the implication is that **the feeling the designer intended to induce, vibrates synchronously with the experience that is induced when he inhabits the design world. The designer pre-structures the problem space by identifying a quality of atmosphere he desires to induce in the user.** This is a sense of design. When the designer inhabits the design world, he is applying his senses to the situation, seeking body knowledge, that will inform his design decisions. It is a visceral, hedonic experience that is developed over years of practice.

The concept of the application of the senses to enter feelingly into an imagined world is not a new concept. For example, though he did not have the neuroscience to back him up, the 16th century mystic, Ignatius of Loyola (1968), writing between 1522–1524, recommended the *application of the senses* as a method for entering more deeply into a contemplative state. His suggestion was to enter into an imaged state feelingly as a means to garnish another level of meaning from the (imagined) situation. There is a visceral quality to the experience he recommended his students to seek during contemplation. He recommended engaging the imagined situation by locating oneself in a particular place in the scene. Taking account of the *atmosphere*: the weather, the smells, the feeling of the ground under one's feet, the weight of the cloths on one's back, the sounds, and to even to try to feel how the others in the scene are feeling. Loyola was recommending the use of what we now call empathy, that is facilitated through mirror-neurons not only allowing us to feel the feelings of another, but to also activate the same mechanisms in our brains that are activated when we experience the world. One could say that Loyola was teaching his students how to apply and develop a sense of aesthesis, to inhabit an imagined place feelingly.[339]

There is growing interest in and familiarity with embodied cognition amongst designers and theorists. Some have been referred to in this research: Eberhard, 2007; Mallgrave, 2013, 2011; Pallasmaa, 2015, 2009, 2005; Perez-Gomez, 2016, 2015. Perez-Gomez (2015) writes regarding architecture education:

The new central concern [in design education] should be to prepare the future architect to use her imagination to make poetic artifacts and spaces with character, resonant with the human situations they house, engaging dimensions of consciousness that are in fact usually stifled by conventional educational paradigms, rather than simply planning efficient buildings." (pp. 229-230)

---

[339] As a one hour exercise for second year design students, I invite them to close their eyes and try to stand in front of the building (usually a house) they are designing. Then after a minute or so, keeping their eyes shut, I suggest that they approach the building, being attentive to the feeling of the ground under their feel, the sound of the crushed gravel, the shade of the trees, the time of day. Then I suggest that they open the door. But stop for a moment and feel the quality of the material of the door knob, then look at it, what does it look like. Is it metal? Now, I suggest, step into the house. What is the first thing you feel. Close the door, now take off your shoes (if it is in China), is there any place to put them? What about your jacket? While you are sitting down, or leaning on the wall, taking off your shoes, what do you see. And so it goes for about an hour. The point of the exercise is to invite the students to learn to use and develop their aesthesis ability to assess the quality of the atmosphere they are creating. A related exercise is to tell them that they are invisible, and to watch how the children use the space. Then to watch the grand parents. Then the parents. And so on. These are exercises that accomplished designers do intuitively. But I don't think it hurts to introduce students to this amazing cognitive power while they are still in school.

It seems that body-knowledge is being re-introduced back into the design process.

Aesthetic resonance describes how *aesthesis* functions within the design process. Aesthesis is at work when the designer assesses the aesthetic quality of interior and exterior representations of the emerging design solution and finally the competed building/built environment. The designer, making use of the same cognitive systems that allow him to assess the quality of the room he is sitting in, wander around his mental representation, looking, touching, tasting, smelling, feeling his way through, seeking congruence, correlation, resonance between what he intended and what he is experiencing. Aesthesis was defined above as *apprehension by all the senses, enabling an understanding through non representative concepts of that which is perceived by embodied consciousness* (Perez-Gomez, 2016, pp. 17-18). This is what the designer does. Or as Dewey puts it, it is *an attitude of the perceiver,* that provides information about an a*tmosphere* or object; be it an internal representation of an intended atmosphere or object, an external representation of an intended atmosphere or object, or an atmosphere that is induced by a building/built environment. Aesthesis is the cognitive mechanism that facilitates the assessment of the quality of an atmosphere, imagined and real. Aesthesis is the cognitive mechanism that assesses an atmosphere and allows us to make a judgment about its experiential quality.

§ 10.3   A Design Scenario

A design scenario might proceed like this: In the process of defining the problem, the designer brings a predetermined sense of coherence and quality of aesthetic experience, as well as a way of thinking about the problem to the problem situation. Depending on the designer's experience, he may or not be conscious of this.[340] These may be a preference for using a grid, modular or proportional system, narrative, generative idea, or any other devise, that will facilitate the making of a cohesive plan. The designer may also, based on the building type, past experience, personality of the client, the intended users, etc., think/feel like this building should *possess* this or that feeling, or quality of atmosphere. Of course, the building does not possess a feeling/or quality of atmosphere, the building induces a quality of experience through it architectural characteristics and how the user experiences them.

---

340   It would seem to me, that an experienced, mature designer would be self-aware of his preferences, and have the discipline to acknowledge them, and then put them aside, so as not to unduly bias how he defines the problem space and frames the problem. I have no way of substantiating this, and I have not found any research that supports it. It is a question for further research.

It is a normative expectation that the expert designer is skilled at making use of architectural elements to induce an intended quality of architectural experience/atmosphere. As the designer works on the problem and a design world emerges, he inhabits the design world feelingly. The expert designer is not seeing plans and sections and elevations in the design world. He uses these conventions (tools) to externalize his mental image. The designer is experiencing an emerging world making use of all his sense systems. As he inhabits this world, and considers the design criteria and constraints, he assembles them, arranges them, moves them around. There are an unlimited number of combinations possible. He looks for evidence of emerging coherence and engages his desired quality of aesthetic experience to bias or limit the possible solution paths. He tests the resonance between his desired aesthetic experience against the experience his mental approximation is inducing. Likewise, as the design traverses one or another solution path, he arrives at moments when *it just doesn't feel right*. It is an odd feeling. One wonders how can something that has never existed before not *feel right*? But that is the way it feels. Something is not working. The designer frames and reframes the problem. Makes moves, assesses them (sees), and makes new moves. Still it just doesn't *feel right*. The designer returns to the problem space, adjusts the problem definition, includes a new variable into the mix. Things start falling place. It is starting to feel right. And so it goes.[341]

The predetermined aesthetic experience with which the expert designer pre-structures the problem can also be challenged or evolve. Midway through the conceptual design phase, the designer may realize the he was *thinking about the problem* all wrong. He expects this. The feeling he desires is a heuristic tool. He has the discipline to let it go if its not working (if not with some resistance). A new revised feeling emerges. It is tested. It is a better fit with the problem situation. Things start coming together. He inhabits the design space. It feels right. It resonates. It is exciting. He enters into the optimal experience called *flow*. He is inhabiting the design world feelingly.

The design world (internal approximation) becomes too complicated to hold in working memory. Aware that what seems to work well in his imagination does not always match reality, he needs to externalize the internal representation, to test if it really works as well as it seems. He needs also to look at the external representation for new or missed opportunities. The designer also needs input from the client/owner/user to know if the emerging design induces the intended quality of experience in others.

---

[341]   The novice designer with limited experience, minimal mastery of domain-related situated knowledge and being problem-focused, cannot rely on feelings to produce a reliable solution. The beginner is more dependent on domain-specific declarative/conceptual knowledge, analysis, trying to please the design tutor to make-sense of the problem. He has preconceptions with which he – perhaps with a certain degree of naïvete – pre-structures the problem, but with limited situational experience, there is a likelihood that these will not work.

He is also interested in the efficiency of the plan and other demonstrable characteristics. But, what he really wants to hear, is that the client/owner/user *likes* the emerging design. That the feeling it induces resonates with the client/owner/user's expectations. He needs the client/owner/user to be able to inhabit the design world as he does. But this is not easy. So he makes external representations intended to allow the client/owner/user to inhabit the design world. But, non-designers do not have a refined ability to experience a design world feelingly (aesthesis), design sense. So he **inhabits the design world in different modes**: as designer, as owner/client/user; as designer observing designer, as designer observing owner/client/user. This is a highly developed skill. In each of these *modes of inhabitation*, he seeks to experience the design world from a different perspective. Insofar as he has mastered this ability, he increases the likelihood that the client/owner/user will be satisficed with the experience of the actual building. Finally the designer inhabits the actual building. And tests to feel if there is *resonance* between how he thought it would feel and how it actually does feel. This is the consummation of the act of designing.

§ 10.4 Feeling as a Functional Cognitive Bias in the Design Process

Aesthesis and the desire for a sense of cohesion function as *cognitive biases* in the design process. Design moves are deemed successful or promising insofar as the feelings evoked by the emerging design proposal are *resonant* with the intended aesthetic experience and produce a sense of cohesion. The intensity of the experience of resonance creates a feeling of excitement (as in *being hot on the trail*), which provides emotional motivation (intensity) to continue in pursuit of this rather than that direction. Aesthesis functions throughout the design process: from the moment of determining the problem space, to framing the problem, through the iterative "see-move-see" process of solution-seeking and development, through the technical phase of determining structure, systems, materials and methods of construction, through site visits and evaluation of the completed building built environment.

Throughout this process aesthesis plays a critical role in the design decision-making process not unlike a wine tasting experience where one is determining which wine will go best with dinner, or which wine to buy for a friend. One starts with a pretty specific expectation/anticipation for the taste (and price range) of the wine (pre-structuring). It is accepted from the beginning that it is unlikely that there will be a perfect match. A match that is both satisfying and sufficient.

Its not so much a compromise, but an acknowledgment of the complexity involved in balancing multiple criteria that offer the greatest likelihood of resulting in the intended (anticipated) experience.

To continue with the wine analogy, one could rely on reviews from leading experts or respected magazines, the recommendations of the wine steward, technical data, research and analysis; or one could pick up the bottle, look at its color, feel its weight, attend a tasting, discuss the flavor, tannins, the acid, the body, the color, the nose, etc., to get some input from someone with a respected – recognizing that the responsibility for the choice belongs to the buyer. Only the buyer knows the precise flavor that is being looked for. But that's not the end of it. Up to now, use has been made of all the resources available to the buyer (conceptual/practical) to make an deliberate choice. How effective his choice was, is finally determined by tasting the wine and then testing the anticipated experience against the actual experience.[342] In this movement from comparison to choice, he is seeking aesthetic resonance. Does it live up to expectations. Søren Kierkegaard (1843/1987) writes, "If I had a humble spirit in my service who, when I asked for a glass of water, brought me the world's costliest wines blended in a chalice, I should dismiss him, in order to teach him that my pleasure consists, not in what I enjoy, but in having my own way." In the end the question is no if it is good – there is a lot of good wine out there – but if it is what I wanted, anticipated, expected.

This experience of resonance relies on an understanding and *feel* for how architectural elements, materials, color, volume, proportion, light, sound, etc., work together to evoke an intended aesthetic experience; an ability to think multi-dimensionally and externalize design concepts; an ability to apply one's senses to enter into and assess/discern the quality of the aesthetic experience of the (emerging) imagined or externalized solution; and the knowledge of how and the skill to (subtly) adjust the various architectural elements in a manner that will result in a building that evokes the desired quality of aesthetic experience. This requires a highly developed sense of design. This is design expertise.

---

[342]   Above this ability to discern quality within the parameters of a normative expectations for performance was referred to as connoisseurship. Consoli (2014) explains that there are two different theories that are usually used to explain aesthetic pleasure and appreciation: The first argues that "liking and esthetic [sic.] pleasure are a function of the interpreters' processing dynamics, in particular the fluency and ease of the processes." The *interpreters processing dynamics* is what is referred to in this research as aesthesis. The second theory holds that "liking or preference for a stimulus is based upon the arousal potential of the stimulus." Arousal potential was discusses above with Berlyne's use of the Wundt curve. Based on current research from neurocognitive science Consoli argues that: "(1.) Esthetic [sic.]pleasure constitutes a subjective feeling grounded in and caused by the interpreter's processing dynamics; (2.) The crucial parameters and variables of the processing dynamics that are able to produce appreciation appear to be opposites: high art stimulates disfluency, low art fluency; and (3.) Expertise represents the key component to understanding and appreciating disfluency" (p. 95). The ability to distinguish the quality of an esthetic experience is acquired.

§ 10.5 Summary

We inhabit, make sense of, and experience the world, our buildings, and built environments with our bodies. The first way a user experiences a building is with his body, seeing a facade in the distance, touching the door knob, climbing the steps, stepping into the lobby, working in an office, looking out a window in a school, sewing cloths in a factory, trying to sleep in a prison cell, giving birth in a hospital, seeking solace in a church, temple or mosque. Each has an atmosphere, for better or for worse, that was intentionally (or unintentionally) made by a designer. The experiential quality of these environments are the result of decisions made during the design and building process. The cognitive ability we use we assess a built environment/atmosphere is aesthesis. Aesthesis functions not only as a mean to assess an external built atmosphere, but also functions to assess the quality of an internal imagined atmosphere. The designer makes use of aesthesis to determine if the quality of the internal approximation of his design proposal correlates with the experience he intended. The designer also makes use of aesthesis to assess the experiential quality of externalized approximations of his design proposal against that which he intended. This use of aesthesis as a means to assess the quality of a design proposal against the that which is intended is called aesthetic resonance. Aesthetic resonance functions throughout the design process as both a motivating factor that establishes the goal to be achieved, and as a heuristic that influences design decisions. Both the deliberate development of a refined sense of aesthesis through connoisseur sometimes referred to a sense of design – and the ability to enter feelingly into the design world to assess the experiential quality of the emerging design solution against that which is intended – aesthetic resonance – are necessary to acquire design expertise.

11 Conclusion

Based on a review of current research in design theory and cognitive science, critical reflection on 25 years of teaching and professional practice, and in dialogue with colleagues, the above sought to describe how design expertise is acquired and the function and place of aesthesis within the design process. The thesis established that the proper end of architectural design is the making of building/built environments. That the normative performance expectations for architecture design as an occupation establish that it is reasonable to expect that a design professional can provide a coherent solution that satisfies design criteria, constraints and technical requirements, and that induces intended aesthetic experience. That expert performers rely heavily on tacit embodied knowledge. The above challenged Cartesian dualism, arguing with cognitive scientists for a change in the way we think about human cognition as existing in a disembodied state, to doing away with the concept of the mind as other, and embracing an embodied way of thinking about human cognition. The above presented multiple ways of describing design, especially as a process. And then went on to describe processes, problem-solving, systems theory methods and methodology. Some traditional ways of thinking about design were challenged, and some old theories reclaimed. Finally, a description of design that is derived from Polanyi, Hillier, and Schön, and influenced by theories of embodied cognition was presented. This laid the ground work for challenging the idea of natural talent as the determining factor that made it more likely that someone would success at designing. And, with the same theory, illustrated that through thousands of hours of deliberate practice it is possible to restructure one's brain and train one's body such that even the most difficult of maneuvers appear effortless. And it illustrated the ability to assess a complex situation without invoking explicit rules, procedures and heuristics, but rather being able to use one's feelings and usually be right. Finally, it was shown how this embodied way of knowing functions in the design process in both seeking a sense of coherence, and being drawn to and intended quality of aesthetic experience. The term aesthetic resonance was introduced to describe how the embodied knowing of designers (aesthesis) both pre-structures the design problem and allows the designer to inhabit the design world feelingly. It is argued that this ability to inhabit a design world feelingly is what is meant by a sense of design.

By presenting research and posing arguments from design theory, expertise, embodiment, aesthetic judgment, and by posing a theory of aesthetic resonance I sought to defend four claims: (1.) Design is an acquired skill that follows well-established models that describe the acquisition of expert performance, (2.)

As architectural design is fundamentally about making places (buildings) for human use and habitation, which are experienced through embodied cognition, design solutions are (properly) experienced not so much as abstract ideas (concepts), but rather as tactile, actual objects. (3.) A successful design is not only a coherent solution that solves for clearly defined (functional, technical, environmental, economic) criteria but also one that possesses aesthetic qualities. (4.) Aesthesis (body knowledge) plays a critical role in the design process. The ability to assess the quality of an atmosphere (aesthesis) within the design process (as internal and external representations) is essential to the acquisition of design expertise. Aesthesis is the way an expert designer knows what to do, knows that an approximation of a building that never existed looks the way it was supposed to.

In making these claims I argued for the importance of recognizing the developmental process that students of (architecture) design must move through to acquire design expertise; the need to challenge Cartesian dualism that promotes abstract formalism; and to acknowledge the fundamental role that aesthesis plays within the design process (aesthetic resonance).

By providing a theoretical basis for understanding how design expertise is acquired and by introducing the concept of aesthetic resonance, it is my sincere hope that this thesis will provide a useful conceptual framework, that will influence how design educators, students and professional think about designing, and be a resource for all those seeking to participate in designing a built environment worthy of the dignity of all people.

Works Cited*

Ackerman, D. (2004, 6 14). ESSAY; I Sing the Body's Pattern Recognition Machine. *New York Times*.
  Retrieved from http://www.nytimes.com/2004/06/15/science/essay-i-sing-the-body-s-pattern-
  recognition-machine.html?_r=0

Adams, K. M. (2015). Design Methodologies. In K. M. Adams, *Non-functional requirements in systems analysis
  and design*. (pp. 15-43). doi: 10.1007/978-3-319-18344-2

Akin, Ö. (1979). An exploration of the design process. *Design Methods and Theories* 13(3/4).
  doi:10.1068/b190503

*Akin, Ö. (1986). *Psychology of architectural design*. London: Pion Limited.

Akin, O., & Lin, C. (1995). Design protocol data and novel design decisions. *Design Studies*, 16, 211-236.
  doi: 10.1016/0142-694X(94)00010-B

Alexander, C. (1964). *Notes on the synthesis of form*. Cambridge, MA: Harvard University Press.

Alexander, C. (1984). The state of the art in design methods. In N. Cross (Ed.), *Developments in design methodology* (pp. 300-316). Chichester: John Wiley & Sons.

Alexiou, K., Zamenopoulos, T., Johnson, J. H., & Gilbert, S. J. (2009, 11). Exploring the neurological basis of
  design cognition using brain imaging: Some preliminary results. *Design Studies*, 30(6).
  doi: 10.1016/j.destud.2009.05.002

American Institute of Architects. (1997). *AIA Document B141-1997*. Washington DC: American Institute
  of Architects.

American Institute of Architects. (2014). *The architect's handbook of professional practice*
  (Fifteenth Edition ed.). R. L. Hayes (Ed.) Hoboken, NJ: Wiley.

American Institute of Architects. (2016). *Architectural graphic standards* (12th Edition ed.). D. J. Hall (Ed.)
  New York: John Wiley & Sons.

**Anderson, M. L. (2003). *Embodied cognition: A field guide. Artificial Intelligence*, 149, 91-130.
  doi: 10.1016/S0004-3702(03)00054-7**

Anderson, R. (2016). The rashomon effect and communication. *Canadian Journal of Communication*, 41(2).
  doi: 10.22230/cjc.2016v41n2a3068

Archer, B. (1968). *The structure of design processes*. (Doctoral Dissertation). London: Royal College of Art, 1968.
  Shelfmark: Document Supply DRT 484530. Available on Ethos: http://ethos.bl.uk/OrderDetails.do?uin=uk.
  bl.ethos.484530

Archer, B. (1979). Design as a discipline. *Design Studies*, 1(1), 17-20. doi: 10.1016/0142-694X(79)90023-1

Archer, B. (1965). *Systematic methods for designers*. London: The Design Council

Archer, B. (1999). Design, innovation, agility. *Design Studies*, 20(6), 565-571.
  doi: 10.1016/S0142-694X(99)00025-3

Architecture for Humanity. (2012). *Design like you give a damn* (Aaronson, Deborah ed.). New York: Abrams.

Aristotle. (2004). *The Nicomachean ethics*. (J. A. Thomson, Trans.) London: Penguin Books.

Aristotle. (2009), *On the art of poetry*. (I. Bywater, Trans.) Retrieved from https://www.gutenberg.org/
  files/6763/6763-h/6763-h.htm

Aristotle. (2015). Metaphysics. (W. D. Ross, Trans.) Retrieved from https://ebooks.adelaide.edu.au/a/aristot-
  le/metaphysics/

Arnheim, R. (1987). The state of the art in perception. *Leonardo*, 20(4), 305-307.

Arnheim, R. (1993). Sketching and the psychology of design. *Design Issues*, 9(2), 15-19.
  doi: 10.2307/1511669

Arnheim, R. (2009). *The dynamics of architectural form* (30th Anniversary ed.). Berkeley: University of
  California Press.

Ashby, R. (1956). *An introduction to cybernetics*. New York, NY: John Wiley & Sons.

---

*   Citations highlighted in bold indicate key texts.

Asimow, M. (1962). *Introduction to design*. Englewood, NJ, USA: Prentice Hill.

Backhaus, W., & Menzel, R. (1992). Conclusions from color-vision of insects. *Behavioral and Brain Sciences, 15*(1), 28-30. doi: 10.1017/S0140525X00067273

Badke-Schaub, P., & Eris , O. (2014). A theoretical approach to intuition in design: Does design methodology need to account for unconscious processes? In A. Chakrabarti, & L. Blessing (Eds.), *An anthology of theories and models of design* (pp. 353-370). London: Springer.

Badke-Schaub, P., Daalhuizen, J., & Roozenburg, N. (2011). Towards a designer-centered methodology: descriptive considerations and prescriptive reflections. In H. Birkhofer (Ed.), *The future of design methodology* (pp. 181-197). London: Springer-Verlag.

Badke-Schaub, P., Roozenburg, N., & Cardoso, C. (2010). Design thinking: A paradigm on its way from dilution to meaninglessness? *Proceedings of 8th Design Thinking Research Symposium: Interpreting design thinking* (pp. 39-50). Sydney: University of Technology, Sydney.

Baiche, B., & Williman, N. (Eds.). (2000). *Ernst and Peter Neufert architect's data* (3rd Edition ed.). Oxford: Blackwell Science.

Bailey, D. (1997). *When push comes to shove: A computational model of embodiment acquisition of action verbs.* (Doctoral Dissertation, University of California Berkeley). Retrieved from http://www1.icsi.berkeley.edu/~dbailey/diss.pdf

Banham, R. (1980). *Theory and design in the first machine age.* **Cambridge, MA: The MIT Press.**

Bartlett, F. C. (1958). *Thinking*. London: George, Allen and Unwin.

Bayazit, N. (2004). Investigating design: A review of forty years of design research. *Design Issues, 20(1),* **16-29. doi: 10.1162/074793604772933739**

Beardsley, M. (1966). *Aesthetics from classical greece to the present.* University of Alabama Press.

Beilock, S. (2010). *Choke: What the secrets of the brain reveal about getting it right when you have to.* Simon & Schuster: Free Press.

Beitman, B. D. (2009). Brains seek patterns in coincidences. *Psychiatric Annals, 39*(5), 255-264. Retrieved from http://www.drjudithorloff.com/Free-Articles/Psychiatric-Annals-Brains-Seek-Patterns.pdf

Berlyne, D. E. (1970). Novelty, complexity, and hedonic value. *Perception & Psychophysics, 8*(5), 279-286. doi: 10.3758/BF03212593

Berlyne, D. E. (1971). *Aesthetics and psychobiology*. New York: McGraw Hill.

Bernstein, R. (1976). *The restructuring of social and political theory*. New York: Harcourt, Beace, Jovanovich.

Bertalanffy, L. v. (1968). *General systems theory: Foundations, development, applications*. New York: Basic Books.

Best, D. (2005, 12). Aesthetic and artistic, two separate concepts: The dangers of 'aesthetic education'. *Research in Dance Education, 5*(2). Retrieved from: http://jashm.press.illinois.edu/14.2/14-2Aesthetic_Best67-82.pdf

Bickard, M. H. (2008). Is embodiment necessary? In P. Clavo, & G. Antoni (Eds.), *Handbook of cognitive science: An embodied approach* (On-line ed., pp. 29-40). Elsevier. Retrieved from https://www.elsevier.com/books/handbook-of-cognitive-science/calvo/978-0-08-046616-3

Bickhard, M. H. (2009). The biological foundations of cognitive science. *New Ideas in Psychology, 27*, 75-84. doi: 10.1016/j.newideapsych.2008.04.001

Bloom, B. (Ed.), (1985). *Developing talent in young people*. New York: Ballantine Books.

Bloomer, K., & Moore, C. (1977). *Body, memory, architecture.* **New Haven: Yale University Press.**

Blouw, P., Solodkin, E., Thagard, P., & Eliasmith, C. (2015). Concepts as semantic pointers: A framework and computational model. *Cognitive Science, 40*(5), 1128-1162. doi: 10.1111/cogs.12265

Bochenski, J. M. (1965). *The methods of contemporary thought*. Dordrecht, Netherlands: Reidel.

van Boeijen, A., Daalhuizen, J., Zijlstra, J., & van der Schoor, R. (Eds.). (2013). *Delft design guide*. Amsterdam, Netherlands: BIS Publishers.

Böhme, G. (1993). Atmosphere as the fundamental concept of a new aesthetic. *Thesis Eleven, 36*, 113-126. doi: 10.1177/072551369303600107

Boulding, K. (1964). General systems as a point of view. In M. D. Mesarovic (Ed.), *Views on general systems theory: Proceedings of the second systems symposium*. New York: John Wiley & Sons.

Box, H. (2007). *Think like and architect*. Austin: University of Texas Press.

Boyer, E. L., & Mitgang, L. D. (1996). *Building community: A new future for architecture education and practice*. Princeton: The Carnegie Foundation.

Braha, D., & Maimon, O. (1997). The design process: Properties, paradigms, and structure. *IEEE Transaction on Systems, Man and Cybernetics – Part A: Systems and Humans, 27*(2), 146-166. doi: 10.1109/3468.554679

Branford, V. (1914). *Interpretations and forecasts: A study of survivals and tendencies in contemporary society*. London: Duckworth & Co.

Brawne, M. (2003). *Architectural thought: The design process and the expectant eye*. Oxford: Architectural Press.

Bridge, H. (2010). Empathy theory and Heinrich Wölfflin: A reconsideration. *Journal of European Studies, 41*(1), 3-22. doi: 10.1177/0047244110391033

Broadbent, G. (1973). *Design in architecture: Architecture and the human sciences*. London: John Wiley & Sons.

Broadbent, G. (1984). The development of design methods. In N. Cross (Ed.), *Developments in Design Methodology* (pp. 337-345). New York: John Wiley & Sons.

Brooks, R. A. (1991). Intelligence without reason. *AI Memos*. Retrieved from http://hdl.handle. net/1721.1/6569

Brown, T. (2008, June). Design thinking. *Harvard Business Review, 86*(6). Retrieved from https://hbr. org/2015/09/design-thinking-comes-of-age

Buchanan, R. (1995). Wicked problems in design thinking. In V. Margolin, & Buchannan, Richard (Eds.), *The Idea of Design, Design Issues Reader*. Cambridge, MA, USA: MIT Press.

Buchanan, R. (2001). Design research and the new learning. *Design Issues, 17*(4), 3-23. doi: 10.1162/07479360152681056

Buchanan, R., & Margolin, V. (1995). *Discovering design: Explorations in design studies*. Chicago: University of Chicago Press.

Bundgaard, P., & Stjernfelt, F. (2010). Logic and cognition. In P. Cobley (Ed.), *The Routledge companion to semiotics* (pp. 57 - 73). New York, NY: Routledge. Retrieved from http://s3.amazonaws.com/academia.edu. documents/37742512/The_Routledge_companion_to_semiotics.pdf?AWSAccessKeyId=AKIAIWOWYYG-Z2Y53UL3A&Expires=1491445143&Signature=hxBeduPe%2Bn%2FL%2FgLMouTFAxNxP5k%3D&re-sponse-content-disposition=inline%3B%20filename%3DThe_Routledge_companion_to_semiotics. pdf#page=80

Burke, E. (1756). *A philosophical enquiry into the origin of our idea of the sublime and beautiful*. London: R. & J. Dodley.

Carpenter, W. (1997). *Learning by building*. New York: Van Nostrand Reinhold.

Carr, D. (1999). Art, practical knowledge and aesthetic objectivity. *Ratio, XII*, 240-256. doi: 10.1111/1467-9329.00090

Cela-Conde, C., Agnati, L., Huston, J., Mora, F., & Nadal, M. (2011). The neural foundations of aesthetic appreci-ation. *Progress in Neurobiology, 94*, 39-48. doi: 10.1016/j.pneurobio.2011.03.003

Chase, W. G., & Simon, H. A. (1973). Perception in chess. *Cognitive Psychology, 4*, 55-81. doi: 10.1016/0010-0285(73)90004-2

Chatterjee, A. (2011). Neuroaesthetics: A coming of age story. *Journal of Cognitive Neuroscience, 23*(1), 53-62. doi: 10.1162/jocn.2010.21457

Chatterjee, A. (2014). *The aesthetic brain*. New York: Oxford University Press. doi: 10.1162/jocn.2010.21457

Ching, F. (2007). *Architecture: Form, Space, and Order* (3rd Edition ed.). Hoboken, New Jersey, USA: John Wiley & Sons.

Churchman, C. W. (1968). *The systems approach*. New York: Dell Publishing.

Cinzia, D. D., & Vittorio, G. (2009). Neuroaesthetics: A review. *Current Opinion in Neurobiology, 19*, 682-687. doi: 10.1016/j.conb.2009.09.001

Clark, A. (1997). *Being there: Putting brain, body, and world together again*. Cambridge, MA, USA: The MIT Press. Retrieved from http://www.amazon.com

Clark, A. (2001). *Mindware*. Oxford University Press.

Clark, A., & Chalmers, D. (1998). The extended mind. *Analysis, 58*(1), 7-19. Retrieved from http://www.jstor. org/stable/3328150

Clay, F. (1908). The origin of aesthetic emotion. *Sammelbände der Internationalen Musikgesellschaft, 9*(2), 282-290.

Collins, H. (2010). *Tacit and explicit knowledge*. Chicago: University of Chicago Press.

Colvin, G. (2008). *Talent is overrated: What really separates world-class performers from everybody else*. New York: Penguin.

Consoli, G. (2013) Recent evidence on perception and esthetic appreciation: The role of value and expertise in canon formation. *i-Perception. 5*, 94-96. doi: 10.1068/i0637jc

Consoli, G. (2014). The emergence of the modern mind: An evolutionary perspective on aesthetic experience. *The Journal of Aesthetics and Art Criticism, 72*(1), 37-55. doi: 10.1111/jaac.12059

Consoli, G. (2015). From beauty to knowledge: a new frame for the neuropsychological approach to aesthetics. *Frontiers in Human Neuroscience, 9*(290). doi: 10.3389/fnhum.2015.00290

Cook, D. (1980). *Some Contributions of General Systems Theory, Cybernetics Theory and Management Control Theory to Evaluation Theory and Practice. Research on Evaluation Program Paper and Report Series. Interim Draft.* Retrieved from https://eric.ed.gov/?id=ED206686.

Corbusier, L. (1926/1970). Five points towards a new architecture. In *Programs and Manifestos in Twentieth Century Architecture.* Cambridge: MIT Press.

Corbusier, L. (1923/1986). *Toward a new architecture.* (F. Etchells, Trans.) New York: Dover.

Couch, Mark B. (n.d.). Causal role of theories of functional explanation. *The Internet Encyclopedia of Philosophy* Retrieved from http://www.iep.utm.edu/func-exp/#H4 (explanations/criticisms) April 18, 2017.

Coyne, R. D., Roseman, M. A., Radford, A. D., Balachandran, M., & Gero, J. S. (1990). *Knowledge-based design systems.* Reading, MA: Addison-Wesley.

Coyne, R., & Snodgrass, A. (1991). Is designing mysterious? Challenging the dual knowledge thesis. *Design Studies, 12*(3), 124-131. doi: 10.1016/0142-694X(91)90020-W

Croley, D. J. (1958, 12). Aesthetic Judgment and Cultural Relativism. *The Journal of Aesthetics and Art Criticism, 17*(2), 187-193. doi: 10.2307/427519

Cross, N. (1977) The automated architect. Viking Penguin.

Cross, N. (1982). Designerly ways of knowing. *Design Studies, 3(4)*, 221-227. doi: 10.1016/0142-694X(82)90040-0

Cross, N. (1984). Introduction. In N. Cross (Ed.), *Developments in design methodology* (pp. vii-x). Chichester: John Wiley & Sons.

Cross, N. (1990). The nature and nurture of design ability. *Design Studies, 11*(3), 127-140. doi: 10.1016/0142-694X(90)90002-T

Cross, N. (1993). A history of design methodology. In M. J. de Vries, N. Cross, & de Groot (Eds.), *Design Methodology and Relationships with Science* (pp. 15-17). Kluwer Academic Publishers.

Cross, N. (1993). Science and design methodology: A review. *Research and Engineering in Design, 5*, 63-69. doi:10.1007/BF02032575

Cross, N. (1999). Natural intelligence in design. *Design Studies, 20*, 25-39. doi: 10.1016/S0142-694X(98)00026-X

Cross, N. (2001). Designerly ways of knowing: Design discipline versus design science. *Design Issues, 17(3)*, 49-55. doi:10.1162/074793601750357196

Cross, N. (2004). Expertise in design: An overview. *Design Studies, 25*(5), 427-441. doi: 10.1016/j.destud.2004.06.002

Cross, N. (2007). From a design science to a design discipline: Understanding designerly ways of knowing and thinking. In R. Michel (Ed.), *Design research now* (pp. 41-54). Zurich: Birkhauser.

Cross, N. (2011). *Design thinking.* New York: Berg.

Cross, N., & Roozenburg, N. (1992). Modeling the design process in engineering and in architecture. *Journal of Engineering Design, 3*(4), 325-337.

Cross, N., Christiaans, H., & Dorst, K. (1996). *Analyzing design activity.* West Sussex: John Wiley & Sons.

Csikszentmihalyi, M. (1996). *Creativity: Flow and the psychology of discovery and invention.* New York: Harper Perennial.

Csikszentmihalyi, M. (2008). *Flow: The psychology of optimal experience.* Harper Collins e-books.

Cuff, D. (1992). *Architecture the story of practice.* Cambridge: The MIT Press.

Cummings, G. B. (1955). Standards of professional practice in architecture. *The Annals of the American Academy of Political and Social Science, 297*, 9-16. doi: 10.1177/000271625529700103

Cummins, R. (1975, 11 20). Functional analysis. *Journal of Philosophy, 72*(20), 741-765. Retrieved from http://links.jstor.org/sici?sici=0022-362X%2819751120%2972%3A20%3C741%3A-FA%3E2.0.CO%3B2-Q

Cummins, R. (1983). *The nature of psychological explanation.* Cambridge, MA: MIT Press.

Curedale, R. (2012). *Design methods 1.* Topanga, CA: Design Community College, Inc.

Curedale, R. (2012). *Design methods 2.* Topanga, CA: Design Community College, Inc.

Curedale, R. (2016). *Design thinking process and methods* [2nd Edition ed.]. Topanga, CA: Design Community College Inc.

Curry, T. (2014). A theoretical basis for recommending the use of design methodologies as teaching strategies in the design studio. *Design Studies, 35*(6), 1-15. doi: 10.1016/j.destud.2014.04.003

Curry, T. (2014a). A theoretical basis for how to approach teaching the fifth thesis/capstone studio (Chinese version). *World Architecture*, 08, 104-115.

Damasio, A. (1994). *Descartes' error: Emotion, reason, and the human brain*. New York: Penguin Books.

Damasio, A., & Damasio, H. (2006). Minding the body. *Daedalus, 135*(3), 15-22.

Daniels, A. (2015). *Expert performance: Apologies to dr. Ericsson, but it is not 10,000 hours of deliberate practice*. Retrieved 3 12, 2017 from www.aubreydaniels.com

Danto, A. C. (2002). The abuse of beauty. *Daedalus, 131*(4), 35-56. Retrieved from http://www.jstor.org/stable/20027805

Darke, J. (1979). The primary generator and the design process. *Design Studies, 1(1)*, 36-34. Retrieved from doi: 10.1016/0142-694X(79)90027-9

Darwin, C. R. (1859). *On the origin of species by means of natural selection, or preservation of favoured races in the struggle for life*. London: Murray.

Darwin, C. R. (1871). *The descent of man, and selection in relation to sex*. New York: D Appleton & Co.

Darwin, C. R. (1872). *The expression of the emotions in man and animals*. London: D. Appleton.

Davis (2015) Why architects can't be automated. *Architect Magazine* [On-line Edition]. Retrieved from http://www.architectmagazine.com/technology/why-architects-cant-be-automated_o

Davidson, J. E., & Sternberg, R. J. (2003). *The psychology of problem solving*. New York: Cambridge University Press.

de Groot, A. D. (1978). *Thought and choice in chess* [2nd Edition ed.]. The Hague: Mouton Publishers.

de Vries, M. J. (1997). Design methodology in university science, technology and society programs. *IDEAS Newsletter*. Retrieved from http://www.jstor.org/stable/43603852

Dervin, B. (1997). *An Overview of Sense-making Research: Concepts, Methods, and Results to Date*. Retrieved 02 25, 2017, from http://faculty.washington.edu/wpratt/MEBI598/Methods/An%20Overview%20of%20Sense-Making%20Research%201983a.htm

Descartes, R. (1637/1999). *Discourse on method and related writing*. (D. Clarke, Trans.) London: Penguin Classics

Designboom. (2014, 9 15). *Interview with graphic designer Garry Emery*. Retrieved 2 14, 2017, Retrieved from http://www.designboom.com/design/interview-with-graphic-designer-garry-emery-09-25-2014/

Deutsch, O. E. (1965). *Mozart: A documentary biography*. (P. Branscombe, & E. Blom, Trans.) Stanford, CA: Stanford University Press.

Dewey, J. (1934/2005). *Art as experience*. New York: Penguin Books.

Dewey, J. (1938/2015). *Experience and education*. New York: Free Press.

Dewey, R. (2007-14). Psychology: An Introduction. Retrieved from http://www.intropsych.com

Dissanayake, E. (1999). Making special: An undescribed human universal and the core of a behavior of art. In B. E. Arts, B. Cooke, & F. Turner (Eds.). Lexington: ICUS.

Dixon, J. (1987). On research methodology towards a scientific theory of engineering design. *AI EDAM, 1*(3), 145-157. doi: 10.1017/S0890060400000251

van Doesburg, T., & Van Esteren, C. (1994). Towards a collective building. In U. Conrads (Ed.), *Programs and manifestos on 20th-century architecture*. Cambridge, MA: MIT Press.

Dong, A. (2009). *The language of design*. London: Springer.

Dong, A., Collier-Baker, E., & Suddendorf, T. (2015). Building blocks of human design thinking in animals. *International Journal of Design Creativity and Innovation*. doi: 10.1080/21650349.2015.1011700

van Dooren, E., Boshuizen, E., van Merriënboer, J., Asselbergs, T., & van Dorst, M. (2013). Making explicit in design education: generic elements in the design process. *International Journal of Technology and Design Education*, 1-19.

Dorst, K. (2004). On the Problem of Design Problems - problem solving and design expertise . *The Journal of Design Research, 4(2)*. doi: 10.1504/JDR.2004.009841

Dorst, K. (2010). The nature of design thinking. *Interpreting design thinking: Design thinking research symposium proceedings*, (pp. 131-139). http://hdl.handle.net/10453/16590

Dorst, K. (2015). *Frame innovation: create new thinking by design*. Cambridge, MA, USA: The MIT Press.

Douven, I. (2016). Abduction. In E. N. Zalta (Ed.), *The Stanford Encyclopedia of Philosophy* (Winter 2016 ed.). https://plato.stanford.edu/archives/win2016/entries/abduction/

Downton, P. (2003). *Design research*. Melborne: RMIT University Press.

Dreyfus, H. L. (1992). *What computers still can't do: A critique of artificial reason* (3rd Edition ed.). Cambridge, MA: The MIT Press.

Dreyfus, H. L., & Dreyfus, S. E. (2004). A phenomenology of skill acquisition as the basis for a Merleau-Pontian non-representationalist cognitive science. Retrieved February, 13, 2015. http://neuro.bstu.by/my/Tmp/2010-S-abeno/Papers-3/Is-AI-intelligent/Dreyfus/Phenomenology/Dreyfus%2520-%2520Non-Representationalist%2520Cognitive%2520Science.pdf

Dreyfus, S. E. (2004). The five-stage model of adult skill acquisition. *Bulletin of Science, Technology & Society, 24(177).* doi: 10.1177/0270467604264992

D'Souza, N. (2007, July). Design intelligences in architectural design. *International Journal of Architectural Research, 1*(2), 15-34. Retrieved from http://www.archnet-ijar.net/index.php/IJAR/article/viewFile/13/13

Duckworth, A., Peterson, C., Matthews, M., & Kelly, D. (2007). Grit: Perseverance and passion for long-term goals. *Journal of Personality and Social Psychology, 92*(6), 1087-1101. Retrieved from https://www.sas.upenn.edu/~duckwort/images/Grit%20JPSP.pdf

Dutton, D. (2003). Aesthetics and evolutionary psychology. In J. Levinson (Ed.), *Oxford handbook for aesthetics.* New York: Oxford University Press.

Eastman, C., Newstettel, W., & McCracken, M. (Eds.), (2001). *Design knowing and learning: Cognition in design education.* Elsevier Science. doi: 10.1016/B978-008043868-9/50000-0

Eberhard, J. P. (2007). *Architecture and the brain.* Atlanta: Greenway Communications.

Edgar, T. (1979). *Apprentice to genius: Years with Frank Lloyd Wright.* New York: McGraw-Hill.

English Oxford Living Dictionaries (2017) https://en.oxforddictionaries.com/

Ericsson, A. (2008). Deliberate practice and acquisition of expert performance: A General overview. *Academic Emergency Medicine, 15*(11), 988-994. doi: 10.1111/j.1553-2712.2008.00227.x

Ericsson, A., & Pool, R. (2016). *Peak: Secrets from the new science of expertise.* Boston: Houghton Mifflin Harcourt.

Ericsson, A., Krampe, R., & Tesch-Romer, C. (1993). The role of deliberate practice in the acquisition of expert performance. *Psychological Review, 100*, 393-394. Retrieved from http://projects.ict.usc.edu/itw/gel/EricssonDeliberatePracticePR93.PDF

Ericsson, K. A. (1995, 5). Long-term working memory. *Psychological Review, 102*(2), 211-45. doi: 10.1037/0033-295X.102.2.211

Ericsson, K. A. (1996). The acquisition of expert performance: An introduction to some of the issues. In K. A. Ericsson (Ed.), *The road to excellence: The acquisition of expert performance in the arts and sciences, sports, and games.* New York: Psychology Press.

Ericsson, K. A. (2003). The acquisition of expert performance as problem solving: Construction and modification of mediating mechanisms through deliberate practice. In J. Davidson, & R. Sternberg (Eds.), *The psychology of problem solving* (pp. 31-83). Cambridge University Press.

Ericsson, K. A. (2004). The influence of experience and deliberate practice on the development of superior expert performance. In K. A. Ericsson, N. Charness, & P. Feltovich (Eds.), *Cambridge handbook of expertise and expert performance* (pp. 683-703). Cambridge: Cambridge University Press.

Finke, R. A., Ward, T. B., & Smith, S. M. (1992). *Creative cognition: Theory, research, application.* Cambridge: MIT Press.

Fodor, J. (1980). *The language of thought.* Cambridge, MA: Harvard University Press.

Fodor, J. (1987). Fodor's guide to mental representation: The intelligent auntie's vade-mecum. *Mind, 94*(373), 76-100. Retrieved from http://www.federaljack.com/ebooks/Consciousness%20Books%20Collection/Jerry%20A.%20Fodor%20-%20Fodor%27s%20Guide%20to%20Mental%20Representation.pdf

Folkman, M. N. (2013). *The aesthetics of imagination in design.* Cambridge, MA: MIT Press.

Frampton, K. (1995). *Studies in tectonic cultures: The poetics of construction in nineteenth and twentieth century architecture.* Cambridge, MA: MIT Press.

Frantz, R. (2003). Herbert Simon: Artificial intelligence as a framework for understanding intuition . *Journal of Economics Psychology, 24*, 265-277. Retrieved from http://EconPapers.repec.org/RePEc:eee:joepsy:v:24:y:2003:i:2:p:265-277

Freeberg, D., & Gallese, V. (2007). Motion, emotion and empathy in esthetic experience. *Trends in Cognitive Sciences, 11(5),* 197-203. Retrieved from http://hdl.handle.net/10022/AC:P:8652

Gabora, L. (2002). Cognitive mechanisms underlying the creative process. *Proceedings of the fourth conference on creativity and cognition.* 126-133. Retrieved from https://pdfs.semanticscholar.org/2ca2/58f235abe26010dfe10e7f36a01b0379fcb8.pdf

Gage, M. F. (2011). Aesthetic theory: Essential texts for architecture and design. New York: W. W. Norton

Gallagher, S. (2005). *How the body shapes the mind.* Oxford: Clarendon Press.

Gallese, V., & Gattara, A. (2015). Embodied simulation, aesthetics, and architecture: An experimental approach. In S. Robinson, & J. Pallasmaa (Eds.), *Mind in architecture*. Cambridge MA: MIT Press.

Galton, F. (1869). *Hereditary genius*. London: Macmillan.

Galton, F. (1874). On men of science, their nature and their nurture. *Proceedings of the Royal Institution of Great Britain, 7,* 227-236. Retrieved from http://galton.org/essays/1870-1879/galton-1874-men-of-science.pdf

Galton, F. (1883). *Inquiries into human faculty and its development*. London: Macmillan.

Gänshirt, C. (2007). *Tools for ideas*. Berlin: Birkhauser.

Gardner, H. (1983). *Frames of mind, the theory of multiple intelligences*. London: Heinemann.

Gardner, H. (1987). *The mind's new science*. New York: Basic Books.

Gardner, H. (1993). *Creating minds*. New York: Basic Books.

Gedenryd, H. (1998). *How designers work - Making sense of authentic cognitive activities. Cognitive Science.* Retrieved from https://lup.lub.lu.se/search/ws/files/4819156/1484253.pdf

Gerkan, M. v. (1998). *von Gerkan, Marg und Partner: Architecture 1995-1997* (German and English Edition ed.). Basel: Birkhauser.

Gero, J. & Kannengieser, U.(2008). An ontological account of Donald Schön's reflection in designing. International Journal of Design Sciences and Technologies, 15 (2) 77-90. Retrieved from http://citeseerx.ist.psu.edu/viewdoc/download?doi=10.1.1.528.7213&rep=rep1&type=pdf

Gero, J., & Maher, M. L. (2016). *Modeling creativity and knowledge-based creative design*. New York: Routledge.

Gibson, J. J. (1986). *The ecological approach to visual perception*. New York: Psychology Press.

Gieser, T. (2008). Embodiment, emotions and empathy. *Anthropological Theory, 8*(3), 299-318. doi: 10.1177/1463499608093816

Gladwell, M. (2008). *Outliers: The story of success*. New York: Little Brown & Co.

Glaser, R. (1992). Expert knowledge and processes of thinking. In D. F. Halpern (Ed.), *Enhancing thinking skills in the Sciences and the Mathematics* (pp. 63-75). Hillsdale, NJ, USA: Erlbaum.

Glaser, R. (1996). Changing the agency for learning: Acquiring expert performance. In K. A. Ericsson (Ed.), *The road to excellence: The acquisition of expert performance in the arts and sciences, sports, and games*. New York: Psychology Press.

Glazer, N. (1974, July). The schools of the minor professions. *Minerva, 12*(3).

Godfrey-Smith, P. (2001). Environmental complexity and the evolution of cognition. In R. Sternberg, & J. Kaufman (Eds.), *The evolution of intelligence*. Lawrence Erlbaum, Associates. Retrieved from http://www.its.caltech.edu/~theory/Godfrey-Smith.pdf

Goldschmidt, G. (1991). The dialectics of sketching. *Creativity Research Journal, 4*(2), 123-143. doi: 10.1080/10400419109534381

Goldschmidt, G., Sebba, R., Oren, C., & Cohen, A. (2002). *Who should be a designer?* Retrieved from https://www.nite.org.il/files/reports/e294.pdf

Goldschmidt, G. (2003). The backtalk of self-generated sketches. *Design Issues, 19(1)*. doi: 10.1162/074793603762667728

Goldschmidt, G. (2014). *Linkography: Unfolding the design process*. Cambridge, MA: The MIT Press.

Gombrich, E. (2000). *Art and illusion* (Eleventh Edition). Princeton: Princeton University Press.

Gombrich, E. H. (1987). They were all human beings: So much is plain: Reflections on cultural relativism in the humanities. *Critical Inquiry, 13*(4), 686-699. doi: 10.1086/448416

Gottfried, J. A. (2011). *Neurobiology of sensation and reward*. Boca Raton, FLA: CRC Press. doi: 10.1201/b10776-1

Gould, S. J., & Vrba, E. S. (1982). Exaptation: A missing term in the science of form. *Paleobiology 8*, pp. 4-15. doi: 10.1017/S0094837300004310

Grant, D. P. (1972, August). Systematic methods in environmental design: An introductory bibliography. (M. Vance, Ed.) *Council of planning Libraries, Exchange bibliography, 302*. Retrieved from https://archive.org/stream/systematicmethod302gran/systematicmethod302gran_djvu.txt

Guindon, R. (1990). Knowledge exploited by experts during software system design. *International Journal of Man-Machine Studies, 33,* 279-304. doi: 10.1016/S0020-7373(05)80120-8

Gulari, M. N. (2015). Metaphors in design: How we think of design expertise. *Journal of Research and Practice, 11*(2). Article M8. Retrieved from http://jrp.icaap.org/index.php/jrp/article/view/485/423

Gun, T. G. (1982) The mechanization on design and manufacturing. *Scientific American, 247* 114-130. ERIC Number: EJ267488

Habraken, J. (1985). *The appearance of the form*. Cambridge: Atwater Press. Retrieved from http://www.habraken.com/html/appearance_of_the___.htm

Hall, A. (1962). *A methodology for systems engineering*. Princeton, NJ: Van Nostrand Reinhold.

Heschong, L. (1989). *Thermal delight in architecture*. Cambridge, MA: The MIT Press.

Hildebrand, G. (1999). *Origins of architectural pleasure*. Berkeley: University of California Press.

Hill, N. M., & Schneider, W. (2006). Brain changes in the development of expertise: Neuroanatomical and neurophysiological evidence about skill-based adaptations. In A. Ericsson, N. Charness, P. Feltovich, & R. Hoffman (Eds.), *The Cambridge Handbook of Expertise and Expert Performance*. Cambridge: Cambridge University Press. doi: 10.1017/CBO9780511816796.037

Hillier, B., Musgrove, J., & O'Sullivan, P. (1972). Knowledge and design. *Environmental Design: Research and Practice, EDRA 3*. (pp. 29/3/1 - 29/3/14). Los Angeles: University of California.

Hollard, V., & Delius, J. (1982, 11 19). Rotational invariance in visual pattern recognition in pigeons and humans. *Science, 218*, 804-806.

Hofstadter, A., & Kuhns, R. (1964). *Philosophies of art and beauty: Selected readings in aesthetics from Plato to Heidegger*. Chicago: University of Chicago Press.

Hume, D. (1777). Enquiry concerning the principle of morals. In *The David Hume Collection: 17 Classic Works* (Kindle Edition ed.). Waxkeep Publishing. Retrieved from https://www.amazon.com/David-Hume-Collection-Classic-Works-ebook/dp/B00CO9IA6Q/ref=sr_1_fkmr1_2?s=digital-text&ie=UTF8&qid=1492713928&sr=1-2-fkmr1&keywords=In+The+David+Hume+Collection%3A+17+Classic+Works+%28Kindle+Edition+ed.%29.+Waxkeep+Publishing

Hume, D. (1817). *Treatise on Human Nature: Volume II*. London: Thomas and Joseph Allman.

Huppatz, D. J. (2015). Revisiting Herbert Simon's "Science of Design". *Design Issues, 31*(2), 29-40. doi: 10.1162/DESI_a_00320

Husserl, E. (1970). *Logical investigations*. (J. Finlay, Trans.) London: Routledge.

Hyungil, A., & Picard, R. (2005). Affective-cognitive learning and decision making: A motivational reward framework for affective agents. In *Affective computing and intelligent interaction* (pp. 866-873). Springer. Retrieved from http://affect.media.mit.edu/pdfs/05.ahn-picard-acii.pdf

International Union of Architects. (2014). *UIA accord on recommended international standards of professionalism in architectural practice*. Paris: International Union of Architects. Retrieved from http://www.uia-architectes.org/sites/default/files/AIAS075164.pdf

Ishizu, T., & Zeki, S. (2011). Toward a brain-based theory of beauty. (E. J. Warrant, Ed.) *PLoS ONE, 6*(7). doi: 10.1371/journal.pone.0021852

Jackson, R. (1929, 1). Locke's distinction between primary and secondary qualities. *Mind, 38*(149), 56-76. Retrieved from http://www.jstor.org/stable/2249224

Jahoda, G. (2005). Theodore Lipps and the shift from "sympathy" to "empathy". *Journal of the History of Behavioral Sciences, 41*(2), 151-163. doi: 10.1002/jhbs.20080

Jastro. (1901/2015). *Fact and fable in psychology*. New York: Houghton Mifflin. Retrieved from https://archive.org/details/factfableinpsych01jast

Johnson, M. (2007). *The meaning of the body*. Chicago: University of Chicago Press.

Johnson, M. (2015). The aesthetics of embodied life. In A. Scarinzi (Ed.), *Aesthetics and the embodied mind*. London: Springer.

Jones, J. C. (1992). *Design methods* (Second ed.). New York, NY, USA: John Wiley & Sons.

Jormakka, K. (2012). *Design methods*. (B. Bielefeld, Ed.) Basel: Birkhauser.

Kahn, L. I., & Twombly, R.C. (2003). *Loius Kahn: Essential Texts*. New York: Wiley & Sons.

Keen, K. (1992). Competence: What is it and how can it be developed? In J. Lowyck, P. de Potter, & J. Elen (Eds.), Instructional design: implementation issues, 111–122. Brussels, Belgium: IBM International Education Centre.

Kierkegaard, S. (1843/1987). *Either/Or*. (H. V. Hong, & E. H. Hong, Trans.) Princeton, NJ: Princeton University Press.

Kirschner, P. (2002). Cognitive load theory: Implications of cognitive load theory on the design of learning. *Learning and Instruction, 12*, 1-10.

Klein, Moon, & Hoffman, (2016). Making sense of sense making. *IEEE Intelligent Systems, 21*(4), 70-73. doi: 10.1109/MIS.2006.100

Koberg, D., & Bagnall, J. (2003). *The universal traveler: A soft-systems guide to creativity, problem-solving and the process of reaching goals*. USA: Axzo Press.

Koffka, K. (1935). *Principles of gestalt psychology.* London: Lund Humphrie.

Kohler, W. (1947). *Gestalt psychology: An introduction to new concepts in modern psychology.* New York: Liveright.

Kolko, J. (2011). *Exposing the magic of design: A practitioner's guide to the methods and theory of synthesis.* Oxford: Oxford University Press.

Komar, V., & Melamid, A. (1997). *Painting by numbers: Komar and Melamid's scientific guide to art.* Berkeley: University of California Press.

Korsmeyer, C. (1998). *Aesthetics: The big questions.* **Malden, MA: Blackwell**

Kosslyn, S., Pinker, S., Smith, G., & Schwartz, S. P. (1979). On the demystification of mental imagery. *The Behavioral and Brain Sciences, 2,* 535-581. doi: 10.1017/S0140525X00064268

Kostof, S. (1977). *The architect: Chapters in the history of the profession.* **New York, NY, USA: Oxford University Press.**

Krampe, R., & Charness, N. (2006). Aging and expertise. In A. Ericsson, N. Charness, P. Feltovich, & R. Hoffman (Eds.), *Cambridge handbook of expertise and expert performance.* Cambridge: Cambridge University Press.

Krupinska, J. (2014). *What an architecture student should know.* (S. Danielson, Trans.) New York: Routledge.

Kuhn, T. (1962). *The structure of scientific revolutions.* Chicago: University of Chicago Press.

Kvan, T., & Jia, Y. (2005). Student's learning styles and their correlation with performance in architectural design studio. *Design Studies, 26*(1), 19-34. doi: 10.1016/j.destud.2004.06.004

Lakatos, I., & Musgrave, A. (1970). *Criticism and the growth of knowledge.* Cambridge: Cambridge University Press.

Lakoff, G. (2003). *Metaphors we live by.* Chicago: Chicago: University of Chicago Press.

Lakoff, G., & Johnson, M. (1999). *Philosophy in the flesh.* **New York: Basic Books.**

Langrish, J. (2016). The design methods movement: From optimism to Darwinism. *DRS 2016, 50th Anniversary Conference* (pp. 1-13). Brighton: Design Research Society. Retrieved from https://static1.squarespace.com/static/55ca3eafe4b05bb65abd54ff/t/574f0971859fd01f18ec63c1/1464797554420/222+Langrish.pdf

Larson, G. S., & Tehrani, J. L. (2013, 9). Exapting exaptation. *Trends in ecology & evolution, 28*(9). doi: 10.1016/j.tree.2013.05.018

Lawson, B. (2005). *How designs think: The design process demystified* **(4th ed.). London: Routledge.**

Lawson, B. R. (1994). *Design in mind.* Oxford: Architectural Press.

Lawson, B., & Dorst, K. (2009). *Design expertise.* **Oxford: Architectural Press.**

Lerner, J., Li, Y., Valdesolo, P., & Kassam, K. (2015). Emotions and decision making. *Annual Review of Psychology, 66*(1), 799-823. doi: 10.1146/annurev-psych-010213-115043

Leslie, T. (2010). Dankmar Adler's response to Louis Sullivan's "The Tall Office Building Artistically Considered": Architecture and the "Four Causes". *Journal of Architecture Education, 63*(1), 83-93. doi: 10.1111/j.1531-314X.2010.01102.x

Lieberman, B., & Vrba, E. (2005). Stephen Jay Gould on species selection: 30 years of insight. *Paleobiology, 31*(sp5), 113-121. doi: 10.1666/0094-8373(2005)031[0113:SJGOSS]2.0.CO;2

Limbeck-Lilenau, C. (2016, 6). *Perception as representation. A conceptual clarification of intentionalism.* Retrieved 3 09, 2017, from e-Journal Philosophie der Psycholgie: Retrieved from http://www.jp.philo.at/texte/LimbeckC1.pdf

Lipari, L. (2015, 1). Human perception: making sense of the world. *Utne Reader.* Retrieved from http://www.utne.com/mind-and-body/human-perception-ze0z1501zhur

Little, S. (2015). *10 Signs that you should become an architect.* Retrieved from http://freshome.com/2015/01/19/10-signs-that-you-should-become-an-architect/#ixzz4abmFiHeY

Loyola, I. (1968). *Spiritual exercises.* **(L. Puhl, Trans.) Loyola Press.**

MacIntyre, A. (2007). *After virtue: a study of moral theory* (Third Edition). Notre Dame, IN: University of Notre Dame Press.

Maier, A. M., Wynn, D. C., Andreasen, M. M., & Clarkson, P. J. (2012). A cybernetic perspective on methods and process models in collaborative designing. Retrieved from https://www.repository.cam.ac.uk/bitstream/handle/1810/243209/CyberneticPerspectiveOnMethodsAndProcessModelsInCollaborativeDesigning.pdf?sequence=1&isAllowed=y

Maier, J., & Fadel, G. M. (2009). Affordance-based design methods for innovative design, redesign and reverse engineering. *Research in Engineering Design, 20*(4), 225-23e9. doi: 10.1007/s00163-009-0064-7

Mallgrave, H. F. (2011). *The architect's brain.* **West Sussex: Wiley-Blackwell.**

Mallgrave, H. F. (2013). *Architecture and embodiment*. New York: Routledge.

Mallgrave, H. F. (2015.). "Know thyself": Or what designers can learn from the contemporary biological sciences. In S. Robinson & J. Pallasmaa (Eds.) *Mind in architecture*. Cambridge: MIT Press.

March, L. J. (1976). The logic of design. In L. J. March (Ed.), *The architecture of form*. Cambridge, UK: Cambridge University Press.

Margolin, V. (2010). Design research: Towards a history. *Design Research Society Conference*. Retrieved from http://www.drs2010.umontreal.ca/data/PDF/080.pdf

Maritain, J. (1943). *Art and Scholasticism*. (J. F. Scanlan, Trans.) New York: Charles Scribner & Sons.

Marples, D. (1960). *The decisions of engineering design*. London: Institute of Engineering Design.

Marshall, J. S. (1953, 12). Art and aesthetic in Aristotle. *The Journal of Aesthetics and Art Criticism, 12*(2), 228-231. doi: 10.2307/426876

Martindale, C. (1990). *The clockwork muse*. New York: Basic Books.

McCarthy, J. (1966). Information. *Scientific American, 215*(3). doi: 10.1038/scientificamerican0966-64

McCormick, R. (1997). Conceptual and procedural knowledge. *Journal of Technology and Design Education*, 141-159. doi:10.1023/A:1008819912213

McCormick, R. (2004). Issues of learning and knowledge in technology education. *International Journal of Technology and Design Education, 14*(1), 21-44. doi: 10.1023/B:ITDE.0000007359.81781.7c

McCormick, R. (2006). Technology and knowledge: Contributions from learning theories. In J. Dakers (Ed.), *Defining Technological Literacy* (pp. 31-47). Palgrave MacMillan.

MacFarlane, A. (2013). Information, knowledge & intelligence. *Philosophy Now* 98. Retrieved from https://philosophynow.org/issues/98/Information_Knowledge_and_Intelligence

Meadows, D. H. (2008). *Thinking in systems*. (D. Wright, Ed.) White River Junction, VT, USA: Chelsea Green Publishing.

Melchionne, K. (2007). *Acquired taste*. Retrieved 3 13, 2017, from Contemporary Aesthetics: http://hdl.handle.net/2027/spo.7523862.0005.011

Merleau-Ponty. (1962). *Phenomenology of perception*. London: Routledge.

Merrienboer, J., Jelsma, O., & F., P. (1992). Training for reflective expertise: a four-component instructional design model for complex cognitive skill. *Educational Technology Research and Development, 40*(2), 23-43.

Miller, G. A. (1956). The magic number seven, plus or minus two: some limits on our capacity for processing information. *63*, 81-97. doi: 10.1037/h0043158

Mitchell, W. J. (1990). *The logic of architecture*. Cambridge, MA, USA: The MIT Press.

Mitrovic, B. (2009). Architectural formalism and the demise of the linguistic turn. *Log*, 31-39. http://www.jstor.org/stable/41765632

Mitrovic, B. (2013). *Visuality for architects: architectural creativity and modern theories of perception*. Charlottesville: University of Virginia Press.

Moholy-Nagy, L. (1947). *Vision in motion*. Paul Theobald & Co.

Mumford, M. (1989). Form follows nature: The origins of American organic architecture. *JAE, 42*(3). doi: 10.2307/1425061

Murty, P. (2006, October). Discovery processes in designing. (Doctoral dissertation). Retrieved from https://ses.library.usyd.edu.au/bitstream/2123/1809/4/01front.pdf

Narayanan, S. (1997). *Embodiment in language understanding*. (Doctoral dissertation). Retrieved from http://www1.icsi.berkeley.edu/~snarayan/thesis.pdf

Nazidizaji, S., Tome, A., & Regateiro, F. (2015). Does the smartest designer design better? Effect of intelligence quotient on students' design skills in architectural design studio. *Frontiers of Architectural Research, 4*(4), 318-329. doi: 10.1016/j.foar.2015.08.002

Newell, A. (1980). The heuristic of George Polya and its relations to artificial intelligence. *International Symposium on the Methods of Heuristic*. University of Bern. Retrieved from http://repository.cmu.edu/cgi/viewcontent.cgi?article=3446&context=compsci

Newell, A., & Simon, H. A. (1972). *Human problem solving*. Englewood Cliffs, NJ: Prentice-Hall.

Newell, A., Shaw, J. C., & Simon, H. A. (1958). Elements of a theory of human problem solving. *Psychological Review, 65*(3), 151-166. doi: 10.1037/h0048495

Newell, A., Shaw, J. C., & Simon, H. A. (1958). The Processes of Creative Thinking. *University of Colorado* (p. 82). Santa Monica: Rand Corporation. Retrieved from http://shelf1.library.cmu.edu/IMLS/BACKUP/MindModels.pre_Oct1/creativethinking.pdf

Newell, A., Shaw, J., & Simon, H. A. (1958, October). Chess-Playing Programs and the Problem of Complexity. *IBM Journal of Research and Development, 2,* 320- 335. doi: 10.1147/rd.24.0320

Nimkulrat, N., Niedderer, K., & Evans, M. (2015). On understanding expertise, connoisseurship, and experiential knowledge in professional practice. *Journal of Research Practice, 11(2).* Retrieved from http://jrp.icaap. org/index.php/jrp/article/view/530/429

Noe, A. (2005, 10). Against intellectualism. *Analysis, 65*(4). doi: 10.1111/j.1467-8284.2005.00567.x

Ogalvie, J. (1999). Cognitive coherence. *Trends in Cognitive Sciences.* 3(5) 171. doi: 10.1016/S1364-6613(99)01322-4

Orians, G. H., & Heerwagen, J. H. (1992). Evolved responses to landscapes. In L. Cosmides, & J. Tooby (Eds.), *The adapted mind: Evolutionary psychology and the generation of culture* (pp. 555-579). New York: Oxford University Press.

Ostman, J. (2013). It's all in the brain: a theory of the qualities of perception. (Doctoral dissertation) Retrieved from http://umu.diva-portal.org/smash/get/diva2:621594/FULLTEXT01.pdf

Owen, C. (2006). Design thinking: Notes on its nature and use. *Design Research Quarterly, 1*(2), 16-27. Retrieved from http://designthinking.typepad.com/dialogues/files/design_thinking_article.pdf

Oxford Dictionary of English. (2016). Oxford University Press. Retrieved from https://en.oxforddictionaries.com

Ozor, F. U. (2008). *Social constructs.* (T. Gale, Producer) Retrieved December 28, 2016, from *International Encyclopedia of the Social Sciences:* http://www.encyclopedia.com/social-sciences/applied-and-social-sciences-magazines/social-constructs

Pallasmaa, J. (2005). *The eyes of the skin.* West Sussex: John Wiley and Sons.

Pallasmaa, J. (2009). *The thinking hand: Existential and embodied wisdom in architecture.* New York: John Wiley & Sons.

Pandya, S. K. (2011). Understanding the brain, mind and soul: Contributions from neurology and neurosurgery. *Mens Sana Monographs, 9*(1), 129-149. Retrieved from http://www.msmonographs.org/article. asp?issn=0973-1229;year=2011;volume=9;issue=1;spage=129;epage=149;aulast=Pandya

Papanek, V. (1984). *Design for the real world: Human ecology and social change.* London: Thames and Hudson.

Pape, H. (1990). Charles S. Peirce on objects of thought and representation. *Nous, 24,* 375-396. doi: 10.2307/2215771

Pass, F., Renkl, A., & Sweller, J. (2004). Cognitive load theory: Instructional implications of the interaction between information structures and cognitive architecture. *Instructional Science, 32,* 1-8. doi: 10.1023/B:TRUC.0000021806.17516.d0

Passingham, R. (2016). *Cognitive neuroscience: A very short introduction.* Oxford: Oxford University Press.

Peirce, C. (1873, January 26). *Charles S. Peirce on representations.* (J. Ransdall, Ed.) Retrieved from the Peirce Gateway: http://www.iupui.edu/~arisbe/menu/library/bycsp/logic/ms212.htm

Perez-Gomez, A. (1992). *Architecture and the crisis of modern science* (Sixth Printing ed.). Cambridge, MA: MIT Press.

Perez-Gomez, A. (1998). Introduction to architecture and modern science. In M. Hayes (Ed.), *Architecture theory since 1968.* Cambridge, MA: MIT Press.

Perez-Gomez, A. (2015). Mood and meaning in architecture. In S. Robinson, & J. Pallasmaa (Eds.), *Mind in Architecture: Neuroscience, Embodiment, and the Future of Design.* Cambridge, MA: MIT Press.

Perez-Gomez, A. (2016). *Attunement: Architectural meaning after the crisis of modern science.* Cambridge, MA: MIT Press.

Pierce, C. S. (1931). *Collected papers of C S Peirce.* (C. Hartsborne, & P. Weiss, Eds.) Cambridge, MA: Harvard University Press.

Pinker, S. (2002). *The blank slate.* New York: Viking Penguin.

Pinker, S. (2005). So how does the mind work? *Mind & Language, 20*(1), 1-24. doi: 10.1111/j.0268-1064.2005.00274.x

Pinker, S. (2009). *How the mind works.* New York: W. W. Norton & Co.

Pionotti, A. (2010). Empathy. In H. R. Sepp, & L. Embree (Eds.), *Handbook of phenomenological aesthetics* (pp. 93-98). Springer Science+Business Media.

Plato. (1956). Meno. In *Great dialogues of Plato* (W. H. Rouse, Trans.) New York: New American Library.

Plato. (2008). Philebus. (B. Jowett, Trans.) Retrieved from https://www.gutenberg.org/files/1744/1744-h/1744-h.htm

Plato. (2012). Laches. In *The complete works of Plato* (B. Jowett, Trans.). Retrieved from https://read.amazon. com/?asin=B0082T0J5W

Polanyi, M. (1966, January). The logic of tacit inference. *Philosophy, 41*(155), 1-18. Retrieved from http://www.jstor.org/stable/3749034

Polanyi, M. (1969). *Essays by Michael Polanyi*. Chicago: University of Chicago Press.

Polanyi, M. (1972). *The study of man*. Chicago: University of Chicago Press.

Polanyi, M. (1974). *Personal knowledge*. Chicago: University of Chicago Press.

Polanyi, M. (2009). *The Tacit Dimension*. Chicago: University of Chicago Press.

Polya, G. (1945). *How to solve it: A new aspect of mathematical method*. Princeton, NJ, USA: Princeton University Press.

Popper, K. (2002). *Conjectures and refutations*. New York: Routledge.

Popper, K. (1959). *The logic of scientific discovery*. London: Hutchinson.

Popper, K. (1996). *The myth of the framework*. New York: Routledge.

Portillo, M., & Dohr, J. H. (1994). Building process and structure through criteria. *Design Studies, 15*(4), 403-416. doi: 10.1016/0142-694X(94)90004-3

Pressman, A. (2012). *Designing architecture: The elements of process*. New York: Routledge.

Prochaska, J. O. & Velicer, W. F. (1997). The transtheoretical model of health behavior change. *American Journal of Health Promotion*. 12(1), 38-48. Retrieved from https://pdfs.semanticscholar.org/d8d1/915aa556e-c4ff962efe2a99295dd2e8bda89.pdf

Protzen, J.-P., & Harris, D. J. (2010). *The universe of design: Horst Rittel's theories of design and planning*. New York: Routledge.

Pugin, A. W. (1841/2006). The true principles of pointed or Christian architecture. In H. F. Mallgrave (Ed.). *Architectural Theory* [Vol. 1]. Oxford, UK: Blackwell. 385-386.

Pye, D. (1978). *The nature and aesthetics of design*. Bethel, CT: Cambium Press.

Pylyshyn, Z. (2003). Return of the mental image: are there really pictures in the brain? *Trends in Cognitive Sciences, 7*(3), 113-118. doi:10.1016/S1364-6613(03)00003-2

Pylyshyn, Z. W. (2004). Explaining mental imagery: now you see it, now you don't. *Trends in Cognitive Sciences, 7*(3), 111-112. doi:10.1016/S1364-6613(03)00004-4

Pylyshyn, Z. W. (2004). Mental imagery. In R. L. Gregory (Ed.), *Oxford companion to the mind* (Second ed.).

Ramachandran, V. S. (2011). *The tell-tale brain: A neuroscientist's quest for what makes us human*. New York: W.W. Norton.

Ramachandran, V. S., & Hirstein, W. (1999). The science of art: A neurological theory of aesthetic experience. *Journal of Consciousness Studies, 6*, 15-51. Retrieved from www.imprint.co.uk/rama

Rand, A. (1996). *The fountainhead* (25th Anniversary Edition ed.). New York, NY: Signet.

Rawsthorn, A. (2009, May 30). The demise of 'form follows function'. *New York Times*.

Razzouk, R., & Shute, V. (2012, 9). What is design thinking and why is it important? *Review of Educational Research, 82*(3), 330-348. doi: 10.3102/0034654312457429

Regier, T. (1995). A model of the human capacity for categorizing spatial relationshiops. *Cognitive Linguistics, 6*(1), 63-88. doi: 10.1515/cogl.1995.6.1.63

Riscica, M. (2017, 3 6). *10 Reasons why you should not become an architect*. Retrieved from Young Architect: http://youngarchitect.com/2014/03/24/why-you-should-not-become-an-architect/

Rittel, H. (1984). Second-generation design methods. In N. Cross (Ed.), *Developments in design methodology*. Chichester: John Wiley & Sons.

Rittel, H. (1988). *The reasoning of designers. International Congress on Planning and Design Theory*. Boston. Retrieved from http://www.cc.gatech.edu/fac/ellendo/rittel/rittel-reasoning.pdf

Rittel, H., & Webber, M. (1973). Dilemmas in a general theory of planning. *Policy Sciences, 4*, 155-169. doi:10.1007/BF01405730

Robinson, S., & Pallasmaa, J. (Eds.). (2015). *Mind in architecture*. Cambridge, MA: MIT Press.

Rock, I., & Palmer, S. (1990, 12). The Legacy of Gestalt Psychology. *Scientific American*, 84-90. PMID: 2270461

Rodriguez, E. (1999). Perception's Shadow: long-distance synchronization of human brain activity. *Nature, 397*, 430-433. doi: 10.1038/17120

Roland, P. E. (1995). Visual memory, visual imagery, and visual recognition of large field patterns by the human brain: Functional anatomy by positron emission tomography. *Cerebral Cortex, 5*, 79-93. PMID: 7719132

Roland, P. E., & Gulyas, B. (1994). Visual imagery and visual representation. *Trends in Neuroscience, 17*, 281-287. PMID: 7524211

Roth, M., & Cummins, R. (2017). Neuroscience, psychology, reduction and functional analysis. In D. Kaplan (Ed.) *Explanation and integration in mind and brain science*. Oxford: Oxford University Press. Retreived from: https://docs.google.com/viewer?a=v&pid=sites&srcid=ZGVmYXVsdGRvbWFpbnxyb2JlcnRjdW-1taW5zcGhpbG9zb3BoeXxneDo2NxneDo3N2E3ZGIxNTQzNzk3NzU0

Roozenburg, N., & Cross, N. (1991, 10). Models of the design process: Integrating across the disciplines. *Design Studies, 12*(4). doi: 10.1016/0142-694X(91)90034-T

Roozenburg, N., & Dorst, K. (1999). Describing design as a reflective practice. In E. Frankenberger, P. Bad-ke-Schaub, & H. Birkhofer (Eds.), *Designers. The key to successful product development* (pp. 29-41). London: Springer.

Rowe, P. (1987). *Design thinking*. Cambridge, MA: MIT Press.

Royal Institute of Dutch Architects. (2006). *The architectural profession in the Netherlands*. (O. Sluizer, & Visser, Betsy, Eds.) Amsterdam: Royal Institute of Dutch Architects, BNA. Retrieved from http://www.bna.nl/fileadmin/user_upload/BNA_International/BNA_International_for_you/2006_BNA_The_Architectur-al_Profession_in_the_Netherlands.pdf

Rusch, H., & Voland, E. (2013). *Evolutionary aesthetics: an introduction to key concepts and current issues*. Retrieved http://www.fupress.net/index.php/aisthesis/article/view/13773/12808

Ryle, G. (1949). *The concept of mind*. Chicago: University of Chicago Press.

Sanfey, A., Lowenstein, G., McClure, S., & Cohen, J. (2006). Neuroeconomics: cross-currents in research on decision-making. *Trends in Cognitive Sciences, 10*(3). doi: 10.1016/j.tics.2006.01.009

Sartre, J.-P. (1946). *Existentialism is a humanism*. (P. Mairet, Trans.) Retrieved from http://homepages.wmich.edu/~baldner/existentialism.pdf

Schilpp, P. A. (1974). *The philosophy of Karl Popper*. La Salle, IL: Open Court Publishing.

Schön, D. (1985). *The design studio: Explorations of its traditions and potential*. London: RIBA Publications Limited.

Schön, D. (1988, July). Designing: Rules, types and worlds. *Design Studies, 9*(3), 181-190. doi: 10.1016/0142-694X(88)90047-6

Schön, D. (1991). *The reflective practitioner: How professionals think in action* (first edition 1983). Surrey, England: Ashgate.

Schön, D. (1992, March). Designing as reflective conversation with the materials of a design situation. *Knowledge-Based Systems, 5(1)*. doi: 10.1016/0950-7051(92)90020-G

Schön, D. (1992). The theory of inquiry: Dewey's legacy to education. *Curriculum Inquiry, 22*(2), 119-139. doi: 10.2307/1180029

Schön, D., & Wiggins, G. (1992, 4). Kinds of seeing and their functions in designing. *Design Studies, 13*(2), 135-156. doi: 10.1016/0142-694X(92)90268-F

Searle, J. (1994). *Rediscovery of the mind*. Cambridge: MIT Press.

Searle, J. R. (2015). *Seeing Things As They Are*. Oxford University Press.

Seeley, W. (2014). Empirical aesthetics. In M. Kelly (Ed.), *Oxford Encyclopedia of Aesthetics* (2nd Edition ed.). Oxford University Press.

Semper, G. (1989). *The four elements of architecture*. (H. F. Mallgrave, & W. Herrmann, Trans.) Cambridge, UK: Cambridge University Press.

Sennett, R. (2009). *The craftsman*. London: Penguin Group.

Seung, S. (2012). *Connectome: How the brain's wiring makes us who we are*. Boston: Houghton Mifflin Harcourt.

Shapiro, H. (2010). John Dewey's reception in "Schönian" reflective practice. *Philosophy of Education Archive*, 311-319.

Shapiro, L. (2011). *Embodied cognition*. New York: Routledge.

Shepard, R. (1971). Mental rotation of three-dimensional objects. *Scientific American, 171*, 701-703. PMID: 5540314

Shepard, S., & Metzler, D. (1988). Mental rotation: Effects of dimensionality of objects and type of task. *Journal of Experimental Psychology, 14*(1), 3-11. PMID: 2964504

Shimamura, A. (2012). Towards a science of aesthetics. In A. Shimamura, & S. Palmer (Eds.), *Aesthetic science: connecting minds, brains and experience* (pp. 3-28). New York: Oxford University Press.

Simon, H. (1962, 12 12). The architecture of complexity. *Proceedings of the American Philosophical Society, 106*(6), 467-482. Retrieved by http://www.jstor.org/stable/985254

Simon, H. (1972). Theories of bounded rationality. In C. B. McGuire, & R. Radner (Eds.). New York: New Holland Publishing.

Simon, H. (1973). The structure of ill structured problems. *Artificial Intelligence, 4*, 181-201. doi: 10.1016/0004-3702(73)90011-8

Simon, H. (1977). On how to decide what to do. *The Bell Journal of Electronics*. doi: 10.2307/3003595

Simon, H. (1980). Cognitive Science: The Newest Science of the Artificial. *Cognitive Science, 4*, 33-46. doi: 10.1016/S0364-0213(81)80003-1

Simon, H. (1996). *The Sciences of the Artificial* (Third ed.). Cambridge, MA, USA: MIT Press.

Simon, H. A. (1959). Theories of decision-making in economics and behavioral science. *The American Economic Review, 49*(3), 253-283. Retrieved from http://www.jstor.org/stable/1809901

Simon, H. A. (1988). The science of design: creating the artificial. *Design Issues, 4*(Special Issue), 67-82. doi: 10.2307/1511391

Simon, H. A., & Chase, W. G. (1973). Skill in chess. *American Scientist, 61*(4), 394-403.

Singleton, J. (1989). Japanese folkcraft pottery apprenticeship: Cultural patterns on an educational system. In M. Coy (Ed.), *Apprenticeship: From theory to methods and back again*. Albany: State University of New York Press.

Smith, I. M. (1964). *Spatial ability. Its educational and social significance*. London: University of London.

Snodgrass, A., & Coyne, R. (1997). Is designing hermeneutical? *Architecture Theory Review, 1*(1), 65-97. doi: 10.1080/13264829609478304

Spiller, N., & Clear, N. (Eds.). (2014). *Educating Architects: How tomorrow's practitioners will learn today*. New York: Thames & Hudson.

Stanley, J., & Williamson, T. (2001). Knowing how. *The Journal of Philosophy, 97*, 411-44. Retrieved from http://www.jstor.org/stable/2678403

Straus, E. (1970). The phantom limb. In E. Straus, & D. Griffith (Eds.), *Aisthesis and aesthetics* (pp. 130-48). Pittsburgh: Dusquesne University Press.

Stueber, K. (2017). *Empathy*. (E. N. Zalta, Ed.) Retrieved 03 12, 2017, from The Stanford Encyclopedia of Philosophy (Spring 2017 Edition): https://plato.stanford.edu/archives/spr2017/entries/empathy/

Sullivan, L. H. (1896, March). The tall office building artistically considered. *Lippincott's Magazine, 57*, (pp. 403-409).

Sussman, A., & Hollander, J. (2015). *Cognitive architecture*. New York: Routledge.

Sutton, K., & Williams, A. (2010). *Implications of spatial abilities on design thinking*. Montreal, Quebec: Design Research Society.

Sweller, J. (2008). Human cognitive architecture. In J. M. Spector, M. D. Merrill, J. v. Merriënboer, & M. P. Driscoll (Eds.), *Handbook of research on educational communications and technology* (pp. 369-381). Routledge.

Sweller, J. (2016). Cognitive load theory, evolutionary educational psychology, and instructional design. In D. C. Geary, & D. B. Berch (Eds.), *Evolutionary perspectives on child development and education* pp. 291-306. Basel: Springer.

Sweller, J., van, M. J., & Paas, F. G. (1998). Cognitive architecture and instructional design. *Educational Psychology Review, 10*(3). doi: 10.1023/A:1022193728205

Takano, Y., & Okubo, M. (2006). Mental rotation. In *Encyclopedia of Cognitive Science*. New York: Wiley.

Terzidis, K. (2007). The etymology of design: Pre-Socratic perspective. *Design Issues, 23*(4). doi: 10.1162/desi.2007.23.4.69

Tetlow, J. (2017). *Application of the senses*. Retrieved 03 14, 2017, from Ignatian Spirituality.com: http://www.ignatianspirituality.com/24156/application-of-the-senses

Thagard, P. (2002). *Coherence in thought and action*. Cambridge, MA: MIT Press.

Thagard, P. (2005). *Mind: Introduction to Cognitive Science*. Cambridge, MA, USA: MIT Press.

Thagard, P., & Schröder, T. (2014). Emotions as semantic pointers: Constructive neural mechanisms. In F. Barrett, & J. A. Russell (Eds.), *The psychological construction of emotions*. New York: Guilford.

Thagard, P., & Verbeurgt, K. (1998). Coherence as constraint satisfaction. *Cognitive Science 22(1)*. doi: 10.1207/s15516709cog2201_1

Thompson, E. (2007). *Mind in life: biology, phenomenology, and the sciences of mind*. Cambridge, MA: Harvard University Press.

Tinbergen, N. (2005). On the aims and methods of ethology. *Animal Biology, 55*(4), 297-321. doi: 10.1111/j.1439-0310.1963.tb01161.x

Tomiyama, T., Gu, P., Jin, Y., Lutters, D., Kind, C., & Kimura, F. (2009). Design methodologies: Industrial and educational applications. *CIRP Annals - Manufacturing Technology, 58*, 543-565. doi: 10.1016/j.cirp.2009.09.003

Tooby, J., & Cosmides, L. (2001). Does beauty build adapted minds? Towards an evolutionary theory of aesthetics, fiction and the arts. *Substance, 94/95*, 6-27. doi: 10.1353/sub.2001.0017

Tootell, R. B. (1982). Deoxyglucose analysis of retinotopic organization in primate striate cortex. *Science, 218*, 902-904. doi: 10.1126/science.7134981

Turing, A. (1990). Computing machinery and intelligence. In M. A. Boden (Ed.), *The philosophy of artificial intelligence*. New York: Oxford Press.

Tzonis, A. & White, I. [Eds.] (1994). *Automation-based creative design*. Amsterdam: Elsevier Science

Varela, F., Thompson, E., & Rosch, E. (1991). *The embodied mind*. Cambridge, MA: MIT Press.

van de Ven, A. (2017). The innovation journey: You can't control it, but you can learn from it. *Innovation: Organization & Management, 17*(1), 39-42. doi: 10.1080/14479338.2016.1256780

Vickers, G. (1995). *The art of judgment: A study in policy making*. London: Harper & Row.

Vischer, F. T. (1866/1998). In C. Harrison, P. Wood, & J. Geiger (Eds.), *Art in theory 1815-1900: An anthology of changing ideas*. Oxford: Wilely-Blackwell.

Vischer, R. (1994). In R. Vischer (Ed.), *Empathy, form, and space: Problems in German aesthetics, 1873-1893* (H. F. Mallgrave, & E. Ikonomou, Trans.). Santa Monica, CA: CA: Getty Center for the History of Art and the Humanities.

Visser, W. (1990). More or less following a plan during design: Opportunistic deviations in specification. *International Journal of Man--Machine Studies, 33*, 247-298. doi: 10.1016/S0020-7373(05)80119-1

Visser, W. (2010). Simon: Design as problem solving activity. *Collection, 2*, 11-16. Retrieved from http://www.parsons- paris.com/pages/detail/624/Collection-2>

Vitruvius. (1998). *On architecture.* **(F. Granger, Trans.) Cambridge, MA: Harvard University Press.**

Vygotsky, L. (1978). *Mind in society: The development of higher psychological processes*. Cambridge, MA: Harvard University Press.

Wagemans, J., Feldman, J., Gepshtein, S., Kimchi, R., Pomerantz, P., van der Helm, P., & van Leeuwen, C. (2012). A Century of Gestalt Psychology in Visual Perception II. Conceptual and Theoretical Foundations. *Psychol Bull, 138*(6), 1218-1252. doi: 10.1037/a0029334

Walker, J. (2009). Defining the object of study. In H. Clark, & D. Brody (Eds.), *Design studies: A reader* (pp. 42-48). New York: Berg.

Walton, K. (1970). Categories of Art. *The Philosophical Review, 79*(3), 334-367.

Watson, D., & Crosbie, M. (Eds.). (2005). *Time-saver standards for architectural design* (8th Edition ed.). New York: McGraw-Hill.

Weber, R. (1995). *On the aesthetics of architecture: A psychological approach to the structure and order of perceived space.* **Aldershot: Avebury.**

Welsh, W. (2008). On the universal appreciation of beauty. (J. N. Erzen, Ed.) *International Association for Aesthetics, 12*, 6-32.

Wessell, L. P. (1972). Alexander Baumgarten's contribution to the development of aesthetics. *The Journal of Aesthetics and Art Criticism, 30*(3), 333-342. Retrieved from http://www.jstor.org/stable/428733

Weston, R. (2003). *Materials, form and architecture*. New Haven: Yale University Press.

Wiener, N. (1965). *Cybernetics*. Cambridge, MA, USA: MIT Press.

Wilson, F. R. (1999). *The hand: How Its use shapes the brain, language, and human culture*. New York: Vintage Books.

Wilson, M. (2008). How did we get from there to here? An evolutionary perspective on embodied cognition . In P. Calvo, & T. Gomila (Eds.), *Handbook of cognitive science* (pp. 375-393). Elsevier. doi: 10.1016/B978-0-08-046616-3.00019-0

Wilson, R. A., & Foglia, L. (2017). *Embodied cognition*. (E. Zalta, Ed.) Retrieved 03 15, 2017, from Stanford Encyclopedia of Philosophy: https://plato.stanford.edu/archives/spr2017/entries/embodied-cognition/

Winch, C. (2010). *Dimensions of expertise: A conceptual exploration of vocational knowledge*. London: Continuum.

Wittgenstein, L. (1958). *Philosophical investigations*. (G. E. Anscombe, Trans.) Oxford: Basil Blackwell.

Wölfflin, H. (1994). Prolegomena to a psychology of architecture. In R. Vischer (Ed.), *Empathy, form and space: Problems in German aesthetics, 1873-1893* (M. H. F., & E. Ikonomou, Trans., pp. 149-162). Santa Monica, CA: Getty Center for the History of Art and the Humanities.

Wong, B. (2010). Points of view: Gestalt principles (Part 1). *Nature Methods, 7*(11), 863. doi: 10.1038/nmeth1110-863

Wood, D., Bruner, J., & Ross, G. (1976). The role of tutoring in problem solving. *Journal of Child Psychology & Psychiatry & Allied Disciplines, 17*(2), 89-100. doi: 10.1111/j.1469-7610.1976.tb00381.x

Wynn, D., & Clarkson, J. (2005). Models of designing. In J. Clarkson, & C. Eckert (Eds.), *Design process improvement*. London: Springer.

Xenakis, I., Argyris, A., & Darzentas, J. (2012). The functional role of emotions in aesthetic judgment. *New Ideas in Psychology, 30*, 212-226. doi: 10.1016/j.newideapsych.2011.09.003.

Yilmaz, S., Seifert, C. M., & Gonzalez, R. (2010). Cognitive heuristics in design: Instructional strategies to increase creativity in idea generation. *Artificial Intelligence for Engineering Design, Analysis and Manufacturing, 24*, 335-355. doi: 10.1017/S0890060410000235

York, W. (2013). Cognitive science, aesthetics, and the development of taste. *Cognitive Science*. Retrieved from https://pdfs.semanticscholar.org/9578/9def5f3e19aff925c904456575f9d8be4b5d.pdf?_ga=1.238654021.437389223.1492722767

Yukhina, E. (2007). Cognitive abilities and learning styles in design processes and judgments of architecture students. (Doctoral Dissertation) Sydney: University of Sydney, Faculty of Architecture.

Zangwill, N. (2014). *Aesthetic judgment*. (E. N. Zalta, Ed.) Retrieved 03 13, 2017, from Stanford Encyclopedia of Philosophy: https://plato.stanford.edu/archives/fall2014/entries/aesthetic-judgment

Zeisel, J. (2006). *Inquiry by design: Environment, behavior, neuroscience in architecture, interiors, landscape and planning*. New York: Norton & Co.

Zumthor, P. (2006). *Thinking architecture*. Basel: Birkhauser.

Curriculum Vitae

1 Education

- Delft University of Technology, Faculty of Architecture and the Built Environment, Netherlands: Ph.D. (2017)
- Harvard University, Graduate School of Design, Cambridge: Loeb Fellow (2000-01)
- Jesuit School of Theology, Berkeley: M.Div. (1994)
- Xavier University of Louisiana, New Orleans: Th.M. (1990)
- Loyola University of Chicago: *De Universa*, Philosophy (1988)
- The Pratt Institute, Brooklyn: B.Arch. (1984)
- LaSalle College, Philadelphia, PA: Certificate in Youth Ministry (1981)

2 Professional Registration and Memberships

- National Council of Architecture Registration Boards (NCARB): Cert. #43157
- Registered Architect: USA State of Michigan (#13030137886), Wisconsin (7538) and New York (029005-1)
- American Institute of Architects (AIA): Member #30106099

3 Professional Experience

- 2015 – 2016, Professor of Practice, Tsinghua University, School of Architecture, Beijing
- 2014 – 2016, Deputy Director, Tsinghua University School of Architecture, Master of Architecture in English Program (EPMA)
- 2009 – 2015, Associate Professor, Tsinghua University, School of Architecture, Beijing
- 2003 – 08, Distinguished Visiting Professor, Budapest University of Technology and Economics, School of Architecture
- 2005 – 08, Founder/Director, Szent Jozsef Studio Kollegium, Budapest
- 2002 – 04, Artist-in-Residence, Fordham University, Department of Theater and Visual Arts, New York
- 1999 – 01, Professor with Tenure, University of Detroit Mercy, School of Architecture, Detroit
- 1994 – 2000, Associate Professor, University of Detroit Mercy, School of Architecture, Detroit
- 1994 – 96, Adjunct Associate Professor, University of Michigan, CAUP, Ann Arbor
- 1994 – 01, Founder/Director, UDM Detroit Collaborative Design Center, Detroit
- 1992 – 93, Visiting Assistant Professor, University of California, College of Environmental Design, Berkeley
- 1988 – 91, Assistant Professor, University of Detroit, School of Architecture, Detroit

4 Honors, Fellowships and Awards

- Fulbright Scholar Award, Budapest University of Technology and Economics (2003-4)
- Honorary Degree, Archeworks, Chicago (2003)
- Dedalo Minosse International Award, Homeboys Industries, Los Angeles (2002)
- NCARB Grand Prize for Creative Integration of Practice and Education (2002)
- Loeb Fellowship, Harvard University, School of Design, Cambridge (2000-01)
- Proclamation, Office of the Mayor of Detroit (2000)
- AIA Detroit, Honor Award, Van Elslander Family Center, Detroit (2000)
- AIA National, Young Architect Award for Design and Community Service (1999)
- AIA Detroit, Honor Award, NAAB Exhibit and Team Room, Detroit (1997)
- AIA Detroit, Young Architect Award for Design and Community Service (1997)
- AIA New York, Honor Award, St. Ignatius Academy, New York (1996)
- Whose Who in American Business (1996)
- AIA Detroit. Honor Award, St. Ignatius Academy, New York (1996)
- AIA Michigan, Honor Award, St. Ignatius Academy, New York (1996)
- Interiors Magazine, Annual Honor Awards, Best School, St. Ignatius Academy, Bronx (1996)
- AIA Detroit, Honor Award, Thunderhead Camp, Oma, (1995)
- Whose Who In American Higher Education (1994)

5 Publication

- "Cube of Brackets," Domus (11/2015) 38-43
- "A Theoretical Basis for How to Approach Teaching the Fifth Year Thesis/Capstone Studio," World Architecture (08/2014) 104-115 (Chinese)
- "A Theoretical Basis for Recommending the use of Design Methodologies as Teaching Strategies in the Design Studio," Design Studies 35 (2014) 632-646; Chinese translation: World Architecture (08/2015)
- "From Design to Construction", New Architecture (04/2011) 18-21
- "Architecture as Ministry," New Village (Issue 3, June 2002)
- "Designing a Building for a Nigerian Church," Faith and Form (Winter 1991) 36-40

- Ricci Café, Movable Café Unit, Beijing (2013): Design/Construction Documents for a prefabricated cafe unit for on-site assembly
- Ricci Café, Beijing Open Pavilion (2012): Design of a prefabricated cafe unit for on-site assembly
- B.A.R.C. - Greening the Metropolis, Urban Design Relay, Caofeidian (2011)
- Orchard Hotel, Beijing: Concept Design and Design Development (2010)
- The Beijing Center for Chinese Studies, Beijing (2009): Concept design for new building
- Horanszky Utca Jesuit Residence, Budapest (2008): Concept, Programming, Design Development, Custom Furniture/Cabinet Design and Fabrication
- Sodras Utca Jesuit Dining Room/Interior Design, Budapest (2005): Concept, Programming, Design Development, Fabrication of Custom Cabinetry (Design/Build)
- Homeboy Industries Office Renovation/Interior Design: Los Angeles (2000): Concept, Programming, Design Development
- Covenant House Michigan, Campus Master Plan: Detroit (2000): Concept, Programming, Process, Design Development
- Covenant House Michigan, Rights of Passage Transitional Housing, Detroit: (2000): Concept, Programming, Process, Design Development, Construction Documents
- Covenant House Michigan, Temporary Administration and Crisis Center: Detroit (1999): Concept, Programming, Process, Design Development
- Adams Butzel Community Complex Addition and Renovation: Detroit (1998): Concept, Programming, Process, Design Development
- Living as One, Community Education Program on Urban Sprawl: Published workshop materials, including publication information manual, slide show, workshop curriculum (1998)
- Van Elslander Family Center: Detroit (1997): Concept, Programming, Process, Design Development, Construction Supervision
- Van Elslander Family Center: Detroit (1997): Interior Design, Architectural Casework design, fabrication and installation (Design/Build)
- People United as One Plaza Apartments: Detroit: (1997): Concept, Programming, Process, Design Development
- Detroit Community Reinvestment Strategy: Detroit (1997): Workshops, Visioning, Graphic Analysis
- Detroit Community High School, Detroit: Outdoor Study Center (1997): Conceptual Development, Project Design, on-site installation with student participation
- St. Ignatius High School, Cleveland: Chapel Design (1997): Design competition for new campus chapel
- Lancing-Reilly Hall, Detroit: Architectural Casework (1997): Specialty casework design, fabrication and installation
- NAAB Team Room Exhibit, Detroit (1997): Exhibit design, construction and installation

- Brightmoor Infill Houses, Detroit: 3 & 4 Bedroom House Design (1997): Schematic Design, Design Development and Construction Documents
- Think Twice Duplex, Detroit: Infill House Design (1998): Schematic Design, Design Development, Construction Documents
- St. Conrad Catholic Church, Melvindale: Building Renovation (1997): Schematic Design, Community Process
- Nativity Mission Center, New York: Interior Renovation (1996): Conceptual Development, Project Design and Fabrication, on-site installation with student participation
- Imani Motown Restaurant, Detroit: Renovation/Adaptive Reuse (1996): Conceptual Design, Design Development, Community Workshops
- St. Ignatius Academy, Bronx: Interior Renovation/Adaptive Reuse (1995): Conceptual Development, Project Design, Fabrication and on-site installation with student participation
- St. Anne's Cathedral, Oakland: Building Design (1994): Concept Development with Marvin Buchannan, Donlyn Lyndon and Charles Moore
- Garnett Residence, Berkeley: Kitchen Renovation (1994): Kitchen Design and Cabinet Construction
- Thunderhead Camp, Oma: Cabin Construction (1993): Building design and construction with college interns and junior high school student participation
- Thunderhead Camp, Oma: Main Hall Renovation (1993): Project Design, Construction Documents and supervision
- St. Augustine/St Monica Church, Detroit: Entrance Design (1992): Conceptual Design and Design Development
- Detroit Province Offices, Detroit: Office Renovation (1991): Project Design, Construction Documents, Site Observation
- Porterfield Marina Village Club, Detroit: House Design (1991): Project Designer
- Black Catholic Museum, Detroit: Conceptual Design (1990): Programming and Pre-design
- Christ the King Catholic Church, Lagos: Building Design (1989): Programming, Pre-design, and Design Development
- Holy Family Catholic Church, Chicago: Building Design (1988): Programming, Pre-design, and Design Development
- Camp Monserrat, Lake Placid: Outdoor Study Center Project (1985): Design and Construction with student participation

Lightning Source UK Ltd.
Milton Keynes UK
UKOW07f2144160617

303428UK00004B/42/P

9 789492 516633